'My father had one career his entire life; I ht
over a variety of interesting careers. Life, I would argue, is indeed a
journey of choice.'

The author of *A Journey of Choice*, Hein Scheffer, was born in South
Africa in the 1960s and lived there for over forty years before emigrating
to the UK with his wife. The story of his personal life is intermingled
with depictions of the memorable events from that period as well as a
wide-ranging and well-researched description of his native country's
tortuous, 350+ year history.

Hein was witness to many seismic changes to South Africa, including
the perpetuation of an Apartheid regime in the face of sustained
international condemnation and the rise of anti-Apartheid resistance
movements, some of which pursued violent methods. Perhaps most
significant has been the country's emergence as 'the rainbow nation',
which arguably began in 1990 with the release of Nelson Mandela from
his long imprisonment on Robben Island.

There have been many books written about South Africa's recent history.
What you get in *A Journey of Choice* is the unusual perspective of a
middle-class Afrikaner, born into a well-respected, God-fearing and
conservative family, whose personal relationships gradually led him to
question the foundations on which the entire life and culture of his
family were based. Hein Scheffer shows us how he grew to understand
that the only way South Africa could achieve its full potential, would be
for all South Africans, irrespective of the colour of their skin, to be
treated equally before the law, with mutual respect, dignity and
opportunity for all in even measure.

Candid and self-reflective, *A Journey of Choice* depicts the struggles and
successes of an ordinary man in extraordinary times.

Dedication

I published a first version of my manuscript (spanning 40 years) in 2009 – by Griffel Media in South Africa, under the title Choices, 0981417779, 9780981417776, - which was dedicated to my mother.

I would like to dedicate *A Journey of Ch*oice to my parents and my lovely wife Renate.

Foreword

Hein Scheffer is a very good man!

That is the response I most often hear when I refer to Hein in discussion with former colleagues, mutual friends and others with whom he has interacted over these many years.

"The first steps to be a good man is this: You must deeply feel the burden of the stones someone else is carrying" ~ Mehmet Murat Ildan.

This sense of empathy is inherent in Hein's chosen profession as how could one be a successful human resources practitioner without being richly blessed with the sound and diverse qualities that make one to be empathetic? However, these qualities run far deeper that simply an important aspect of his professional life. I believe these qualities define his life.

In 1996 Hein joined my team as our Regional Human Resource Manager at a successful Casino, Hotel and Entertainment complex in the then Ciskei "Homeland" in Southern Africa. It was a turbulent time. South Africa was still in the throes of the birth pain aftermath of the "dawn of democracy" lead by the charisma and wisdom of Nelson Mandela as we grappled with "Madiba Magic". The Ciskei was being absorbed in the Eastern Cape Province in the "New South Africa", our company was experiencing exponential growth opportunities with all the "growth pains" and challenges that times of turbulence and change provide.

Hein and I both developed and grew in our chosen professions. I continued to climb up the corporate ladder. Hein chose the braver route, becoming an entrepreneur and started his own business in human resource consulting and then, braver still in hospitality management. He never did shirk the braver choices in life, a testament to his courage, fortitude, confidence in his own ability and incredible tenacity.

Hein and Renate relocated to England, under extremely trying circumstances and conditions that would have crippled a lesser man. However, not Hein, he soldiered on, often against the odds, the "establishment" and the vagaries of life in a new, foreign land. He faced life threatening health issues and personal tragedies yet, in the immortal words of Churchill, "He never gave up".

The journey of life lead to our paths crossing again in 2011 when I was developing a beautiful manor house hotel in the Cotswolds and Hein and Renate were living "just up the road" in Lytham St Annes. We made contact, they came to visit and we reconnected. Life was good.

Hein studied. Renate supported him. They moved home. Hein studied some more, doors opened, opportunities were presented and Hein was "back in business". We were delighted and rejoiced in our friends' successes, we wept in his times of despair, bereavement and ill health. We celebrated birthdays together and we visited each other whenever possible, always in awe and respect.

Life's journey separated us by geographical distance but never in emotional distance. We remain in awe and stand in respect of this remarkable man who through thick and thin, highs and lows, pleasure and pain has driven himself to success and happiness. His personal commitment and total dedication to achieve that upon which he sets his heart is an inspiration to us all, an example of how one can overcome adversity and "ill fortune".

Life is all about choices. The choices one makes, as we travel the troubled path of our destinies, define the outcomes, often unforeseen, often unexpected and totally unpredictable. This book will give you an insight and understanding how the life of a remarkable man exemplifies the very essence of life being "A Journey of Choice".

And, of course, behind every successful man stands an equally remarkable lady… we salute you Renate as Hein could never have embarked upon this incredible journey without you!

Graham Vass
Development Manager for Mantis and former General Manager, Sun International

Hein Scheffer

A JOURNEY OF CHOICE

AUSTIN MACAULEY PUBLISHERS™

LONDON • CAMBRIDGE • NEW YORK • SHARJAH

A CIP catalogue record for this title is available from the British Library.

ISBN 9781788483148 (Paperback)
ISBN 9781788483155 (Hardback)
ISBN 9781788483162 (E-Book)

www.austinmacauley.com

First Published (2018)
Austin Macauley Publishers Ltd™
25 Canada Square
Canary Wharf
London
E14 5LQ

Table of Contents

Chapter 1
The Beginning, Robben Island, Early Experiences and the Cullinan Diamond

"When he sailed into Table Bay aboard the Golden Hind in 1580 Sir Francis Drake proclaimed it to be 'The fairest Cape… in the whole circumference of the earth'[1]

In 1652, the Dutch East India Company established a feeding station at the Cape of Good Hope. The climate was more tempered than that of Europe and was well placed on the sea route to India. This resulted in a variety of Europeans immigrating to the Cape Colony at the foot of Table Mountain, which saw the birth of what is known today as South Africa.

Dutch was the primary language, with a number of minorities of French Huguenots, Germans, Khoi natives (previously referred to as Hottentots), and Malay slaves. Most of the Europeans arrived as unmarried soldiers or employees of the Dutch East Indian Company. At the Cape, they would marry Dutch, Malay, or Khoi wives and were absorbed into the main body of Dutch speakers. As a result, both German and French surnames are common among the Afrikaners, the modern-day descendants of the Dutch. But, neither group established a separate identity at the Cape during the early years. Many Germans, especially those from northern Germany, would have found Dutch very similar to their home language of *Plattdeutsch*, so there was little incentive to forming a separate subgroup within the population.[2]

Altogether, there were about 4,000 Germans that immigrated to the Cape during the Dutch period, almost all of them male. They came from all the German-speaking areas of Europe. A number of books have been written about the early German immigrants to South Africa, most notably Dr Hoge's *Personalia of the Germans at the Cape.*[3]

My maternal family line goes back nine generations to 1691 to Willem van der Vyver, who was born in Haarlem, Northern Holland in the Netherlands. He arrived in the Cape of Good Hope, South Africa in 1714 and married Elizabeth Bastiaanse on 31/07/1719 in Drakenstein.

My paternal family line goes back seven generations, to just before the

---

[1] Bell, et al, Insight Guide South Africa, 2008
[2] Deutsche Einwanderer in der hollandischen Kapkolonie 1651–1806
http://www.safrika.org/Personalia_de.html
[3] Dr J. Hoge, Personalia of the Germans at the Cape, 1652–1806 Cape Town : Archives of the Union of South Africa, 1946

arrival at the Cape of Good Hope of Christiaan Johannes Scheffer, from Einbeck, Hanover, in modern day Lower Saxony. He married Margaretha Elizabeth Scheffer (nee Steenvat) on 31 March 1802, in Cape Town. She was the daughter of Johann Steenvat, who came from Bavaria, and 'Rachel from the Cape', who was born circa 1764.[4] It is said that Rachel from the Cape was a Malay girl from Batavia from the old Netherlands East-Indies (present day Indonesia).

* * *

Two hundred years later, during the early morning of Monday, 25 October 1965, the first contractions started. My parents rushed to the maternity unit of the Aliwal North Public Hospital situated in the Northern Cape in the Republic of South Africa. Later that morning, at 11:15 AM, the youngest of four children in a middle-class conservative Afrikaans family was born – a healthy, strong baby boy. I got my name from my father's eldest brother, Johann Heinrich Scheffer, in line with the family tradition.

My father was a career civil servant and spent nearly 50 years working for the South African government. He started his working career immediately after leaving school, with only a standard eight (grade 10), joining the Department of Justice in Pretoria as a messenger. After two years of service, he joined the Department of Prison Services from where he retired nearly 50 years later – a strict disciplinarian, a proud military man, and a devoted civil servant.

My mother was a conservative, traditional housewife who formed the backbone of our family; a strong woman who ensured that my father completed his studies whilst she attended to their four children. She lived a God-fearing life, had a voice like an angel, a wild imagination and a brilliant sense of humour. In short, my mother was a well-balanced person, who could laugh (and she did laugh a lot), cry, sang beautifully, and she worked very hard in both her family and professional life. She dedicated most of her life to family research. My mum always wanted to research all four of our family lines. These are the van die Vyver (see Annexure 1) – my mum's father's family; the De Jager family – my mother's mum's family (see Annexure 2); the Meyer family – my father's mum's family (see Annexure 3); and the Scheffer family – my family line (see Annexure 4). However, she only managed to complete the last three families, whilst I completed the van der Vyver line. My mother can only be described as remarkable.

My mum had her own difficulties growing up in Port Natal (KwaZulu-Natal). She came from a very conservative Afrikaans family. My grandfather, Johan David van der Vyver, was an Afrikaans schoolteacher and later headmaster, but also one of the Afrikaner leaders of Port Natal in the 1940s. He was a difficult man who was interned by the then Union Government during the Second World War, at Koffiefontein, together with John Vorster

---

[4] Cecilia Scheffer, Geslagsregister van Christiaan Johannes Scheffer

(a former prime minister and later State President of South Africa) and other prominent Afrikaners of the time, who were suspected of being pro-Nazi.

* * *

At the time of my birth, we stayed at the Goedemoed Prison Reserve situated in the Northern Cape, where my father was in charge of logistics. My two brothers, the eldest Chris, some nine years older than me and the second Johan, only sixteen months older than me were happy that the male presence in the household was again being taken to a higher level. However, my only sister, Suzanne, who was nearly five years my senior, had prayed for a baby sister to join the family. I was told that when she heard that the third boy in our household was due to arrive imminently, she was less than impressed. This first reaction to my arrival played a major role in our relationship throughout childhood and still does so today. My sister's choice of anger and resentment formed my perceptions of both of us, and that experience would to a large extent influence and become my reality.

* * *

Memories of the first years of my life are naturally vague except for what our parents told us based on their experiences of those early years.

Not long after my birth, my father was transferred to Robben Island where he was initially in charge of the stores on the island. Later, he became Deputy Commanding Officer until he was transferred at the end of 1966. Robben Island not only played a spectacular part in the history of South Africa during the second half of the 19th century, but it also impacted my own family in terms of its beauty, history and also what it resembled. This would only become more apparent to me in years to come. Therefore, I will revisit this prison island including Nelson Rolihlahla Mandela, who was an inmate on the island from 1964 to 1982, in more detail later.

* * *

However, in 1981, when Johan and I were 17 and 16, respectively, we returned to the island again. We were on vacation with our parents in Cape Town and stayed in a guesthouse at Pollsmoor Prison. (This was the same guesthouse where Nelson Mandela was accommodated during the last term of his incarceration before being unconditionally released in 1990.)

It was a cold wet morning when we went to the island. We left Cape Town harbour early in the morning on the ferry *Susan Kruger*. The *Susan Kruger* and the *Dias* were two ferries used to transport prison service staff and prisoners between Cape Town and the island. This was Johan and my first trip on a boat, which made it even more exciting. Cape Town's city bowl was covered in a blanket of fog. The low-hanging clouds and thick fog were made more prominent by the city lights which were still glowing in the early morning. The smell of fresh seawater crisp in the air. But the short trip between Cape Town and Murray's Bay Harbour on the island was soon over. At the harbour, we were met by prison service officials. At that time, my father held the rank of Colonel, so we were treated like 'government royalty'.

After disembarking from the *Susan Kruger*, we walked through a stone construction which welcomed visitors to Robben Island with the words 'Welcome / Robben Island / We serve with pride / Ons dien met trots / Welkom'. We were put into a white prison service vehicle and escorted to the guesthouse on the island. We were blissfully unaware of the stature of people on the island, except that the prisoners kept there were 'very dangerous' and posed a 'national threat' to the white people of South Africa. Harriet Deacon[5] described the island as being regarded as "...a hell, purgatory or rural Eden by various groups at particular times." Oliver Tambo is quoted in the same book to have commented in 1980 that "the tragedy of Africa, in racial and political terms, [has been] concentrated in the southern tip of the continent – in South Africa, Namibia, and, in a special sense, Robben Island." In 1981, however, we were uninformed and 'comfortably numb' if I may use the Pink Floyd phrase, with our belief in the political system of the day – the political affirmation by the church and our ignorance of the true facts.

When recalling that first trip to the island, I can remember going from the harbour into the small village where we found a large white English style Anglican Church that was inter-denominational. Next to the church was the primary school where my sister Suzanne started her schooling career. Both my brother Chris and Suzanne attended the school during our stay on the island. Adjacent to the school was a general dealer, post-office, bank, and petrol station. Further down the road were the historic graveyards from when the island was used as a leper hospital.

Of further interest were the old cars on the island. It was common practice amongst prison service staff to trade cars when transferred to and from the island. We found a rusted old Anglia with a license disk of 1966 still being utilised during our visit in 1981.

All Governments ruling over the Cape since the early 1650s utilised the island for various and different functions. The island was used as pantry, as a post-box, a banishment centre for lepers and as a prison for political prisoners.

Although my mother had the difficult task of raising four children on Robin Island, two of whom were young and chronically ill, she always spoke fondly of the island, primarily about its beauty, vegetation, animals and beautiful view of Table Bay. In a newspaper article[6], my mother made the following comments about Robben Island:

"The Other Side of Robben Island"

---

[5] The Island, 1996, Harriet Deacon – A History of Robben Island
[6] Daily Dispatch, 15 March 1982, East London, written by Ronel Scheffer

Robben Island has through the years served as an island for outcasts, a leper station and a defence station. In the early 1960's it became a top security prison. To many South Africans the offshore prison, and island as a whole, is a symbol of oppression. It is an establishment spoken of with dread by many throughout the world. But an East London woman, who spent nine months on Robben Island, feels differently. Ronel Scheffer [no relation] reports.

Cecilia Scheffer will go back to Robben Island any day. Her nine-month stay on this infamous island, where many of South Africa's security prisoners are serving long sentences, was too short for the wife of the new commanding officer of the East London Prison, Colonel Chris Scheffer.

There's more to Robben Island than its top security jail, says Mrs Scheffer. The 570 hectare speck of land off Table Bay has a charm of its own.

Come spring, and the barren and scrubby landscape is transformed into an arum lily paradise. Buck, ostriches and rabbits roam freely on the island, and the ever present seagulls are a source of both annoyance and amusement.

Daily Dispatch, 15 March 1982, East London, written by Ronel Scheffer

"You don't dare take visitors sightseeing if you're not armed with umbrellas. Even a former prime minister got the full seagull treatment on his head," said Mrs Scheffer.

It was in 1966 that Colonel Scheffer's job took him and his family to Robben Island. He was appointed deputy commander of the island prison.

When the Scheffer's got off the boat, they were greeted by, among others, two giant tortoises. It was only a sample of the island hospitality they would later become accustomed to, says Mrs Scheffer.

She arrived on the island with two babes in arms. "We had travelled for almost two days and I had run out of nappies and clean clothes for the babies. I was frantic." The island community came to her rescue in due course.

"I haven't come across friendliness like that in my life ever again," said Mrs Scheffer. Life on Robben Island is as "civilised" as in the city of Cape Town 11 kilometres [6.83m] away across the water. The homes made available to Prison Service's employees are comfortable. There's a well-stocked store, a school and a church (used by all denominations) on the island. And, for the convenience of those who have business to tend to on the mainland, a boat runs daily between Cape Town harbour and the island. The 45-minute boat trips through the rough waters surrounding the island have generated many good tales.

On one occasion Mrs Scheffer, who admits that she was always been a rather poor sailor, had to take a group of women on a tour of a fish factory on the mainland.

"It was a Wednesday – strangely enough there was always a gale blowing on Wednesdays. All the women were in hats, feathers and gloves – as we used to dress in those days.

"The swells were enormous and the boat was tossing and turning. One minute you were high up and the next you were down."

Mrs Scheffer decided to spend the turbulent journey on the top deck. "It was just me and a young man standing there. As the boat struggled through the swells I saw him going white, and I suppose I must have been white in the face too. I was hanging on for dear life."

But it wasn't very long until hats, feathers and gloves started flying in all directions. Mrs Scheffer managed to stay fairly composed until she got the first whiff of the fish at the factory. "I don't think I've ever prayed against illness as hard as I did on that day."

Mrs Scheffer finds it difficult to explain what made living on Robben Island so different and so enjoyable.

"You're surrounded by water. You can't just get into your car and drive off. You experience things you wouldn't have come into contact with elsewhere."

When the South African Seafarer sank in 1966 the Robben Island community had a good view of the whole drama. During her stay on the island, a whale was washed out on the rocks. Incidents like these and also the lifestyle of the closely-knit community often make Mrs Scheffer wish her husband would be transferred to the island again. "No matter how long you've been on the island, you go down to the jetty to meet the boat whenever it comes in." She has fond memories of long walks along the rocky shore, collecting driftwood and bamboo for "flower arrangements."

"The island is not for the gardener. The water is too brackish. The only flower that grows there is the Bokbaai vygie. And I managed to get a fig tree growing."

Evenings were spent either with women's club activities, seeing the occasional film or playing sport.

After nine months on Robben Island Colonel and Mrs Scheffer decided to move. Two of their children had developed chronic chest problems, and the island's climate did not improve matters. Needless to say Mrs Scheffer was very reluctant to leave.

She has been back to the island on a couple of visits and says: "If the opportunity to live there comes our way again, I'll jump at it."

Does she have any recollections of contact with some of the long term prisoners? "No that was my husband's baby." The answer was brief, in keeping with Prison Service's policy on prison affairs.

It's hard to say whether Mrs Scheffer, an earnest woman, ever felt any sympathy for men like Nelson Mandela and Walter Sisulu, who are serving life in the island jail. It is another of the questions she is not permitted to answer.

What she did mention was: "I always treat a prisoner with respect as I would treat any human being. I always keep in mind that it could have been my father or my brother...."

During that return visit to the island, I enjoyed my first taste of Abalone mince served on rice, a strange but tangy fish and an experience I recall with fond memories. We spent one full day on the island, walking around. My parents showed us our house at the end of a long row of houses. My father took us to the cemetery where we saw the graves of many lepers who died on the island and visited the lighthouse on Minto Hill. We had a look at the R.I. Battery (with two 9.2″ guns) protecting the western shore of the island. We never went near the prison and at that time, were not curious to do so either. After all, we had grown up on prison reserves and were not really interested in what was going on inside. We knew they housed dangerous criminals and that was enough. My father often reminded us that prisoners were not in prison because they were picking daisies; we were conditioned not to have too much sympathy for prisoners.

Little did we know, however, that the future first democratically elected President of the Republic of South Africa was on the island, and most of the black role models whom, today we view with respect, were there with him. Neither we nor the prisoners at the time had any idea of what the future would hold, what freedom would mean for them and for South Africa.

Remarkably, years later, Nelson Mandela wrote:

"When I walked out of prison, that was my mission, to liberate the oppressed and the oppressor both. Some say that has now been achieved. But I know that this is not the case. The truth is that we are not yet free; we have merely achieved the freedom to be free, the right not to be oppressed. We have not taken the final step of our journey, but the first step on a longer and even more difficult road. For to be free is not merely to cast off one's chains, but to live in a way that respects and enhances the freedom of others. The true test of our devotion to freedom is just beginning. I have walked that long road to freedom. I have tried not to falter; I have made missteps along the way. But I have discovered the secret that after climbing a great hill, one only finds that there are many more hills to climb. I have taken a moment here to rest, to steal a view of the glorious view that surrounds me, to look back on the distance I have come. But I can rest only for a moment, for with freedom come responsibilities, and I dare not linger, for my long walk is not yet ended."[7]

Isn't it remarkable that a man who posed such a grave threat to national security could utter words of such wisdom, such leadership, and such humanity? This was a man who was an alleged terrorist – a man who was meant to be sentenced to death for being a terrorist, but ultimately was given a life sentence.

In reality, prior to 1994, all who were outside the then National Party, or who were not members of the Afrikaans Dutch Reformed Churches, were considered Communists, famously referred to as 'die rooi gevaar', the red danger, and/or the Anti-Christ.

---

[7] Long Walk to Freedom, (1994, pg. 617)

The members of the African National Congress (ANC) were most definitely regarded as Communists (and some of them were) and, thus, enemies of the State. In reality, however, and with the clarity of hindsight, all that the ANC of the 1960s and 1970s wanted, and specifically people like Nelson Mandela and later Steve Biko, was to be respected as humans, as equals, as citizens, and as leaders. The black population, represented largely by the ANC, paid for their birthright and their land with their blood, in the same way as the Dutch, German, French, and English settlers paid with theirs. However, in the process, people like Nelson Mandela taught the rest of mankind what it means to treat your enemy with respect, what it means to forgive, and to what lengths one man can go to prevent a bloodbath in a country torn apart.

As babies, both Johan and I suffered from severe asthma and the doctors felt that the humid air of the island and Table Bay was not healthy and would hamper our recovery. As a result, my father requested a transfer from the island some nine months after our arrival. My mother loved the beauty of the island and often dreamed of going back. My father was regularly transferred, as was the custom, from one prison station to another.

* * *

After our time on the island, my father was transferred to ModderBee Prison in the East Rand, near Johannesburg. I can only recall our house on the prison reserve, as a standard three-bedroom prison service house. Across the road from us lived a colleague of my father. Johan and I were friends with their son Roelfie. However, I remember Roelfie, their house, and the time at ModderBee because of an incident with a garden fork. All three of us were playing at Roelfie's house. Johan was four years old, I was three, and Roelfie was of a similar age. While we were playing in the garden at the back of Roelfie's house, Johan tried to handle a garden fork but accidentally pinned his foot to the ground. Two of the prongs of the fork went through Johan's foot. At the sight of this, we became hysterical, as only three and four-year-old boys could. My father was fortunately home from work. My father took the fork out of Johan's foot, picked him up, and ran to the medical centre down the road from our house. They cleaned Johan's foot and it looked more seriously than what it was.

It was also during this time that my godparents gave me my first dog. A dachshund puppy called Heinz. Heinz remained with our family for the next thirteen years.

* * *

After ModderBee, my father was transferred to the Orange Free State (now called the Free State), where he was stationed at Kroonstad prison. I spent two years in a pre-primary school where my teachers reported, repeatedly with concern, that they were worried that I did not mingle with the other children. Although I was not considered too much of an introvert, it was reported that I would amuse myself, watching the other children, rather than playing with them. As a young child, this was of no real concern to me. Whilst I might have been classed a 'loner', I was content in my pre-primary environment. However, this manifested more strongly in years to come, and whilst it caused some challenges, on reflection, I am now content with my own company.

The following year saw the beginning of my school career at the Volkskool Primary School in January 1972. I recall my first day as exciting. I was allocated to Miss van Zyl's class, and the Headmaster was a Mr Naude. However, my mother told me years later, that I obviously knew what I wanted in life and Miss van Zyl's class was unacceptable to me. She had only recently completed her studies and had little experience as a teacher. As I was not impressed with my allotted teacher who was supposed to provide me with a sound foundation at the beginning of my schooling career, I promptly went to the Headmaster. It is said that I informed Mr Naude that I did not want to be in Miss van Zyl's class as she was inexperienced and I had no intention of going through life with a substandard education. Clearly I was a young man who knew what he wanted in life. Mr Naude, however, convinced me that Miss van Zyl's was very capable and I need not worry.

The foundation to my education would be good.

In those days, a very strong bond existed between my mother, Johan and me. Suzanne was like most sisters are to a seven-year-old brother, an irritating necessity. She had a terrible temper, and for good measure she was heading into puberty at the time. Chris was in high school and felt much older than us.

Suzanne was always very protective of her own space. In the car, I normally ended up in the middle, between her and Johan, and had to ensure that there was space between us. She did not want any part of my body to touch her in the car or invade her space. She constantly believed that the boys were treated better than her. She felt we were the favourites of both our parents and that she was always the victim in our family, misunderstood and unloved. As a result, the relationship between Suzanne and the boys was strained.

It was this abundance of negative energy that moved me to stay clear from her in those early years. She often criticised the manner in which I walked and talked. She told me that I looked feminine, had feminine hands, and often referred to me as a 'nancy boy'. Yet, whilst being ever cautious of her sharp tongue, I always sought an opportunity to befriend her. However, I also started to constantly rate and evaluate myself according to her assessments.

* * *

At the end of 1972, my father was transferred to Bloemfontein. Johan and I initially went to Jim Fouché primary school. During the next two years, we attended an evening with our parents to see Heintje Simons, the Dutch boy singer who was on tour of South Africa. He held a performance with the South African Drakensberg Boys choir. I was mesmerised and wanted to join the Drakensberg Boys Choir School, however this was not meant to be.

The next five years of school were difficult, as neither Johan nor I enjoyed sport very much and being in a pro-sporting school, we were not fully accepted by our peers. To add insult to injury, I started to play the piano and showed great potential, whilst Johan played the organ.

My keen interest in the piano did not go down well at school as this was not something that growing young boys should aspire to.

My sister had a field day with us, or at least, with me. As I was initially quiet, I became even more of a loner at school and became very self-conscious about everything I did, the way I walked, talked, used my hands, and even my facial expressions. I practiced in lifts, in front of mirrors, or just walking down the street to try and look cool. I developed an insecurity about myself that would haunt me for years to come.

* * *

The Sharpville riots in Soweto near Johannesburg on 16 June 1976, sparked the beginning of a violent road to a free and democratic South Africa for all its citizens. Today, the 16th of June is celebrated to mark the anniversary of this tragic event when hundreds of youths were killed, including Hector Peterson, and thousands more injured by the South African police, following a mass demonstration against Bantu Education and the compulsory use of Afrikaans as teaching medium.

At this time, Chris was studying law at the Free State University, Suzanne was in standard eight (Grade 10), and Johan and I entertained each other. We were good friends and generally content with life, although I did not particularly liked school. We had a very close bond. He always protected me, or if I was worried or scared, Johan comforted me. I always felt safe when he was near. We shared a room, and whilst there was only sixteen months' difference between us, he always had the ability to console me. This bond continued for the remainder of our lives together.

* * *

We were all indoctrinated with the teachings of the Nederduitsch Hervormde Kerk van Afrika (Dutch Reformed Church of Africa), a very conservative Church founded on the teachings of Luther and Calvin and heavily influenced by the politics of the government of the time. I said earlier that my mother was a God-fearing woman, and she ensured that we all become God-fearing Scheffers. We attended church twice every Sunday and on Saturday before Holy Communion, as well as all New Year's Eve services every year at midnight.

Whilst in Bloemfontein, we often went to the officers' mess on Sunday afternoon for lunch. This became a tradition and was the place where our parents taught us table etiquette, especially with three or more courses, how to drink wine, how to utilise multiple sets of knives and forks, and the proper manner in which one should eat the last of your soup. The foundation for my manners was taught during this time. I can recall that whilst I didn't like the taste of red wine at the time, I am grateful for this education as I enjoy a good quality red wine today.

In Bloemfontein, Suzanne prepared for the final year at school and was generally difficult and particularly short-tempered with us boys. I often wondered why this was. I thought she did this intentionally to irritate my father, to gain his attention, and to frustrate my mother. Maybe she needed more love. Maybe she just needed a firm hand. Whilst I would like to profess that I was an exemplary child, in honesty I was probably a mummy's boy. However, as part of my punishment, I remained doomed to live under the tyranny of a difficult sister for most of my school years.

After our initial two years in Jim Fouche Primary School, Johan and I transferred to Dr Viljoen Primary School, as it was closer to home. It also provided schooling facilities to a large number of orphans who resided in the orphanage adjacent to the school.

I generally developed a stronger relationship with some of my teachers than with most of my schoolmates. One such teacher was a Miss Bester, a very friendly and kind person. Years after I completed my schooling, I visited her at her home in Bloemfontein. She told me a story from my days as one of her students. Taking into account that I did not enjoy school, and I was a loner in class, I often became 'sick' in an attempt to avoid going to school. On returning to class, after one of these spells, she inquired what the doctor said about me. I confirmed with all seriousness that I was diagnosed with hypochondria. It sounded serious to me. She smiled with sympathy.

During this time, my mum went to see a fortune teller, which is something good Afrikaans Christians were not allowed to do. However, she apparently told my mum that she had four children and that the youngest would rise above the rest, achieve a high position, be someone of whom she would be very proud of (it sounds a bit like the Bible story of Joseph). Now I accept that this is not something my mum should have told me. I am not even sure if this is truly what the woman told her, whether she really went to a fortune teller, or if she was just making conversation with her little boy. However, these words stuck with me all my life and actually encouraged me to constantly evaluate where I was in my life and what I was doing. They became inspirational, as if I wanted to give meaning to this story. I wanted it to be true. I wanted to be special, achieving heights that would impress my mum and gain me the respect and approval of my father, my siblings, and most importantly, Suzanne.

My father was in his early forties when we stayed in Bloemfontein. He played tennis, rugby and badminton, whilst absolutely married to his job. Taking into account that he was responsible for the Free State Command of the Prison Service, he was often away on business, and the relationship between him and his children was distant. His focus on life was firstly his work, secondly my mother, and thirdly his children, or at least, that is how we perceived it to be. I felt more fear for my father than admiration at that stage. Fortunately for both my father and I, our relationship improved in years to come. However, we had to work hard to break down the barriers to eventually get to a point where both of us respected each other for the individuals we are, and established a fantastic loving relationship.

* * *

Just before I went to standard five (grade seven), and Johan had to start high school, my father was again transferred to Pretoria as Chairman of the Release Board at Pretoria Central Prison – yet another city and another school for me and Johan. Chris stayed behind in Bloemfontein to continue with his studies in law, and Suzanne began her studies as a student nurse. This left Johan and I alone as lords and masters of the house, with my parents.

I concluded my last year in primary school at the Jopie Fourie Primary School in Skanskop Pretoria, whilst Johan started high school at the CJ Langenhoven High School. My last year at primary school was relatively uneventful, apart from the bullying I had to face on a daily basis. Johan had a good year at school with excellent mathematic results and a very good general school report.

Johan and my reign at home was short-lived as Suzanne became pregnant by a young Air Force guy and moved back home for most of the latter part of the year. My father was devastated that his only daughter had gotten pregnant, whilst my mother spent most of the second half of that year working hard to locate Suzanne's boyfriend who was on border duty in South West Africa (Namibia). She liaised with the Air Force officers to have him re-assigned for duty in Pretoria so that David and Suzanne could get married and prepare for their unborn child. In an Afrikaner family in the late 1970s, not getting married was not an option.

Towards the last quarter of that year, Suzanne spent most of her weekends with us at home whilst the plans for the wedding took place. Taking into account that both David and Suzanne were under age, written permission of both sets of parents was necessary. This could not be faxed but had to be granted in original form, and as Dave's parents lived in Cape Town, this seemed problematic so soon before the wedding. Eventually, the wedding took place on Sunday, 30 December 1978 after the morning services in the Du Toit Street Nederduitsch Hervormde Kerk, in Pretoria. It was not a happy occasion. Suzanne could hardly be described as a happy person, although one could forgive her, considering that her hormones were now more out of control than usual.

That December saw Johan, my parents and I moving to Zonderwater Prison outside Cullinan, a diamond mining community some 45 minutes' drive from Pretoria.

Cullinan is also the place from where the world famous Cullinan Diamond comes. Years later when visiting the Cullinan Mine, we would learn that the original gem weighed 3106 carats, or about 1.33 pounds. It was discovered on 26 January 1905 by the then-mine superintended Captain Frederic Wells. He received £3500 for his discovery. The diamond was named after the owner of Premier Mines, Sir Thomas Cullinan and eventually sold to the government of the Transvaal Colony for £150,000.00, who presented it to King Edward VII on his 66th birthday on 9 November 1907.

* * *

It was time for me to start high school and most of the prison service children took the bus to attend Erasmus High School in Bronkhorstspruit. A relatively small country town providing infrastructure to the local farming communities in the Eastern Transvaal or modern day Mpumalanga. Again Johan and I had the run of the house as Suzanne now lived with her husband and baby girl in Pretoria.

Chris had abandoned his studies in Bloemfontein, joined the South African Police, and was in the Police College beginning his new career. Generally, life was good again for Johan and me.

The two years that I spent at Erasmus High School were both enjoyable and frustrating. Yet again, we were in a new school, in a new town, and had to adapt to a new environment, something that would be repeated a number of times in the next couple of years.

* * *

However, in later years I would be grateful for all the transfers we had to undergo and different schools we had to attend, as I would need all the resilience I could muster to set up a life in a new country, across continents, where we knew only five people in an entire new land. At the time, however, I hated it.

* * *

Johan and I befriended two brothers, Michael and Stefan Berg, German boys who lived in Cullinan with their mother and half-brother. Michael was the eldest, a tall lean boy who had the good looks of a young David Beckham, and Stefan was also a good looking boy with an excellent sense of humour. Michael and Stefan had a friend named Jacques Grobler, who stayed in the school hostel as his parents lived in Botswana. Johan and Michael were in the same class, and Stefan, Jacques, and I became friends. I was intrigued by the German language, music, and food. Stefan's mother, Tante (Aunt)

Renate, also had the most fantastic 'foreign' chocolates which she gave to us when we visited.

During those two years, we formed a little gang of friends in Cullinan. We learned how to smoke together, got into trouble together. We stayed over at each other's homes and did what young boys do. Stefan and I generally were in trouble every Wednesday at school as our carpentry skills were not that great. The woodwork teacher, with a nickname of 'Patat' (which, directly translated, means 'sweet potato') gave us hidings on a weekly basis when we attended his horrific class. This sadistic man would hit us and without fail ask Stefan whether the hiding burned, to which Stefan without fail answered, "No, sir, it bites."

Once a month, on a Saturday, we all walked to the mine hall to watch the movie of the month. We would walk alongside the railway tracks, talking, joking, and just having carefree times. One specific movie I will never forget was the first *Superman* movie. In 1980, it was still permissible to smoke in public places, and we all smoked, or rather tried. We watched how Clark Kent saved the world by being superhuman, good, honest, passionate, and dedicated to his mission in life. We watched how he made Lois Lane fall in love with him. We watched in awe how good triumphed over evil.

During my second year in Erasmus High School, I discovered that numbers were not my forte. I had difficulties with both Mathematics and Accountancy. I regrettably did not have the choice with regards to Mathematics, but I did have the choice between Accountancy and Typing. I decided to take Typing. One could say that a lot of my unfortunate events in school could be placed at my own door, as a boy taking Typing was unheard of. Nevertheless, since I was a keen piano player, I did have the benefit of rhythm and supple fingers, which aided me in the typing class. The benefit of my typing skills will manifest in years to come.

* * *

When school started on 16 April 1980, everyone thought it would be a normal school day. Johan and I travelled to school in our bus from Zonderwater. When we arrived at school we learned that the school bus, which left from Rayton, had been involved in a massive accident. Mr Kruger, the headmaster at the time, wrote.

"Today was indeed a dark day in the history of our school. This morning one of our busses was involved in a serious accident on the Forfar-Rayton gravel road. An accident with a large sand truck resulting in the death of three of our learners however, if one looks at the state of the bus, one could only thank God that not more learners were killed."[8]

---

[8] Erasmus High School, Headmaster's Journal, April 1980: Mr Kruger

The entire school attended the funerals. The three pupils who died, Alida Steynberg, Martha Hitge, and Annette Lubbe, were all in standard six (Grade Eight). Another died later in the then-H.F. Verwoerd Hospital in Pretoria. The school flag was lowered to half-mast for the next two weeks. On 21 April 1980, a memorial service was held in the school hall, and Mr Kruger recorded on 9 May 1980.

"We have just received the tragic news that another girl from our school, who was in the bus accident, died yesterday evening. She was Johanna Adriana Strydom."

Whilst it was unclear what happened on that fateful morning, from the stories told by some of the children on the bus, it seemed that the bus approached a hill with the morning sun rising in the road dead ahead of it. The driver's vision was blurred and the bus collided with an oncoming truck filled with sand. The bus was totally wrecked, with some of the benches ripped out. The entire side behind the bus driver was ripped open. Mr Kruger was correct; it was indeed a miracle that not more children were killed on that day.

During this time, Suzanne gave birth to her first child, Ursula Cecelia Swart, who was born on 20 July 1979. Chris developed a serious relationship with his girlfriend, Rina and on 15 June 1980, Suzanne turned 21. As this is a memorable occasion in the life of every adolescent, Suzanne arranged with my father to host her 21st birthday party in the club-house of the tennis club at the prison reserve at Zonderwater. My father prepared his speech to congratulate his only daughter on her 21st birthday, the winter air crisp outside, whilst we all danced to the music of Smoky and Suzi Quatro, among others.

An unfortunate miscalculation came just before my father made his speech, when Chris took the stand and announced that he and Rina were getting married, and right there on Suzanne's big night, Chris unwittingly stole the moment and converted Suzanne's birthday of a lifetime into his own engagement party. Although Chris is not a devious individual, and whilst it is clear in my mind that he did not intend to sabotage Suzanne, this error of judgment on his part remained part of Suzanne's irritation and blame against the boys for years to come.

* * *

During the school vacations, Johan and I visited one of my father's brothers who had a farm in the Witbank area in the old Eastern Transvaal. Uncle Hercules was a Regional Human Resources Manager at a large mining company, and his wife, Aunt Levina, was an occupational health nurse at an industrial company in Witbank. They had two children, cousin Hercules and his sister Brendina. It was great to visit them on their farm, as both Johan and I were real city boys and the farm life was a great experience for us. I had a large number of hang-ups when it came to food.

However, my aunt taught me to eat everything she made, as we had to eat what was on our plate. Today, I can honestly say that there is nothing I do not eat from a western dietary perspective, except tripe and black pudding.

* * *

Something that I did enjoy doing during our time in Cullinan, was to visit the local Magistrates Court. I developed a keen interest in law and spent many a school holidays sitting in the local Magistrate Court – listening to the various court cases, how the state set out its prosecution, and how the defence tried to create reasonable doubt. I loved those holidays. I thought that being a public prosecutor is one of the greatest jobs there could be. When the court adjourned for lunch, I would go home, make myself a cup of coffee, and drink it standing up as I needed to get back to court. When I arrived at court, I bowed respectfully at the Magistrate before quietly taking my seat and listening to the arguments. I was sure that one day, I would become a lawyer.

In October 1980, Chris and Rina got married, and my parents, Johan, Ursula, and I drove to Vryburg. I had broken my left arm at school and had my arm in a cast. En route to Chris's wedding, we drove through Ventersdorp, where I saw the large white Nederduitsch Hervormde Kerk in which I was baptised. Outside Ventersdorp, near Coligny, we first stopped at Schefferspos, the area where my father grew up. This was my first visit to my father's birthplace. My father showed us the old farmhouse where they lived. Inside the old ruin was an old wooden coat rail my grandfather had made and a cast-iron bath. The latter was the same old bath my father bathed in when he was a little boy. There was very little left of the house but the stone kraal next to it was still visible with the grindstone at the back where my grandmother ground maize. The dam and windmill in front of the house were all still there. It felt as if we had stepped back into time. At the end of that year, my father was again transferred.

* * *

We moved back to Pretoria. Johan and I were enrolled at Overkruin High School, which is situated in one of the northern suburbs of the capital. The area was affluent, dominated by white conservative middle and upper-class citizens, with beautiful homes, carefully planned gardens, and spoiled children. Johan started with standard nine (Grade 11), while I went to standard eight (grade 10).

Except for the normal school humiliation, considering that I was now the only boy in the entire school taking typing as a subject and not participating in any form of sports, 1981 was a good year for me. I auditioned for the very prestigious eighty-voice Northern Transvaal Youth Choir (NTYC) and won a place. Suddenly, I had friends with the same interests as me, who did not particularly mind that I was not part of the school's rugby team. Instead, they welcomed me as part of the group for my talent, my voice.

During the March school holidays the NTYC had a choir camp at a school near the Hartebeespoort Dam, some forty minutes west of Pretoria. This was a fantastic week as I made a variety of friends with whom I could relate and who recognised me for my talent rather than my inadequacies. The camp was filled with five days of singing, holiday romances, and great fun. After the camp, Johan, my parents, and I went to Cape Town for a vacation and visited Robben Island for the first time since Johan and I were babies. We had a great time, and things were generally good.

* * *

My uncle after whom I was named, owned a very up-market furniture business called *Hein Scheffer Furniture*, situated on the corners of Skinner and Andries Streets in Pretoria. The business specialised in high quality wooden furniture, which remained in families for generations. The business had been in Pretoria since 1966, the name 'Hein Scheffer' became associated with good quality furniture. For the first time in my life, people started associating me with good quality furniture. Whenever I identified myself as 'Hein Scheffer', I was often asked whether I was related to the furniture people.

* * *

In October, the NTYC was booked to tour South West Africa/Namibia which was a great success, in addition to enjoying my first flight. We visited Grootfontein in the north of Namibia, performed in a Church in Windhoek and visited and performed at both Swakopmunt and Walvisbay on the west coast. On my return, I heard the bad news that my father had been transferred again. This time we had to move to East London, a harbour city on the Buffalo River in the Eastern Cape. This was terrible news for me. For the first time in my school career I had made true friends, enjoyed the NTYC, and had a girlfriend. I had a sense of belonging, and in my mind, the coast is a place you go to for holiday, not a place where you lived. To make things worse, we were working very hard at the NTYC to prepare for our first overseas tour. It was envisaged that the choir would tour Europe in April 1982 and my father's transfer to East London conflicted with my own plans for the remaining years of my school career.

Chris lived five kilometres from us in Pretoria North and was now well-established in his career in the South African Police. By then, a good relationship had formed among Chris, his wife Rina and me. I campaigned very hard to stay with them to finish my schooling in Pretoria. Chris and Rina had no objection but my father wanted to hear nothing of this plan. His only comment was that:

"Whilst you stay in my house, you will do what you are told, and I am telling you, we are moving to East London!"

I really hated my father's autocracy. He never negotiated nor consulted with us. It was my perception that things were always his way or no way at all.

29

This last year in Pretoria, Suzanne and David experienced marital problems resulting in their daughter, Ursula, living with us for most of that year. She was a very cute little girl, only three years old, and already experiencing the difficulties of life. I spent most of my holidays caring for her. I always introduced her to my friends as my 'god-child' as a very special bond developed between us. She also became my father's 'little princess'. My parents, in discussion with David and Suzanne, decided that Ursula would move with us to East London to enable them to sort out their marital problems. Ursula eventually remained with my parents for the rest of her childhood years.

Whilst Johan's school results at the end of standard nine (Grade 11) were reasonably good, mine, at the end of standard eight (Grade 10), were terrible. I failed Mathematics and English and the threat of having to repeat standard eight became very real. I negotiated hard with my teachers and eventually was allowed to pass to the next year. However, my mathematics teacher made me promise that I would never take any subject that involved figures. I promised, said my goodbyes to the kids in my class, and prepared to relocate to the Eastern Cape.

Chapter 2
Some Perceptions, The Church Street Bomb and Building Life-Long Friendships

In December 1981, we arrived at the Fort Glamorgan Prison Reserve in East London. My father held the rank of Colonel and was made Commanding Officer of the Eastern Cape command for the Prison Services. The day we arrived, a persistent soft rain fell and all our furniture was off-loaded in the rain. The official residence for the Commanding Officer was impressive in terms of prison reserve standards, with a spectacular driveway past the front door. It had a beautiful garden with high trees in front and at the back, with a separate private entrance at the rear of the house which led to the garage and back door.

East London had one exclusively Afrikaans High School so both Johan and I were to finalise our schooling in Grens Hoërskool. I was to go into standard nine (Grade 11) and Johan had to start his final year (Grade 12) in a new province, a new city, and a new school. The education syllabus for South African schools for the last two years, standard nine and ten (Grades 11 and 12), were very closely linked. These are also not always perfectly synchronised between two provinces. It was thus not ideal to move school during these two final years of schooling. Both Johan and I had at least one difficult year ahead of us, but nothing we could not overcome. After all, we had moved so many times before, and another new school, new teacher, new town, new province, and making new friends had now become part of who we were.

My mother took us to enrol at Grens, and I had to select my final subjects. As one of my best subjects was typing, I obviously wanted to continue with this for the next two years. Johan continued with the subjects that he selected at Overkruin and was duly enrolled at Grens High School. The Headmaster at Grens, however, had a problem with my subject choice. This conservative Afrikaans educationist was not used to boys who took typing. Although I insisted that I wanted to continue with typing, the headmaster decided that I must start with either Xhosa or Biology at the beginning of standard nine. This was ridiculous as I knew that my linguistic aptitude was limited, and Biology was not something I wanted to start with in standard nine. I was adamant; I wanted to continue with typing. The headmaster refused.

We had to find an alternative school for me and were directed to Commercial High School, later to be renamed Stirling High School. The Headmaster at Commercial was Mr Bernie Simpson, a very traditional English headmaster. I was accepted and whilst I was allowed to take typing as a subject, I had to select an alternative subject in the place of Mathematics. Taking into account my disastrous track record in this field, I decided to take Mercantile Law. Although I was happy with my subject choice, I had to face a different challenge, I had to attend a dual-medium school and my English was non-existent. Throughout my school career, I had attended conservative Afrikaans schools. Also, the method of teaching in the Free State where I began my schooling was predominantly phonetic, and whilst this method of speaking English might have been acceptable in Afrikaans schools, it would not be allowed in a very English school in a very English city.

My first day in this new school was terrible. Most of the children in my class had been together since the beginning of high school, or at least since the previous year. There were only seventeen Afrikaans children in our grade. Eventually, I made friends with Harry van Heerden and Marius Rademan who had been in the same class the previous year. Both of them had a wicked sense of humour. Harry loved laughing at his own jokes and came from an upper-class Afrikaner family.

Marius was nicknamed 'Ponti'. He was incredibly tall and large – not fat, just a very big boy. Ponti was Harry's exact opposite. He never took part in sports, very much like me. He seldom laughed at his own jokes, although he had an excellent sense of humour, and an incredibly sarcastic one at that. During the first year we met, the South African Broadcasting Corporation (SABC) showed a local program which included a chameleon called 'Ponti', so the big boy from school somehow got the name of a small chameleon and remained Ponti to this day. He might not have become a well-paid Executive with lots of cash in hand; in fact, he struggled most of his life to raise his two children, to stay afloat, and, eventually, moved to the United Kingdom. But he became the best father to his young children I have ever known.

My first few weeks in Commercial High were challenging, at best. Harry, Ponti, and the girls in our class spent their days joking about my accent, about what I did, how I walked, and how I talked. It seemed that whatever I did provoked gales of laughter from them, not because I was the funniest kid in school, but because they found me 'different' or 'strange'. They took great joy in harassing me on a daily basis, not in an ugly sense poking fun at me, but laughing with me, although sometimes I thought they were just laughing at me.

Harry told me that he came from a very poor family, and as we had a number of children in our school that came from poor families, there was no reason for me not to believe him. In an attempt to make friends in this strange and foreign environment, I brought sandwiches to school every day, and thinking that Harry came from a poor family, I ended up giving my sandwiches to him on a daily basis for a good couple of months. Needless to say, Harry and Ponti then enjoyed my sandwiches during break and had a good laugh at my expense.

Our English teacher in standard nine was Miss Webb, a good-hearted teacher, passionate about her job. Her teaching job was more of a calling than a career. When I arrived, I am sure she must have wondered on various occasions whether she had angered God to get such an un-teachable Afrikaner as a pupil. Her calling seemed to become a curse. Miss Webb took great care of her students and had a very difficult time teaching this Afrikaner boy who could neither speak nor read English. Fortunately, because we were the Afrikaans class in a predominantly English school, we were not forced to have to study Shakespeare. Imagine, I could not speak, read, or write normal English. How confused would I have been if I had to be tortured with the English of the Middle Ages.

After the first semester at Commercial, it became very clear that I was not adjusting. I was about to fail English and Miss Webb became very concerned. Although my results for my other subjects were good, English was a prerequisite to pass one's year. To add insult to injury, my sister announced that she and David were getting a divorce and she wanted to move back home. It was unbelievable. My last two years of school and my childhood nightmare was about to return to my doorstep. I was outraged. There was nothing I could do, as my parents did what any supportive parent would do for a child in distress and agreed that Suzanne could move in with us in East London. As a result of my constant failures in English, and my challenges in making friends, the daunting prospect of Suzanne returning home and my longing for my friends in the NTYC, led me to take matters in my own hands.

I wrote a short essay on everything that had happened in my life, the difficult times in Bloemfontein, the harassment by my sister, all the moves from one town to the next, one school after the other, the problem of leaving Pretoria and the NTYC whilst it was heading for an overseas tour in which I wanted to take part, and my father's militaristic approach to our upbringing. I decided to make an appointment with Mr Simpson and to present my case to him for assistance as my father was a member of the Parents Teachers Association (PTA). I wanted to go back to Pretoria.

Mr Simpson agreed to meet with me. I went to his office rather nervously, sat down, and confirmed that I was in need of his assistance. He listened as I related my life story briefly to what appears to be an attentive and caring man. His facial expression gave no clue as to what he was thinking and at the end, and, to my shock he replied:

"I have listened to what you have said. It is clear that you have applied your mind, and I am impressed with the fact that you prepared for this discussion. I noted that you have made some notes prior to our meeting. However, if you were my son, I would have given you a fucking hiding…"

I was so startled at this response that I did not utter a single word. I just looked at him in horror. Here I thought I had the man on my side. I presented, what I considered to be, an excellent case, and closed with a perfect reason why he should help me. My father was clearly not on my side, and if Mr Simpson was not going to help me, who would? I had depended on a positive response and had no idea he was going to dismiss me with such contempt. However, he was not finished with me yet. After my initial shock, he told me to leave his office, go home and think about what I had said. He instructed me to consider "all the good things [my] parents had done" for me in my life so far and to think about any good which may have come from us moving from place to place and constantly having to meet new people. He then committed himself to come to my aid, and stated that he wanted to see me the next morning at 8:00 in his office for a follow-up meeting. During this meeting he promised that after I had applied my mind as instructed, and if I still wanted to leave East London, he would talk to my father. Again, I was startled, as this was what I wanted but I had not expected this kind of response. He confirmed what I wanted to hear, that he would speak to my father about sending me back to Pretoria, but the tone of his voice was such that my longing for Pretoria did not sound like a victory but rather a possible banishment in disgrace.

I went home, spending most of the afternoon in my room and did not speak to anyone. I thought long and hard about what I wanted to achieve with this meeting with Mr Simpson. I considered and reconsidered all the merits of my plea and the torture of Harry and the gang, and for the first time I came face to face with the harsh reality of having to make a choice which potentially could alter my life – a choice that only I could make.

At about 9:30 the next morning, Mr Simpson sent for me as I did not report to him at 8:00 as he instructed. When I arrived at his office, he looked irritated that I failed to report to his office. He told me to sit down and said in an unyielding voice, "I told you to be in my office by 8:00. You were not." He continued in the same tone and asked, "What do you want to do with your life?" I looked at him from my chair and cautiously stated that I would like to remain in Commercial High School, if I may, and confirmed that I had thought about it and regretted all the things I said the previous day. I confirmed that I understood that I had wonderful parents and a lot to be thankful for. I told him that I struggled with English, which I knew was no secret, but I again asked him if I may stay. He looked at me with a stern face and responded, saying, "You are most welcome to stay." He then surprised me and said that I should meet with him every Tuesday afternoon after school in his office, as he would help me with English, and then he dismissed me. That was it.

No reference was ever made to that discussion again. I attended Mr Simpson's office every Tuesday afternoon for the next couple of months, where he taught me to read, pronounce, write, and understand English. I wrote various essays and had to complete numerous comprehension tests for him. Every now and again, he would chuckle as my accent was not quite English. However, Mr Simpson helped me with care and patience, like only a truly devoted teacher could.

* * *

After my disastrous first meeting with Mr Simpson, I had to face my father and the issue of Suzanne returning home. I am not sure if Mr Simpson ever told my Dad what was said in his office but my father was accommodating when we debated Suzanne's return home. I objected, Johan was indifferent, and both my parents were concerned for their daughter, as good parents ought to be. I offered an alternative and suggested something, which I never would have considered before. I suggested that I should go to 'Boshoff House', the hostel linked to Commercial High School. My father agreed conditionally. However, he asked me to give my sister a chance saying that he understood that these two years were supposed to be Johan and my years at home, whilst 1983 (the following year) was supposed to be my year alone as Johan would have left home to attend Pretoria University. We agreed that Suzanne would be given a fair opportunity, but if it did not work out, I would be allowed to go to boarding school.

* * *

One Sunday afternoon, Harry and Ponti were driving around in Ponti's car and were clearly bored, so they came to visit me at our house at Fort Glamorgan. According to the standards of that time, we had a grand house. We had a formal lounge suitably furnished with heavy wooden furniture on a pale blue carpet. My mother loved blue. My parents were sleeping as we always did in our home on Sunday afternoons. I heard a car at the front of the house and was shocked when I saw that it was Harry and Ponti. I was even more shocked when I opened the front door and they told me in a very suspicious tone that they had been in the neighbourhood and decided that they would come and visit me. What's the catch, I thought? But I invited them into the formal lounge. We sat talking for about half an hour when Harry suddenly grabbed his throat and fell on the floor. He rolled around on the floor as if suffocating and only after he burst into his trademark laughter, did I realise that this was his way of telling me that he was thirsty. I laughed, feeling a bit stupid, and offered to make some coffee. I left them in the lounge and proceeded to make coffee. This was the beginning of a lifelong friendship. Harry continued to tell the story of him grabbing his throat for years to come and made a lot of people laugh.

* * *

In the interim, my sister arrived in East London and got a job at the Frere Hospital. To everyone's amazement, the relationship between us seemed fine. She treated me like a human; she liked my friends, and particularly liked Ponti. She went on doing her own thing, whilst every now and again we went out together. We actually became good friends in East London. It seemed as if my preconceived ideas of Suzanne invading my space during the last year of school were incorrect. I saw a side of her that was great. She was a lot of fun, and for the first time in our lives, we lived in harmony. Thus came the first realization that past practices do not always predict future behaviour, and whilst our past experiences are direct contributors to our perceptions, these do not always have the correct influence on our realities.

* * *

On 23 September 1982, I became a prefect. Harry was our head boy. The following year, Harry and his lieutenants ruled Commercial High School. We had an absolute ball and in hindsight, these two years were the best years of my schooling career. I campaigned for the school to either establish its own Choir or host an Eastern Cape Youth Choir, which did not materialise in my time, but I am pleased to see that today Sterling High School boasts a large Music Department, offering a variety of cultural activities.

I joined the local Technical College on a part-time basis where I took singing classes with a remarkable lady by the name of Marian Keys. I participated in various singing competitions and was part of Beverly Cross's musical 'Half a Sixpence', which had a six-week run in the Guild Theatre in East London. My friends thought that I was 'cool' in my own strange way, and they were the best friends I could ever ask for. Even today, I think back to those days with fond memories.

* * *

In May 1983, Ponti invited me to go with them to a Baptist revival service held at the Oxford Baptist Church. Taking into account that I was a member of the Nederduitsch Hervormde Kerk van Afrika, a very conservative Afrikaans church in South Africa at the time, this 'outing' could be viewed as an abomination. The service was loud, musically enhanced, and that evening something happened to me.

Throughout my life in the Hervormde Kerk, we were taught what the Bible said and that God selected white people as his chosen people to bring the gospel to Africa. Black people were not allowed in our church. We had to attend church twice a Sunday, wearing a Sunday suit and tie, and adhering to the strict rules defined and dictated by the Church fathers.

I often went to church wondering at the end of the sermon what I had learned. Not all, but most of the Afrikaans ministers, based their sermons on politics and addressing the issues of the day, depending on what was happening in the country at the time. That, however does not mean that everything I learned in church was of little value. I learned the basis of my moral values and was taught the scriptures, the meaning of the Bible, which ultimately formed my religious foundation. However, visiting a 'sect' like the Baptist Church was very heavily frowned upon by my church fathers, not to mention my own father.

During the evening at the Oxford Baptist Church, the pastor gave an impressive sermon dealing with forgiveness and salvation. When the call came for people who wanted to claim Christ as their personal Saviour, I went forward and received prayers and experienced something so special that I was walking on clouds. I was ecstatic, as I accepted Christ into my life as my Saviour. That evening, when Ponti's mum dropped me at home, she came in and as loudly as only she could, announced to my parents that I had gone with them to the Baptist Church and received Christ as my Saviour. My father looked dumbstruck, my mother was without words, and when Ponti's mum asked my father whether he had accepted Christ as his Saviour, my father was notably irritated. This was not the kind of thing that we were taught to talk about in our Church. These were private matters. My father did not say anything, but was clearly not impressed that I had attended a Baptist Church. The Baptist Church was viewed by our church as a 'sect' and not the place for good Afrikaans Christians to be.

My evening of enlightenment was short-lived and resulted in a tremendous feeling of guilt. I knew that attending any other church than the Dutch Reformed Church was 'wrong'. As a result, and in an attempt to deal with the guilt, I made an appointment with our minister and told him what I had done. I told him that I attended the Baptist Church and that I volunteered to accept Christ as my Saviour. Whilst he did not criticise me for the latter, he warned me that the Baptist church liked to seduce young people with music and charismatic sermons. He warned me that I should refrain from going there again and sent me on my way. With the clarity of hindsight and the current state of the Hervormde Kerk, perhaps my old church should have embarked a couple of years ago on getting young people to join even if they did it with music and charismatic sermons. Today, the Hervormde Kerk is struggling to keep its doors open, whilst the Baptist Church, like so many other denominations, recognises that the needs of young people must be addressed to keep them coming to church. We live in changing times, and the Church cannot afford to lag behind. Ultimately, and this is my perception, the aim of the Church should not be to protect age-old traditions, but rather to change with time, so as to continue spreading the Word of God. After my visit to our minister, I felt confused that no one seemed happy that I found Christ and that I wanted to be a Christian. Surely this is what all Christian churches teach and hope that their followers will achieve. I did go a few times with Ponti and his parents to the Baptist Church, and whilst it was a bit too jovial and noisy for my liking, I felt rejuvenated every time I attended.

* * *

The next year was generally a relaxed year. I had my friends, Suzanne had a new boyfriend, who was the organist from our Church, my parents were busy with their work, Johan was studying in Pretoria, and Chris and Rina were raising their first born in Pretoria.

Then, on the morning of 20 May 1983, disaster struck. The African National Congress (ANC) planted a bomb outside the Air Force Head Office in Church Street, Pretoria. This was done on instructions and with approval from Nelson Mandela[9]. The bomb exploded shortly after 4:30. Most of the military personnel and other civil servants were queuing at bus stations, ready to go home. Johan, at this exact time, was across the road in a florist. The building was made entirely from glass panels, on the pavement in front of the Prison Service Head Office across the road from the Head Quarters of the South African Air Force. Both the buildings were similar in size. From the evidence of the damage caused, it was clear that the force of the explosion was tremendous. The destruction it caused between these two concrete giants was devastating. The car contained 40kg of explosives that detonated two minutes prematurely; killing two ANC cadres, whilst 19 other people were killed and more than 200 were injured.

We heard about the incident on the news, but at the time, Johan was living in College Hof, men's hostel, adjacent to the Pretoria University. Although the entire country listened to the news, we did not for one minute think that Johan was in the area of the explosion. Things like this, we believed, only happened in American movies, or to other people. Not to us. About an hour after the explosion my father received a phone call from Johan from Church Square where the Paul Kruger statue is situated some 800m from the site of the explosion. Johan told my father that he had been there. He confirmed that he was all right but had difficulty in hearing. Johan reckoned that there was nothing wrong with him, except that he was not sure how he got from the florist to Church Square, presumably running, whilst being in shock.

My father made arrangements for Johan to come home and he boarded a flight a few days later bound for East London. On arrival Johan looked fine, but his hair was starting to fall out in clumps. By this time, we had seen the devastation the bomb had caused; we could not believe that Johan was still alive but now understood why he was losing his hair, though this was a small price to pay compared with some of the victims of the Church Street Bomb.

Whilst the ANC intended this incident to target military personnel, a lot of civilians were struck down, not to mention the psychological scares this caused for the families of the people killed and/or injured. We were very grateful that Johan survived.

Shortly after this tragic incident and taking into account that Johan was not successful in his studies to become a theologian, he returned to East London. A National Party friend of my father and Member of Parliament, Peet De Pontes, facilitated Johan's appointment to the Department of Home Affairs in East London. This relationship in years to come would result in disaster, devastation, and unimaginable heartache for our family.

---

[9] The Long Walk to Freedom, (1994, pg. 506)

On 1 July 1983, my father announced that he had been promoted to the rank of Brigadier. We were all delighted.

Ponti and I decided that we needed pocket money and obtained casual employment in the liquor off-sales of the Orange Grove Hotel, adjacent to East London airport. We earned R20.00 a weekend.

During October 1983, my father's brother and my godfather, Hein Scheffer, passed away, which brought an end to my legendary 'uncle in the furniture business'. As we were busy preparing for the supplementary exams, I could not attend the funeral and stayed home alone for a week or so.

This was the same time as the matric farewell dance that took place on Friday, 14 October 1983. As the matric farewell dance was very important to us, we organised our partners, and taking into account that Commercial had too few boys for the number of girls in school, the girls were allowed to bring partners from other schools. As the boys had to be given the same privilege, I got a date with a girl from Grens. She was a sweet girl, and very beautiful, but when I had to introduce her to Harry, Ponti and the rest of the crowd, I could not remember her name. Names have never been my forte and as a result our 'romance' was short-lived.

My father had yet again been transferred to Pretoria. This time he was appointed as the Chairman of the Central Release Board, with a seat on the Central Release Advisory Board. Suzanne stayed on in East London, and eventually married the organist of our Church, Robert Taylor and had two beautiful daughters together.

My final exams in East London went well. The night our marks were published, we waited at the offices of the local newspaper *The Daily Dispatch*, with great anticipation. When I got home, I was ecstatic and woke my parents up. My mother was overwhelmed with joy and joined us for champagne to celebrate this magnificent achievement in every child's life.

After school, Harry and Ponti decided that they would move to Port Elizabeth. Harry and Heather went to study Accounting, whilst Ponti enrolled at the then Port Elizabeth Technikon for a National Diploma in Public Relations. My father wanted to hear nothing of the fact that I wanted to go and study in Port Elizabeth as paying for a hostel or boarding house would have been a waste of money, considering the fact that I could study from home. So, that was the end of my wonderful and interesting stay in the Eastern Cape, and more specifically, East London. I made friends I would keep for life; I experienced events that I would recall with fondness and to this day look back on my time in East London as some of the happiest of my life. These events and friendships, will, in time to come, empower me to move across continents.

From the day I was born to the day we moved back to Pretoria, in 1983, we lived in twelve different houses, eight different cities, situated in three of the four provinces or five of the current nine provinces. Today if people ask me "where did you grow up?", I often answer "in South Africa" as we stayed in such a variety of places, from Robben Island to Pretoria. Of all these cities and places we lived in, at heart I remain a citizen of East London in the Eastern Cape, and will always think back to my two years in this windy city with fondness and good memories.

Chapter 3
Beginning Higher Education

1984 was the beginning of my higher education. I was not sure what to study and considered a number of careers whilst in school. Originally, in my primary school days, I wanted to become a priest, but I was never one for languages, and to study to be a priest, I would need to be able to pass Greek, Hebrew, and Latin. So I decided I wanted to become an attorney.

During the time that we stayed in Zonderwater and while attending classes at Erasmus High School, I spent most of my school holidays visiting the local magistrate's court in Cullinan. Although the legal profession was my preferred career, one of my teachers felt that I was not clever enough and strongly recommended that I should change my choice of career. It was said that I would be setting myself up for failure if I pursue a career in the legal profession. This harsh reality eventually put an end to my goal to become an attorney. So my last option was to become a teacher, and for most of my high school career, I resigned myself to that fact. I attended an interview with the relevant schooling authorities in the Eastern Cape and was granted a government bursary to become a teacher. However, the day I had to sign my papers, one of my teachers at Commercial High, Mr Hill, suggested I should study Personnel Management. I was unsure what this meant. However, he explained that it was like teaching, except one just deals more with adults. So, I thought that that should be okay. I did not sign my papers to accept my bursary from the Department of Education and applied to a local bank for a study loan. On our return to Pretoria, I enrolled at the Pretoria Technikon for a three-year National Diploma in Personnel Management.

I was again unhappy to relocate, very much like the situation two years before when we had moved to East London. Then I did not want to move to East London, as I had all my friends in Pretoria in the NTYC. This time around, my friends from the NTYC had all moved on and we were too old for the choir. All my friends were now in East London.

After going back to Pretoria, my parents moved into the standard prison services home allocated to my father according to his rank and position.

I wanted to stay in hostel and secured a place at Lezard – the same hostel where the now famous Afrikaans musician Steve Hofmeyer stayed. On 16 February 1984, we had our first day at Technikon and my tertiary education began. We started with orientation for the National Diploma in Personnel Management. Our first year started under the guidance of Mrs Sonia Swannepoel. In between our first round of classes, a number of guys from my first year's group took a break at the courtyard cafeteria on the old Du Toit Street campus. The outside tables were under a canopy of grapevine and I thought I might as well start meeting new people, making new friends, again.

Hennie was a year older than me and did his national service in the South African Navy before starting with his studies. He was a charismatic character. His remarkable wit underlined his personality. He was clearly more experienced in life, having already completed his national service and served in the war between South Africa, in South West Africa/Namibia, and the South West African People's Organisation (SWAPO), in Angola. He had a wealth of information and seemed to know something about everything. The things he talked about were always both interesting and highly entertaining. This day saw the birth of another friendship that would last for many years, and which directly affected who I would become.

Although our group of friends consisted of about ten people, Hennie became the one individual that kept this friendship together. I had always enjoyed the company of extroverted people, as this gave me the opportunity of being slightly removed, an observer, even a participant, but not leading the conversation. I found being put in the spotlight stressful, something that I could do, and had to do throughout my career, but generally not something that I voluntarily would seek out to do.

Hennie loved to talk about his days in the South African Marines, his sexual achievements, making jokes, and generally, he just loved talking. He stayed at Monitor, one of the Technikon's hostels, situated at the new campus in Pretoria West. In-between classes, we spent our time listening to Hennie's stories. He told us about his service on the Angola border and how he was injured and lost some of his teeth. He told us about midnight marches and military routine. Taking into account that I still had to do my national service, I was both mesmerised and petrified by these tales. Hennie also told us about a girl he met whilst on vacation after he completed his national service. He described her as a beautiful goddess. Her name was Halina, the only child of a wealthy Polish migrant, residing in Houghton, Johannesburg.

As time went by, my friendship with Hennie grew and a strong bond developed between us. Hennie was the commanding general and I the supporting lieutenant who viewed him with unreserved respect and admiration. Everything I wanted to do in life, he seemed to have already done. I was a willing follower, with Hennie as our leader.

By March 1984, I was living at home again. Hostel life did not work for me, so my father reluctantly agreed that I could move back home. I wanted to have my own pocket money, to have the freedom to buy my own cigarettes, without having to explain to my father what I was doing with my money. I needed a job and considering that I worked at the off sales of the Orange Grove Hotel whilst at school, I found a position as a cashier at Rebels Liquor Store in Esselenstreet, Sunnyside, where I worked on weekends.

However, one day, I saw an advertisement for auditions for the opera choir with the Performing Arts Council of Transvaal (PACT). As I had been a member of the NTYC I made an appointment and started preparing for an audition. I loved singing, I loved opera, and I thought it would be great if I could get a position in the ad-hoc Opera Choir at PACT. It would be great, I thought, if I could be doing something I loved, whilst being paid for it. At this time, Giuseppe Verdi's opera '*La Traviata*' was on at the State Theatre. I bought a ticket to see what it was that the opera choir did and instantly knew I wanted to do that. It was beautiful.

The song I used for my audition was a piece I learned under Marian Keys at the East London Technical College. It was Giuseppe Giordani's *Caro Mio Bjen* (*My Dear Beloved*).

The choirmaster was Marcel Seminara and the pianist was Matilda Hornsveld. I was incredibly nervous and whilst singing I felt I was totally out of my league. Even though my mum was very proud that I was invited to an audition, I was not sure if my attempt to be a member of an opera choir would be successful.

Two gruelling weeks went by before I received a letter from PACT. I was prepared for the standard "thank you for attending, but we regret to advise" tone. The letter advised me that I had been selected as a new member of the ad-hoc choir and that I would hold the position of an ad-hoc baritone. This was fantastic and both my mother and I were overjoyed. I was to be paid for every rehearsal and nearly double for every performance. I could now earn my own money, whilst doing something that I enjoy tremendously. The duration of the next year saw me performing in six operas, Umberto Giordano's *Andrea Chénier*; Gaetano Donizetti's *Lucia di Lammermoor*; Giuseppe Verdi's *Rigoletto*; Richard Wagner's *Tristan und Isolde*; Giacomo Puccini's *Turandot* and *La Bohemme*. I sang in two *Singing Christmas Trees*, was selected as a cast member for the musical *The King and I*, decided not to do it, and sang in Handel's *Messiah* whilst I was an extra in Puccini's *Tosca*.

* * *

When I started at the State Theatre in Pretoria, it was the first time that I had been with a group of people that were mostly gay. I was petrified to be among so many gay people or just even to be associated with them, as this was one stigma I feared most. It was fine to be called 'nancy boy' by your sister or rivals at school, but to openly admit that you are gay seemed unthinkable. This, in a country where most acts of homosexuality were considered criminal in law and an absolute repugnance in the eyes of the church. It was said to be an unforgivable sin before God. That was before the law was consolidated and revised by the Criminal Law (Sexual Offences and Related Matters) Amendment Act, 2007. However, the position of the church did not change.

I felt intimidated, but fortunately, I met Willie Roets, a wonderful artistic character with a wicked sense of humour who was some twenty years older than me and became my guardian angel. Willie's wife Barbara was a ballet teacher and the two of them together were very special. Willie took me under his wing and 'protected' me in the nine kilometres of corridors, which spanned the hallways of the State Theatre in Pretoria.

By June 1984, my life was altered forever. An event took place that would change my life fundamentally. Whilst horrifying, it was an event that changed a mummy's boy into a man.

Chapter 4
6 June 1984 – The Day That Changed My Life

We were busy with mid-year exams. I did well academically, passed all my semester tests, and had adjusted well to my tertiary surroundings.

My father settled into his role as the new Chairman of the Prison's Parole Board at Head Office and had a brand new Mercedes-Benz as his 'company car'. As a result, he wanted to sell his eight-year-old BMW 518. Although I was allowed to use the car every now and again, I was cautioned to look after it, as it was due to be sold soon.

On Wednesday, 06 June 1984, at 9:00 in the morning, we wrote a three-hour paper on 'Business Principles in Practice'. I felt confident and was in high spirits. I agreed with Hennie that I would meet him at the hostel after the exam. After completing our papers in less than two hours, I drove from the Du Toit street campus to Hennie's hostel in Pretoria West. We reflected on the exam and at about 12:30, I left the hostel to return home. I was happy as I thought it went well with my exam. I drove from the Pretoria West Campus toward Potgieter Street, where the prison reserve is situated at the southern bottom end of this main road entering Pretoria.

When I reached Potgieter Street, I turned right due south and drove toward the prison reserve. I went under the rail bridge and approached the robot (traffic light) after the old military headquarters. Here I had to turn right into the prison reserve. My indicator was on, and a car was in front of me. Both the car ahead of me and I waited for oncoming traffic.

There was no turning indicator on the traffic light at that time. This would have allowed the traffic turning right out of Potgieter Street to do so more safely. However, after the oncoming traffic had passed, the car in front of me turned right and drove off. I looked dead ahead, there was no oncoming traffic. My indicator was still flashing; there was a car on my left-hand side waiting for our green light to change so that he could cross the intersection from the left. As the road ahead of me was clear, I started moving forward. Moving slowly. The next few moments were burned into my memory, in slow motion. Moments that would haunt me for many years to come.

I saw no vehicles coming down from the Johannesburg highway (motorway) into Potgieter Street, so I started turning and, looking where I was supposed to go, a young man on a motorbike came racing down Potgieter Street. In reflection, and in my estimation, his speed had to be in excess of 120km (75mi) per hour. The time that had lapsed from the moment I looked up to check for oncoming traffic, to the moment of impact, was seconds. The motorbike literally appeared from nowhere and crashed at high speed with a deafening sound.

When the driver of the motorbike realised that he was heading into a crossing with a vehicle in the middle of it, he tried to turn the bike in an attempt to avoid the collision but hit the BMW full on the centre of its left side. I just saw glass everywhere as both the windows on the left of the car exploded.

I was not sure what had happened at the moment of impact; however, the car continued to move slowly forward after the impact. Eventually, I slammed on the brakes. I sat mesmerised trying to come to terms with what had just happened, in disbelief and confusion. I had no idea what had hit me.

I got out of the car and ran around it; I saw the motorbike on the ground, with the driver on the ground. He was moving slowly and clearly in pain, but thankfully alive. His bike was smashed, the battery exploded with battery acid eating away at the yellow paint of my father's car. The car, that was due to be sold within a week or so, was reduced to a wreck.

Within seconds, there were people on the scene, and a prison service official in uniform asked me what happened. In shock, I said, "I don't know," and was left alone. Everyone seemed to focus on the man in the road, and I just stood there. I realised that I had to tell my father and asked someone if I could go to make a phone call. I was told to go, and I ran up the road toward the first row of prison reserve town houses on the left hand side of the road. I ran until I found a house with an open front door. I rushed in and asked the lady who stayed there if I could use her telephone.

I phoned my father's office. He was not available as he was in a Parole Board meeting. I was clearly in shock, but needed to get hold of my father. I shouted at the woman on the other end of the phone and demanded that I speak to him. I told her that I had been in a car accident and needed to speak to him immediately.

When my father took the phone, I was not sure if he was irritated because I had called him out of his meeting, or shocked to learn that I had been in an accident. He sounded very formal and factual, but did inquire about my well-being. I told him that I was all right but very worried about the owner of the motorbike who seemed badly injured. My father told me to stay at the scene of the accident. I ran back to the scene some 200m down the road and again looked in horror at the biker on the road. The shattered motorbike and the deformed BMW stood in quite witness to the frantic events around it. Paramedics arrived and attended to the man in the road. I kept asking them whether he would be all right but they just ignored me. Eventually one of them confirmed that he was very seriously injured. I had no idea what to do; I just stood there, horrified and scared.

The ambulance arrived, shortly after my father. My father went directly to speak to the military personnel attending to the injured motorbike driver. He did not talk to me and I was convinced that he was going to kill me for what had happened to the BMW. It looked as if they had given the man oxygen and stabilised his neck and head before loading him on a hard orange board into the ambulance. I again asked the paramedics if the injured man would be all right and again was told that he was very seriously injured. After the injured man was taken away in the ambulance, my father told me to get into the car and we drove home. No one spoke.

On arriving home, I went into the house looking for my mum. My father was inspecting the damage to the BMW. When I found my mum, she was lying on the couch in the TV room, having an afternoon nap. I woke her, and told her that I had been in an accident. That I thought I might have killed a man. I explained what had happened and begged her to talk to my father. I knew he must have been furious with me for what happened to his car.

My mum was remarkably calm. She immediately got up and asked me to explain to her what exactly happened. She checked whether I was alright and immediately went to the kitchen to prepare a glass of sugar water. She went outside to speak to my father. They talked, but I stayed inside the house. When she came back, she took me into their bedroom and phoned my father's sister-in-law, Aunt Livina. She briefly explained what had happened and handed me the phone. My aunt spoke to me quietly. She told me that I need not worry and that she would phone some people to find out where the ambulance had taken the injured man. She promised to find out how he was doing and to let me know. She also told me that I needed to get back into a car and drive. The last instruction was something I could not do. She spoke firmly and said that she would phone me later. I had to give the phone back to my mum. I remained standing in the bedroom, waiting for my father to explode. But he did not.

My mum informed my father that she was taking me to the chemist to get some tablets for me. My father, I think, phoned Chris, who was stationed in the police in Pretoria somewhere. Before we left, I phoned Hennie and told him that I had been in an accident. I told him that I thought I was in huge trouble and asked him if he could come over to our house. He agreed.

My mum then told me to get into my father's Mercedes. After what had just happened, I did not want to go near a car. My mum ordered me to get into the driver's side. I objected, but my mother wanted to hear none of it and instructed me to get in and drive us to the chemist. I nervously obliged, started the car, reversed out of the driveway, and drove to the chemist.

On our return to the house, Chris and a Warrant Officer from the South African Police Force were there. Hennie also arrived. Although we didn't really talk, it was comforting to have him there. I don't know why I phoned him to come over, but I was grateful that he had made the effort, and his moral support was appreciated.

Later that evening, between Chris and Aunt Levina, it was discovered that the injured biker was a 21-year-old permanent force soldier. He was admitted to 1 Military Hospital at Voortrekkerhoogte, and was pronounced dead an hour after the accident. The local newspaper[10] had a small single announcement, under the heading 'Motorcyclist Killed', written by 'the crime reporter' who confirmed:

---

[10] Pretoria News, 7 June 1984

Motorcyclist Killed

A young man died on the way to hospital after a motorcycle accident in Potgieter Street. The man, whose name has not yet been released, died on the way to 1 Military Hospital, Voortrekkerhoogte soon after 2 pm yesterday.

Later we found out that the young man's name was Bradley Rowe. After it became known that Bradley had passed away, the police informed me that I may be charged with culpable homicide. Whilst the death of any young person at the age of twenty-one is always tragic, the thought of being charged for culpable homicide at the age of 18 was mind numbing. After all of this, my father's approach toward me softened and the next couple of days became a blur. I was in the middle of mid-year exams and was due to write Industrial Relations the following morning at 9 AM.

My first reaction was that I could not write any more exams. However, my mother felt that I should carry on as normally as possible and insisted that I go and write the three-hour paper. Prior to the exam the next day, I went to see both my Personnel Management and Industrial Relations lecturers, Mrs Sonia Swannepoel and Mr Robert Otto, respectively, and told them what had happened. Both were very supportive and understanding. I wrote my Industrial Relations paper and passed despite the circumstances.

The next day at class, one of my classmates, Anina, or Borries as we called her, heard from Hennie what had happened the day before. Borries came to me and just quietly gave me a card. When I opened it, it had a simple message of support, telling me that I had a friend in her, and that if I wanted to talk, she would be there for me. She had no questions nor was she interested in the gruesome detail of what had happened. She just saw me as a friend in distress and offered her unconditional support. I was overwhelmed.

The first Sunday after the accident, we went to church in Du Toit Street, as was the custom in our house. My mother spoke to the minister and told him what had happened the previous Wednesday. After the service, the minister took me aside and prayed for Bradley, our respective families, and me. I did not really want to see or speak to anyone. While the minister prayed for me, I cried quietly. The guilt was devastating. As much as I wanted this nightmare to be over, I could only think of the family and friends of Bradley who that Sunday mourned their son. I heard the sound of the crash in my head over and over. I felt as if I was going crazy. I honestly had not seen the motorbike coming down the road.

The following weekend, Hennie invited me to go home with him to visit his parents, and I thought it would be good to get out of the house. We spent the weekend lounging around at his parent's place. His mother made Cremora fridge tart and we watched MTV the entire weekend. It was good to be with Hennie and his family; they were very supportive. One thing, however, was for sure – I would never forget the 6th of June for the rest of my life.

I continued with my classes and went to the State Theatre every evening to practice for whatever opera we were busy with. Singing with us was a young state prosecutor called Karin. Willie suggested, on a number of occasions, that I should speak to her, as she was able to explain the legal process to me in preparation for what might come. For a long time I did not want to talk about it and just carried on with life as if nothing had happened. My emotional immaturity at the time, in conjunction with my inability to deal with what had happened, was manifesting in various forms. I started having nightmares, anxiety attacks, and becoming paranoid when driving.

My mother knew that something was not right and took me to our house doctor, who referred me to a psychologist for therapy. He was a devoted Christian and from the onset it was clear that he practiced psychology from a Christian perspective. This was comforting for me, as, the Bible verses in his room were reassuring. However, we spoke little about the accident and a lot about my father, my sister, and brothers. Eventually, after various sessions, he explained to me that my paranoia was because of the guilt I felt, that I was not going crazy, and that in time, everything would be all right.

Back at the State Theatre, Karin was always friendly to everyone, and as Willie suggested, I agreed to talk to her about the accident. I wanted to find out what was going on and what the process would be, if the state decided to prosecute. Eventually, one evening at a final dress rehearsal, I mustered

enough courage to talk to her. I told her what happened on the 6th of June and what I had been told by the police. She was kind and supportive and told me that she was the prosecutor in the Pretoria criminal court for traffic related offences. She also explained that in all likelihood, she would be the prosecutor in the event that the state would go ahead with criminal charges against me. She explained in detail what would happen the day in court, what the process would be, and what the realities of a guilty charge could be.

During this time, Hennie was very supportive; he firmly established himself as the leader of our group, with the rest of the gang and I in tow. He even showed interest in my involvement at the State Theatre and was employed by PACT as an extra for a number of the operas in which I sang. Hennie's wit and easy way of interacting with people gave me renewed confidence to talk to the people I worked with. This soon made me realise that most of them were normal hardworking people. The gay people I worked with were not freaks, perverts, or a threat to society, as suggested by the politicians of the time, the church, or our homophobic friends at Technikon. The majority of them were actually great fun. Focused, hardworking and talented people.

* * *

At the time, my association with PACT made me wonder if people could choose to be gay or whether they were born gay. The latter was ridiculed by both the state and the church as a weak excuse for perversion and sinful behaviour. However, it made more sense to me, as I could not believe that any person in his right mind in South Africa, in the mid-1980s, would choose to live a lifestyle resulting in total isolation from society that would evoke constant criticism from the churches, and rejection from broader family circles and friends. Whilst in some cases, under the law at that time[11], if caught and convicted, it was considered a crime for men to engage in any sort of erotic contact in situations where more than two people were present.

I looked at the definition for the term 'gay' and found the following descriptions: *"(1) homosexual (2) relating to homosexuals (3) light-hearted and carefree.* I went to look for the word 'homosexual', which was defined as *"feeling or involving sexual attraction to people of one's own sex"*[12]. I had a better insight into a large grouping of the people that I worked with.

Later in life, I would actively and consciously strive to alter my behaviour and attitude towards others. I realised that the psychological make-up of human beings was not simplistic at all. I learned to become more tolerant and that as I hated to be judged, I also should not be so judgmental of others. These principles are, in fact, confirmed in the Bible, the Torah, and the Koran and are generally values of people with and without faith. In time to come, it will become my belief that we should treat people with respect, irrespective of their religious opinions or orientation in life, in the way we would like to be treated.

My singing in the Opera Choir was great for stress relief and very good for my personal growth, whilst helping me to deal with my own psychological issues.

* * *

On 25 October 1984, Karin phoned to inform me that she had spoken to her superiors. My file had come back from the office of the Attorney General and it was confirmed that the state intended to charge me with culpable homicide. The date for the court case was set for 16 November. I was petrified. This was the worst birthday present I had ever received.

During the week following my birthday, my father took me to a prominent attorney in Pretoria whom he requested to instruct my mother's brother, a leading professor in law and an advocate to the High Court, to be my council.

Prof Johan van der Vyver is my mother's only brother. He worked initially in the Law Faculties of both Potchefstroom and Wits Universities until 1995, when he was appointed as the I.T. Cohen Professor of International Law and Human Rights at Emory University, Atlanta, Georgia. He also served as a fellow in the Human Rights Program of The Carter Centre from 1995-1998. He is the author of many books and more than two hundred law review

---

[11] Section 20A, Immorality Act, 1957
[12] Compact Oxford Dictionary, (2008, pg 417 and 485)

articles, popular notes, chapters in books and book reviews on human rights and a variety of other subject matters.[13]

He is a brilliant and respected legal mind, both in South Africa and abroad. Today, he is globally respected and recognised for his views on human rights, international and political law, a man for whom I have the deepest respect. Oom (uncle) Johan indicated that he would help us and guided me through the judicial process of a culpable homicide court case.

The BMW was fully repaired and was still in my father's stable. The previous buyer no longer wanted it so I used it as a means of transport.

Mr Otto, one of my lecturers, regularly inquired how things were going and when I told him that I had been charged and had to appear in court, he offered to be a character witness at my hearing. Although my legal team never made use of this offer, I thought it was a kind gesture.

During the next couple of weeks, I became more and more anxious about the pending court case and emerged myself in my studies and my work at the Theatre. This resulted in me passing all my first year subjects with flying colours. In addition, my psychologist advised my parents that following the court case I should go away and have a break. I chose to go and visit Ponti for three weeks in Port Elizabeth.

A week before the court case, I contacted Bradley's parents. Mrs Rowe answered the phone. I introduced myself and informed her that the court case was set for 16 November. She did not talk much but thanked me politely for letting her know. I felt better for doing this, irrespective of the fact that I was shaking with nerves.

The day of the court case, I dressed in a dark suit and took a calming tablet, prescribed by our doctor. Both my parents and Hennie were in court to support me.

Prior to the hearing, Oom Johan told me to listen carefully and answer all questions honestly and directly, explaining that once I was called to the witness stand, he would guide my testimony, after which the prosecutor would have the opportunity to cross-examine. He instructed me to direct all my answers to the Magistrate and told me that if I did not understand a question, I should say so and ask for clarification. As South Africa does not have a jury system, a single Magistrate would decide my fate. I was incredibly nervous, so were both my parents.

On arriving in court, I was showed to the bench reserved for the accused. There were a number of unfamiliar people in the courtroom. Two ladies were sitting toward the middle of the public gallery and were clearly much stressed. I assumed that they were members of the Rowe family. They made no eye contact with me.

Karin withdrew from the case, as we were still working together at the State Theatre and she assisted me with the process. One of her colleagues took the case, a blond female prosecutor. Karin sat at the back of the courtroom.

---

[13] *http://www.law.emory.edu*

The prosecutor began the state's case and confirmed that Bradley "was a young man in the prime of his life, who was a respected young leader in his community and a keen sportsman". She submitted, "His life was prematurely ended due to the negligent driving of the accused." She stated that I "did not take due care when crossing the intersection and as a result of [my] negligence", she submitted that I "caused harm to come across his way, which directly resulted in the accident and the premature end of his life". She called the accident an "unnecessary incident, which could have been prevented". The state prosecutor presented nauseating and very graphic evidence from the coroner's report on Bradley's injuries and submitted that I should have seen the motorbike coming down Potgieter Street. She presented a picture to the Magistrate of 'blatant negligence and disregard for traffic rules'. She made me sound as if I disregarded life in general and deliberately caused the untimely death of a 21-year-old man in the prime of his life, ignoring the fact that I was, at the time, only 18 years old.

Oom Johan called me to the witness stand and asked me to introduce myself for the record to the court. He clarified my date of birth to establish my age and asked me what my profession was. I confirmed that I was a full-time student at the Pretoria Technikon where I was studying toward my National Diploma in Personnel Management. He then asked me to explain to the best of my abilities, what happened on the day of 6th June at around 1:00 PM. I explained as clearly as I possibly could that I had written an exam at 9:00 in the morning, that I went to visit my friend at the Technikon hostels in Pretoria west, and that I drove home in my father's BMW at about 1:00 PM. I explained that whilst approaching the Prison in Potgieter Street, there were one or two cars in front of me waiting at the traffic light to turn green, after which I waited for the car in front of me to clear the intersection. I looked up into Potgieter Street to see if there was any oncoming traffic, as I needed to turn right into the Prison Reserve. I told the court that I saw no traffic when it was my turn to cross the robot into the road leading into the reserve. I relived the sound of the crash, the glass shattering, the shock, the motorbike lying in the road and the driver on the ground, that I had run to phone my father, and that, eventually, the ambulance had taken the injured driver away. I told the court that later that day I learned that the driver had died at 1 Military Hospital at Voortrekkerhoogte, and that his name was Bradley Rowe.

Oom Johan asked me to explain what I had done the week prior to the court case. I told the court that I had phoned the house of the Rowe family in Benoni to inform Mrs Rowe that the date of the court case was set down for the 16th of November and that she responded politely when she thanked me for the call. On asking why I phoned her, I answered, "because I felt it was the right thing to do, they had a right to be here."

The prosecutor began with her cross-questioning and tried to trick me in changing my testimony with a hundred and one questions. All her questions were just about the same but worded slightly differently, presumably in an attempt to confuse me. I listened attentively and answered her questions whilst addressing my answers to the Magistrate. Eventually, her questions became so confusing that I addressed the Magistrate and indicated that I was not sure what the prosecutor wanted me to say as I had answered all the questions honestly and to the best of my ability, yet she kept on asking the same questions over and over. The Magistrate reprimanded the prosecutor. She then decided to attack the fact that I phoned the Rowe family. She tried to show that it proved I was guilty of negligence. I did feel terrible guilt, not of negligence, but for the loss of Bradley's life, and that was why I phoned them. I agreed with her that I had a deep feeling of guilt, as they had lost their son, brother, family member and friend. However, I disagreed with her claim that I was negligent. I phoned them because I felt they had a right to be there. They had a right to know what happened that terrible day in June. They needed to deal with their loss as I had to deal with this terrible event that had happened, and the consequences thereof in my life.

Oom Johan re-directed briefly before he closed by submitting that at the time of the accident I was only 18 years old, that I come from a reputable family, and that my father was a high ranking officer in the Prison Services. He explained that I was raised according to Christian principles and that I was in the wrong place at the wrong time. He called Karin as a character witness and she confirmed that I sang with her in the Opera Choir. She testified that she had got to know me as a kind, sensitive, and caring individual who would not purposefully harm any individual. Oom Johan ended his closing argument by requesting the court that if the state could not prove beyond a reasonable doubt that I was negligent in my actions on that dreadful day, the charges against me should be dropped. However, he submitted that in the unlikely event of the court finding in favour of the state, a custodian sentence would be inappropriate and as such proposed that a suspended sentence should be considered.

In hearing Oom Johan's submission, I went cold, as I now thought that there was a distinct possibility that I may go to prison, if found guilty. The events in the court became a blur; my legs shook uncontrollably. I stood staring into space and prayed quietly that this nightmare would end. The anguish and stress was becoming unbearable. Whilst all of this was carrying on inside me, I made sure not to portray any emotion to the court and tried to regulate my increased tension with deep breathing.

The prosecutor had the final word, and at the start of her closing argument, she took a newspaper article from one of the ladies, who I can only assume must have been Bradley's mother, and with the court's permission, read the newspaper clipping. The article confirmed the tragic events of 6 June 1984 and that Bradley Rowe (21) was a much-loved member of the community of Benoni where he and his family lived. The article mourned the untimely death of this brilliant sportsman, and confirmed that he would be terribly missed by all who knew him. The article described his death as an absolute tragedy.

The Magistrate called a recess and confirmed that he would present both his verdict and sentence, if necessary, after lunch.

I was going out of my mind with fear, and my parents were equally worried. Oom Johan tried to keep us calm.

After the lunch break, we returned to court. The Magistrate came in, we all stood up, and I remained standing to hear his verdict. My legs were shaking so much that I held on to the wooden barrier on top of the bench.

The Magistrate confirmed that he viewed me as a credible witness, who answered the questions put to me honestly and directly. He acknowledged that the court was impressed with the fact that I phoned the Rowe family to inform them of the hearing. This, he said, demonstrated that I felt real remorse for what happened but pointed out that the larger society also needed to be protected and as such, a suspended sentence would be inappropriate.

My legs became like jelly. I interpreted these comments as my one way ticket to Pretoria Central Prison. I was only 19 years old and the prison, next to which I grew up, now became a reality for me, for something that I did not intend to happen. I did not see any oncoming traffic. I did not see the motorbike. What more did I need to do to convince the court of my innocence?

In closing, the magistrate confirmed his finding of "guilty as charged". I was found guilty of culpable homicide in that I caused the 'unlawful killing of a human being without malice aforethought'. He immediately proceeded to sentence me to a R300 [£666] fine or 100 days imprisonment. Plus a further R600 [£1332] or 200 days imprisonment, which was conditionally suspended for five years. By this time I was not registering anymore and was not sure what any of this meant.

The prosecutor did not look pleased and the Rowe family were equally unimpressed. I was immediately escorted out of the court, together with my father and Oom Johan. The three of us went to the cashier, where my father paid the R300 fine.

That evening, my parents took me to Jan Smuts Airport where I boarded a plane to Port Elizabeth to go and visit my friend Ponti.

The court case and the events preceding this day were incredibly traumatic for both my family and I. What it did to the Rowe family stayed with me for the rest of my life. More than thirty years after this event, and for the remainder of my life, I still have to confirm, on each visa application, and every job application in the public sector, what the outcome of that fateful day. For me, this never became easier Thirty years later, when people heard of the conviction, their immediate response still made me feel like a criminal.

On 17 November, I woke up in a student's home situated at 45 Newton Street, Newton Park in Port Elizabeth. Here, Ponti lived with a group of students and some of our old school friends from East London who were either studying or working in Port Elizabeth.

I suddenly found myself in a place where there was no judgment, no questions, no pressure. I was again among my friends. The next three weeks were a relief; we spent a lot of quiet time in the sun, not on the busy beaches, not among many tourists, just me and my friends, in the back yard of the house in Newton Street.

Finally my respite came to an end, and I had to return to Pretoria, to my studies and home to the entrance to the prison reserve on the corner of Potgieter Street and Skanskop Road, to face the realities of what happened in June that year.

Chapter 5
Visiting Europe for the First Time

In January 1985, we started our second year at Pretoria Technikon. The Technikon authorities established their first unisex hostel for second and third year students. I convinced my parents that I should move to this hostel and both Hennie and I moved into Kollege Hof. This was fantastic as the hostel was more like a block of flats with a communal dining room. Friends often visited, we had braais (barbeques), and generally enjoyed a carefree student life. Most students went home every weekend; however, I considered my 'flat' as my home and enjoyed the quiet time alone. I spent weekends cleaning and did go to see my parents but returned to my 'flat' most evenings.

During the first term of that year, Hennie and I decided to go overseas. My godfather, *Hein Scheffer,* who died in 1983, had left me R2000.00, so I told my parents that I would like to use this money to go overseas. I had saved all the money I earned whilst singing at the State Theatre, and although I had a very rough first year at Technikon, I passed all my subjects despite my personal circumstances. My parents agreed that we could go explore Europe.

In preparation for our tour to Europe and all it has to offer, Hennie took me to Hillbrow, a very hip suburb in Johannesburg at the time. Our outing educational, to watch the *Rocky Horror Picture Show,* a prohibited movie banned by the South African censor board. I watch this cult movie with absolute enchantment.

One evening, a number of students from other hostels were having a social at 'Denise', the ladies hostel adjacent to ours. Hennie and I met a guy, sitting alone on a 'lovers-bench', playing his guitar, oblivious to the people around him. That evening we met Dietloff Giliomee, a student in Electrical Engineering and a brilliantly talented musician, writer, and human being.

It is an interesting truth that all humans, irrespective of our education, status, or intellect, have a deep-rooted need to belong. We have an urge to be part of a social order of some sort, a desire to be part of a social circle. Abraham Maslow defined this desire in his 'Hierarchy of Needs'[14] in 1943, as one of the five levels of personal needs; a systematic progression in achieving our full potential.

As I was accustomed to moving from place to place, I was never really perturbed about belonging to a social group; however, my time in the NTYC and the subsequent years in East London taught me that it is great to have good

---

[14] Theory of Human Motivation, 1943

friends and to belong to a social circle. I guess the fact that we went to church, every Sunday, also contributed to understanding the benefits of being part of a wider congregation. After all, we all want to be accepted, preferably the way we are rather than the way that others believe we should be. It is, however, unfortunate that peer group pressures at times stifle our development. Instead of allowing the influences of others to develop our personalities, we allow opportunity to pass us by.

I developed a subordinate or rather subservient role to Hennie in that he was the leader and I the follower; whatever he said was gospel, not because he commanded that, but because I allowed that to be. Instead of learning from Hennie, as I believe we learn from people around us, and developing my own personality and attributes, I set myself to his standards and followed him blindly. This behaviour was cleverly worded by Dietloff in a song that I asked him to write, about our circle of friends. Dietloff wrote about our student days, but the words of a campfire song is as applicable today as it was in 1985. The lyrics of the song called *Young Days* verbalised our circle of friends as follows:

Young Days[15]

Your life depends,
on all those people that you meet;
Your crowd get sorted,
into a virgin's lover's treat;
You fix your grin,
because the crowd you're in;
They've become your sun and rain –
And when the dark days come,
your crowd is fading out, and holding hands is never thought about!
Ten years from now,
You'll think of all the love you shared;
Knowing they're gone,
makes you cold depressed and scared;
You await the pain,
like summer for the rain;
Your dreams lies scattered in your thoughts –
And in your heart you'll find, there's no one left to hold,
Still, winter can't lay off the cold.

Dietloff – 1985

This song verbalised my need for approval, support, love, and acceptance from my circle of friends. It could be argued that, to a large extent, this applies to all the people that we meet in our lives, be it our parents, siblings, friends,

---

[15] D. Giliomee, Young Days, November 1985

spouses, bosses or colleagues. We need to belong, be accepted, be appraised whether by social order, our families, at work, and/or be accepted by our spouses or life partners. Regrettably, what I had not yet learned was that whilst it is great to belong to a social circle, to learn from the people around me is much more important.

The next three months saw us planning our tour to Europe. I had a pen-friend in Solingen, Germany, called Petra Brenner. Petra and I had been pen-pals since standard six (grade eight) when I attended Erasmus High School. I wrote to her and asked if we could come and visit. She confirmed that it would be great to eventually meet.

Whilst we were supposed to pay attention to our studies, the pending European tour was all-absorbing. The results of my first semester tests were less than impressive but I scraped through with good marks in Industrial Relations. After all, there was still time to improve on the year marks in preparation for the final exams in November. Our date for departure to Europe was set for the 15th of June 1985.

* * *

However, I had to face the memories of the 6th of June. The first anniversary of that dreadful day, I had a quiet internal struggle as this date approached and was not sure what to do. *Do I make contact with the Rowe family, again? Just to tell them that I have not forgotten their pain. That I will never forget. That I think of them? Surely, I would be the last person from whom they would want to hear.* I wanted to do something to remember this terrible day, if not for myself, then at least in memory of Bradley.

At 12:30 in the afternoon on 6 June 1985, I stopped in Brooklyn at a florist where I bought a bunch of red roses. I drove down Queen Wilhelmina Drive toward fountain circle and headed out towards Voortrekkerhoogte. The roses were on the passenger seat next to me. The events of a year ago played through my memory like a movie. The emotion and pain haunted me as strongly as the year before. After I passed the Voortrekker Monument on my right hand side, I turned right, just before the Iscor Head Office, and headed toward Potgieter Street. This must have been the same route that Bradley had taken a year ago, before he drove toward Potgieter Street on that fateful day. As I entered the southern point of Potgieter Street, I looked down the length of the street and saw the traffic light at the entrance to the prison reserve. The road was now being altered and road works were underway to make it a double motorway into Pretoria. I drove toward the prison reserve, and at about 1:00 PM, I passed the dreadful site where Bradley's life ended a year ago and my life was altered forever. I opened my window, took the roses, and gently dropped them on the road. As I drove on, I saw the red roses in the middle of the road, I saw the BMW, I saw the motorcycle, I saw Bradley... I cried.

On 15 June 1985, Hennie and I boarded Lux Air, on route to Luxembourg and a vacation of a lifetime. We visited five countries in twenty days. On our arrival in Luxembourg, we travelled by coach to Amsterdam station. We found our hotel and as we walked into the foyer, we saw a poster of Nelson Mandela with a slogan "Free Nelson Mandela". We presented our newly issued South African passports to the man at the reception desk. But were startled when we were told the hotel was full, irrespective of the fact that we had a pre- paid booking, whilst another member of staff took our suitcases and placed these outside the door in the street. We were not welcome. This caused a bit of a damper to the start of our vacation, as we were in a country that we had never been to before. Treated in a rather hostile manner by the Dutch staff. Hennie and I found another hotel, called the Hotel Adolesce. The hotel was an old canal house converted into a hotel in the heart of Amsterdam. I was exhausted and grateful that we had found a place to stay. Hennie wanted to go out and explore Amsterdam. I stayed at the hotel and Hennie went out exploring. The next day he showed me the places he saw, and it became apparent that our hotel was very close to the famous red-light district.

Coming from a very conservative background, this was an absolute shock to my system. We saw prostitutes, both male and female, offering their 'services' from windows; we saw adult films in both Dutch and German, and even stood in front of a very menacing black satanic temple.

From Amsterdam, we travelled by bus to Oostende from where we took a ferry to Dover and the British Isles. We spent two days in London and ate McDonalds at Piccadilly Circus, visited Buckingham Palace, drank beer in Soho, and walked in St. James' Park.

After returning to the continent, we took a train to Germany and ended up in Cologne. We thought we were very close to Solingen, but were mistaken. We walked next to the Rhine River toward the famous Cathedral in Cologne, where we crossed the bridge and somehow ended inside an ammunition factory where we were arrested by the factory security. In very broken German, I explained that we were students from South Africa and that we were on our way to Solingen and were lost. After lots of explaining and demonstrating, we were escorted out of the premises and directed on to a country road. We eventually found ourselves on the famous 'Autobahn', where we hitchhiked in an attempt to get a lift to Solingen. The motorists were less than accommodating, as pedestrians are illegal on the autobahn, let alone allowed to hitchhike. It was not long before a German policeman picked us up and was kind enough to drop us at the nearest train station. We took a train bound for Solingen.

In Solingen, Petra Brenner and her father came to collect us at the station. It was a strange feeling, as Petra and I had been writing to each other for more than five years, yet this was the first time that we had met.

The Brenners lived in a small apartment in no 4 Damashke Strasse, Solingen. Herr Brenner made arrangements for Hennie and me to stay at a nearby Guest House. Frau Brenner was astonished that both Hennie and I were white, whilst our impeccable table manners and general good conduct impressed her immensely.

During the next five days, we were treated to walks in forests and visits to the town of Solingen. Petra worked at the radio station of a local hospital and invited us to visit. The program presenter treated us like celebrities and invited people to phone in to talk to the two visiting South African students. No one phoned. Irrespective of this, we had a great time.

After a wonderful week with the Brenners, we boarded the train bound for Italy. Herr Brenner gave Hennie and I each a silver bottle opener from Solingen. On my arrival back in South Africa, I had a small hole drilled into one of the corners of the opener and made a key- holder out of it. I still use this for my keys.

On route to Italy, we were mesmerised by the scenery of the German countryside and could not believe the beautiful vineyards on the mountain slopes within, the then, West Germany. During our train trip, Hennie discovered that he had misplaced his passport and we soon realised that we would not be able to leave West Germany to enter Italy. Hennie suggested that he would get off at the next station and suggested that I should go ahead to Italy without him. He proposed that we would meet up again once he had sorted out his passport. I did not want to go into a foreign country on my own nor did I want to leave Hennie in West Germany on his own, so we decided to disembark at the next station, which was Frankfurt-am-Main.

On arriving at the spectacular Frankfurt-am-Main Hauptbanhoff, we secured our luggage in a locker, contacted the South African Consulate, and made our way through the streets to the Consulate. We walked past the Frankfurt Opera House, eventually arriving at the Consulate; we explained our dilemma and were directed to a waiting area. I helped Hennie with the completion of some of the forms they handed to us and made an error with his names. I recorded his names as Hendrik Petrus Crowther, instead of Hendrik Pieter Crowther. This created some suspicion with the officials at the Consulate and they started questioning us independently. Eventually they confirmed Hennie's identity with Pretoria and said that his replacement passport would be ready in five days. Five Days! We only had two weeks left of our vacation and still had to get to Italy. With five days delay it soon became apparent that we would not make it to Italy. In addition, we were not sure if we would have had sufficient funds to sustain ourselves for an additional week in Frankfurt.

The receptionist at the Consulate, called Katherine, took a liking to Hennie and I, and saw that we were in a bit of a predicament. She invited us to stay with her in her flat for five days until the issue of the replacement passport. We accepted her kind offer gratefully. When we arrived at Katharine's flat, we were shocked at its state. There was underwear and a large number of empty bottles of wine everywhere. It was evident that she recently had had a huge party in her flat.

Before leaving the Consulate, Katherine had told us that when we got to her flat, we must excuse the mess and to help ourselves to the potato salad in the fridge. We opened the fridge and found a twenty-litre bucket filled with real traditional 'sauer potato salad'. This, I must admit, was a great treat as we were starving and the salad tasted excellent.

That evening, Katherine arrived from work and again apologised for the state of her flat. She made a feeble attempt to clean it, removed the underwear, and started preparations for dinner. Later that evening, Katherine's boyfriend, John, arrived. He was a large, dynamic and very friendly Afro-American living with her in Germany.

Taking into account that this was 1985, PW Botha was State President of South Africa, it was the height of apartheid – the forceful implementation of race segregation in South Africa. We knew that if we were in South Africa, we would be breaking a number of laws. Hennie and I spent a pleasant evening with Katherine and John. It was the first time in my life that I had spent an entire evening, in a social setting, in the company of a black man. A man who spoke fluent German, drank German beer, sang German folk songs and was a well-spoken, well-read, and well-travelled human being. An epiphany.

The next morning, Hennie and I thanked both Katherine and John for their hospitality but indicated that we would like to explore Frankfurt. We found a youth hostel near the city centre, the Frankfurt station, and the Consulate. We walked around, looked at bookstores, attended a public cinema where we watched German porn, eating German sausages and drinking beer. Tension started to mount between Hennie and me, as I felt disappointed that we could not go to Italy, whilst Hennie felt agitated because he had lost his passport.

Once we got Hennie's replacement passport, we decided to skip Italy and boarded a train for Paris. We arrived in the late afternoon and I was totally mesmerised by the size and beauty of the city. We made friends with other students we met in a park. We had no more money and were relieved when they invited us to join them in their youth hostel. We managed to stay for two nights before being found out by the hostel management who duly evicted us. The next night, Hennie and I slept in a park as our funds were now dangerously low and we still had about three days before we could board our plane back home.

That evening, with hardly any money left, we sat in a pub, drank beer, and ate the peanuts on the bar counter for dinner.

The following day, we booked a single hotel room in the Beaubourg area, in the fourth arrondissement of the city. We could not afford two rooms. We spent the day on a market plain in front of the Centre Georges Pompidou[16]. A very modern and state-of-the-art, high-tech, cultural building. A large public

---

[16] http://www.centrepompidou.fr/

library where we asked to see what they had on South Africa. The attendant confirmed that they had a number of videos on 'apartheid'. We watched a video which was supposed to be about South Africa but focused purely on the political system of apartheid showing a large number of 'dead black people' on Church Square. We thought this to be anti-South African propaganda at its best. Not far from this centre, we also visited the world famous Notre Dame Cathedral[17]. Outside, we bought prints of Paris and the Cathedral.

That evening, we had no money for dinner and hung around a McDonald's restaurant. We saw a black family having dinner with four children, and when they got up to leave, Hennie and I went in for the kill and helped ourselves to their leftovers. Dinner was good and we knew that the next day we could start heading home.

We were very relieved to board our bus to Luxembourg, to start our journey back to Johannesburg. Our twenty-day tour was history. That evening on the plane, we had dinner twice and drank wine and beer. I had lost nine kilograms and on our return to Jan Smuts Airport. My mother and Ursula came to collect me, whilst Hennie's mum and Halina collected him. We were both pleased to be back home but were also relieved that we could go our own ways for a while.

Being home from Europe brought us back to reality. I went back to Kollege Hof, cleaned our rooms, and prepared for the new semester to start.

At the end of 1985, I stopped singing in the Opera Choir. In January 1986, I started to work as evening duty manager at the Buffet De La Opera Restaurant, situated in the marble foyer of the State Theatre in Pretoria. This started a life-long passion for the hospitality sector.

The former coordinator for the Opera Department was now responsible for the catering functions within the State Theatre and arranged for me to meet PACT's Catering Manager, a very dynamic and friendly individual called Amanda. Amanda and the Executive Chef knew each other from her days when she did her hotel school in-service training, and a strong bond developed between them. In the beginning, I felt out of place, but soon proved my worth as one who managed the evening shift of the restaurant's activities effectively on my own.

I spent just about every evening during the next two years at the State Theatre and completed the balance of my studies in its corridors. I enjoyed my work as Restaurant Duty Manager tremendously. I learned a great deal from Amanda. She was a great mentor and later became a good friend who would also have a dramatic influence in my life in time to come.

The Buffet De La Opera hosted functions for up to 500 people in the marble foyer, and did the catering for the annual Opera Ball. A very glamorous debutante ball, held on the Opera stage itself, resulting in the crowning of Miss Jacaranda annually.

---

[17] http://www.notredamedeparis.fr/

The beginning of 1986, I felt somewhat out of place with the second year class, as all my friends had moved on to their third year. In the Personnel Management II class, I knew none of the students. On my left hand side, against the wall, sat a guy who looked a lot like Bruce Willis. I greeted him, and at the end of the class, we introduced ourselves, and then I met Andre Waters.

Johan was transferred to Pretoria and worked at the Head Office for the Department of Home Affairs, which enabled him to purchase his own two-bedroom flat in Sunnyside.

Ponti's girlfriend became pregnant which brought an end to his jolly times in Port Elizabeth, as they tied the knot in anticipation of the birth of their first child. Ponti and Renita moved in with his parents, who had a large home in Sunninghill in East London. I could not attend the wedding as it was in the middle of our semester tests and I did not have the funds to fly to East London either. They moved into their own flat and prepared their home for the new arrival. I flew down to East London just before Renita was admitted to the hospital. During the time prior to the baby's birth, I helped Ponti at home whilst attending to Renita's every need. Carla Francois Rademan was born on 8 April 1986, a beautiful baby girl.

I studied very hard during 1986, as my father was not impressed with the fact that I had failed my previous year, and reminded me that I was responsible for the repayment of my study loan and could not afford to waste another year. I continued to work at the restaurant about six nights a week.

Towards the middle of the year, I decided that I wanted to move into my own flat. I no longer wanted to study full-time and wanted to get a job, whilst completing the remainder of my studies part-time. I found a flat on the corner of Du Toit and Church Streets, directly across from the Technikon and shared my flat with Dawie Vermeulen, a friend of mine from Overkruin High school. I applied for a position with the Department of Foreign Affairs, and was appointed as a personnel clerk in October 1986.

On 25th October 1986, I celebrated my 21st birthday at the Pioneers Park Open Air Museum. We made stir-fry, drank copious amounts of beer and wine, and partied until the early hours of the morning.

During November that year, Hennie was finishing his studies and applied for various personnel-related positions at a variety of companies. I still did my shifts as duty manager at the restaurant in the evening at the State Theatre. The restaurant was very busy with the Christmas showcase, traditionally a pantomime, or musical, the performance of the annual singing Christmas Tree shortly before Christmas and the New Year's performances on the 31st of December. These were great times. Ronel Erasmus, the modern day gospel singer, played the piano in the Marble Foyer. Amanda and I had a lot of fun with the guests and I recall this period of my life with nostalgia.

Back in the Eastern Cape, Harry and Heather completed their studies and got married; they settled in East London and started to build what would become one successful business after the other.

Suzanne and Robert got married later in that year in East London, and Robert's son, Robert Jr., a school friend from the Drakensberg Boys' Choir and I sang at their wedding.

Chapter 6
The Beauty and Pain of Adoption

During March of 1987, a friend of Johan and I, whom I will call Catherine, became pregnant with twins. She told us that her boyfriend was under pressure from his family to deny his responsibility. His mum did not support the relationship and refused to let them marry. At the time, Catherine was a law student at Pretoria University and had strong roots in the Western Cape. She needed to continue with her studies and was not able to care for two little girls without the help of their father. She paid for her own studies and could not afford to be a single mother. Both Johan and I became very close to her during this time. We helped her through her pregnancy, with the assistance of my mum.

Eventually, on the 29th of March 1987, the girls were born. Only Johan and I were at the hospital with Catherine. Most of the people at the hospital thought that I was the father. I played my part and held her hand, supporting her, as she was in pain after the caesarean. Following several discussions with my mum and a number of social workers, Catherine agreed that her two daughters be adopted. In years to come, we learned that the girls brought great joy to their adoptive family; however, their departure broke Catherine's heart. As time went by, I saw that the loss of her girls remained with her and she often talked about them, especially around their birthday.

At the time of their birth, I promised her, although I had no right to do so, that one day there will be contact between her and her girls. Whilst Catherine regretted giving up the girls, this event in her life ensured that she became a fighter. She was ultimately rewarded with another child, and she embarked on a fantastic academic career as author and became a Professor in law.

On reflecting on 'the beauty of adoption', it is evident to me that people react differently to potentially the same circumstances. Children who are adopted, at times reject their parents for not telling them that they were adopted. Yet, those parents were there when they were babies and assisted them to grow up. Surely, it must be better to give a child up for adoption if you cannot look after that child, rather than having an abortion, or allowing the child to grow up in a park in absolute poverty. Life these days is far too easily terminated through abortion; the latter in my view, should never have been made so easy.

Sometimes it is very difficult to do the right thing, but adoption is a bittersweet gift. I have seen how difficult it is for a biological mother to give her children away. Yet, it is wonderful for adoptive parents to be able to adopt a child they otherwise would not have.

Whilst abortions are legal in the United Kingdom, South Africa and most of the western world, adoption is a much better gift any mother could give her child whom she cannot raise on her own.

It is my view, through my experience with Catherine and through my own personal experiences, that the act of giving a child for adoption is a remarkable gift. During adoption, and specifically if you are an adopted child, it should be remembered that your biological mother had nine months to contemplate what she must do before she actually finalised the adoption. The adoptive parents, especially in the United Kingdom, had to wait much longer for the arrival of their adoptive child. They had probably tried to conceive their own child. When this did not work, they possibly started with various medical interventions to fall pregnant. Ultimately, when their third or fourth, and in some cases fifteenth, in-vitro fertilization (IVF) failed, the adoption option is debated. This on its own is a difficult and very long process. My wife and I in later years had to follow the same route.

* * *

We registered with a variety of adoption agencies in South Africa. Some immediately told us that the waiting list was more than two years and that they would not consider us, unless we were prepared to adopt a Black child. Eventually, we ended up with an agency in Johannesburg who confirmed our registration and invited us to attend an informal meeting during which a variety of questions were asked by a social worker. Information was exchanged about who we are, what it is that we want from this adoption, and a large variety of topics that were very personal. One could even define this as an invasion into our own privacy; however, no adoption agency or social worker will approve an adoption if they are not convinced that the adoptive parents will act in the best interest of the child. Ultimately, social services is entrusted, by the biological mother, or in most cases by the state, to ensure that her child is placed with parents who will give the child a suitable life, filled with love and support.

During this evaluation process, the social worker inquired about what kind of work we did, what our circumstances were, in addition to us having to supply a full medical report and references from our employers at the time. We had to get references from family and friends, people who knew us well, and had to declare if we had criminal records or not.

Regrettably, the waiting lists with all agencies were just too long. White babies were scarce; people opted for abortion, the killing of a human being, rather than giving that life a wonderful second chance. Ironically, pro-adoption campaigners often publish eloquently worded reasons why abortion is the right of the mother, but persistently fail to deal with the right of the child.

Eventually, some agencies phoned and confirmed that they were taking us off their list as we were just too far down and actually returned our documentation and personal information to us by post. Fortunately, my wife and I agreed that one does not have to have children to be happy, and the fact that we could not have children also did not mean that we were doomed to be unhappy. We did try years later again, but again without success. This resulted in the writing of *A Letter to my Daughter* which I wrote in 2011 and became a finalist in the Brit Writers Awards in 2012 (see Chapter 25).

* * *

Adoption is clearly not a light-hearted matter. It is a long process, full of investigations, personal reviews, internal considerations, and at times, a very rewarding process. As for the case of Catherine's daughters, suitable parents were found for the twins, there was contact between them and Catherine, and the fact that loving parents raised them, was a comfort for Catherine.

Years later, I met a very dynamic girl from Kenya, who I will call Kaweria (meaning 'Loving One'). At the age of eighteen, Kaweria learned that she was adopted. However, for reasons unknown to me, her own sister adopted her, and when Kaweria visited her 'grandparents', she was actually visiting her own parents. When she found out that she had been adopted, Kaweria was very bitter and cried for days on end. After she had dealt with the initial shock and disappointment, and this is the remarkable part, she became an incredibly dynamic, self-motivated, and respected young lady, proud of who she was, what she had achieved in life, and a role model to many. She effectively made a choice in her life, when she decided that:

"I will not allow my circumstances to dictate my happiness, or bitterness or even my future. I will take charge of my circumstances and ensure that I remain in control of my happiness, my future and make every event in my life a learning experience. From each incident I take the good and learn from this and consider the negative and learn from this. In my life, this has worked."[18]

This woman became a highly respected member of my staff. Her aptitude and attitude are clearly evident in who she eventually became.

It is true that these experiences influence our perceptions of life; however, the realities of our lives are predominately influenced by the choices that we make. In my view, happiness comes from within. You need not be the biological child of your parents to be happy, or the fact that you are adopted should and/or does not make you automatically unhappy.

---

[18] Quotation from a private conversation

Chapter 7
From a Carefree Vacation to the Realities of Apartheid

On Friday, 9th June 1967, the Defence Amendment Bill was enacted, which made military service compulsory for all white males who were between the ages of 17 to 65. Since that day, the government notified every white male over the age of sixteen to report for duty as either part of the South African Defence Force (SADF), the Prison Services, or the South African Police (SAP), to enforce the government's stance against liberation movements, anti-apartheid activists, and the 'communists threat'[19].

By February 1987 Dietloff was already doing his time in the South African Air Force. I received my call-up papers and was ordered to report to the South African Infantry Battalion situated outside Palaborwa in the Northern Transvaal. The previous year, my call-up papers told me to report for duty at the infantry base outside Oudtshoorn that is situated in the Karoo, a dry and very hot part of the country, near the world famous Cango Caves. But fortunately, my final papers confirmed that I was drafted to the South African Navy and had to report to Saldanha Bay on the west coast of South Africa for my basic training.

* * *

During this time, Ponti, Renita and their daughter, Carla, moved to Klerksdorp. Ponti was appointed manager of a magazine distribution company. He was a dedicated husband and wonderful father; Renita a very glamorous girl, who enjoyed the nicer things in life. One weekend, I decided to go and visit them in Klerksdorp. On arriving, we talked until the early hours of the morning. Carla was a beautiful little girl, very cute, very energetic and very trying. It soon became clear that Ponti was the dominant parent in this marriage and was very protective of his daughter. That Saturday morning, Ponti had to go to work and Renita and I stayed at home with Carla. Carla was very difficult and demanding; however, Renita did not pay much attention to her. Ponti did not believe in any form of physical punishment, which was still custom and practice in those days. I was raised in a strict military home, where my father's word was law. We

---

[19] http://www.sahistory.org.za/dated-event/military-service-becomes-compulsory-white-south-african-men

received frequent hidings and whilst I hated them at the time, I do believe most of them were deserved and they ultimately contributed to me becoming a good upstanding citizen.

Eventually, Carla became too much for me. After she threw her fourth temper tantrum, which Renita again ignored, I took matters in my own hands and gave the young girl a solid smack on the bottom. She was shocked, as I don't think that she had had a hiding in her life before. She was instantly quiet. The day progressed normally until later that afternoon when Ponti came home. The minute he walked through the front door, Carla started screaming as if someone had just given her a hiding. Ponti was shocked, as was I, until she calmed a bit, only to tell him "Heino, hit me". Ponti was very disgusted that I smacked his daughter and duly reprimanded me. I was defiant, confirming that if he could not teach her manners, I would.

* * *

Prior to the commencement of our national service in February 1987, Andre and I decided to go on vacation. We took a tour through South Africa before we had to report to our respective military camps. We had a great time, traveling the country, enjoying each other's company, and reminiscing about our student days and speculated about our pending national service.

While I was saying my goodbyes at home, Andre was doing the same to his girlfriends and family. In Klerksdorp, Ponti was also preparing for his incorporation into the defence force as his applications for exemption based on his health failed and it had become apparent that he had to report for his national service, as well.

Harry completed his accounting degree in Port Elizabeth and was sent to do his national service at the offices of the Receiver of Revenue for two years. It seems that Harry got the best deal of us all.

Arriving in Cape Town, an aunt of mine came to collect me and I spent my last weekend of freedom in Malmesbury. The following Monday morning she took me to Saldanha, where I reported for national service at the SAS Saldanha training base situated in the harbour and the Bay of Saldanha on the west coast.

The first week of my national service was stressful, though uneventful. For some reason I was grouped with the troops from the Eastern Cape. There were guys from East London, Port Elizabeth, Grahamstown and other towns from the Eastern Cape. There were about eight hundred servicemen in total. The first few days saw us having medical examinations with fairly limited activities. Former President PW Botha's son, Rossouw Botha, was also part of our intake. The majority of the servicemen were between seventeen and nineteen. They consisted of surfers, wash-outs, academic drop-outs, school leavers, drug users, and graduates at all levels, including a doctor in botany. Normally, only immediate school leavers and volunteers were selected to go to the marines, whilst all graduates were utilised in their respective fields in the 'blue navy. The marines wore brown uniform like infantry soldiers, whilst the rest of the navy personnel wore blue uniform. Those who studied law normally became a legal officer, or as in my case, I was destined to become a personnel officer. There were only a few graduates, our ages ranging between 22 and 25.

The entire naval intake was sent to SAS Saldanha where we were examined. From here, a group of marines were chosen to be trained as infantry soldiers and from whom the future South African divers would later be selected. Traditionally, one would volunteer to go to the marines like the then State President's son. Rossouw Botha very publicly announced that he was ready to do the right thing and defend his country, to protect it from the 'rooi gevaar' (red danger) of communism and the anti-Christ. I was less valiant, and just kept a low profile, as I was not in the defence force out of choice, but because the law dictate that I will serve. I definitely did not join the Navy to volunteer to become a marine. I was not too worried, as I knew that as a graduate, it was unlikely that I would be drafted.

On the second day in SAS Saldanha, we had to go for hair-cuts and complete our medical examination. The Navy had to make sure that we were clean-shaven before they could send us to war. One of the guys in front of me had long hair. He looked older than me, very confident, very British, with a cool personality, not phased at all. There was a strange cockiness about him. They cut his hair and gave him a piece as a memento. His hair was not that short, but he looked much neater after his haircut. Perhaps some of my father's militaristic character had rubbed off on me, as I preferred his short neat hair to his long untidy look. However, at least neither of us was in the infantry, nor would we be incorporated into the marines. Later that day, when we underwent our medicals, I was certified healthy, fit and ready to be killed. I saw the Englishman again; he was also fit for war, still cocky and irritatingly in control of his circumstances. Here I was stressing quietly about the impending basic training, and this Englishman, who in my book at that point equated to a liberal communist, seemed un-phased, calmly prepared for what was coming our way. Whilst we didn't talk or make any real connection, I later learned the Englishman's name was Cuan Sawyer. Unbeknown to me, this Englishman would have an incredible influence in my life.

The next day, we saw more people arriving, with more hair being cut, with more medicals performed, and more uniforms being issued. We heard Able Seamen, Leading Seamen and Petty Officers shouting instructions, whilst Ensigns and Lieutenants were strutting their stuff all around the base. Taking into account that I grew up in a military home, I felt quite at ease with the uniforms, the military ranks, and the parade grounds. But I felt uncomfortable about the future as I had no idea what was waiting for us during the next seven weeks. However, it soon became apparent that the next twenty-four hours would send both the Englishman and I into very different pathways.

We were all instructed to report for a mass church service the first Sunday on the base. We were crammed into a recreational hall where the instructors addressed us and indicated that they needed five hundred volunteers to make up the annual marine intake. They again asked the President's son why he had volunteered for the marines, and cocksure as he was, he confirmed that he wanted to defend his country and protect it against the evil forces of communism. He confirmed that he was proud to be able to volunteer, and for a moment he sounded patriotic, nearly inspirational. The instructors confirmed that it was moving to know that there were patriotic and loyal young men. Soldiers, who were willing to defend their country, their government, their religion, against communism, the anti-Christ and other evil forces which were constantly 'threatening' South Africa.

I said earlier that I came from a conservative Afrikaner family, with my religious education primarily in the Dutch Reformed Church. Imagine my surprise when an Anglican Bishop from Cape Town was to address us. None other than Archbishop Desmond Tutu led the service. But it was no ordinary service, as he seized the moment to address us on apartheid and all its evils. For a born and bred Afrikaner, it sounded like blasphemy at a brand new level. I listened in absolute horror, as not only was this Bishop addressing a new group of defenders of freedom and the Afrikaner system, but he was directly talking to us, in English, about the wrongs of the government, apartheid, and the evil system that we were here to defend. I prayed that God would forgive him as he clearly did not know what he was doing.

* * *

In those days, anything and everything that was not underwritten by the National Party was either from the devil or was considered communists, the latter being inspired by the devil anyway. Thus, the government of the day had many 'devils' to fight, a battle they would dismally lose in years to come. It was a political system that denied people dignity and basic human rights, a war that cost the tax payers millions of rands, which ultimately would result in a defeated government, a total loss of power, a dissolved party, a disillusioned section of the population, and all of this would eventually see the birth of what is known as *'the rainbow nation'*[20], a term that Nelson Mandela gave to South Africa to capture the diversity of its people in terms of language, culture, and race.

* * *

The instructors reiterated that there was time until Monday 8:00 AM to volunteer, and unless the required number of five hundred marines volunteered for training, they would select at random from the remaining servicemen in the 'blue navy'.

---

[20] 'Rainbow nation' is a term that Nelson Mandela gave to South Africa to capture the diversity of its people in terms of language, culture and race.

The marine base was called Klipvlei (stone valley), about two kilometres (1.24mi) from SAS Saldanha at the same base but further inland. It was situated at the foot of a hill called Lakenkoppie (sheet hill), after the white sheet flag that was planted at its top. We saw marine instructors stomping around at the base and it was as if they went out of their way to scare the living daylight out of anyone daring to look at them. I was grateful that I had first been able to study and that there was no way that I would see the inside of Klipvlei.

We were up at 5 the next morning and served breakfast which included fish. Saldanha Bay being on the coast, with Irvin & Johnston (I&J) fishery situated in its harbour, had a constant smell of fish in the air. So, fish for breakfast was something I eventually got used to, but not something that would spark one's appetite so early in the morning. After breakfast and an early morning dormitory inspection, we were instructed to re-group on the main parade ground. Once everyone had arrived, we were ordered to sit down, while all the marine volunteers were ordered out of the group. There were only three hundred volunteers and they needed two hundred more. They then started reading the names of those individuals who had been selected to go to the marines, whether they wanted to or not. The names were read, Bosch M; Canton J; Davis A; Ferland G; Jacobs R; Johnston S; Mann H; Odendaal E; Richardson S; Rossouw D; Scheffer J...the rest was a blur. The only thing I can remember that what I said, before jumping to my feet and running toward my new marine platoon, was..."f**k"...!

Within minutes we were grouped in platoons and instructed to collect our belongings and start running. We were about two kilometres [1.25mi] away from SAS Saldanha. Away from the 'blue navy', heading down the road towards the marine base. We were running to Klipvlei. I was so screwed. The average age group of the marines was between seventeen and nineteen! I was twenty-three years old, and was not prepared to be an infantry soldier.

Once we arrived at Klipvlei, we were introduced to our instructor, Leading Seaman John Basnett. He was twenty years old, very well-built, with wide shoulders, strong arms, and, clearly, a lot of stamina. He fit his part perfectly as a proud marine. He was as strong as an ox and was clearly looking forward to making men from the bunch of pathetic excuses for marines he had been dealt. I knew we were not going to get along – one could say it was written in the stars. And there were a lot of stars at night in Klipvlei.

* * *

Hennie told me that when basic training started, I should keep a low profile and help people as far as possible. I should determine what I was good at and make sure that I became excellent in that. For example, if I could iron better than making my bed, I should perfect the art of ironing and get someone who was better in making beds to make my bed, by ironing their clothes. So I needed to determine quickly what I could do well.

* * *

We were given a sleeping kit and instructed to make our beds, so once I was finished, I helped the guy at the bottom of my bunk to make his bed. I felt totally out of place. Most of them were English-speaking, and English has never been my strongpoint. They were fit sportsmen who had mostly just finished school. The majority of them played first team rugby, cricket and water polo, or were provincial swimmers or surfers. I had never really played sports.

Within the next twenty-four hours, we were given instructions to collect uniforms, and our basic training started, from how to make a bed, iron our uniform, to classroom training and parade work. We were up at dawn and lights were normally out by ten. Our dorm consisted of very fit and energetic youngsters who were ready to go to war.

* * *

One guy in our platoon was Etienne Odendaal. His father was a Dutch Reformed Church Minister in Oudtshoorn. He was the typical naughty son of a minister. Odendaal was constantly in trouble, but with such wit and good humour, his punishment seemed more like entertainment to all of us, including the instructors, and in some warped way, to himself as well.

There was also John Stephenson, who should never have been sent to the marines, but regrettably ended up in Klipvlei. John came from a troubled home in the Eastern Cape and had problems adjusting to the military, in general. We became good friends and I found John to be a kind and warm-hearted individual, his only downfall being that he was never meant to be a national service man. Whilst he had done everything in his power to get out of national service, he eventually was shipped out to Simonstown, where he became a chef. John unfortunately had a drug problem, and I was told that after he was caught preparing his drugs in Simonstown, he was marched off to the Commanding Officer's office. Whilst waiting outside, the story went, he was told that he would spend most of his natural life in a military jail. John's own problems, compounded with his drug problems, and the fact that he now faced a long time in a military jail, became too much for him to handle, resulting in him taking a drug overdose outside the Commanding Officer's office, causing a heart attack and John's premature death.

* * *

John Basnett developed a particular dislike toward me. I could not keep up with the physical training, and he discovered that my father was a Brigadier. So he took great joy in humiliating me in front of the platoon in an attempt to provoke a reaction. Fortunately, poor a soldier as I was, I have always had an ability to keep quiet and not to rise to the occasion, at least most of the times. One day we did something wrong, and after many times being sent up

Lakenkoppie, Leading Seaman Basnett climbed into me. He mocked the way I spoke and imitated my mannerisms, emphasising that from his point of view, my mannerisms were far too feminine for a soldier and that I was clearly not fit to be called a marine. He must have investigated my past, as it also became apparent that he was aware that I had been in a car accident in 1984 and that someone had been killed. He further knew that I was convicted of culpable homicide, so when it became clear that I was losing my cool and that he was hitting a nerve, he asked me, "So what are you going to do, graduate, are you going to kill me?" I glared at him; he glared back after which he packed up laughing. For the next day or so he left me alone. But I disliked this overloaded testosterone junky of an instructor very much.

After three weeks at Klipvlei, we were allowed a weekend pass. I spent most of my passes in Malmesbury with my family, as going home to Pretoria was too far. In any event, most of my weekend passes were spent sleeping and eating.

One Sunday I had to do quartermaster duties, and the officer on duty was Ensign Werner Schultz. We started talking. He asked me what I had studied, how old I was, and what kind of music I liked. I learned that he was also from Pretoria and whilst his family were second generation Germans, he was an Afrikaans- speaking South African. Ensign Schultz was surprised to learn that I enjoyed Pink Floyd and that was just about the only music I listened to whilst doing my basics. We eventually became friends, as close as an Officer and an enlisted seaman could become.

At the end of our seven week basic training, we were due to be transferred to Simons Town, where specialised marine training awaited us. We had a passing out parade at SAS Saldanha with the blue navy, marking the end of basic training for those in the blue navy and the end of the first phase of our training. My parents came down from Pretoria, with my father, as a Brigadier, being the second most senior officer in attendance. I really hoped for good weather, as my father loved parades. Whilst I was not much of a soldier, I could hold my own with the best of them on a parade ground. I really wanted the passing out parade to be a grand affair. Whilst it was my perception that my father was not too impressed with his youngest up to that point of my life, I knew he would be proud and impressed with me on the parade ground.

However, this dream was short-lived, as it rained the entire day of our passing out until after the parade. The occasion was scaled down dramatically and was moved inside a massive hanger. We could not do any of the impressive marches and basically marched into the hanger and out again. That was it.

While we took part in the passing out parade, our 'friends' from the blue navy, including the cocksure Englishman, were also there. I saw Cuan for the first time in seven weeks when he commented about the fact that I had lost so much weight. I weighed a remarkable 69kg, with a body length of 1.84. That is skinny all right. They looked at us, with some pity, without saying much.

They had it very good in the blue navy and it truly looked as if they were on vacation.

On returning to Klipvlei, we were instructed to clean our dorms and pack for our transfer to Simons Town. I dreaded the thought of taking my marine training to a new level. The introduction had been bad enough.

That evening was the first time that I saw a glimmer of humanity in Leading Seaman Basnett. He talked in a gentle manner to his troops about what awaited us in Simons Town, and that it was a privilege for us to be made marines of the South African Navy. He joked with us and for a brief moment appeared human. Before we had dinner that evening, he came to me and whilst I prepared for yet another verbal attack, he calmly said, "Graduate, you are not going to Simons Town; you will transfer to the blue navy tomorrow morning. Good luck." I could not believe my ears. I thanked him, and he said "You're welcome."

Whilst I personally disliked John Basnett, he was a marine of whom the South African Navy could be proud of. Nothing he asked of his troops was too much for him to do. He always led by example and would demonstrate, in detail, what he expected from us. Be it at the swimming pool, during water training in the harbour, on the parade ground or in the classroom.

I often wondered what happened to Leading Seaman Basnett, as in later years I was told that his platoon had become one of the best during that intake. Basnett taught his marines well, and they became a platoon of great success whilst being deployed for operational duty in South West Africa / Namibia and Angola.

In my career in human resources, I often used Leading Seaman Basnett as an example when doing management training, in that management should always be able to do what they expect from their staff to do, never to ask of their employees to do tasks for which they are not prepared or cannot do. In essence, to lead by example. This, Basnett did well.

I saw Ensign Schultz once more at SAS Saldanha before he left with the rest of the marine officers to Simons Town. He gave me his contact details and said I should get in touch with him after my national service was over. His family stayed very close to my parents in Pretoria. I saluted him and he left. I never saw him again during our national service.

Eventually my drafting instructions came and I was sent to SAS Immortelle, the Naval Head Office in Pretoria. I was assigned to the personnel division of the Navy and worked for about six months as a personnel clerk.

The relationship between my father and I improved almost instantly and whilst my father never said so, I think he liked to see me in uniform. We travelled on the same bus to work in the morning and in the afternoon. At the beginning, it felt odd when he arrived at the bus station in the afternoon and I saluted him. He was a flag officer, and at that point, I was an Able Seaman.

After about three months back in Pretoria, Andre had his passing out parade from the South African Medical Corps outside Potchefstroom. I decided to go and visit him, and on my arrival, learned that he had been elected platoon sergeant. He had some strange but very amusing friends.

At this time, Christiaan work as part of the Police's Special Protection Unit and was a bodyguard and driver to the then State President PW Both.

In July, we prepared to celebrate my father's sixtieth birthday. Suzanne and Robert offered their home in Garsfontein. All the family were invited and some of the senior ranking officers from the Prison Services were in attendance. Robert's father (Oom Dad) was a retired national intelligence officer and was good friends with the then-minister of foreign affairs, Min. Pik Botha, MP, who was also among the guests. My father was overwhelmed with the surprise. We managed to assemble all of his brothers and sisters and a large number of his friends to celebrate his sixtieth birthday.

We bought my father a rifle for his birthday, while Dietloff wrote a birthday wish, which he set to music. Dietloff and I pre-recorded the birthday song and played to my father on the 28th of July 1988.

For the balance of this year, I worked in Pretoria. The second half of that year was done at the Defence Force Headquarters where I worked on a variety of human resource-related projects. Towards the end of that year, I was transferred to Salisbury Island, the naval base in Durban, KwaZulu-Natal, where I completed the second year of my national service.

Just before leaving for Durban, I was promoted to the rank of Leading Seaman and was instructed to conduct an investigation for Captain Stapelberg, the Head of Personnel, on instruction from the Chief of the Navy. The scope of my project was to investigate the status of general assistants, or labourers, as part of the ships company. This followed on from the legalisation of Black trade unions, by PW Botha which was done back in 1979.[21] By the time I went to the Navy, in 1988, nearly all general assistants were black. Neither the then-Labour Relations Act, nor the military ordinances recognised black people as employees, and in the naval context, as part of the ship's company. This increasingly became a problem as pressures mounted to incorporate black people into the definition of a worker in South Africa's labour legislation. The same were to be applied in the military personnel code. This project was very exciting for me, although I was not prepared for the difficult times I would have during the next ten months, whilst doing this project and implementing the recommendations approved as a result.

Systematically I came to the realisation that the system of apartheid was fundamentally flawed. I am sure that older people of South African decent would disagree and could list a number of examples where separate development was practised, where people with different languages and cultures lived apart from others and no word was said about them. No claims of racism were made, no sanctions were imposed, and no human rights charters were recited. None of these examples would even raise an eyebrow at the United Nations. It was accepted, that people with the same cultures, traditions, language and beliefs, like to associate with their own people. If one considers the people from the United Arab Emirates, Mauritius, Austria, Germany, or the Dutch – they all live together in their respective countries,

---

[21] https://www.theguardian.com/news/2006/nov/02/guardianobituaries.southafrica

protect their own language and beliefs, diverse as they might be. In some cases, they even force their religion onto others. Alternatively, they do not grant freedom of religion to all. They govern themselves, be it through unilateral decree or in terms of a democratically elected government. They are all nations who lived within specific borders, governed by them, whilst they respect the dignity of others. But that was not what apartheid was about. So I started questioning my own beliefs and reviewed the history of South Africa from a different perspective. I wanted to understand how apartheid was established. I discovered that it was a number of factors that contributed to the ultimate development of apartheid, and which directly came to influence my own beliefs.

Whilst I believe that there is nothing wrong with own rule and self-determination, what apartheid had become was not present in any of the countries above. It was not ordained by the Bible as we had been taught, and it had nothing to do with self-determination. This self-preservation theory eventually became a self-destructive paranoia.

Chapter 8
The Death of a Giant

On Wednesday, 5 October 1988, my mother woke me up at about 7 in the morning. She told me that we had to go to Delmas, a small mining community in Mpumalanga, as her father was dying. He was in his eighties and had suffered several strokes since the age of 72. He was a very tough man, large and impressive, the former Afrikaner leader in KwaZulu Natal in the 1940s, but now his end was near. Even though I had a car, which my father had bought me, my mother suggested that we take my father's Mercedes. Since my accident with the BMW, I was hesitant to drive the Mercedes, as it was my perception that my father was not keen that I drive his car.

However, my mother and I drove the 60km (37mi) to Delmas with neither of us saying much en route. When we arrived at the hospital, we were directed to my grandfather's bed where we joined my grandmother, mum's two sisters and brother. We were shocked to see this large, strong man fighting his last breath. Everyone stood around the bed. The doctors confirmed that there was nothing they could do. They tried to keep my grandfather comfortable, and suggested that the only thing we could do was to wait. We stood in silence around his bed.

I watched my grandfather, anxiously recalling how he influenced my life and the impact that he had on my mother. I thought of the times that I had visited them, as a young boy, a student and as an adult, on his smallholding just outside Bapsfontein, a small farming community not far from Pretoria. My grandfather had been an Afrikaans schoolteacher and in his day, a very good orator. He was well-respected by his peers within the Afrikaner community. After his first stroke, when he was in his early seventies, he turned to God. He could no longer speak fluently and often mumbled, with irritation that no one could understand what he said. This was very frustrating for him, as people often asked him to repeat himself. My grandfather eventually spent most of his last days in his study, where he read the Bible and prepared talks about life after death.

He and my brother Johan, who was named after him, had a special bond. I did not enjoy the same affection from my grandfather and he made it clear that he was not too keen on having me around at times. However, although I often became bitter toward him, my mother always said that we should respect our elders and that it was not for us to judge others, as only God will judge all of us. So we kept on going to visit my grandparents.

As a 22-year-old, I have never seen someone dying. As I looked at my grandfather, I felt a deep sadness for my grandmother, as she had not had an easy life with him. My perception of my grandfather was that he was a very egocentric and hard man. My mother and her siblings were also taking strain, each one of them busy with their own thoughts. My grandfather's eyes would roll behind his eyelids, from one side to the other. I wondered if he was dreaming, or whether he was starting to see what is on the other side of this life.

* * *

I had a lot of negative feelings towards my grandfather. He had treated my grandmother very harshly, irrespective of the fact that she had cared for him during the last ten years of his life with kindness, patience and dedication. My grandmother was a petite old lady. It was astonishing that she managed to look after this big, strong but incredibly stubborn old man with such dedication. My mum often said that my grandmother should go to heaven alive. She endured more hell on earth than what any normal human being could cope with. In addition, my mum's stories about her childhood did not increase my grandfather's popularity in my book.

Whilst I am the first to admit that my mum had a very imaginative mind, a number of the stories she told us during our lives were confirmed by relatives and were not merely her perceptions, but were her experiences, and collectively became her realities. My mother was born out of wedlock in 1929 and with a clubfoot. As it was in the United Kingdom at the time, being born out of wedlock in South Africa was viewed with great shame, unlike today. This was especially true if the child came from a well-respected Afrikaner family who were viewed as leaders in their community. At first, when my grandparents learned that my grandmother was pregnant, my grandfather left town. My great-grandfather had to get him and force him to marry my grandmother. After the wedding on 10 July 1929 and following the birth of my mother on the 16th of September 1929, they lied about her date of birth. For the first six years, mum and her sister, who celebrated her birthday on the 9th of October, celebrated their birthdays on the same day, as if they were twins. This way, my grandparents hid their scandal of having a child out of wedlock. At least they thought they had.

As my mother grew older, she desperately tried to win the favour of her father. She told us that he was ashamed of her and locked her in a room when people came to visit. However, mum was equally stubborn and repeatedly climbed through a window, made coffee, and served this to the guests. He would then give her a hiding after the guests left because she embarrassed him by coming out of the room. I once asked Oom Johan (my mother's only brother) about these stories and he played them down by saying that my mum had a very fertile imagination. On reflection, this may have been true; however, the reality is that mum's perceptions, if not experiences, became her realities, irrespective of whether they were true or not. That is human nature.

When my mother spoke to my father earlier that morning, he indicated that although he was busy at work, he would try to come out to Delmas during the day. He asked us to keep him posted on what was happening. At about 12 in the afternoon, my mother asked me to phone my father and confirmed that my grandfather was dying and that my father should come to Delmas. He was sincerely concerned and asked how we were doing. After I told him that we were all right, he inquired how we got to Delmas. I told him that we had taken the Mercedes and where the VW Golf key was. He didn't say anything and I didn't think anything more of it. My father, however, did not come to Delmas.

Later that afternoon, my grandfather seemed to become calmer. He looked more relaxed. His eyes were no longer busy and he looked as if he was asleep. Oom Johan suggested that my grandmother should eat something and offered to take her to a coffee shop in the foyer of the hospital. My mother and I, with her sisters, stayed at my grandfather's side. Our eyes remained fixed on him, on his every move, whilst we were entertaining our own thoughts about this remarkable, and often unpleasant, man.

* * *

As my mum was born with a deformity and the medical profession was not as advanced then as it is today, it was difficult to restore a clubfoot to its normal and full functionality. In those days, they had to do several operations which resulted in my mother being in the hospital for long periods of time. The fact that my mum was a bit of a tomboy those years also did not help. Mum did not always do what the doctors told her to do. When she was about sixteen, she spent most of that year in a hospital in Durban, where she almost became a resident. She had plaster on her left leg for more times in her life than what she would care to remember, and as a result, the growth of this leg was stunt, resulting in the other leg growing longer and stronger.

My mother told us that my grandparents hardly ever came to visit her in the hospital. During the year of her stay in the hospital, South Africa was still under British rule. The British authorities at the time did everything possible to undermine the Afrikaner. Afrikaans were frowned upon wherever one went. At this time, my mother said that there was a Sister Goodman at the hospital who had a special dislike for her. On one specific day, the dinner menu was chicken and rice. According to my mum, cooked in the rice was a large worm, which was apparently a big problem in those days. When Mum saw the worm in her food, she told Sister Goodman that she was not used to food that contained worms and refused to eat her meal. The sister was a large, no-nonsense English registered nurse and was not about to be told by a cheeky 16-year-old Afrikaner girl what she was and was not going to eat. According to my mother, Sister Goodman force-fed her, including the worm, just to be spiteful, and to confirm that the English were in power and not the

Afrikaners. The story then had it that my mother vomited and Sister Goodman forced my mother to eat her own vomit. Whether the latter was true or not, the story became my mother's truth. Since that day, mum never ate chicken again. When I heard this story for the first time, I hated my grandfather for abandoning my mother for such a long time and for allowing people like Sister Goodman to mistreat mum so badly. No young girl needed to suffer so much.

* * *

After Oom Johan and my grandmother left for lunch, we did not talk much around my grandfather's bed. I stepped out of the room for a moment, only to be called back by my aunt looking for a nursing sister. The mighty Johan van der Vyver had died.

I phoned my father and told him that grandfather had died and confirmed that we were going to Bapsfontein before returning home. My mum, her brother, and sisters wanted to support my grandmother and needed to notify the rest of the family. My dad asked me to drive carefully.

That evening, mum and I arrived home and were both exhausted. I was physically and emotionally drained and had witnessed something that day that I have never experienced before. On our arrival home, my father was busy watering the trees. He greeted us and after my mum went into the house, I went to greet him. After he greeted me, he asked, "Why did you use my car?" I was so shocked at the question that I just looked at him, not knowing how to reply. My father repeated his question and added that he had bought me a car. He was clearly unhappy that I took the Mercedes. It was true that he had bought me a car and that there had been no reason why we did not use the Golf instead. I tried to explain that my mum agreed that we could use the Mercedes, but my father did not seem to listen. I was so taken aback, that he was more worried about his car, than being concerned about his traumatised wife and son.

Normally, I would not challenge my father, as anyone who grows up in a military home knows not to challenge a superior officer. However, this was a watershed day in my strained relationship with my father. I absolutely exploded and told my father that I could not believe that he could be worried about his car when my mother and I had just witnessed someone dying. I could not understand how he could be cross with me for driving his car. Would he have acted the same if my mother had driven the Mercedes, surely not? I felt personally insulted. I stormed into the house and my mother wanted to know what was going on. Johan also looked rather shocked. I told my mother what my father said and vowed never to drive his car again.

My father, I can only assume, must have realised that his reaction had not been appropriate, came into the house and apologised. He looked and sounded sincerely sorry for what happened whilst I equally regretted my outburst.

Johan was about to leave to visit Oom Hercules and Tante Livina on their farm outside Witbank. I thought it best to leave my parental home. I needed to get out so I packed a bag and left with Johan for a few days until the funeral.

My grandfather's internment was the first funeral I attended where I could stand at the back and look at the people attending. I felt removed from the reality of the death, which hung in the air. I can only ascribe this to the fact that I had physically watched my grandfather die and now realised that what we were burying were only his earthly remains. After the funeral, I went home with my parents, peace returned to our lives, and a better relationship between my father and I began. I think in some way we both realised that we should change our approach to each other. We started to work towards a relationship of mutual respect.

Chapter 9
A Historic Overview of Apartheid

From what I was taught in school about the history of South Africa, and in terms of websites[22] and a number of books[23] written in novel form about South Africa and its people, the following led to the establishment of apartheid.

It is well known that the southern tip of Africa is a region blessed with an abundance of natural resources, including fertile farmlands and unique mineral resources. In the seventeenth century, all of the above made South Africa a prized possession for the colonial forces of Europe. South Africa is the largest platinum producer[24] in the word, and a significant producer of diamonds and gold. Its climate is great with lots of sunshine, green lush forests, open landscapes, wine lands, mountains, and a fantastic shoreline.

First the Dutch and later the British colonised the southern tip of Africa. The Dutch did not take the constant British harassment lightly. The descendants of the original Dutch colony could not stand English rule and moved out from under British oppression and established themselves outside the British colony. These Dutch descendants were later joined by settlers from Germany and France and became known as Boers. The term 'boer' actually means 'farmers'. These 'farmers' later became generally known as Afrikaners. Regrettably, the English did not want to leave them alone. The Boers tamed the wild southern frontiers of Africa, which in those early days were largely uninhabited or sparsely habituated. They fought the locals at the time and established their own country. The British, based in the Cape colony, invaded and reclaimed new territories as part of the British Empire. The Afrikaners later established their own states in the Republic of the Orange Free State and the Republic of Transvaal.

Again the British waited for the Afrikaners to tame the hinterland and then invaded. This was especially true after the discovery of diamonds and later gold around 1900, when Britain invaded the Afrikaner states, which sparked the Anglo-Boer Wars.

On 31 May 1910, the British colonies and the Boer Republics were unified as one Union. The constitution that was approved by the respective powers, being the Boer Republic leaders and Britain, made provision for an all-

---

[22] *http://www.sahistory.org.za* [accessed 17/01/2016]
[23] The Covenant – Michener; A History of South Africa – Welsh; An Illustrated History of South Africa – Readers Digest
[24] *http://www.platinum.matthey.com/about-pgm/production* [accessed 17/01/2016]

powerful government consisting only of white men which paved the way for the South African government to introduce various legislation that would disenfranchise African people. Up to 31 May 1928, the South African (British) Blue and Red Ensigns were the flags of the Union of South Africa. Later that year, the Orange, White and Blue was adopted by the British Governed Union as the new flag of the Union of South Africa. [25]

It was the alienation of black people, that prompted Nelson Mandela, in his time, to write to the then prime minister, Hendrik Verwoerd, on 20 April 1961 and later again on 26 June 1966, in which he objected in the strongest terms against the *dual and dishonest [policy] which are opposed by millions of people here and abroad...*"[26]

The Afrikaners suffered under British oppression. This was preceded by a period of hell following the Boer Wars and the destruction of Afrikaner morale with their women and children in the English concentration camps. They were reduced to little more than poverty-stricken tenants in their own country. The Afrikaners became anxious to preserve what they held dear and when the Union of South Africa was formed in 1910, they enjoyed great respect from a large variety of countries in Europe and Asia. It is these experiences under British oppression that later turned into a self-destructive paranoia.

The establishment of the 'White Republic', as Mandela referred to it in his second letter to Verwoerd, was the beginning of strategists in the National Party to refine apartheid as a means to cement their control over the economic and social system. Starting in the 1960s, a plan of 'Grand Apartheid' was systematically executed, emphasising territorial separation and police repression.

What is important to understand is that the system of separate development, or apartheid as it was later called, comes from the English class system and was not something designed by a group of conservative white Afrikaners but was initially practiced by the English who referred to the locals in the countries they colonised as 'indigenous aliens', 'uncivilised and uncontrollable natives'.[27]

However, it was the Afrikaner who wrote the concept of apartheid into the laws of the land with the enactment of the apartheid laws in 1948. This saw the beginning of racial discrimination as an institutionalised system, whereby the minority dictated to the majority of the population. By now, the land was no longer uninhabited, as in the middle 1600s, the migration of Black groupings also flooded down from the north in search of wealth and prosperity. The black population of South Africa also contributed to the building and development of South Africa as we see it today. Not much is written about their contribution, but they contributed extensively, nevertheless.

---

[25] *http://www.loeser.us/flags/south_africa.html* [accessed 17/01/2016]
[26] *http://www.sahistory.org.za/letters/second-letter-nelson-mandela-hendrik-verwoerd-26-june-1966* [accessed 17/01/2016]
[27] *http://www.sahistory.org.za/archive/black-uncivilized* [accessed 17/01/2016]

The apartheid or race laws touched every aspect of social life, including a prohibition of marriage between non-whites and whites, and the sanctioning of 'White-only' jobs. In 1950, the Population Registration Act (which received Royal Assent on 22 June 1950 from King George VI), required that all South Africans be racially classified into one of three categories. White, coloured (person of mixed race) or black. The latter consist of a number of subcategories.

The identity book that was issued to South Africans also made provision for a 13-digit identity number, appearing on the first page of the identity document. This represented the individual's date of birth, sex, and population group. The latter were grouped in seven population groups. (i) White; (ii) Cape Coloured; (iii) Malay; (iv) Griqua; (v) Chinese; (vi) Indian; (vii) Other Asian; and (viii) Other Coloured. Blacks were not considered as part of the population but as 'native aliens'.

Classification into these categories was based on appearance, social acceptance, and descent. For example, a white person was defined as "in appearance obviously a white person or generally accepted as a white person."[28] A person could not be considered White if one of his or her parents were non-White. The determination that a person was 'obviously White' would take into account 'his habits, education, speech, and demeanour. A black person would be from or accepted as a member of an African tribe or race, and a coloured person is one that is of mixed race, neither black nor white.

The then department of home affairs was responsible for the classification of the citizens. Non-compliance with the race laws was dealt with harshly. All blacks were required to carry 'passbooks', containing fingerprints, photo, and information on access to non-black areas. These pass books were similar to the 'papers' that were carried by Jews under the Nazi era. South African passbooks had its origin from the Cape Colony permits, issued to keep the natives out of the colony, introduced by Earl George Macartney, on 27 June 1797, the then-governor in the Cape from 1797–1798,.[29]

These very passbooks would be the ones that Mahatma Gandhi refused to carry during his visit to South Africa in Natal and which sparked his quiet and peaceful revolt. This revolt of Gandhi ultimately contributed to India's independence and self-determination.

In 1951, the Bantu Authorities Act, No 68 of 1951, established a basis for the establishment of the 'homeland system'[30]. This system saw the demarcation of specific pieces of land, which the then-South African government earmarked as independent states, to give the black people in South Africa a 'country' of their own. Hendrik Verwoerd clarified the meaning of 'apartheid' as 'good neighbourliness'. Whilst this might sound noble, it also was fundamentally flawed, as this basically meant that people had to be uprooted from where they had lived for most of their life, to be resettled in a

---

[28] *http://www-cs-students.stanford.edu/~cale/cs201/apartheid.hist.html* [accessed 17/01/16]

[29] Report of the Inter-departmental committee on native pass laws, p.2 [accessed 17/01/16]

[30] *http://www.sahistory.org.za/archive/bantu-authorities-act-1951*

piece of land where there was no or very little infrastructure, with almost no possibility of getting meaningful employment. Taking into account what the English did to the Afrikaner during the Boer Wars, one would think the Afrikaner would have been more sensitive to the needs of their fellow countrymen. However, sadly, it did not seem as if non-White people were viewed as 'fellow-countrymen'. Former South African citizens were assigned to these 'homelands' and given new citizenship, effectively stripping them of their birth right as South African Citizens, not something anybody would easily accept. To add insult to injury, people were often incorrectly assigned to these homelands, as their passbooks reflected the wrong origin, so a Zulu became a Xhosa and a Sotho became a Tswana. That made the difference of whether you would be uprooted from a suburb in Johannesburg like Sophiatown, which was earmarked for white residents or white development and be relocated to the homeland of the 'independent' Republic of Transkei, the Republic of Ciskei or the Republic of Bophuthatswana, to mention only a few. These 'banana republics', as they became known, preceded the withdrawal of all political rights, including citizenship, held by a Black South African, as these privileges were transferred to the new 'independent' homeland, whilst the South African Parliament held complete hegemony over the homelands' administration.

In 1953, the implementation of this demonic system was taken to a new level. This year saw the implementation of the Public Safety Act[31] and the Criminal Law Amendment Act [32] which empowered the government to declare stringent states of emergency and increased penalties for protesting against or supporting the repeal of a law. These penalties included fines, imprisonment and whippings.

* * *

Ironically, according to my 1972, HAT Dictionary (Handwoordeboek van die Afrikaanse Taal), which I would translate as the 'practical dictionary of the Afrikaans language'. The word 'racism' is defined as 'the assumption that character and ability are determined by race – a philosophy that assumes that a specific race is considered superior and therefore entitled to rule over other lesser races'.[33]

* * *

In 1976, a large group of Blacks in Sharpeville refused to accept Afrikaans as the medium of education, as well as the principles of Bantu Education. This uprising resulted in the killing of 700 youths with more than 4,000 injured. The 16th of June 1976 would in later years be described as "the spark that

---

[31] Public Safety Act, No 03 of 1953
[32] Criminal Law Amendment Act, No 08 of 1953
[33] HAT, (1972, pg 681)

ignited the winds of change in South Africa". This was the day that signalled the failure of apartheid as a system and set the scene for the ultimate birth of a democratic South Africa where all would be viewed as equal before the law.

The time period of 1976 to 1981 saw the creation of four of these homelands, which denationalised nine million South African citizens.[34]

I can recall in 1976, a debate took place at my parent's home in Bloemfontein, where the effect of the homeland system was discussed. The conclusion was that the Whites were indeed the majority in South Africa, as all the Black people would ultimately have their own counties. They would be allowed to work in South Africa, but their political rights, the right to vote etc. would be exercised in their 'own country'. They would have self-determination in their own country, irrespective of the fact that most of them hadn't even been born there. They were simply being repatriated. That sounded fine to me as an eleven-year-old boy. I could not understand why the Black people were so upset in Sharpeville that year. As a young boy at the time, it just did not make sense why they were so angry. They had all the rights in the world, in their own independent republics, in their own countries.

As Black people now had their own countries, they required passports to visit South Africa. White people, on the other hand, could enter the homelands with their South African identification document, and were not required to obtain a passport. As a result, the system failed before it even started. The homeland governments joined the gravy train that was passing, but constantly criticised the South African government about racism and human rights breaches.

The penalties imposed on political protest, even non-violent protest, were severe. During the states of emergency, which continued intermittently until 1989, anyone could be detained without a hearing by a low-level police official for up to six months. Thousands of individuals died in custody, frequently after gruesome acts of torture. Newspapers carried low-key articles about detainees who tried to run away from the police and were shot, or people resisting arrest. Alternatively, detainees would mysteriously fall out of buildings, allegedly committing suicide, or simply just disappear. Those who went to trial were sentenced to death, banished, or imprisoned for life, like Nelson Mandela.

Although the apartheid policy was highly effective in achieving its goal of preferential treatment for whites and elevating the white population to a self-created supremacy, it was totally ineffective in achieving for Afrikaners their so desperately desired self-determination.

I think that is what the older generation did not understand about the concept of apartheid in the South African context. There is nothing wrong with wanting to live among your own people, protecting your religion, language and culture, in the country of your birth, but it is criminal, inhumane and un-Christian to uproot people from the country of their birth and

---

[34] Tharushi Hewaarachchi on Prezi, 19 December 2013

dump them in another 'country' just because their presence is offensive to your own agenda. Not to mention the absurdness that whites were considered the chosen race, superior to the native people of Africa. No one will have peace or prosperity in such circumstances. Hence, apartheid was deeply flawed, and if one considered the South African context, then indeed a sin against humanity. James Michener wrote in the Covenant that the fate of South Africa would either be decided through the barrel of a gun, or through a negotiated process. All the people of South Africa were relieved that it was the latter, a 'peaceful evolution to a modern multiracial state' as said predicted by Michener.[35]

---

[35] The Covenant, James A. Michener, (1980), pg. 865 and 866)

Chapter 10
Political Insight and Religious Belief

In 1987, only three years after the illustrious President PW Botha crossed the Rubicon and destroyed the value of the Rand, I was tasked to conduct a project on how best to incorporate the general assistance into the ships-company. My assignment in the Navy saw me relocating to Naval Command East, situated in Durban, and having to conduct my investigation at all the naval units from Richards Bay to Simons Town.

When I arrived at Salisbury Island, the new accommodation for the junior staff was being constructed, and I was assigned to a dormitory. There were twelve beds, but only five 'residents'. They consisted of three Indian Seamen, me, and none other than the Englishman that was in Saldanha with me a year ago, Cuan Sawyer.

Like all new places I started at, be it at the various schools I attended, Technikon, and now the Navy, I kept to myself quietly greeting the people around me and reservedly kept busy with my own affairs. I spoke more with the Indian guys than with Cuan. Every now and again, Cuan tried to make a comment or attempt contact with me, but I mostly interpreted his attempts as sarcasm. I tried to stay out of his way, as I knew we would not get along. He was too much of a self-opinionated individual for my liking. He seemed un-phased at the beginning of his basic training, and more than a year later, he seemed the same about life, in general.

Two weeks after our arrival, we were allocated double rooms in the new junior ratings living quarters. I was looking forward to moving into the new block and could deal much easier with living with one stranger than living in a dormitory with five or even twelve strangers. I arrived back from the Bluff which is the south end of the Durban Harbour, on which the regional headquarters for Naval Command East was situated, to find that my roommate was none other than Cuan Sawyer.

I immediately went to the Master at Arms to lodge a complaint in that I could not share a room with a liberal, English-speaking 'communist' like Cuan Sawyer. Reflecting on this incident, I must confess I am embarrassed about my behaviour. Needless to say, the room allocation was left as is and Cuan and I started what unexpectedly became a life-long friendship.

Our rooms were standard hostel rooms with a bed and built-in wardrobe on the left and right sides of the door, with a single study table between the beds, and one chair, directly in front of the only outside window. We each had a steel bed, with a fairly thin mattress, but comfortable beds, nevertheless, each covered with its own mosquito net. During the year that I shared that room with Cuan, we initially did our own thing. He had his English friends, and I befriended some of the Indian guys in the corridor, just because there were no Afrikaans-speaking guys in the naval base at the time. Eventually, Cuan started inviting me to go out with him and his friends and although reluctant in the beginning, I went out a few times with them.

I always suspected that Cuan had 'other' extramural activities after work but was never sure where he disappeared to every day after our return from the Bluff. One day when I walked into the room, I found Cuan at his wardrobe. He was taken by surprise and fell forward into the wardrobe. Only after I inquired what was going on, did I notice that Cuan was now lying inside his wardrobe and cracking up with laughter. Cuan's mysterious disappearances every evening became apparent. He was stoned.

I was initially shocked as firstly the consumption of dagga (marijuana) was and still is illegal and, secondly, we were inside a government, or even worse, military facility. I think the law dictated that if you were found within a specific radius of dagga, you were deemed guilty, and the burden of proving your innocence became yours. The arrogance of this Englishman was just too much for me.

Cuan knew that I was conservative by nature, and tried to hide his habits from me. However, he never tried to influence me to smoke with him. Every now and again, he would disappear, and later, it became apparent that Cuan and his partners-in-crime went to the roof where they smoked their joints before returning to the room.

With the ice broken, Cuan and I started to talk more, on a large variety of topics, mostly when he was stoned, as Cuan was quiet by nature. I also learned that his demeanour was not being un-phased or even arrogant, but rather that he was emotionally very mature. He had a wonderful ability to manage his own emotions, not taking the anxiety of others onto himself, whilst he dealt with his own situation in an analytical and factual manner. Prior to our national service, he studied at Rhodes University where he obtained a degree in Computer Science.

We eventually established a good group of friends. There was Peter Callaghan, a very artistic and eccentric individual who went to Bolivia as an exchange student in his last year of school. Then there were Mark Holgate, Giovanni Maccioni, Adrian Fourie, Mark Neethling, and Eric Cleminston. Together with me and Cuan, we became a very jovial bunch of friends. It seemed that all my insecurities of the past just vanished, as I became part of a group of friends who knew little about me, but accepted me just the way I was. I did not try to impress them; they did not try to impress me. We just became friends.

As most of the guys did not have their own transport, my Volkswagen Golf was an added advantage, and one Friday evening, we all decided to go to town after we had received our monthly salaries of a full R125.00 [c. £30 at an exchange rate of 4:1] per month. I never allowed anyone to smoke in my car, but as we drove out of the naval base, Cuan lit a cigarette, no ordinary cigarette, but one of his special ones. "Guns and Roses" was playing on the radio and we all eventually had a drag. Later we decided to go and watch the midnight show of Pet Cemetery, which I was told is supposed to be a horror movie. But taking into account the refreshments at hand, it was one of the funniest movies I have ever seen.

Through all the discussions we had on the base, Cuan enjoyed teasing me or putting a controversial argument forward, just for the sake of provoking debate. I enjoyed that and attempted to defend my personal views, both political and religious philosophy, and tried very hard to convince him that my argument was the correct one.

In our time in Durban, Cuan and I probably had only two heated debates, one on politics and the other about religion. It is difficult to separate these two topics in any event, especially in South Africa.

One Saturday evening, like so many nights during that year, we were having debates in our room and Cuan wanted to know why I went to church every Sunday. He also wanted to know why the Dutch Reformed Church did not allow people of colour to go into the Church or to become members. I argued with conviction that it was necessary for the preservation of one's own traditions, language, customs, and culture, irrespective of the fact that the Coloured population spoke Afrikaans and had to go to their own Afrikaans Mission Churches. I defended the philosophy of the Church law that banned people of colour from becoming members, irrespective of the fact that those same Coloured, Indian, and Black people to a lesser extent, were equally 'defending' the safety of our country by being part of the National Defence Force System.

Whilst this heated debate continued, Cuan slowly planted a seed in my mind that my argument was flawed, that the aim of going to church was to learn about the Word of God and had absolutely nothing to do with the preservation of tradition, language, customs, or culture. The aim of a Christian, according to a far from stupid Cuan, was to live or at least aim to live in the image of Christ.

The next morning, I got up and prepared to go to church. As I drove off the base, I saw a Coloured Seaman, Luke Abrahamson, standing outside the base waiting for a lift. I stopped and asked him where he was going. He indicated that he was on his way to Church as well and was grateful for a lift. As we drove, Luke explained to me that his Church was also one of the three sister Churches.

* * *

There are three historic Afrikaans Churches founded on the teachings of John Calvin and Martin Luther, being the Nederduitsch Gereformeerde Kerk, Nederduitsch Hervormde Kerk van Afrika and the Gereformeerde Kerk van Afrika, all three very close in doctrine, but divided in politics. All three of the above church groupings had 'mission' churches for people of colour, and Luke was a member of the Nederduitsch Gereformeerde Mission Church. So it was possible that we could belong to the same church. However, whilst the white members could attend a service in a mission church, the non-White members of the mission church could not freely attend services in the White churches.

* * *

As we drove, it became apparent that Luke's congregation was situated much further away and that it was unlikely he would get to church on time. The easiest and most Christian thing to do, was to invite Luke, a Seaman in the South African Navy, dressed in his Navy blacks, to join me at my church. But I couldn't, as I was White, and he was coloured. It was not allowed.

On arriving at my Church, I explained to Luke that unfortunately I would have to drop him off at the corner of the road, as that was as far as I was going. The Dominee (Minister) at the congregation I attended at the time was a remarkable clergyman, and I enjoyed listening to his sermons. However, that day I was deeply disturbed at what had happened before I entered the church building. I always found the minister's services to be captivating, delivering very powerful, non-political sermons. However, that day I thought about Luke and what I had just done before entering the church. I did something that went totally against what I had been taught as a Christian. I failed as Christian to do what was right to a person longing to hear the Word of God. I denied this Coloured guy, standing proudly in his South African Naval uniform, the right to worship in the House of God, because a group of white Afrikaners said so.

* * *

Of interest about this congregation is that it was the same Church my late grandfather and grandmother went to when my mother and her three siblings were children whilst growing up in Durban. I joined this congregation because my grandfather had been the Afrikaner leader in Port Natal in the early 1940s. From the first day I attended church there, I was made to feel as part of the family, nearly an honorary member, due to the fact that I was the grandson of the famous Johan van der Vyver of Port Natal.

* * *

After the service on the day in question, we had a church meeting. I normally was on the quiet side at church meetings, but this day, I had something to say. Or rather to ask. At the end of the meeting, when the agenda item 'general' was reached, I raised my hand and said, "I would like to inquire about what I was supposed to do this morning. As I left the naval base, a fellow serviceman was standing outside the gate waiting for a lift to go to church. As very few of us have our own transport whilst doing our National Service, I offered him a lift, and when I arrived outside the church, I had to drop him off as his church was some ten kilometres further down the road. It is unlikely that he could have walked and reached his church on time and so he probably missed a very good church service this morning." The elders and the dominee seemed confused and surprised by my statement, as they seemed to think that the question was rather stupid. Without thinking, the dominee responded with "Why did you not invite him here?", which was the question I was waiting for. I responded, "I am not sure if I would have been allowed to as he is a Coloured."

The elders were furious and the dominee looked very uncomfortable. It seemed to me that both the dominee and elders perceived my intention to be provocative. They had that famous look of old-school Afrikaners being caught out. They probably thought the nice boy who came from the van der Vyver family had now turned Communist. As I have stated, in those days in South Africa, everything and everyone that was against the National Party was branded a Communist. In addition, all three of the Afrikaans churches were ferocious supporters of the National Party and the government system; anything against the church was also viewed as against the government. The elders were offended that the grandson of Johan van der Vyver could insult the Church to such an extent.

When I realised that I had set the cat among the pigeons, I repeated the initial question, "What was I supposed to do?" I continued. "He wears the same uniform as me, he stays in the same quarters as me, he eats in the same mess hall as me, during the day we work in the same offices, he even speaks the same Afrikaans, yet I am barred from inviting him to attend a church service with me, because he is a 'non-White'. Was our Bible not as applicable to him, and therefore the commands count both ways, considering Corinthians 13:13 *"so now faith, hope and love abide, these three; but the greatest of these is love.*[36] Where is the love in what happened this morning?"

The dominee tried to explain the terms of the church law as unemotionally as possible, at the same time trying to avoid an incident in church. I confirmed, "Next time, I will invite him, as this is the House of God, not the house of man." I was surprised at my own defiance, which provoked evil glares from the elders and members of the congregation. The dominee indicated that he wished to meet with me afterwards to discuss the matter in more detail, in an attempt to put a lid on the matter.

There was no meeting with the dominee after church but we did agree to meet during the following week. I left the church premises after the church meeting without having the customary coffee. As fate ordained, as I drove down the main road, Luke was still standing where I had left him. Luke and I drove back to the base in silence.

* * *

---

[36] Corinthians 13:13 – New English Version

Years later, I read the autobiography of Randall Wicomb, a South African Afrikaans musician who was raised White, but came from a mixed race family. This caused him years of anxiety. In his book *Kleur* (Colour), he said, *"people of all colours, sex and age have a deep desire for acceptance and motherly love. However, our existence is poor in love whilst music and words are the medium through which this is expressed."*[37]

* * *

On arriving back at the base, I told Cuan what had happened and what I had done.

Surprisingly, he was shocked but very impressed, as within a short period of time, I had changed. From accepting the establishment, accepting what my parents, the system, the church, the government, and everyone else were telling us, and thinking for myself and asking…"why?"

This opened the door for Cuan and my second heated debate on the history of the land. I constantly took a dig at him for being English, as it was a matter of public record what the British did to South Africa, the Afrikaners, and the rest of the world they colonised.

I felt more comfortable about these debates, as I enjoyed history and knew South African history fairly well. Eventually, Cuan gave me a book to read, an English book called *The Covenant, the epic tale of the history and the development of the people of South Africa* written by James E Michener. It took me some six months to read the 1080 page novel, but it was the most fascinating book I have ever read.

During the year we stayed in Durban, Cuan fell in love with an Indian girl, whom I'll call Rushida, and who worked with us at Naval Command East. She was equally intrigued by this bright and witty, though strange, Englishman. Rushida had a friend Samantha or Sam who worked in the same office block as I did. So Cuan, Rushida, Sam, and I often went out for drinks and dinners together. Cuan saw a lot of Rushida, and as her parents would not approve of her relationship with a White boy, their meetings had to be discreet and secret. Cuan also potentially faced repercussions from the South African Government, as inter-racial relationships were strictly forbidden, and in fact, at that time, still against the law. Cuan became besotted with Rushida and wanted to meet her parents and pursue the relationship, but she was petrified. She had fallen in love with a White boy which was forbidden by both the law of the land, and by the traditions and beliefs of her own people.

I found this rather intriguing and can recall a lengthy debate between me and Sam when I wanted to know why it was unacceptable and branded racist if Whites did not want to mix with people of colour, but it was acceptable and explained as a 'cultural thing' if Indian people refused to mix with White people. The same argument could be extended to Black people from

---

[37] Kleur, My Lewe, My Lied, Ranmdall Wicomb, *et al* (2015, p.79)

one tribe and another, i.e. the Zulus and the Xhosas. It seemed that it was thought that only White people were racist and people of colour were not. However, the harsh reality is that all people could be racist.

Although we did not resolve this conundrum, at the time, we did agree that all people could be racist and that, it was a myth that racism was reserved for a White–Black relationship. Racism, is ultimately founded in one's own beliefs, prejudices, status, traditions, tribe, culture, and lifestyle.

* * *

Years later, and following a similar conversation as the one with Sam, the question was raised as to the difference between racism and classism? Which made me wonder what does race, ethnicity or class means. The Oxford Compact Dictionary defined them as follows : -

Race : - *(1) each of the major divisions of humankind, having distinct physical characteristics. (2) racial origin or distinction. (3) a group of people sharing the same culture, language, etc.; an ethnic group. (4) a group of people or things with a shared feature: a race of intelligent computers. (5) Biology a subdivision of a species.*

Ethnic : - *(1) relating to a group of people who have a common national or cultural tradition. (2) referring to origin by birth rather than by present nationality, i.e. ethnic Albanians. (3) belonging to or characteristic of a non-Western cultural tradition, i.e. ethnic music.*

Class : - *(1) a set or category of people or things having a common characteristic, i.e. a new class of antibiotics (2) a system that divides members of a society into sets based on social or economic status (3) a social division based on social or economic status, i.e. the ruling class...* [38]

Ultimately, there does not appear to be much difference.

* * *

What was and remained important, in my view, is that we are all human beings. We are created in the image of God, so we are taught, irrespective of whether we are Christian, Hindu, Muslim, or Jew. No government should decide by law that one group is better than another, or that one group of people should enjoy preferential treatment above another, purely calculated on the colour of their skin.

I was equally amazed at the wealth of the Indian community in South Africa at that time, if one considers that they were imported between 1860 and

---

[38] Oxford Compact Dictionary (2008, pg. 840, 341, and 176)

1911 as labourers for the sugar plantations of Natal.[39] They were brought to South Africa, mostly against their will, alternatively in desperation to find some form of employment, and arrived in this foreign land with absolutely nothing but the clothes on their bodies. The Indian people were subjected to the same Apartheid laws as the local Black and Coloured people, yet they managed to rise above their situation to become affluent business people, attorneys, accountants, teachers, architects, merchants and the like. I wanted to know from Sam why this was so. Why did the Black people in South Africa not achieve the same at that time? Could it be that Gandhi's passive resistance [40] and the Black population's slogans of 'first liberation then education'[41] made the difference?

Both the Indian and the Coloured communities seemed to have been 'too Black' to be recognised by the old regime, and today, they are viewed by the current government to be 'too White'.

* * *

I eventually had my meeting with the dominee about the incident at Church. I confirmed that I was questioning some practices of the church and to date had been unable to get acceptable answers to my questions. I was often worried that I was not doing the right thing and that my salvation was not secure. I questioned the teachings of the church and was amazed by the people around me, in that Muslims and Jews were often much more dedicated in their beliefs, rituals, and religious practices than we Christians were. I debated with him on what would have happened if I had been born and raised by Muslim parents in a Muslim home? Would I have been condemned, as I was not a Christian? Surely God, as a loving God, created all people and would not condemn me for being raised and educated by my Muslim parents. I knew the Bible taught us that no one would get to the Father and His Kingdom unless they accepted Christ the Son as our Saviour, as in accordance with John 14:6 Christ said *"I am the way, and the truth and the life. No one comes to the Father except through me."* However, it is also written in Colossians 3:11 that *"Here there is not Greek and Jew, circumcised and uncircumcised, barbarian, Scythian, slave, free; But Christ is all and in all"*. Christ himself said in John 12:46, *"If any one hears my words and does not keep them, I do not judge him; for I did not come to judge the world but to save the world"*. Thus, the one and only God would judge all of us in relation to what we knew and what we had done during our lives. In my view, from a Christian's perspective, I did not think that someone would be automatically condemned just because he was a Muslim, a Jew or a Hindu, etc. However, I also have faith that God will ensure that everybody will hear the word, even if it is through our actions, our mistakes in life, and in the unlikely event that

---

[39] http://www.sahistory.org.za/indian-indentured-labour-natal-1860-1911#sthash.zzl0KKmd.dpuf
[40] http://www.sahistory.org.za/article/gandhi-and-passive-resistance-campaign-1907-1914
[41] http://www.sahistory.org.za/topic/congress-south-african-students-cosas

people never hear the word of God, I also have faith that God will judge accordingly.

I do believe that the Bible is often read out of context and various religions often justify their own doctrine. Governments, politicians, and lunatics often defend their policies through the manipulation and subjective interpretation of what they want their holy scriptures to teach. Therefore, I believe that one should be very careful when defining one higher than the other, as all men, white, brown, Afrikaans, Zulu, Xhosa and Brit, are created equal before God the Father and were all equally saved by God the Son.

* * *

Whilst our meeting had been initiated by the incident a few Sundays back, I had a number of questions about my religion, about my church, about the laws of the land and about the future, which I hoped that he could answer. I wanted to know who had drafted the church law, who had decided what went into the Bible, and how we knew that it had not been manipulated by man over the past centuries. The dominee explained to me how the Bible was put together and said that the Church fathers decided many years before, and with the guidance of God's divine intervention, which books should be incorporated into the Bible and which should be left out. Our Church fathers were the Roman Catholic Church, as all Christian Churches have their original roots in the teachings of the Roman Catholic Church, which can be traced as far back as the Apostle Peter, to whom Christ said "*on this rock I will build my church*" (Matthew 16:18)

However, I learned that it had not been the Church fathers, but rather the opportunistic Roman Emperor Constantine who funded and progressed the compilation of the modern-day Bible and the Christian faith as we know it.

In 325 AD, Constantine summoned all the bishops of the east and the west of Nicaea. At this council, the branch of the Christian faith known as Arianism was condemned as a heresy, and the only admissible Christian creed of the day (the Nicene Creed) was precisely defined, and with this Creed, Christianity was declared to be the official and only faith of the entire Roman Empire.[42]

A pagan leader, Constantine, is described as somebody who was only baptised on his deathbed by Eusebius, bishop of Nicomedia, on 22 May 337 AD, at the imperial villa at Ankyrona. It is said that Constantine remained very tolerant of the older pagan religions, like son worshiping. It seems that Constantine's support for Christianity was more of a political move to back the more popular religion at the time, as it were, as his sudden turn towards Christianity allegedly helped him win a battle against the numerically stronger army of Maxentius during the Battle at the Milvian Bridge in about October 312 AD.

---

[42] www.roman-empire.net/decline/constantine-index.html

Whether Constantine paved the way for the Bible to be completed is questionable but that it evolved over a period of time from 200 BC to about 367 AD appears more probable. Jonathan Black also confirmed this in his 2010 edition of The Secret History of the World (Ref p. 312).

In fact, it is claimed that it was not until 367 AD that the church father Athanasius first provided the complete listing of the 66 books belonging to the canon or standard Bible.[43] Christianity had become a popular religion at that time, and he was basically just backing the winning horse of the day. This does not seem much different to the Afrikaans churches that for many years defended government's policy via selective scriptures from the Bible, to appease the people of their "empire".

* * *

During our discussion pertaining to church law and the events of a few Sundays back, the dominee confirmed that he also had experienced problems with the compilation of the Bible when he studied theology. He explained that he learned that: "It became very apparent that the more one study theology, the more one realises how little one knows and that a lot of issues pertaining to religion and faith should not be dissected in its smallest detail but should be accepted in faith."

We debated the position of the Government and the Church concerning the segregation of races. Eventually it became clear that the church law and other laws of the land would stand, and that neither I nor the dominee could do anything about it. I declared my intention to resign my membership of the church. I felt that I could no longer associate myself with a practice that is neither Christian nor humanly acceptable. It seems now truer than ever that God created man but man created culture and man and his culture often fails in terms of God's will.

After I finished my coffee, the dominee said in a quiet but sincere voice, "Remember, you cannot affect any change to the church from outside the church. If you resign your membership, then you disassociate yourself from the church and there is then no reason why the church should listen to you. If you feel so strongly about your views, then stay in the church and be a voice from within. You will have more success than otherwise." Whilst the dominee might have had sympathy with my dilemma in terms of Luke and the realities of the church law, he knew, and I realised, that the Dutch Reformed Church will not change as a result of my objections. Neither he, nor I, would effectively influence any amendment to the historic laws of our conservative church.

In years to come, I often thought about this discussion with the dominee in Durban and I read extensively about history, antiquity and freemasonry. I eventually came to the conclusion that one must be careful not to try and scrutinise every letter of the Bible. Whilst our own experiences or perceptions

---

[43] http://www.biblica.com/en-us/bible/bible-faqs/how-were-the-books-of-the-bible-chosen/

were not necessarily the reality from a Biblical perspective, this Holy Book is much more complicated than meets the eye. The Bible, in my view, although possibly manipulated or incorrectly translated by man, the ground text remains the Word of God, whether Constantine was part of its compilation or not, or whether our interpretation thereof is tainted by our culture, politics, and own agendas. The message is clear in that, through the Cross, God loved the people He created so much that he sent His only Son to die so that we could live. Sometimes you have to believe because you believe, and that is why you believe. Isn't that what faith is all about?

* * *

I went back to the naval base and carried on with my duties. In the evenings and over weekends, I read my book and read about the establishment of the Free State and Transvaal Republics – the treaty, which Piet Retief negotiated with Dingaan, the then-Zulu King, and the battles between the Zulu and British Kingdoms. I read about the constant British persecution of the Afrikaner Boers. As soon as the now well-established Afrikaners thought they had established their own place in the sun, the British were on their heels again. Sinister deals between British commanders and the local chiefs were often done in bad faith to the detriment of both the local Chiefs and the Afrikaners alike.[44]

What was so remarkable about the manner in which Michener wrote this book was the way in which he described facts from the perspective of the various parties. The Dutch did what they thought was the right thing to do, based on their beliefs, their culture, their own agenda, whose practices, in general, were to the benefit of the East India Company. The Afrikaners did what they thought was right in terms of their own self-preservation, guided by their interpretation of the Bible and their past experiences in this new land. The British did what they thought was right in terms of their mission to conquer Africa from Cape to Cairo. Whilst the Xhosas, Zulus and other local tribes did what they believed was right for their people, within their culture, beliefs and own agendas.

The National Party, when they emerged in the 1940s, took all their past experiences into account and considered what our forefathers had endured since their arrival in Africa, and decided that never again would they be oppressed by any other foreign nation. They were no longer Dutch, French or German settlers; they were hardened Afrikaners who established firstly the Union of South Africa, which incorporated the Cape Colony, Port Natal and the Boer Republics, (Zuid-Afriaanse Republic of Transvaal and the Republic of the Orange Free State) and the protectorate of South West Africa / Namibia. Regrettably, however, instead of building a united South African nation, where all people were equal and respected, we legalised oppression doing all those things of which we accused the British, and, ultimately, created a

---

[44] The Covenant, James E Michener (1980)

country and nation divided. Unbeknown to us, it seems as we crossed a Rubicon, which is defined as *"a point of no return"*[45] long before PW Botha made his famous speech of the same name.

After six months, I finished reading *The Covenant*" which ended in the late 1970s predicting that South Africa would see a free and democratic country in time to come, a country in which all men would be equal, and where the concept of one-man-one-vote would apply. Fortunately for South Africa, a democratic state would ultimately be achieved in 1994 through inter-party negotiations and as a direct result of the vision of the then-President FW de Klerk and the statesmanship of Nelson Mandela.

The project I worked on whilst doing my national service was equally enlightening, as I was required to interview a large variety of military and civilian personnel, from Rear Admirals to general assistants. The old-school military stalwarts were against the inclusion of general assistants (generally Black labourers) as part of the ship's company; whilst the majority of the general assistants felt that they were just as much part of the ship's company as the military personnel.

This project required of me to address very senior commissioned officers on basic principles of human rights, even though I was a non-commissioned junior rating. This was very difficult as I had to sell a concept that was in principle unacceptable to the majority of them.

The upside of this project was that I had several first-hand opportunities to speak to Zulus who were many years my senior, and as they saw the constructive nature of my project, they opened up during interviews and gave me a rare glimpse of a side of the South African population that I had never known. I found the Zulu people I spoke to during this time to be hard-working people, who only wanted the best for their families, who wanted to see their children grow up successful, whilst making a constructive and positive contribution to the development of the nation. I met people who were proud of their association with the South African Navy, irrespective of the fact that the Navy, at that point in time, did not recognise them as being part of the 'ship's company'.

The project had to cover all the naval units from Richard's Bay to Port Elizabeth. I also had a short visit to Naval Command West, where I had an appointment with the unit commander of SAS Simons Town to inform him of my project, its purpose, its findings, and at that point in time, the proposed way forward.

Most of the time in Durban was spent consolidating the information that I gathered at the respective naval base in Richard's Bay, Amanzimtoti, Durban, East London, Port Elizabeth, and, eventually, Simons Town. Cuan often mocked me, as whenever he walked into my office he saw me writing. Those days only the officers had computers so I had to write all the reports by hand, then take them to Rushida to have them typed, checked for accuracy and

---

[45] Compact Oxford Dictionary (2008, pg. 900)

before I presented the completed sections to either Commander Brand or Lt Commander Naidoo, the two officers who managed my project in Durban.

Talking of Lt Commander Naidoo, it was the first time in my life that I worked for an Indian boss, and his professionalism and consistent application of good management principles was very impressive. It just confirmed to me that it did not matter what the colour of one's skin was; it was our attitude and attributes that made the difference. John Harvey Jones was quoted by Gordon S. Jackson, to have said that:

"Leadership is the priceless gift that you earn from the people who work for you. I have to earn the right to that gift and have to continuously re-earn that right."[46]

I can honestly say that Lt Commander Naidoo earned that right on a daily basis, and whilst I am not sure what became of him in his career as a Naval Officer, he was indeed one of the finest.

* * *

One weekend, Andre and a few of his friends from the military base in Bloemfontein came to visit me in Durban. They drove a pickup truck called 'a bakkie' (a utility vehicle), two sitting inside and the rest 'sleeping' on the back. We spent the weekend visiting some of our favourite places, like the old Med Hotel, eating egg, steak and chips, and drinking copious amounts of beer. The entire weekend was spent in pubs drinking up a storm, like only national servicemen could do.

At the end of October, I concluded my report to the Chief of the Navy and recommended that the personnel code of the South African Defence Force be amended to incorporate general assistants into the base personnel / ship's company. I was very pleased that this project was a success and that my recommendations submitted to Chief of the Navy were approved. As a result, all general assistants were granted their own workplace forums and were fully integrated as part of the workforce. A small step forward to an inclusive South Africa.

Just before November, some four weeks before the official end of our national service, I was offered a position as Assist Food and Beverage Manager with Harrismith Holiday Inn. I have always had a passion for the hospitality industry, and worked on an ad-hoc basis as barman at the Elangeni Hotel in Durban during the second year of my service. The position at Harrismith Holiday Inn was as a direct result of conducting my practical project entitled 'Personnel Management in the Hotel Industry' under the guiding eye of Derek Sutter, the then-Regional Personnel Manager for Southern Sun / Holiday Inn at the Johannesburg Sun and Towers Hotel in downtown Johannesburg in June/July 1987.

---

[46] Never scratch a tiger with a short stick (2003, pg. 109).

During the second week of September 1989, Ponti and Renita were preparing for the birth of their second child. Renita asked me to visit them again, as I did with the birth of Carla, so I took some leave and flew to East London. It was great spending some time with my old friends again, and I enjoyed helping them with Carla while Renita went to hospital. Stefan Marcel Rademan was born on 15 September 1989. I fed Renita pancakes in the hospital and helped Ponti at home with Carla until Renita and Stefan came home. In years to come, I became the godfather of both Carla and Stefan and developed an especially close bond with both these two remarkable human beings.

From October, during our last year in national service, we all started applying for positions in preparation for our re-incorporation into the real world. Thus, when Derek phoned me and told me that a position was available at Harrismith Holiday Inn, I applied successfully with Commander Brand, the personnel officer in Durban, to approve my early release from the Navy to enable me to take up this position. Unfortunately, it was not a personnel-related position, but at least I had a foot in the door to begin a career in the hospitality industry.

Chapter 11
In Remembrance of Barbara

After arriving at Harrismith on the Greyhound, I met the then-Innkeeper Robert de Leeuw ('Tau' or 'Lion', as he was called by the local staff). I was given staff accommodation and a uniform. The accommodation consisted of an old but neat four bedroom house in town, which I shared with the Executive Chef, the Food & Beverage Manager, and the Restaurant Manager. We were not particularly welcomed by our neighbours and during that time had two bricks thrown through the lounge window. This was simply because the Food & Beverage Manager was an Indian man and the Executive Chef was a German who loved the local Black woman. Harrismith, at that time, was a very conservative town on the border of the Free State and Natal. Interracial relationships and sharing of accommodation between races was heavily frowned upon. Although still illegal, it was probably more tolerated in that part of South Africa than what it was in Pretoria.

It did not faze me after my year of liberation under Cuan's guidance and my own acceptance of people as people, rather than as representatives of race or culture. I actually enjoyed the rejection, as I could stay in defiance but with pride, with my colleagues who became my friends at the time.

Although January was full of busy schedules and sports weekends, the 2nd of February 1990 came with a greater impact than the New Year Eve parties. The then-President, FW de Klerk, announced that the government had resolved to release Nelson Mandela. I was both delighted and scared, as I knew what he had stood for when he went to jail, but I also knew what he had done before he went to and whilst in jail.

While working at Harrismith Holiday Inn, I constantly wondered about my destiny, and the words of my mother reminded me that I had to become 'something special'. I was not convinced that Harrismith was the place where I was meant to become great, so I started to look for a job in Pretoria.

After Andre completed his national service, he was appointed as Personnel Officer with PUTCO, a bus company in Johannesburg. Ponti and Renita moved back to East London where Ponti's father helped him to get a position with Mercedes-Benz of South Africa.

On arrival in Pretoria, I successfully applied for a Personnel Officer's position at the Department of Manpower and was responsible for the preparation of submissions for the Bargaining Councils for the Building, Motor and Hotel Industries.

My time at the Department of Labour was interesting. I travelled by bus every morning from my parents' home in Garsfontein to Church Square. I walked to the corner of Schoeman (now Frances Baard) and Paul Kruger Streets to the Laboria Building, the head office for the then-Department of Manpower, renamed by the new government after the 1994 democratic elections to the Department of Labour.

It was here where I met a girl called Riana. She worked in the same directorate as me but in a different division. She held a degree in Industrial Relations and was busy with her Honours through the University of Potchefstroom (now the University of the North West – Potchefestroom campus). Riana was a dynamic girl, with a determined walk and an aura of total self-control. Being the only daughter in her family, with three brothers all much older than her, she had learned to fend for herself. We went out for coffee and later lunch at a local coffee shop across the road from the office.

Johan started studying part-time again and enrolled for a bachelor's degree in Public Administration. During his studies, he made friends with a girl called Retha Botha who studied with him and was a very talented, entertaining, artistic, and at times, melodramatic individual. A colourful character with an artistic flair.

* * *

I still had regular contact with Willie and Barbara who become very close friends of mine. The week before Easter, on 5 April 1990, Ursula and I went to visit them for dinner. Willie and Barbara planned to go to George for a week and asked me to look after their house and to feed Barbara's dachshund, Ludwig. They lived in Suiderberg in a beautifully decorated three-bedroom detached house, situated in a lush South African garden. That evening, Barbara showed me the rooms, where the dog food was and told me the do's and don'ts for Ludwig. I wished both of them a good and relaxing holiday and said our goodbyes.

A week later, Barbra fed Ludwig before Willie, Barbra and a friend of theirs set off for their well-deserved vacation. Willie drove most of the way, but with the trailer loaded behind an old Mazda 323, they could not go too fast. The road became very long and tedious. Although they stopped for petrol and comfort breaks, driving through the night is, at best, tiring. The radio played classical music, softly, and Barbara was comfortably asleep. Eventually, Willie became tired himself and early on Saturday morning decided that he could no longer continue. As Barbara was also sleepy, he asked their passenger to take the wheel and drive the last bit to George.

Barbara raised her head as the car and trailer stopped so that the drivers could change. Her petite body was curled in a comfortable bundle on the back seat of the car. After Willie stopped and switched on the hazard lights, he turned the radio down slightly and got out. His passenger next to him opened the passenger front door and got out. Both men walked around the car while Willie was relieved that they were nearly at their destination. As the doors of the car closed, the driver switched off the hazards, switched the indicator on indicating that they were about to turn back onto the main road, and accelerated. Willie fastened his seatbelt and made himself comfortable. Barbara mumbled something from the back in a sleepy voice and confirmed that the driver would be okay to drive. After she was reassured that he was fine, she fell asleep again. Willie turned the radio slightly louder in order to hear the soothing classical music above the roar of the engine and prepared to close his eyes. He was thankful that he did not have to drive anymore and that he had the opportunity to regain a bit of strength before they arrived in George. Day was preparing to break as the night sky made way for the upcoming sun.

* * *

On Saturday morning, I fed Ludwig and drove into town. That evening I went to visit my parents. Johan and Retha were also there. I decided to stay for dinner and spent an excellent evening at home. Back in Suiderberg, later that night, I made sure that Ludwig had food and water and went directly to bed. The next morning I had some errands to run and drove back to Willie and Barbara's home at about 4:00 on Sunday afternoon. On arriving, I checked on Ludwig and sat in the lounge taking in the beauty of this magnificent house. There was art all around the house, from all over the world. The floors were shining black slate covered with Persian carpets, tastefully decorated. I was not home long before there was a knock on the front door. It was the neighbour, inquiring who I was.

I explained that I was a friend, looking after Ludwig and the house, whilst they were away. The neighbour looked grey. "Haven't you heard?" she asked. I went ice cold because of her body language, tone of voice, and the blankness of her face, I realised that something horrible was about to unfold. "Willie and Barbara were in a terrible accident. Barbara is dead and Willie is in the hospital in George," she said. I could not believe that the jovial Barbara was no longer with us, while it was equally incomprehensible that Willie was in a hospital in George some one thousand two hundred kilometres (745mi) away from home.

"What happened?" I asked. The neighbour explained that the driver who had taken over seems to have fallen asleep behind the wheel. The car went slightly off the road, and when he realised that he had dozed off, he pulled hard on the steering wheel to get the car back on the road but forgot about the heavily loaded trailer. The momentum of the trailer pulled the car out of control and resulted in the car and trailer rolling three or four times. The driver was thrown from the car. Willie cracked his jaw, broke his left arm, and broke just about all of his ribs, while his right leg was crushed – immense internal injuries as well. It seems as if Barbara was thrown from the car and died instantly.

I stood cold and in shock as I listened to this horrific tale. The neighbour ended her terrible tale by confirming that Willie's sister, Sarah, would make contact with me in due course.

105

When the neighbour left the house, I felt ill with disbelief. I could not comprehend the pain and suffering that Willie had to endure all on his own in a hospital far from his home. I wondered if he was awake, if he knew what had happened, and worse, if he knew that the love of his life had died. I wondered what Willie would do and how he would cope. Not only was Willie deeply in love with Barbara they had travelled the world together, they were best friends, and now he was on his own, alone, and it was not even certain that he would make it. I was absolutely shocked.

Later that evening, I stood in their bedroom looking at their wedding photo framed in an antique and heavy golden oval frame, both of them looking radiantly happy. Barbara holding a single long-stemmed red rose, with Willie towering over her – proud, in love and content. I stood for a long time in their bedroom. It was unthinkable that she was no more.

On Monday morning, I went to work. I had the telephone number of Willie's sister. I phoned her to inquire what had happened and how things were with Willie. She briefly explained to me what had happened, more or less what the neighbour told me, and that Willie had been critically injured. I wanted to know if Willie knew about Barbara, but at that point it was unclear if he was conscious. We expected that he would be heavily sedated as he was lying in the Intensive Care Unit (ICU) in George Hospital. I expressed my condolences on Barbara's death and confirmed that if there was anything that I could do to assist, I would gladly help. She thanked me and asked if I could stay on to look after Ludwig and to make sure that the house was looked after while Willie was in the hospital. As it was unclear when Willie would be able to come home, and considering I was staying with my parents in any event, I agreed.

The following week, Barbara's body was cremated while Willie was still in ICU. It seemed cruel that not only had he lost his wife, but he was prevented from attending her funeral due to his own injuries. Johan's friend, Retha, wrote a poem in memory of Barbara:

A Poem for Barbara
We can still hear her laughter
And know in the hereafter
She will brighten up the day
Of any angel coming her way
Although we miss her
As times goes on
The pain will be less
And she'll never really be gone
Cause we will remember – always
Her warmth and funny ways.
It was good to know Barbara
One wishes that by magic
We could have her back here – clowning
But even in heaven they need someone
To keep the angels from frowning.

Rue[47]

---

[47] In Memory of Barbra by Retha Botha, 1990

Willie stayed in the hospital in George for the next three months before he was transferred to the Eugène Marais Hospital in Pretoria.

Life carried on normally in Pretoria and I enjoyed the luxury of the large house in which I stayed. I took the municipal bus to work every morning and went home by bus in the afternoon at 4:00. On arriving back, I walked two blocks from the bus stop to Willie's home and would be greeted by a very enthusiastic Ludwig who was always pleased to see me.

During the next couple of weeks, my romance with Riana grew stronger after I was invited as her partner to a wedding in Potchefstroom. We drove to Potchefstroom where I met a number of her friends, and while I felt a bit out of place, we had a great time. The wedding was held in the City Hall and as fate wanted it, Riana caught the bride's bouquet.

In the following weeks, Riana and I started seeing more of each other at work. I introduced her to Andre whom she introduced to one of her friends, Adri. André and Adri, and Riana and I started going to the movies, going out for dinner, and spending a lot of time together.

André came to visit me regularly during this time and we tackled Willie's garden and trimmed the trees, something Willie would joke about for years, as he claimed that his trees were never the same after Andre and I pretended to be gardeners.

During the fourth month of Willie's hospitalization, he was transferred to the Eugène Marias hospital in Pretoria. I thought it would be good for Willie to see something from home, so I smuggled Ludwig, covered in a blanket, into the hospital so that he could at least see that little Ludwig was in good health. Willie was surprised and overwhelmed when Ludwig appeared from within the blanket.

Eventually, Willie returned home, and although he indicated that I could leave if I wanted to, I offered to stay and look after him for as long as may be required.

Willie underwent several operations, including a bone transplant to the bottom part of his left leg, and recovered to some extent but walked uncomfortably; however, he had his old sense of humour back and always saw the bright side of life. From the time I met Willie, he had shown the ability to rise above his circumstances and always considered others. He never disclosed any of his personal pain or hardship to anyone around him. He was always positive.

When I eventually moved out of Willie's house, he asked me to take Ludwig, as a very special bond had developed between Ludwig and me, and Willie did not want to resume the responsibility of looking after, what was in essence, Barbara's dog. I was delighted and Ludwig and I moved back to my folks in Pretoria East.

Chapter 12
About Perseverance, Attitude and Aptitude

In February 1991, I saw an advertisement in the local newspaper for a post as Personnel Officer at a private hospital. Although I enjoyed my work at the Department of Manpower, the pay was small, and after living in Willie's house for nearly half a year, I wanted to have a place of my own. I applied to the agency who arranged an interview for me at the Sandton Medi-Clinic. On arriving for my interview, it soon became clear that the then Regional Human Resources Manager for Medi-Clinic, Mr Johan Malan, wanted someone with two years personnel experience. I tried to convince him of my activities and experience while being in the Navy and my time at the Department of Manpower. I told him that I was the candidate he was looking for, thanked him for his time, and told him to cancel the other appointments, as he found his man.

He laughed but did not appear convinced and confirmed that he would phone me during the following week. He still had to see a number of other candidates. The following week, I received a phone call and was delighted to hear that Johan decided to appoint me as personnel officer for Sandton Medi-Clinic. On receiving my letter of appointment, I tendered my resignation with the Department of Manpower. Riana was happy for me. I confirmed that I would be looking for a flat in Sandton. Riana did not appear pleased, as she was concerned about the effect the distance would have on our relationship. For me, it seemed to have stagnated, which frustrated Riana. The thought of living in Sandton was great and a good indication that my career was on the way up. I was very excited.

I was responsible for the nursing quarters and was assigned a flat in the nursing quarters got a flat there. I spent my first month of employment with Medi-Clinic, at Morningside Medi-Clinic. I worked with that unit's personnel officer, Gerhard Harmse, a young bodybuilder who was three years my senior. I thought it an excellent practice to make my mistakes in a new job in another unit, to familiarise myself with company policy, politics, and general business practice, before returning more orientated and better prepared to my own unit.

The hospital manager at the time was a strong and dynamic individual. She loved telling stories about her general practitioner days in a government hospital, and although most of her stories were both interesting and entertaining, she tended to take a lot of time telling them. During this period, I learned a valuable lesson of having insight into one's own shortcomings.

One day in March, during a management meeting, we were being pressured by our head office in Stellenbosch to finalise the preparation of the annual salary increases. Taking into account that the hospital had some three hundred employees with another nine hundred relief nurses, it was a rather hectic task. This specific day was the deadline for the submission of increments to Stellenbosch, and the hospital manager decided to tell a long-winded story during a management meeting. While everyone listened attentively, I was getting more and more agitated as I knew that I was not going to finish my increments. Instead of politely excusing myself, I rather abruptly interrupted her and asked her to get back to the agenda for the management meeting as I had a lot of work to do. Needless to say, she asked me to leave the board room immediately. As I left the room, there was a deafening silence, and I immediately knew that during this lesson, I was supposed to shut up!

The management meeting was over within the next five minutes. After returning to my office I started to work, but knew that the hospital manager was about to break down my door. My thoughts were not even processed when she burst inside. I realised that to try and defend what I had done would be futile. Thus, I immediately and sincerely acknowledged what I had done was improper and offered my apologies. She still gave me an earful.

I used this incident for years to come during training, in explaining to others that there are ways to do things, which could be done without causing offense.

Eventually, I moved into a duplex flat (town house) in Randburg, which I shared with Andre.

The hospital manager had a secretary working for her, a lovely girl with natural dark features. She was an absolute bundle of energy and an incredibly optimistic and friendly person. Ronel also had a flat in the nursing quarters and when it became apparent that Ronel had some interest in me, I was keen to explore the possibilities of a relationship.

I invited Riana to come and visit. We had dinner and I told her that I did not think that things would work between us and ended our relationship.

I started courting Ronel and developed strong feelings for this beautiful natural girl. The hospital manager was less than impressed, and I even had a meeting with Johan Malan who pointed out to me that Medi-Clinic was, by nature, a conservative company and personal relationships with colleagues were frowned upon. I insisted that our relationship would not affect my professionalism, nor would it affect Ronel's performance or professionalism. The hospital manager remained unimpressed and my relationship with her deteriorated even more. However, love was blind and Ronel and my relationship bloomed.

* * *

My brother, Johan, got engaged to a girl from Barrydale, and when he and Mariska were married in this beautiful Karoo town, on Route 66 between Oudtshorn and Motagu, Ronel and I decided to go down for the wedding.

This would be the first time that the two of us would be away for a long period of time, all by ourselves. We drove to Verkeerdevlei some 30km outside Bloemfontein where Chris and Rina lived and where Chris was the local police station's commanding officer. Chris took great joy in serving sheep's head for dinner, which he knew would make my stomach turn. Ronel enjoyed Chris's wicked sense of humour and the next morning we departed for Barrydale. We had a great vacation. Hennie, who by then lived in Cape Town, also attended Johan's wedding. It was good to see him again and we all enjoyed Johan and Mariska's wedding, dancing the night away. I was very impressed with Ronel. Her natural beauty, her lovely and bubbly personality, her naughty laugh, everything about her was fantastic.

On our return, I spent weekends with Ronel and her family in Alberton and a very strong bond developed between me and my possible future in-laws.

* * *

Every year at Medi-Clinic, we had a human resources workshop where all the personnel officers from the respective hospitals came together and discussed the various personnel-related issues which were of importance at that time. It was during one of these workshops that I was reprimanded because of my relationship with Ronel, but by the second year, it seemed to have been accepted. During this second workshop, I arranged for a number of us to go to Robben Island, and it was during this visit that I decided that Ronel was to become my future wife.

On my return, I arranged to see Ronel, and I could hear that she sounded different, but I interpreted this as nervousness for what was clearly the natural thing to happen. That evening when I arrived at Ronel's flat, she immediately said we needed to talk. From her body language, I sensed that there was serious trouble in paradise, and I waited with bated breath. Heart pounding. Then the news came. While I was in the Cape, Ronel's former boyfriend had made contact with her and she realised that she still had feelings for him. She decided to terminate our relationship. Ronel did not want to discuss the matter any further.

We continued working together in a professional and cordial manner. Eventually when I told Johan that our relationship was over, I was shocked to hear that he had known this was coming for some time. Isn't it strange that normally everyone else always knows about things of this nature except the person most affected?

With Andre now living permanently in Vereeniging, I decided to give up the duplex and moved upstairs into a one-bedroom flat. Although rather cramped, it became a comfortable bachelor's pad.

As the failed relationship between Ronel and I started to impact negatively on our working relationship, I started to look for alternative employment and, as there were no other vacancies within the group, I explored the possibility with Johan Malan to take a transfer to one of the Rembrandt Group's other companies, but there were no vacancies available either. So I looked further afield. I responded to an ad with Nestlé South Africa whose head office was also situated in Randburg, some four blocks away from the hospital. The position advertised was that of a recruitment specialist and the package included a company car. I was sold. I had to attend five interviews, including a spelling test (which I knew I failed), and a detailed battery of psychometric tests, before my appointment was confirmed.

Andre inquired if he could apply for my position at the hospital and when Nestlé confirmed that I was successful, I made an appointment to speak to Johan Malan. During this meeting, I informed Johan that it was time for me to move on and I had been offered an opportunity that Medi-Clinic could not better. When he agreed, I told him that a friend of mine was interested in my position, and I gave Andre a glowing reference. Johan agreed to meet with Andre but said that, ultimately, the hospital manager would have the final say. André was successful and was appointed Personnel Manager for Sandton Medi-Clinic and was quickly liked by all. He charmed the nursing personnel and seemed to settle in very quickly. I often looked at his relationship with my former colleagues with some jealousy, as I was never able to establish such friendly relationships at work; mine were always cordial, like an outsider, distant but polite, no more, no less.

Eventually, I also settled into my new job at Nestlé and enjoyed the challenges it offered. I was responsible for recruitment for head office and the regions and became friends with Gillian Wood. Gillian was the Employee Assistance Programme lead and become a lifelong friend.

Chapter 13
Marriage, The Death of Chris Hani, Divorce

Towards the end of that year, Dave, Suzanne's first husband, asked me to look after his house in Pretoria while he was on leave. I agreed.

During this week, Suzanne announced her divorce from Robert, her second husband. She phoned at about ten on a Friday evening and told me that she and Robert had already been divorced for about three weeks. I was shocked and knew my father was going to be devastated. Why this affected me so much I cannot say, but I spent most of that night awake, thinking about my sister, her two failed marriages, our troubled relationship, and the effect that this was going to have on my father. Suzanne always had been his blue-eyed girl; after all, she is my father's only daughter and the two of them always had a special relationship.

I rekindled the relationship with Riana. André, Riana, and I decided to go and visit Johan and Mariska for her birthday on 18 December, in Phalaborwa, adjacent to the Kruger National Park. André was reluctant to go as he had no girlfriend at the time and did not want to be the proverbial fifth wheel on the wagon. So I thought I would introduce André to Lynda, a friend of mine from Technikon. Riana also knew Lynda from a wedding of a mutual friend that we attended. Riana and Lynda immediately clicked and became very good friends. So, I introduced André to Lynda and it was agreed that the four of us would go to Phalaborwa for the weekend.

During our trip to Phalaborwa and frequently thereafter, André asked me when I intended to ask Riana to marry me. I remained apprehensive. However, eventually, I could not find any good reason in my own mind why Riana and I could not make a success of a prospective marriage. I phoned Riana and offered to cook dinner for us at her flat and proposed to her. She was ecstatic and agreed to become my wife. We celebrated with JC le Roux sparkling wine. Andre and Lynda arrived a bit later that evening to congratulate us. I still remained nervous.

We went to see Riana's mother. I was especially tense. Her mum did not take kindly to the news and told me directly that she was uncomfortable, as we had broken up so many times before. "Why would it now suddenly work?" I explained that we had resolved all our differences. She told me that she did not want us to come and tell her that we were getting divorced. I told her we wouldn't, and whilst she accepted my response, my future mother-in-law had strong reservations.

The day before our wedding, Riana and I went for breakfast at the Buffet Restaurant in the marble foyer of the State Theatre, where the Executive Chef treated us to a Champaign breakfast. Amanda refused to attend the wedding, even though we invited her, as she felt that our wedding was a mistake.

Then the big day arrived, 29 November 1992. Willie was supposed to sing at our wedding, but had to undergo an operation to have the bone in his formerly crushed leg extended. As replacement he sent his nephew, the now famous Mathys Roets, to sing.

Andre was my best man, and as we sat in the front row of the church waiting for the wedding march to play, I wondered if I had lost my mind. I chewed gum frantically, until Andre told me to take it out of my mouth.

The wedding march started and I saw Riana coming down the aisle. She looked confident, happy, and radiant. I knew that this was the right thing to do. I realised that I love her, that this would work and that I was just over anxious. After taking her hand from her brother, who brought her into the church, we turned and listened attentively to her other brother, who led the wedding ceremony.

The following morning, Andre and Lynda dropped Riana and me at Johannesburg International Airport from where we left for Malawi. And then we were alone.

The flight from Johannesburg to Blantyre was not that long, from where we had to board another plane that took us directly to our resort. The second flight was more interesting, as we had to land on a gravel runway and stopped right in front of the resort.

We found the area we were in to be incredibly clean. We were told by the locals that it was a legal offense to litter, and taking into account that the local population was very poor, they used and re-used every plastic bag or bottle they could find. We quickly discovered why Malawi is referred to as 'The Heart of Africa', as it has majestic beauty and the population is incredibly warm and friendly. However, although we had a great time, I drank ice that was made from lake water and picked up a bug that at one point I thought was going to kill me. Eventually, the resort management wanted me to be attended to by one of the local doctors, but I refused. On our return to South Africa some seven days later, I drove to Sandton Medi-Clinic to see our general practitioner. She took one look at me and promptly placed me on a drip in her rooms, which she pumped manually to get liquids back into my system. I ended up in the hospital for ten days. This was a bad omen if ever I was superstitious.

My friendship with Andre changed dramatically when Riana and I bought our own home. Andre continued to behave like a bachelor, and why not? After all he was still a bachelor, while I was now a married man. The adjustment for me, however, was difficult. Riana adapted easily and took to the tasks of a housewife like a fish to water. We got two Staffordshire Terrier puppies, a male and female, and called them Arthur and Guinevere.

The next February, Andre and Lynda tied the knot. I was honoured to propose a toast to both of them, a toast that I prepared carefully as I felt it was important that I leave with them a special message, something that they could reflect on in years to come. I wished them many years of happiness. André and Lynda were indeed blessed, as in time to come they had two beautiful children.

After only three months, our marriage was in trouble. Riana packed to go home to her mother. Andre and Lynda came to visit at the moment that Riana was packing. I tried to get some support from Andre, but I quickly realised that there would be none. Andre and Lynda left shortly after, Riana left a little later, and I had to deal with being a failing husband. I think I was alone for a couple of days, but loathed myself. I wanted a perfect marriage, with all my children being born before the age of thirty, and here after just six months, I had a wife who loved me dearly but I could not reciprocate, and then I was alone.

When Riana returned a few days later, I agreed to go with her to marriage counselling. The entire process failed, as it was my perception that I was made out to be the only person at fault, the only cause of all our problems.

Our first year of marriage was very difficult and life became very stressful.

In April 1993, Riana and I went on vacation to the Eastern Cape to visit Ponti and Renita in East London. This was the same weekend that Chris Hani was assassinated. It was Saturday, 10 April 1993. Generally we had an uneventful weekend, relaxing with our friends and enjoying the fresh Eastern Cape weather. Then the announcement came over the evening news. "Chris Hani, the Secretary General of the South African Communist Party, was gunned down in the driveway of his home in Boksburg." The general response of the White population surprised me, as for some it was one of joy. Although I did not know the detailed history of Chris Hani at the time, I stood in silence, staring at the television screen, when the then-President of the ANC, Nelson Mandela, released the following statement:

"Today an unforgivable crime has been committed. The calculated, cold-blooded murder of Chris Hani is not just a crime against a dearly beloved son of our soil. It is a crime against all the people of our country. A man of passion, of unsurpassed courage, has been cut down in the prime of his life. During that time he served the cause of the liberation movement with distinction, earning the respect and love of millions in our country. His death demands that we pursue that cause with even greater determination. We appeal to every religious service over this Easter Holiday to commemorate Chris Hani's life and what he stood for. This killing must stop."[48]

On reflecting on this event, and understanding the politics better now than then, what Chris Hani, the ANC leadership, and the struggle stood for originally was a non-racial, democratic South Africa, where all the citizens of

---

[48] SABC, News on 10/04/1993

this beloved country of ours had equal rights, irrespective of the colour of their skin.

South Africa held its collective breath, as Nelson Mandela addressed the nation in a firm but sincere tone. Clive Darby-Lewis and Janusz Walus were arrested not long after this incident, and although initially sentenced to death, their sentences were commuted to life in prison.

* * *

During June 1993, Nestlé decided to send me on a management development programme at a facility outside Escort in Natal. I did not want to attend, as I have a fear of heights and heard that we would have to do abseiling. I could not understand how this would make a better manager out of me and tried everything I could not to attend. However, I could not get out of it and eventually went.

The intervention was an outward-bound experience. It was freezing cold. We were divided into teams and had to do rope work and fall backwards from a ledge into the arms of our colleagues – to build team spirit and trust. Our leadership skills were evaluated and a group of facilitators and trainers were on hand to watch our every move. After every event, we were given feedback and at the end of each day, evaluated and given points as to how we conducted ourselves during the day's activities. Because I was petrified of most of the activities, as the difficult ones just about always involved height or some form of activity that I did not like, I volunteered to do most of my events first. This was not because I was brave, but because I knew that if I saw anyone else doing something that I dreaded and had to witness their fear, I would in all likelihood not be able to do it. So I gave meaning to the cliché 'attack is the best defence'. The activities became fun as I overcame my own fears.

Every evening I was more enlightened about what we had done the previous day and astonished that I was doing so well. I thought a lot about my marriage and where we were in our lives. Eventually on the 14th of June, the day before Suzanne's birthday, we had to do abseiling. We had to descend a 35-metre cliff. Again after the facilitator explained how we should work the ropes around the figure 8 safety ring, I decided to just get this over and done with. The process required that once in the correct position, I had to walk backwards down a slight slope and bring my body horizontal with the ground before lifting my legs over a wooden log and to descend the cliff. The instructor who facilitated this event was a 21-year-old called Anthony Meyer, who loved the outdoors and was very mature for his age.

He had no difficulty telling us what to do and how to do it, despite the fact that most of us were all much older than him. Anthony had blond hair and penetrating blue eyes. While he talked me through the process to get me parallel to the cliff, he made sure that he had close eye contact and that I was doing exactly what he told me to do. Eventually I had to lift my leg over the wooden log and that was where I stopped. I could not move.

By this time, I was also no longer standing but sitting in my harness with my legs stretched out horizontally in front of me against the cliff wall. When it became apparent that I could not move, I asked Anthony to pull me up. He agreed to help me, but indicated that I would have to pull myself up. Anthony stood back and said that unless I pulled myself up, I would have to go down. Once I eventually lifted my foot over the wooden log, I went down the cliff. When I arrived at the bottom, my entire body was shaking. It was not that bad after all.

The next day, we had a free day to reflect on what we had experienced over the past couple of days and I accepted that I had made an error in marrying Riana as it was unlikely for us to ever have a happy marriage.

At the end of the eight days spent living in barracks and enjoying the beauty of the Natal landscape, we had our final evening before returning home. That evening I was honoured for being so negative initially and eventually becoming very positive and enthusiastic, participating in all the events. I had achieved a personal breakthrough in my life that I had never experienced before.

Nothing is ever as difficult as what we make it out to be. The reality is that it is possible to overcome difficult tasks, by dividing these into smaller, easier steps. How do you eat an elephant? Bite, by bite. Once you have taken the first small step towards the completion of any task, the rest normally follow rather naturally.

Arriving home, life carried on normally. At around September, Anthony took me up on an offer to visit us and came to visit me and Riana for a week, and it seemed that everything, eventually, would work out for the best.

* * *

In October, I was transferred to Nestlé's baby milk factory in Bethal. Nestlé had promoted me and transferred us to Bethal in the Eastern Transvaal (now Mpumalanga – a Zulu word for 'the place where the sun rises'). I thought this would be great for our marriage as it would give Riana and me the opportunity to actually get to know each other, as for all the time before our marriage we were never really alone. We were always in the company of Andre and a number of other friends.

Leaving Pretoria for Bethal was a new chapter. Riana resigned her position at the Department of Manpower; we packed and sold our house, and the two of us moved to Bethal.

The trip to Bethal was stressful. We drove, with my mother-in-law and two dogs in the car, through torrential rain. My mother-in-law came with to help us settle in.

On our arrival at Bethal, I took the dogs out and they were both very relieved that this movable cocoon in which they were constrained had come to an end. I asked Riana to hold Arthur for me so that I could close the gates of the yard. While she held him, he 'talked' to her as he often did when he got excited, and one of his teeth nipped her on the cheek. She was furious and claimed that the dog had bitten her. The more I tried to explain that she was just too close to his face and he was merely excited to be out of the car, the less she wanted to know. She demanded that the dog should go. So instead of putting my dog down, I gave Arthur to one of the guys at the laboratory who lived on a farm outside town. I heard in time that Arthur took to his new life on the farm like a fish to water. We had a large old company house and I enjoyed my new position as Human Resources Manager for the factory tremendously. Riana was appointed Personnel Officer with a para-statel board situated in Bethal. Life generally seemed good.

This appointment was the first time in years that I had been on my own, with my wife, in a new town where we knew no one. We just had each other. Part of my assignment in Bethal was to source, identify, train, and develop a Black human resources manager who was to take over from me on completion of my estimated two year assignment.

* * *

We had an occupational health nurse, called Yvonne Austin, working at the factory. A few years before I arrived, her husband had lost his job and they had four children, one boy and three girls. What made this family remarkable was that, although Yvonne was often the only income generator in the house, they never had a shortage of food, love, and happiness. All four of the Austin kids were incredibly well-mannered and a testimony to their parents. In fact, they were all dedicated students who understood very well that unless they worked hard and got good marks, they would not be able to see the inside of a university. The kids loved each other sincerely, and they always stood together as a united family. There was none of the animosity that I had experienced in my own family. While I am sure they did fight, like all children do, this was a unique family, one with character. This family followed Einstein's advice, as quoted by Gordon S. Jackson, when he said:

"Try not to become a person of success but rather a person of value."[49]

Success followed naturally. Yvonne and her husband started their own business a couple of years later, and all their children did well and eventually the family immigrated to Australia.

* * *

Early 1994 marked the beginning of a phase in South Africa's history when the majority of White South Africans started to prepare for the impending 'war' as the first all inclusive, one-man-one-vote, democratic election scheduled for 1994 became a reality. Bethal was no exception, and as

---

[49] Never scratch a tiger with a short stick, (2003, pg. 35)

a very conservative community, the dangers of the communist and Black domination were regular themes in White Afrikaner churches throughout the country. It was also this election that was the motivation behind Clive Darby-Lewis and Janusz Walus' actions to trigger a race war in South Africa, to derail the planned democratic election. The fear of uncontrolled riots and civil war remained the fear of many a White South African. Fortunately, the elections of 1994 took place without major incidents, and the birth of a peaceful democracy took place on 27 April 1994.

* * *

Riana and I, initially, were happy in Bethal. We settled into our new community and were very involved in the activities and social life of the factory. Once a year, all staff who received recognition for their 25-year-service was invited to an award banquet that the human resources department traditionally hosted. Riana and I planned an elaborate theme and menu based on the fifteen southern states of Africa. Every table was themed after a different country: South Africa, Namibia, Zimbabwe, Botswana, Mozambique, Malawi, Zambia, etc. I visited all the embassies in Pretoria and collected national flags from all these countries to adorn the hall. A small flag representing the relevant country was placed on each table. It was an impressive evening.

However, tension between Riana and me continued to increase, and, eventually in October, I went with the guys from the factory on a fishing trip to St. Lucia on the Natal North Coast.

On our return, Riana was strangely calm and seemed lost in her own thoughts. About three days later, she sat me down in the lounge and said that this was not working and that she suggested that we prepare to get divorced. She was very objective and factual, not emotional at all. She proposed that she move out of our bedroom into one of the spare bedrooms. I agreed that it was not working and that we should bring it to an end. I told her not to move out of the bedroom and offered to speak to the factory manager about using one of the company's guest houses that were used for visitors from Johannesburg. She agreed and I left home. I drove to the factory manager's home and explained to him that Riana and I had decided to separate and that I would like to use one of the guest houses as an interim arrangement. He agreed and I moved out of the house that evening.

I thought I would be relieved, but as I walked into the quiet and empty guest house, I realised what an absolute failure I was. I phoned my mum and did not go into detail, just told her that we were splitting up. My mother sounded devastated, as she was very fond of Riana, but said that she would support both me and Riana in whatever we decided to do.

Why I made the second call I am not sure, but I decided to phone Suzanne. After all she had been through two divorces, I guess I thought that if there was anyone who could give me helpful advice on this subject, then it was my sister, as troubled as our relationship had been at times. However, nothing prepared me for the response I received. After I told Suzanne that Riana and I were getting divorced, her immediate response was: "I'm glad. Now you know how it feels to be the bad one." I was so stunned that I could not respond. I phoned Christiaan and told him and Rina what was happening. I was relieved that both of them were remarkably supportive, and the same with Johan. Without taking any sides, Johan provided me with kind words of support. Taking into account Andre and Lynda's friendship with both me and Riana, I decided not to say anything to him at that point.

By this time, my father had arrived home and my mother had told him what happened. My father was clearly upset. He phoned me and wanted to know why we had not worked things out. I did not go into too much detail and kept the conversation short. Eventually, I went to bed and when I woke up the next morning, I felt as if my entire world was turning more slowly. Life seemed to happen in slow motion.

Back at work, I carried on normally and a day or two later, I phoned Riana and told her that I would be coming home on Saturday to do some laundry. When I arrived, I noted Riana was already busy with laundry, so I made breakfast. I could see she was drained. Things were very strained and we did not talk much. All our actions that day were very measured, very calculated, and very painful.

That evening my father phoned again, and though there were some discussions between him and Riana, he respected our decision and in a calm voice, confirmed that he would support whatever we decided to do. Although I knew I disappointed my father, his attitude was a relief.

We remained a married couple in the public eye. We attended a braai (barbeque) at Andre and Lynda's house and agreed beforehand that we would not tell anyone until such time as we had finalised the terms of our divorce and agreed upon the way forward.

Knowing that I needed to move on, I approached Nestlé head office to inquire if I could obtain a position in sales and marketing. I had several meetings with the various sales and brand managers, but they could not accommodate me. Eventually, the factory manager in Bethal released me from my duties and I was transferred back to Randburg as a Training and Development Specialist.

My departure from Bethal was unceremonious, and the last day, after half of our belongings were loaded, was challenging. Guinevere stayed with Riana, and I placed all my belongings in storage. I drove directly to Johannesburg International airport, where I boarded a plane to East London to visit Ponti and Renita for two weeks.

For the next ten days, I spent just about the entire time in bed, sleeping except when I had to go to the bathroom or eat. Ponti and I spent most of the evenings talking, and yet again, he proved to be a remarkable and supportive friend. At this time, Ponti seemed to be the only friend who did not judge me, who did not even criticise me. Although I knew that he really liked Riana, this was my divorce and he did not take sides. He just supported me, even though he did not agree with what was happening.

After I faced a tongue lashing from Ponti's mother about the guidance the Bible gave in terms of divorce and how I had no right to allow this to happen, I eventually returned to Pretoria to start a new life. I bought a house situated in Pierre van Rijneveld and phoned Amanda. When she heard that Riana and I were about to get divorced, she invited me to dinner at a Chinese restaurant. We spent the evening talking and she in so many words said, "I told you so." She seemed relieved that the marriage she condemned originally as a mistake was in fact on the rocks. Amanda immediately told me that she wanted to introduce me to an employee of hers who was a lovely and petite German girl. I was not interested.

Amanda was very kind during this time and helped me to move in to my new house. She spent an entire day helping me wash the cupboards, putting up my paintings, and decorated my house. After settling and carrying on with my life as best as I possibly could, the loneliness and the reality of my circumstances hit home. The friendship with Andre was now notably strained, although Ponti, Dietloff, and Hennie remained friends and did not involve themselves with the merits of my divorce.

Then came the news that Riana had tendered her resignation and also moved to Pretoria in early January. I knew this was bad news for any remaining friendships I had, as people do make a choice when their friends get divorced, and, in our case, some of our friends chose to invite my ex and dropped me off the invitation list. Although her move to Pretoria was generally bad news in my book, she moved into a flat and could not keep Guinevere, so at least I got the dog. On the 9th of January, Riana celebrated her birthday and came around to my house. We had a cordial discussion and it was clear that the pending divorce was taking its toll on both of us. I suspected Riana spent a lot of nights crying, and I spent most of my nights doing the same. Both of us crying, but for totally different reasons.

On Friday the 13th of January 1995, I attended the court proceedings, with Gillian Wood providing me with some moral support. We listened how one marriage after the other was dissolved. There was one specific divorce which stuck with me. It was a 60-year-old woman who filed for divorce. The presiding judge was the Honourable Judge Heher, an old rather British sounding gentleman. He listened as her Advocate (Barrister) took her through the standard questions. But the judge was curious why she wanted to get a divorce at such a ripe age and asked her to clarify her reasons why she had not filed for divorce years earlier. She stated that both she and her husband had agreed some twenty-three years ago that their marriage was not working. However, they had children and agreed not to get divorced until the youngest was fished with university, and now her children were out of the house all she would like was 'to get her life back'. The judge looked at her pensively and closing his folder, said to her in a stern voice: "Madam, I might be able to grant you a divorce, but no mortal being can give you your life back." This simple sentence was so profound for me that the rest of the proceedings became rather blurred. It emphasised that although it is important to work at a marriage, and work hard at it at all times, if a marriage is doomed, to remained married 'for the sake of the children' is stupid, as everyone, including the children, would suffer for years. This further confirmed the point for me that life is not a dress rehearsal. We only have one life and need to make the best of it. There is no second run.

Although I wanted children very badly, in fact nearly desperately, at this point, I was grateful that we did not have children.

After I had my three minutes in front of the judge, my divorce was granted. Gillian and I stopped at a restaurant for a cup of coffee. We did not talk much, as there was little that either of us could say. I thanked her for her support and she returned home to Johannesburg, while I drove to the Holiday Inn where Lynda worked. I informed her that the divorce had been granted and asked her if she would let Riana know. I returned to my house.

I spent a lot of time reflecting about what happened the past couple of days. It had become clear that I was to blame for my own misery. I could not blame what happened on Riana, on my family, or any of my friends. I could not blame my in-laws. As much as I would have loved to externalise my anger and frustration, I could not blame anyone but myself.

In a number of books I have read about emotional intelligence, from authors like Stephanie Vermeulen, Daniel Goleman or if one consider the teachings of Victor Frankl, I have learned two basic rules in life, that when it comes to human behaviour in any relationship, be it as lovers, friends, colleagues or employees, the following are true; we get the behaviour that we tolerate, and others will not change until we change first. It was Gandhi who said: *"Be the change you want to see in the world."*[50] What should we change?

Whatever is needed to have a balanced relationship, wherein the needs of both parties are addressed in equal measure.

Now I could do nothing about my past, but I could change my future. I made a conscious decision not to discuss the merits and content of our divorce with any of our friends. I actively embarked on a process of confirming Riana's goodness, her strong personality, and kindness. She had always been a good friend and wife to me; we were just not meant to be together as husband and wife. I could not be the husband that she wanted me to be.

This caused frustration among my friends and family, as I could hear that various debates were being held about who did what, who was to blame, and what the various reasons for our break-up were. Whether these were comments made by Riana or whether they were pure speculation, was unclear and no longer important. However, I decided that Riana at this point in my life was indeed a better human being than I, and as such, I would always honour and respect her for who I knew her to be.

---

[50] Mohandas Karamchand Gandhi, commonly known as Mahatma Gandhi, was the preeminent leader of Indian nationalism in British-ruled India –www.goodreads.com [accessed 08/12/16]

For years to come, I would regularly think, with sadness, of my ex-wife, as she had loved me dearly, and wanted nothing more than to build a happy traditional Afrikaans family with me.

During this time, for the first time in my life, I suffered with depression. I felt incredibly guilty for the pain I had caused Riana, for the disappointment I had been to my parents and my friends.

I started directing my energies towards building onto my house and tried to make new friends. Leon Jordaan (Jorries), a friend of Riana, never attempted to discuss my divorce with me. He remained a jovial and happy-go-lucky individual who, in years to come, became a very good friend of mine. Jorries reintroduced me to Louwtjie and Jenna, and a variety of their friends, including a girl by the name of Zelda. I started spending more and more time with them and during the first quarter of the year, we attended three weddings, without the funeral. Every time I listened to the various wedding sermons, it was a cold and hard indictment against me.

Riana also attended some of the weddings, and although it seems odd, we always got on well. In fact, after our divorce, we actually saw quite a lot of each other, to the extent that at one point I thought we might possibly get together again, but that would have been as ill- advised as all the other times that we broke up and made up before.

We all make mistakes through life, I took some comfort in the words of Nelson Mandela who said: *"I never fail, I either win or learn."*[51] Making mistakes is not the end of the world. What is important is the learning moments derived from these mistakes, and that we are not debilitated through our own guilt. The key is not to repeat the same mistakes or wrong choices over and over again.

The nature of my personality is that I do not like to disappoint or hurt others. It creates stress for me if others are angry, upset or unhappy with something that I have done or neglected to do. Thus, during the balance of my life, I always worked hard to achieve the support, acceptance, and friendship of others. I would learn that to care for others is a good characteristic, but to feel sorrow for the suffering of others does not relieve them of the slightest pain.

* * *

During this time, Ponti and Renita had moved to Pretoria from East London and settled in their home in Menlo Park. Their kids, Carla and Stefan, were attending primary school, and I was delighted that they had come to my part of the world. I always enjoyed their company.

Amanda continued to pressure me to meet the German girl who worked for her, but when I learned that her name also started with an 'R', I was convinced this would be disastrous. Taking into account that most of

---

[51] *http://awakenthegreatnesswithin.com/50-inspirational-nelson-mandela-quotes-that-will-change-your-life/* [access 08/12/16]

the names of the women in my life began with the letter 'R', (Retha, Ronel, Riana), another 'R' would just be too much. So as much as Amanda pushed, I declined.

Ponti and his kids bought me a black Labrador puppy. It was great to have a little bundle of life in my house.

I started going out with Louwtjie and his friends on a regular basis and enjoyed their jovial company. During this time, Zelda and I began to spend more and more time together. The fact that her name did not start with an 'R' was a great advantage. Zelda was also a party animal. It was this persona that attracted me to her. Zelda often wanted to talk about Riana, but I refused. I often warned her that I was not good to be with and that nothing would come from our 'relationship', but she stood by me. She made me feel special, we laughed, we drank copious amounts of red wine, and spent just about every weekend together.

Zelda gave me one of her mother's Fox-Terrier puppies that they thought was a miniature, but turned out to be just a normal Foxy. So I had two dogs, one Labrador, with lots of staffy blood and a large 'miniature' Foxy. I had no idea what to call either of the dogs until the first Sunday night after the Foxy's arrival. The movie *Amadeus* was screened on TV. My love for classical music and the history of Mozart's life ensured that I watched the three hour movie with attention. As the bizarre life of Mozart unfolded, the Labrador was named 'Wolfgang' and the Foxy was named 'Amadeus', which later just became 'Dias'. Life was starting to get better, Wolfgang, Dias and I, looking out for each other.

In May that year, Zelda and I attended the wedding of Gavin Schmidt, my former colleague from Nestlé, She looked beautiful; her red hair glowed healthily in the sun, while the freckles on her face made her look even naughtier than she naturally was. Some of my friends became nervous that Zelda and I might become more than just friends. She was special, but our relationship would not have survived.

* * *

The emptiness of my house got to me. I loved the company of both Wolfgang and Dias and enjoyed visiting Ponti and his family, but coming home to an empty home was not good for my state of mind.

Suzanne was on a drive to take her daughters away from her ex-husband, who had custody over them. However, she could not afford her own place and I had a three bedroom house. So I suggested that she and the girls should come and live with me. Regrettably, although not so intended, this invitation caused a final blow to my formerly good relationship with her ex, who promptly terminated any form of contact with me. A relationship that was fortunately re-established some twelve years later.

It was truly pleasant to have Suzanne and the girls in my house as it gave my home some atmosphere. The girls were full of energy, and when things became a bit much, I went to visit Ponti, Renita and the kids. It also did my and

Suzanne's relationship the world of good, as we had time to talk to each other, to have fun together, and to build a friendship that would last for the rest of our lives. We became strange friends.

I eventually resigned my position at Nestlé and accepted a position as Regional Human Resources Manager with the Premier Group, with specific responsibility for Blue Ribbon Bakeries. This was the best job I've ever held in corporate South Africa. I reported to the Human Resources Director, who was a brilliant boss, while I took responsibility for seventeen bakeries across two provinces, in both Mpumalanga and the North West Province. Although we had an office in Newtown Johannesburg, I spent most of my time on the road between the bakeries.

Chapter 14
New Beginnings

Eventually, Amanda told me to come and see her at Lion Match, where her company held the catering contract at the factory in Rosslyn, Pretoria. She told me to dress formally as she was going to introduce me to her staff as a potential client. This was not true, as the entire aim of the 'appointment' was to meet this long talked about German girl.

On my arrival at Lion Match, I was introduced to the catering manager, Renate Hoffmann. She was professional, courteous and polite. After about twenty minutes, Amanda indicated that we had to go; we said our cordial goodbyes, and Amanda and I departed.

During June 1995, Renate's company opened a new catering contract at Mercedes-Benz of South Africa (MBSA) in Schoeman Street in Pretoria. Renate was appointed catering manager for her company at MBSA with Executive Chef Shaun Campbell.

Amanda continued to muster all her influence to organise a date that she planned for me and Renate. Even Renate's area manager was roped in to influence or soften Renate's constant refusal to go out with her boss's friend. Eventually, Ponti, who worked at Mercedes-Benz's head office, also entered the debate and told Renate about me. I am not sure what he said to her, but it must be about my good looks, my brilliant sense of humour and all the other kind of attributes that I know my good friend would assign to me. However, she was still not moved. Although Renate liked Ponti, she was not yet ready to meet his 'good friend'. I think my friendship with Amanda had something to do with that.

At this time, my brother Johan came to Pretoria for an operation. As they had to operate on his knee, he could not drive back to Phalaborwa, and asked me if I would take him back home after the operation. I decided to phone Renate at work and ask her if she would like to go with me for the weekend. I figured that she would say yes, (arrogant, yes, I know), as we would be going to my family and we would not be alone, so she would not feel 'threatened'. If the weekend worked, then we would see what came of that. Eventually, I gathered enough courage to phone Renate at her office. It was about 4:00 in the afternoon, and she was busy finalising the last of her daily admin when the phone rang. I told her that it was "Hein Scheffer speaking, the friend of Marius". (She did not know him as Ponti.) She went silent and did not register anything that I said. She just heard my name, and could only remember that I was somehow connected to a furniture business in town. She could not even remember what I looked like. So the rest of the conversation was a bit of a blur. I told her that I would like to take her with me to Phalaborwa. She confirmed that it would be fine and the conversation was kept rather short. I was both surprised and relieved.

The next two days Renate spent some time trying to get my telephone number from Ponti to call me back. Eventually, after Renate gathered sufficient courage, she called. I did not expect to hear her voice and was surprised. She continued, "I've thought about going with you this weekend, but won't be able to make it." She provided no explanation, extended no open door, no promise of a later date, just a "won't be able to make it".

I decided to take Wolfgang along, as he loved traveling in a car and, after all, he was my best friend. So Johan, Wolfgang and I went to Phalaborwa. Johan made himself comfortable in the passenger seat, while Wolfgang slept the entire trip to Phalaborwa. I had an excellent weekend with Johan, Mariska, and their son Juandré. The Sunday when I drove back, I said my goodbyes and took Wolfgang for a last walk before we headed home.

Arriving back home, I attended to my duties within Blue Ribbon which stretched from Nelspruit in the north to Mmabatho in the northwest. I really enjoyed this job as I could travel extensively and did not have to be home alone. We attended quarterly human resources workshops at various game farms, while I was exposed to collective bargaining negotiations with the Food and Allied Workers Union (FAWU) and the South African Commercial Catering and Allied Workers Union (SACCAWU) in negotiations forums of up to fifty people at a time. This kind of practical experiences is not something that one could learn from a text book or in a class room. The management delegation consists of ten people and the union delegation of fifty, the dynamics of negotiation change dramatically. I was even taken hostage by the union representatives of FAWU at the bakery in Temba, just outside Pretoria, and again later at the Middleburg bakery. However, no harm was done.

I called Amanda to inform her that the match-making process had not been successful and that it seemed unlikely that it would work. Amanda wanted to hear nothing of this and so she applied more pressure on Renate's area manager and Shaun. Interestingly, she never spoke to Renate directly about me, always via others.

Ponti also told me that I should not give up so quickly and that I should try and go out with Renate as 'she was remarkable'. I said that I could not quite remember her all that well. After that, Ponti proceeded to describe her to me as "a small, petite girl, with beautiful features". He described her as "sophisticated and in a class of her own" and added that her looks could be described as "spectacularly gentle, not traditionally German at all".

Amanda did not want to take no for an answer and pestered me to stop complaining about being alone, as all I needed to do was to call Renate and ask her out. I told her that I could not, as I did not have her home telephone number. "No problem," Amanda added, and went to work. That following week, Amanda instructed Renate's area manager to "update the personal information of all staff" and in so doing, obtained Renate's private home telephone number which was duly presented to me with instructions to call Renate and to invite her to dinner. Confidentiality laws in South Africa were then, or now, clearly not comparable to those in the United Kingdom.

That Sunday evening, I decided to call Renate at home. She was busy ironing and incidentally had thought of me just before the phone rang. She thought about how manipulative Amanda was in that she influenced everyone around her to interfere with her (Renate's) private life. She answered the phone with the familiar "Renate here…" I greeted her and told her who was speaking. She sounded shocked. I made small talk about my trip to Phalaborwa and said that I had taken Wolfgang along. Renate then inquired about my animals. I told her that I had both Wolfgang and Dias as pets at home, and she told me about her black cat called 'Molly'. I thought I needed to keep her talking, as we had not started off well. So we talked about our animals and I managed to get Renate to tell me about Molly and how she and Molly had become 'family'. Eventually, I asked her again whether we could go out, "perhaps for dinner?" Perhaps it was her love for animals and the fact that I had two dogs which softened her heart, and she agreed to go on a date with me. At the end of the conversation, Renate inquired how I had obtained her phone number. I tried to be creative and said I was a man with many resources and had looked through the telephone directory, but after she told me that her number was not listed, I had to confess that I had obtained it from Amanda.

I provided Amanda with feedback the following day and told her that we had agreed to go for dinner on Friday evening at an Italian restaurant situated in the Old Tram Shed in Pretoria.

That next week, life carried on normally with me visiting all the bakeries and I spent three nights in Nelspruit. It was nice to travel and to see other towns and talk to different people, but returning to my hotel room all alone had its disadvantages, as the empty hotel rooms haunted me to the extent that I could hardly sleep. The following Friday, Renate and I went for an Italian dinner in the Tram Shed. Dinner was not spectacular. Renate wanted to know about my family, so I told her. I ended up talking the entire evening, which created the image in her mind that I was egocentric and self-absorbed. The impression that she created in my mind was one of being withdrawn, quiet, introverted but mysterious. At the end of that evening, she knew just about everything that was to be known about me and my background, while I knew nothing about her, her family, or her friends.

When I received Amanda's phone call the following week asking how dinner went, I told her that I was not interested and it was clear that Renate was equally uninterested.

At this time, Andre was in the job market, and secured an appointment as Regional Human Resources Manager with Netcare, a group of private hospitals. He called me and asked for my advice about it. I was pleased that he had asked, and recommended that he take the position if the pay was better and seeing that he would be based in Pretoria, it was obviously a good position for him. Andre duly tendered his resignation with Medi-Clinic and embarked on his new career at the regional office in Centurion.

I wanted to rekindle old friendships. 1995 was the year during which Andre, Lynda, Dietloff and I were all turning thirty. We decided to hold a combined birthday bash as a number of other friends of ours also turned thirty. As our birthdates varied from May to October that year, we decided to have a combined birthday bash in June. I offered to host this at the tennis club at Pretoria Central Prison. While Zelda and I attended this as a 'couple', I was very surprised when that evening she decided to link up with a friend of Gerhard, who turned out to be Andre's new boss. This was the final nail in the already shaky 'relationship' between Zelda and me. The evening, however, was a great success, especially Suzanne's special birthday cake that she baked for this occasion.

In July that year, my boss had to go to Durban and asked me to look after her home, a very neat two-bedroom townhouse in Kelvin. I invited Renate to come over for a picnic and was pleasantly surprised when she accepted. That morning, Renate drove from Pretoria and as luck would have it, bumped into Amanda at the petrol station where both of them had stopped to fill their cars with petrol. I made enough finger food for six people, while Renate brought cake from the Grapevine restaurant in Pretoria. We watched cartoons, ate food, and drank champagne. That afternoon when Renate drove back, I reflected on the day's events with a new perspective. Up to then I had not particularly liked this quiet introverted girl. However, after that day, I started to think otherwise.

On the 7th of August 1995, *The Tales of Hoffmann*, an opera by Jacques Offenbach, was being performed at the State Theatre in Pretoria. I originally bought tickets to take Dietloff, as it was his birthday. However, for some reason, he could not go, so I decided to call Renate and invited her to go with me. It was a fantastic evening, even though I regret that Renate did not enjoy it all that much. Again, I tried to share something that I truly enjoyed but failed to find out if it would be something that she would enjoy. As I had spent a number of years at the State Theatre during my student years, I knew a lot of people associated with the performing arts. So I spent most of the evening talking to people from my days in the theatre, neglecting to pay attention to my date. Thus, another failed evening, although the music and performance were spectacular.

I went to see Renate later at MBSA, and she mentioned that things she had told me during our dates had somehow got back to Amanda, and, ultimately, to her as well, and she was not impressed. So I started to become more cautious in terms of what I shared with Amanda.

I developed a keen desire to visit Ponti at the MBSA head office and obviously made sure that I was there over lunch and that Ponti had to go and buy cigarettes. I met Renate's Executive Chef, Shaun Campbell, who was a 23-year-old blond guy. Renate described him as a guy who 'had ants in his pants' as he just could not sit still. He also believed he was the coolest dude on the planet, and irrespective of whether you liked Shaun or not, he had the ability to make anyone laugh.

Ponti often went to the MBSA pub night, which was run by Renate's catering company, while Shaun managed the pub. Shaun became the resident 'lover boy' as he had classical pretty boy looks and a personality that was difficult not to like. Eventually, I heard the stories of their pub nights, and there is one specific evening that Ponti, Renate and Shaun attended with a number of Ponti's colleagues from MBSA which apparently was a great evening. They all swore secrecy about this specific evening and I have yet to find out what happened. The only thing I do know was that Ponti arrived late at home, and knew that he was going to be in trouble with Renita, so he plucked a flower in the garden before going into his house and when arriving inside he informed Renita that "I brought you a flower", as if this would fix everything.

Then came October and my 30th birthday. I was dreading this milestone. I always said that by the time that I turned 30, I wanted to be married, have at least two children, and a well-established and stable career. On reflecting on my situation before my birthday, I was divorced, had no children, and had just changed jobs some months before. In terms of the parameters, I had created to determine whether I was on the right path, I was well behind schedule.

Amanda celebrated her birthday the day before mine, so every year on the 24th of October, I think of Amanda when she celebrates her birthday.

The night before my birthday, in 1995, I was taking stock and I did not like what my 'balance sheet' told me. I reflected on every negative aspect in my life thus far, and allowed myself to spiral into a depression that bordered on being ridiculous.

The next morning I called Renate and told her that it was my 30th birthday. Taking into account that all my friends had a combined birthday party in June, I did not want to spend the evening alone and asked her to accompany me to dinner. She kindly agreed.

That evening I went to see my parents briefly after which I went to collect Renate from her flat in Sunnyside. We had a reservation at 'Diep in die Berg' (Deep in the Mountain), a hotel and conference centre in the eastern suburbs of Pretoria. The hotel had organised an evening of classical music with four opera singers performing at the venue. Renate and I spoke about her hobbies, her love for animals, and the fact that she loved Spanish dancing. We enjoyed our dinner and the music was fantastic. Just before the quartet was finished with their performance, one of the ladies sang 'Granada'. Both Renate and I listened attentively, and as I watched Renate taking in this angelic voice, I noted that a tear was running down her cheek. She was mesmerised by the music and at that moment, I realised that she was the one. That this was the woman with whom I wanted to spend the rest of my life. This was the mother of my children. This was my soul mate. There was only one problem; I was not convinced that she shared my point of view.

After dinner, we took a slow walk through the garden and stopped at the duck pond. I placed my hand on her shoulders and thanked her for a remarkable evening. She stood still, just looking ahead into the darkness, before she turned to me, and thanked me for a lovely evening. I realised there and then that if I wanted to get this unique and quiet German girl to fall for me, as I had now clearly had for her, I would have to change my approach drastically. I would have to use the negatives of my past and convert them into positives and learn from all the things that I had done badly, or the mistakes I had made, to enable me to do the right thing, to become a better person, to become the man with whom Renate would fall in love. So, from being a generally egocentric ass, I needed to show her that I was actually a nice guy, that I do take others into consideration, and that life is not just about 'me', but that life would be great if it was about 'us'.

On 16 December 1995, Renate, Shaun, their area manager, their client at MBSA, and a number of MBSA staff attended a party at the house of Renate's client, in the suburb of Irene. Renate went home with me and stayed the night.

That Sunday morning, Shaun and Renate left my house early as Amanda indicated earlier that week that she would come and visit and was due to arrive at 11:00. When she arrived, she brought me a small Christmas cake. I was rather irritated by her interference; however, Amanda played my mood down as being silly. During the next few weeks all hell just about broke loose.

Renate had had enough of all this interference and subsequently sought a position with another company. When she tendered her resignation, Amanda asked her why she was resigning, to which Renate said that "it was time to go". Amanda asked Renate whether she was resigning because of her, a strange question to ask if you were not involved. However, Renate did not want to debate it any further and reiterated that "it was time to go".

The following week, the company human resources representative came to see Renate and wanted to know why she was resigning after being with the company for more than five years. Interestingly enough, the human resources practitioner also asked if Renate's resignation was due to Amanda. Renate decided to lay her cards on the table and confirmed that she had enough of Amanda's interference in her life. She felt that Amanda had manipulated Shaun and had a general management style of divide and rule, and she feared that things would just become worse. The human resources representative asked if Renate would reconsider, to which she answered: "No, it's time to go."

Not long after this visit, Renate received a phone call from her divisional managing director who had had a similar discussion with Renate. Again Renate explained the situation, to which he responded that they did not want Renate to resign and said that they would remove Amanda from Renate's region, and seriously requested Renate to reconsider. Not long thereafter, some of Amanda's responsibilities were re-assigned to another Operations Manager. Renate continued to work for her company for another two years, before leaving to start her own business.

All of these events had a totally destructive effect on my friendship with Amanda, as she always declared war on anyone who crossed her. From that day on, she never spoke to Renate again, and not long after, Shaun also resigned. Fortunately, within the next eight months, Renate was in a position to move to the Eastern Cape and would be given an inter-company transfer to their offices based in East London.

I ended up with a dilemma, as I was upset with Amanda for interfering in everyone's lives. However, I was incredibly pleased and grateful that she had been so persistent in pressuring me to meet Renate. Taking into account that I was now intrigued with Renate and wanted to explore this relationship further, I did not need or want Amanda's constant interference, but equally did not want her controlling personality affecting Renate's career adversely. I tried to restore my friendship with Amanda. I did value her friendship and although she might have upset a number of other people, she did me a very big favour in being so persistent. So I thought, we are only human and humans err, and any error can be rectified if both parties are prepared to acknowledge their mistake, place it behind them, learn from it and move on; that is what forgiveness is all about.

On the 24th of October that year, I had to attend to business in Johannesburg and made sure that I had time to visit Amanda at her office. Because it was her birthday and we had been friends for many years, except the past eighteen months, I arrived at Amanda's office, firstly to wish her a happy birthday, and secondly to mend our friendship. I arrived unannounced, as I was not sure how she would respond to my peace-making effort. Her secretary took me to her office and offered me coffee and cake. Amanda was clearly shocked to see me, and was not pleased with my visit. She told me that she was engaged and that life was very good. She did not share any details about her engagement and changed the topic. There was a clear distance between us and a coldness that I had never felt before. It soon became clear that she did not want to talk to me and that she was not impressed by my sudden visit. The fifteen minute visit was incredibly strained. I tried to make conversation to no avail. She was not interested. I left Amanda's office feeling disappointed. That was the last time I made an effort to make contact with her.

Something that I learned from this experience specifically is that we cannot force people to talk to us. If someone made up their mind not to talk to me, for whatever reason, then there is absolutely nothing that I can do. The lesson learned is that if you try and ask for forgiveness from another, and that person persists in rejecting you or refuses to talk to you, even refuses to listen to you, the loss of the relationship belongs to the other – try three times, if unsuccessful, move on. However, keep the door open for the day they come back to you – always forgive others when they are sincerely asking for your forgiveness – always. Reflecting on all my friendships and the mistakes I have made in some of them and the mistakes that I have made in my own life, following the advice I received from an acquaintance, I wrote the following, which is ultimately also applicable in business relationships, in fact, in any form of association:

Friends – If Only You Have That...

'Firstly you need to have affinity'
The willingness to share your space with others
If only you have that...
'You need capacity'
The willingness to accept others for who they are;
With strengths, weakness, good or bad.
The ability to forgive others for their inadequacies.
If only you have that...
'You need reality'
To understand that friends disappoint each other;
But, they support each other;
They understand each other; and
Accept each other.
If only you have that...
'You need to communicate'
To talk about irritations, disappointments, resentments, good times and bad;
To address the problem without affecting the person;
To understand others and their needs in relation to your own.
If only you have that...

We Could Be Friends[52]

---

[52] J.H. Scheffer, 07/08/2001

Chapter 15
Facing Our Parents and Friends

During November 1995, MBSA had its year-end function at its head office in Schoeman Street. Renate and Shaun prepared a fantastic spread and Ponti made a plan for me to attend as the 'partner' of one of the employees at MBSA. It was a lovely evening, and I spent the evening talking to my 'date' and the guests at our table. I watched Renate from afar and there was a special magic about her as she worked diligently with Shaun to do what they both did best. They were clearly a brilliant team. Renate had a natural ability to motivate her staff, while providing guidance to her team and ensuring that the executives, management and staff of MBSA had a year- end function of note. The Hawaiian theme added to the ambiance of the evening, and the food was delicious. I just could not wait for the dinner and formalities to finish, so that I could get some time with Renate.

That year in December, Renate invited me for dinner on Christmas Eve. Traditionally, in my family, we celebrated Christmas on the 25th of December, but I learned that the Germans celebrated Christmas on the 24th, so it was actually easy, as we could spend Christmas Eve with Renate's mother and Christmas Day with my family. This was a very memorable Christmas Eve, as it was the first time that I actually met Renate's mum. I was petrified, as Renate had warned me that her mother was a traditional German lady who wanted her to have a German boyfriend. Although my name and surname was German, the fact that my German ancestors had immigrated to South Africa from Einbeck, Hanover in Germany in the early 1800s[53] disqualified me as a true German, making me a full-blooded Afrikaans- speaking South African.

Dinner was spectacular, and I immediately clicked with Mrs Hoffmann. She was very kind and while looking like a stereotypical German lady, she is indeed a kind, warm, friendly, and very welcoming person.

Renate was noticeably anxious and it soon became clear that her mum was an outspoken lady and showed little concern about impressing the new boyfriend. In fact, perhaps that was the characteristic that impressed me most. After dinner, we exchanged gifts and Mrs Hoffmann also had a gift for me with a card, which read: 'Dear Hein, Merry Christmas, From Ma Helga'.

I was surprised and pleased at the instant familiarity with which Renate's mum welcomed me in to her home. After dinner, Renate and I joined

---

[53] Cecilia Scheffer, *Geslagsregister van Christiaan Johannes Scheffer,*

Dominique a cousin of mine and Debbie his girlfriend, for the mid-night Mass at the Roman Catholic Church in Hercules, Pretoria. After Mass, we drove back to my house, listening to Christmas carols on the radio without talking. We savoured the moment quietly, each one with our own thoughts, while reflecting on the events that had brought us together. On arriving home, we went to bed and slept like logs. The next morning, we drove to Kempton Park for Christmas Day with my family.

Suzanne decided that she wanted to move to Cape Town and to return her two daughters to their father. This enabled her to get a position with a private hospital in Cape Town.

During June 1996, Blue Ribbon had its annual management conference in Midrand. It was a three-day conference. The eve of the 20th of June was the last evening of our conference. The following morning was Friday, 21 June, and Johan's birthday. All the conference delegates were fragile, and when I left, I drove directly to Renate's flat. En route, I called Johan to wish him a happy birthday. On arriving at her flat, we talked for a little while before we fell asleep and slept for most of the afternoon. I woke up at about 4:00 feeling like a new man. Without waking Renate, I carefully got out of bed and went to the lounge to insert a CD that I had bought of Joshua Kadison, titled 'Painted Desert Serenade'. I set the CD player on the sixth song on the disk, titled 'Beautiful In My Eyes', and went back to bed. While the CD played, I spoke to Renate quietly and whispered sweet nothings into her ear. As all of this carried on, I tried to muster the guts for what I needed to say. What I came to ask…

As the CD continued to play, my anxiety rose. Literally thirty seconds before the end of the song, I quietly whispered in Renate's ear, "Will you marry me?" Renate did not show any facial reaction, but quietly responded, "Look me in the eyes and say that again." I rose onto my arm and looked her in the eyes. "I said, will you please marry me?"

After Renate's initial response, I was prepared for the worst and had already prepared myself mentally for what I would do when she either said 'no', or told me that she was 'not ready for marriage yet'. If she confirmed the latter, I would be supportive and understanding. And I would not feel rejected, as she at least now knew how I felt about her. If she needed more time, I was prepared to wait and did not want to pressure her. If she blatantly said 'no', well, then, our relationship would be slightly in trouble, as a clear and definite 'no' would place a great damper on it. However, I did not intend to be blown off by either answer. After all, there was not much more she could do. She could either terminate the relationship, which I was very confident she would not do, or she could confirm that she needed more time, as she was not ready to give up her flat, her freedom, and that was also fine. After all, I had known since the 25th of October 1995 that I wanted to marry her, and I waited patiently from October '95 to June '96 before I asked her. Surely, if I could wait eight months without pressuring her, I could wait longer if need be.

If one really thought about it, less than a year before, I had told myself that I would never ever marry again. I did not believe that I would ever find someone that would make my feet sweat the way that this petite German girl did. And when I eventually realised that this was the one, I clearly understood that I would have to be careful. I would have to make sure that I nurtured this relationship to maturity and until such time as she was ready to take it to the next level. This was such a time.

Renate looked at me, her eyes penetrating mine as if she wanted to see what was going on deep inside my head. Her facial expression was mysterious, like that of someone who had just woken up from a deep sleep and was totally relaxed, content with her surroundings and with life. She took my hand, opened her mouth, and said "Yes!"

Joshua Kadison sang the last part of what became our song, and the words echoed in the lounge.

You will always be beautiful in my eyes.
And the passing years will show that you will always grow ever more beautiful in my eyes...

That evening, Renate and I went to visit Ponti and Renita and told them our news. They were very happy for us and Ponti immediately joked with Renate that they would have to go for coffee, as he would have to warn Renate about me – fresh coming from one of my oldest friends, who actually facilitated our union.

* * *

The next Sunday, Renate and I went to visit my parents to tell them. I was very nervous, as I feared that my parents would not give their blessing. Like Renate's mother, who felt very strongly that Renate should marry a German-speaking Lutheran. Taking into account that my divorce had only been finalised some six months before, I also feared that my parents would feel that this engagement was too soon. I was always convinced that deep down, they both wished that my ex-wife and I could reconcile our differences.

* * *

Renate and I decided that we would not ask either of our parents if we could get married, but rather would advise them that we intended to get married. We also decided that we would pay for the wedding ourselves and not ask for any financial help from our parents. With this in mind, we stopped at my parents' house first.

After my father had made some coffee, Renate and I and my mother and father sat in the TV room. I kept the process short and respectfully informed my parents that Renate and I intended to get married. Both Renate and I were equally surprised at my parents' warm and overwhelming response. They both seemed very pleased for us and immediately welcomed Renate into the family. We told them that we would like to get married before the end of the year, but that no official date had been set. As soon as was appropriate, Renate and I excused ourselves. When we drove away, we both said that it went much better than what we anticipated. We were, however, not as confident about the next visit at Mrs Hoffmann's house.

On arriving at 108 Van Heerden Street, Capital Park, we greeted Renate's mum and stood with her in the kitchen, until the coffee was made, before we moved into the lounge. After taking about four or five sips of my coffee, and making nervous eye contact with Renate, I started fumbling with words, trying to build up to what I wanted to ask, but nothing seemed to make much sense. Eventually the words fell into place. "Mrs Hoffmann, I would like to ask you for your daughter's hand in marriage." The statement sounded out of place, so unprepared, but I was grateful that it was out.

Her reaction was not what I expected. I had prepared myself for some challenges, about the fact that I was not German, that I could not even speak German, that I would probably have to ask Renate's father – who was living in Germany, or any other relevant comment that a mother would throw against the possible future husband of her only child, to protect her only daughter. Mrs Hoffmann exploded with joy and laughter. She jumped up from her seat and in tears grabbed Renate. "But of course," she said. She hugged Renate and through their tears of joy, both of them hugged me. It was clear that my future mother-in-law supported our union wholeheartedly.

Although both Renate and I were excited, we were both cautious about sharing our news with our respective friends, Ponti excluded. Renate's friends were mostly German and they probably expected that she would marry a German, too. Most of my friends had not forgiven me for my divorce from Riana. So we decided to keep a low profile for a while.

When, eventually, I did tell Andre that Renate and I intended to get married, he was surprisingly happy for me. In fact, all my friends were very happy that Renate and I had decided to tie the knot. So my fears were put to bed and the planning of the wedding could start in earnest.

Renate wanted to introduce me to her friends and organised several fondue parties. However, the nature of my work at Premier often required me to attend to industrial action matters or unit visits on short notice, and I had to cancel about three or four of these invitations at short notice. This caused tremendous embarrassment for Renate, as her friends started questioning whether I actually existed. They knew I worked at a milling and baking company, and Graeme Dennis, one of Renate's colleagues and friends, got his facts wrong when telling the other people about me. Graeme had seen a photo of me and described me as the 'Italian Stallion from Tiger Oats'. The only Italian resemblance I had was a head of thick black hair. I had a full beard and looked anything but Italian. And, as said before, I worked for Premier Foods, not Tiger Brands. However, Graeme was renowned for getting his stories mixed up, which made him a pleasant, unique, spaced-out kind of individual. But, eventually, we all became good friends.

Chapter 16
East London, Before Going to the Chapel

Just after I had returned to Pretoria from Bethal, and before I accepted my appointment with Blue Riboon Bakeries, I submitted an application to Sun International.

I had always had a passion for the hotel industry, and submitted an application for an advertised post of Regional Human Resources Manager for SunBop (A Division of Sun International Southern Africa [SISA] situated in the former Bantustan homeland of Bophuthatswana). Brett Nicholls, the Divisional Human Resources Manager for InterSun, the holding company for this division, called me for my first interview. I was told that I would have to attend a second interview in Mmabatho, where the Regional Office was situated at the time. Mmabatho was the capital of the former homeland of Bophuthatswana, and situated directly adjacent to the historic town of Mafikeng, in the old Western Transvaal (now North West Province). I drove to Mmabatho with very mixed feelings about the countryside and the area in which I was planning to build a new career. On my arrival at the then-Molopo Sun, I was introduced to the Regional Financial Manager, Mike van Vuuren, who conducted the interview. I was unfortunately not successful in my application and the other candidate, a competent and professional human resources practitioner, by the name of Rob Hoffman, was appointed. However, Brett said that he would keep my application on file. I accepted this and moved on. As I could not get a position within Sun International at that point, and the position with Blue Ribbon was offered to me, so I accepted the latter.

Christiaan, Suzanne, and Johan were also happy about the new sister-in-law that was about to enter the family, as were the rest of our family. Dietloff said that as long as I was happy, he would be happy for both of us. Dietloff supported us just because he was a special friend, a friendship that I expect to last for the rest of our lives.

In June 1995, some five months after my initial interview with Brett Nicholls, Brett called and said that they were looking for a Regional Human Resources Manager for the Ciskei, also a former homeland situated in the Eastern Cape near East London. He wanted to know if I would be interested and I was truly torn between two worlds. I had always wanted to work for

Sun International, and had idealised Sol Kerzner as an example of how an ordinary individual could become a great entrepreneur, hotelier and businessman. However, I was also very happy with my job at Premier and truly enjoyed working for Blue Ribbon Bakeries.

I agreed to go for an interview and both Renate and I went down to the Ciskei to meet the Regional General Manager for the Eastern Cape, Mr Graham Vass. I found him to be a remarkable man, short of posture, very neatly dressed, and as cool as a cucumber. Soon, it became clear that Graham liked to talk, and for the duration of the 'interview', he talked about the Ciskei, the region, the politics, the changing times, Sun International, and a variety of topics. He asked a few questions to Renate about her background and where she came from and he wanted to know a bit about what I had done.

As I launched into a well-prepared explanation of my experience and abilities, I quickly realised that I was talking too much and cut myself short in order to give Graham more time to talk, which he duly did. He told me about the four units under his control, the Amatola Sun situated in Bisho, the Mdantsane Sun situated in the township of Mdantsane just outside East London the Mpekweni Sun on the coast near Port Alfred, and the Fish River Sun situated between Mpekweni and Port Alfred. Graham just wanted to determine if I would suit the culture and whether I would be able to fit within his team of regional managers. The interview went very well, and Renate and I returned to Pretoria.

About two weeks after my interview with Graham, Renita had her birthday on the 29th of July and invited a large number of people to their house to celebrate. At about 7:00 that evening, Brett called and said that I had been selected as the preferred candidate for the position of Regional Human Resources Manager for Sun International in the Eastern Cape. I had to make a decision that evening and spent about half an hour with Renate in Ponti's bedroom talking about this dream job that I had been offered in the company that I had tried to get into for years, the ideal position in my company of choice, and that in the Eastern Cape of all places.

Renate was absolutely fantastic and demonstrated a sense of adventure that I did not know she possessed. She said that this job was something that I had always wanted, and if that is what I wished to do, she would be happy to move to the Eastern Cape with me. So, with that, I called Brett, accepted the position, and told him that I would tender my resignation on 1 August at Premier Foods to join Sun International on 1 September 1996.

We then celebrated not only Renita's birthday, but also my new job and the fact that Renate and I not only planned to get married, but that we also intended to move to the Eastern Cape and live in East London, my old safe haven, my home-town.

The last week of July was spent in the Johannesburger Hotel, where Premier Foods was conducting its annual wage negotiations with the Food and Allied Workers Union (FAWU).

Dietloff designed a nifty computer programme for us to calculate the annual increment in relation to the basket of funds available to us, which then made sure that we did not overspend. The Managing Director of Blue Ribbon at the time was Jorries Jordaan, and Dietloff's programme warned us with a catching phrase that if we overspend our mandate, a warning panel flashed the words: '*Jorries is going to f**k you up!*'.

While I enjoyed the experience of being part of a large negotiation team and dealing with the trade unions, I found myself in a dilemma as I knew that I was about to 'jump ship' from Blue Ribbon and was not sure how I was going to tell Terry Lavery, our Human Resources Director at the time. Fortunately, the wage negotiations kept me busy and I did not have much time to think about what was lying ahead. But the fact that I could join Sun International and move to the Eastern Cape gave me a new zest for what I was doing. Fortunately, a settlement was reached with FAWU on 30 July 1996. After the agreement was signed, I told Terry that I had been offered a position with Sun International that I could not turn down and subsequently tendered my resignation.

* * *

As a result of my resignation, Terry asked me to look for a possible replacement and after we had looked at a number of candidates, I recommended that Gerhard Harmse should join Blue Ribbon. I contacted Gerry, who was still the Human Resources Manager at Morningside Medi-Clinic, and arranged for an interview with Terry Lavery. Prior to his interview, I briefed him in detail about the company, the role players, the regions, the regional managers, the unions, and everything he needed to know in order to make sure that he was as well prepared as anyone possibly could be to facilitate a successful interview. However, Gerry is the type of person who needed very little help in selling himself, his experience, and his skills.

Gerry and I became friends when I joined Sandton Medi-Clinic, when he introduced me into Medi-Clinic, its policies, people, culture, and politics. We remained good friends and did not realise at the time that our paths were to cross a few times on both a professional and social level in time to come.

Terry Lavery was duly impressed with Gerry, who was appointed my replacement. However, it was made clear that it was the intention of Blue Ribbon to split my old region into two, but in the interim Gerry was responsible for all seventeen of the bakeries that I had looked after.

Gerry took to his new position, his new colleagues, and his new environment like a fish to water, and I had about a week before I had to start with Sun International. I realised just how easy it was for one person to be replaced by another. I felt betrayed by my colleagues, but could not say that, as I was the one who had resigned. As strange as this might sound, this was the most difficult departure of all my jobs. I really enjoyed working for Blue Ribbon and considered the team as close friends.

It is not the company that makes the employer of choice, but the people driving it. Terry Lavery, Pete Smith, Bill Read, Bruce Shelton and all the other Bakery Managers and other human resources colleagues I worked with at Blue Ribbon, made Blue Ribbon a brilliant employer at the time. They all contributed positively to my personal growth and development.

* * *

The next morning I called Brett Nicholls to finalise the paperwork at his office. I arranged to be at his office at about 11:00 in the morning and left Ponti's house early enough to be in Sandton on time. However, while driving toward Johannesburg, I found that the Ben Schoeman motorway was partly under construction. A new bridge restaurant and filling station was being built at the New Road off-ramp. Although there was sufficient signage that one should drive slowly, the general flow of the traffic was about 140km/h (87mi). Just as I approached the New Road road-works, suddenly the traffic in front of me came to a grinding halt in both the fast and middle lanes. There was a white car in front of me, which I noted was standing still. I slammed on the brakes and as I slid forward, I braced myself for impact. In a split second I glanced in my rear view mirror and noticed another car from the middle lane had also realised that the car in front of him was standing still and thought that the fast lane was still moving. He accelerated out of the middle lane and moved into the fast lane and was heading straight for me. Suddenly everything happened in slow-motion. As I slammed into the car in front of me, the other car slammed into me from behind, making me and my car the proverbial ham in the sandwich. Miraculously, I only suffered whip-lash. However, my car was severely damaged. Needless to say I did not make my appointment with Brett and now found myself without a car.

When I took the appointment with SISA, Renate and I decided that I would move to East London on my own until December 1996, when we would marry in Pretoria. Renate would then join me in our new home in East London. So, we arranged that I would spend a short while staying with Harry and Heather in East London, while looking for a suitable home. However, with the car accident and the fact that my car was to take some four weeks to be repaired, I was stranded. After I called Harry and Heather and explained my predicament, they immediately came to my rescue, confirming that I could stay with them for a month, and could use one of their BMW's to travel to Bisho, just outside King Williams Town, where my new office was situated.

Harry had me picked up by one of his drivers in East London and he and Heather were remarkable hosts. I was made comfortable in their home in Vincent in East London while Harry introduced me to a number of local estate agents to help me to find a suitable home for Renate and me.

On 1 September 1996, I drove to Bisho to take over from my predecessor, Andreas Dinse. I had an early morning meeting with Graeme Vass, who introduced me to the company's employment lawyer, Dr Brian van Zyl, owner of Van Zyl, Rudd and Associates in Port Elizabeth, labour law experts and legal advisors to Sun International.

Harry helped me to get a house in Baysville in East London. It was a very large old house, but I really liked it.

At the beginning of November, I had to fly to Johannesburg from where I boarded a bus to Swaziland to attend my first human resources conference in Sun International. Brett Nicholls introduced me to the other human resources managers and we drove to the Hlanganu Sun situated opposite the Valley of the Kings in Swaziland. During this conference, Christiaan called. At this time, he was working as part of the Police's VIP protection unit, and was assigned to look after the then Premier of the North West Province, Dr Popo Molefe. He called to tell me that he and Rina would not attend our wedding, as it excluded children, and therefore his boys could not attend. Although I heard via my father that Rina was unhappy with this arrangement, both Renate and I felt that we were paying for the wedding ourselves and we had limited space. Eventually I agreed that the boys, who were actually no longer boys but rather young adults, could attend. However, Chris was adamant that Rina did not want to attend and was very offended. Eventually, I spoke to Rina to convince her to change her mind, but she then claimed that Chris did not want to attend and that she would go where her husband went. This kind of 'he-said, she-said' regrettably continued for the next couple of weeks, which led to my eldest brother effectively boycotting the best day of my life, as neither he or his wife could make a decision.

On returning after the HR workshop, I had to get through one more month before I could go back to Pretoria to get married and return with my wife. I had moved out of Harry and Heather's house and settled in my new home in Baysville. During the time I stayed with Harry and Heather, Wolfgang was in the kennels outside East London. During those first couple of weeks, I went to visit him a few times, and every time he saw me he went crazy. When I eventually fetched him to come home, I decided to treat him and took him to Nahoon beach where he played in the sea water and ran up and down the sand dunes. I was initially worried that he might fight with other dogs on the beach, but he was just grateful to be out of the kennel and back with me that he did not even notice the other dogs.

That evening, Harry and Heather invited me to a braai (barbeque) at their house. I told them that I had Wolfgang with me and they said that I could bring him along. Wolfgang sat next to my chair and eventually fell asleep on the floor. He was out for the rest of the evening, and by the time I woke him up to go home, he was so stiff from all the day's activities that I had to carry him to my car.

Eventually December was upon us and on 11 December 1996, I took my leave from work and boarded a South African Airways plane for Johannesburg. Renate and Ponti were at the airport to meet me and it was great to see Renate again. I did not realise how much I had missed her and she looked more beautiful than ever. It was fantastic to be 'back at home'.

On the 12th of December it became apparent that there was some politics brewing in the Hoffmann clan, as my mother-in-law did not want either her mother or sister present at the wedding. Renate's aunt had learning difficulties and was a resident at Irene Homes in Pretoria. She was a wonderful individual who had secured a very special place in both my and Renate's hearts, and though the relationship between my future mother-in-law and her mother was strained, the relationship between her and her sister was non-existent. This placed a lot of tension on Renate in the days before we tied the knot. To add to our stress, Renate's father was arriving from Germany on the morning of our wedding. I had not yet met my future father-in-law. So we did not exactly need more pressure at that time.

Eventually, I just could not take the politics anymore, so I decided to allow the 'control freak' in me to take charge and I spoke frankly to my future mother-in-law. Following a compromise, the tension was alleviated and the arrangements could be finalised. It was agreed that Renate's grandmother would attend the wedding. So it seemed the only hurdle that needed to be overcome was my meeting with my future father-in-law.

The morning of 14 December, I drove to the airport to collect Herr Thorwaldt Breuer, my future father-in-law, whom I had never seen before and had to recognise from a photo. I collected Herr Breuer, his son, René, and a friend, Torsten, from the airport. Herr Breuer looked tired, while René was very quiet. I did not try to talk too much as I was not sure what to say to them. I drove back to the Manhattan Hotel, where Renate, her mother, and Hennie's mother were busy with the flowers and preparations for the reception.

Renate was ecstatic to see her father and brother again. I left her with her father and mother, while I took René and Torsten to Hatfield for a beer. I thought I should start spending some time with my future brother-in-law.

On arriving back at the Hotel, Ponti arrived with more flowers, only to announce that Renita had decided to leave him and had told him that she wanted a divorce, this after ten years of marriage. Although I realised this was rather insensitive, I asked Ponti to put his marital problems on hold for 24 hours and help me to get through my wedding. While Ponti was much stressed, he was, however, great for the duration of the day. He spent most of the day on his cell phone trying to sort out the effect of his wife's early morning announcement. But by the time he had to have my bride at the church, Ponti was as focused on our wedding as he needed to be.

The wedding was to start at 5 PM, and Dietloff and I arrived at the church at 4:45 PM. On walking into the church, I gave Dietloff a sip from a small bottle of Archer's Peach Snaps that Renate had left for me in my room to calm the nerves.

As I walked into the church, I saw Willie sitting in the back of the church. Willie had been in Turkey and I did not know that he was back in the country. It was so good to see him there and unbeknown to us, Willie would become a very close friend to both Renate and I in years to come. Willie effectively became Renate's 'father' in South Africa. My parents were in attendance, and my mother looked as graceful and beautiful as ever. Renate's mum looked equally glamorous. The stage was set for a wonderful and memorable life-changing event.

We greeted some of the family and went to sit in the front of the church. The organist played softly, I looked up at the roof of the church and I prayed quietly,

Dear God, please bless this marriage, this union. Help me to be a good husband to Renate. Help us to be good parents to our children and guide us to ensure that this marriage works.

The wedding march started, Dietloff and I rose and as I turned around, I saw my beautiful, angelic bride coming down the aisle, holding the arm of a very proud father. Behind them, Ursula was dressed in a beautiful bottle green dress, while René was, to my horror, dressed in jeans, a sports jacket, and running shoes.

We said our vows and pledged to take each other for richer and for poorer, in sickness and in health, until death do us part, all with God's help.

Chapter 17
A Traumatic Beginning to the First Year of Marriage

After Renate and I celebrated our wedding with family and friends, we departed to Hogsback in the Eastern Cape where we enjoyed our honeymoon. We took long walks in the forests, rode horses, appreciated the arts and crafts of the local community, and enjoyed each other's company. We moved into our house in Baysville, East London, and had a comfortable and content life.

Renate obtained a transfer to East London with the catering company she worked for in Pretoria. This necessitated that she had to work on weekends some of the time. One Saturday, toward the end of January, Renate was at work and I enjoyed an afternoon nap. The phone rang, and in my state of being half asleep, I answered the phone. It was my brother Johan. He recently resigned from his position with a mining company in Phalaborwa and accepted a better position with a large fishing company in Saldanha Bay, on the Cape west coast. He was bemoaning his new position and indicated that he was not sure if the move from Phalaborwa to Saldanha was the right thing to do. I was openly irritated with him, as I wanted to sleep and he seemed to be fishing for sympathy for a move he made which, to the best of my knowledge, was an improvement on his previous position. Living on the coast, working for a large fishing company, in my mind at least, must be better than living in Phalaborwa, working for a mine. I told him to focus on his new job and to forget Phalaborwa. It was a fresh start, a new beginning, and a fantastic new opportunity for him to build a new career.

Johan was not particularly pleased with my lack of understanding or support for him. He seldom asked for help or advice. He was normally the one who gave me advice and direction. I should have known that something was wrong, but I did not, and as I wanted to sleep, I had no desire to provide my brother with sympathy when I thought he least needed it. We ended the conversation and I resumed my afternoon nap.

Sometimes in life, people ask for help in strange ways. I have pondered my discussion with Johan that day many a times in years to come. If only I truly listened of what he was saying. If only I took note of the fact that something was bothering him. If only I asked the right questions. If only…

Although we stayed in East London, the regional office of Sun International was situated in Bisho, adjacent to King Williams Town, about 60km (37.6mi) from our home. Bisho used to be the capital of the former homeland, the Republic of the Ciskei. I drove between Bisho and East London on a daily basis and enjoyed the quietness of the highway (motorway) in comparison to the havoc I was used to between Pretoria and Johannesburg every day.

On Monday, 10 February 1997, at about 4 in the afternoon, I was on my way back from Bisho to East London. While driving, my phone rang. It was my mum. She was very distressed. I pulled over on the side of the road and inquired why she was so upset. My mum cried uncontrollably on the other side of the line and told me that according to Mariska, Johan's wife, he was missing, feared dead. My mum's words were so shocking that I could not, and did not believe her. Johan apparently left the house early that morning and agreed to drop their eldest son, Juandré, at day-care, but failed to return home. Mariska said that she reported her concerns to the local police but the anxiety and fear in her was mounting.

As my mother at times could overreact, I tried to calm her and told her that I am on my way home. I told her that once I arrived back in East London, I would call to find out what had happened. About thirty minutes later, I stopped at our house and told Renate what my mum said. Just after 5:00 PM, the phone rang, and it was my father, confirming what my mum told me. I asked him to call me as soon as he knew anything. We waited with great anxiety.

Just after 7:30 that evening, the phone rang again, it was my father again. He was calm, but I could hear the anguish in his voice. My father told me that the police found Johan's body and that it looked like he committed suicide. I tried to remain calm, for my father's sake; however, it felt as if my gut was ripped open. Johan was my friend, not just my brother. Renate and I saw him less than eight weeks before at our wedding. I spoke to him less than two weeks before. This seemed surreal.

I knew that Johan had problems at his work in Phalaborwa and that he had some difficulty adjusting to his new position in Saldanha. I also knew that previously he mixed with some unsavoury friends when he worked for the Department of Home Affairs, but committing suicide just seemed unreal.

I made a number of phone calls advising family and friends of what had happened. Renate and I remained in our kitchen, near the telephone, and in shock, while we waited for further news and answering calls of condolences.

In death, Johan facilitated reconciliation between Amanda and me – be it for a short time – as she called to express her condolences, and with a warm and friendly call, the battle-axe was laid to rest. Although we did not really have much contact thereafter, the animosity between us was over. Andre contacted Riana on my request and she was also very supportive. Dietloff offered to fly down to East London to be with us and to drive with Renate and me to Cape Town for the funeral. The support that we received from family, friends, colleagues and associates in this time was heart-warming.

On arriving in Cape Town, we met with Mariska, at their house in Saldanha Bay with their two boys. We tried to make sense of what happened, but nothing seemed to add up – the notes, the manner in which he died, and the alleged circumstances surrounding his death. At the time, it was said that Johan died at about 2 in the afternoon on Monday, 10 February 1997, when he allegedly injected a sufficient amount of air into a vain, forcing a heart attack. Johan's body was discovered in the bay area of Jacobs' Bay on the west coast just outside Saldanha Bay.

The day before the funeral, we travelled to Jacobs' Bay where my mother laid a wreath of flowers at the spot where Johan died. Each one of us pondering, in silence, what went through his mind while sitting at that pristine place? I reflected on the telephone call I received a couple of days earlier and wondered if Johan tried to tell me something. Was he reaching out for help, and I failed to see it? Was he trying to open a conversation, which could have prevented this disastrous tragedy? I reflected on what he was doing from early in the morning when he took Juandré to day-care, until 2 PM which was the time everyone thought he must have died.

People often remarked that suicide is a cowardly act. However, one never knows all the facts and I do believe it takes guts to take such a drastic step. That it is difficult for those who stay behind is obvious, as there are always unanswered questions that remain forever. How does a mother explain events of this nature to her two young boys? How do parents make peace with something so dramatic? So tragic. In life, it is the children who are supposed to bury their parents, not the other way around. This all seemed so wrong.

The funeral took place in Bellville near Cape Town, on Valentine's Day. There were very few people at the funeral, due to the distance from Pretoria, where the large majority of our family stayed. Mariska decided not to have Johan's coffin at the church, which we respected at the time; however, in years to come, I thought it would have been better to have the coffin there, as it helps to have closure. To see, touch, and feel the last evidence of Johan's presence on this earth. Years later, in attempt to get closure, we would learn much more about that dreadful weekend. Today, we only have the memories of a wonderful human being, a dedicated husband, a loving father, and a good friend.

After arriving back in East London, Dietloff returned to Pretoria and life eventually returned to normal. I enjoyed my work at Sun International and visited the four units for which I was responsible on a regular basis.

Our initial marital bliss was disrupted following a burglary at the Baysville house, which happened shortly after we moved in. Following the trauma of Johan's death and the subsequent memorial service behind us, we started looking to buy a house. We moved out of the Baysville house and bought an old restored railway house in Nahoon, where we settled comfortably. Here we did live in peace, with the rest of our family, being my Labrador, Wolfgang, and our three cats, Nuschka, Molly and Bishop. We spent our days in each other's company, the silence at times comforting, knowing that we are happy. Our content 'family' later grew with the arrival of Tessa, a young German Shepherd.

In July that year, Renate and I went to Grahamstown where we visited the annual National Grahamstown Arts Festival. I introduced Renate to Mathys

Roets, the famous singer and cousin of our friend, Willie Roets, and she became an instant admirer of the man with the deep voice. After enjoying the art and music at the festival, we travelled to Hogsback in the Amatola Mountains, to celebrate Renate's birthday, at the same place where we enjoyed our honeymoon before returning to our home.

On the 31st of August, we mourned, with the rest of the world, the death of Princess Diana, the Princess of Wales, and by Christmas, my parents came to visit us for two weeks, my father, trying to be strong, while my mum was notably quieter. We spoke a lot about Johan and reflected on the good and happy times we could recall of him. We all missed him very much, but we kept that pain quietly within ourselves.

Johan's death had a devastating impact on my mum. She never recovered from this traumatic event. On the contrary, I believe this event set in motion a period of decline. Whilst nearly twenty years later, I would have my own difficulties coming to terms with Johan's death, and, eventually, wrote a short story titled 'A Weekend of Ambiguity and Obscurity' in an attempt to make sense of it all. (See Chapter 18)

They say the first year of marriage is always the most difficult. However, because both of us wanted nothing else than a successful marriage, we worked continuously and with diligence to achieve this. Irrespective of the burglary to our first home, and the trauma of Johan's death, we came through the first year with success.

Chapter 18
A Weekend of Ambiguity and Obscurity

It was a Thursday afternoon in February when the legal expert met with management and together they decided to confront the man. He was a gentle man; friendly, likeable, a good father, a loving husband, a remarkable friend, and an outstanding brother. But, he had some questions to answer, some explaining to do. So the legal expert flew to Cape Town, South Africa. He wanted to know what had happened with the chequebook, the money, the paperwork; he needed the truth.

After arriving in Cape Town, the legal expert explored the case with the local police inspector and jointly agreed to confront the man. They went to see him at his place of work. After a brief encounter, it was agreed that the man should join them the following day at the local police station. Friday was easier to leave work early. The man reported to the police station in the afternoon and was questioned by the legal expert, under caution. The picture started to become clearer; however, it was confirmed that they needed to speak to him again in time to come.

Earlier that day, in another town on the Cape Route 62, situated in the scenic Tradauw Valley, a very picturesque tourist route between the Eastern and Western Cape, grandma was looking after the boys. The one, a toddler, the other, a baby. They planned to travel to Saldanha Bay on the west coast the next day. However, they did not know where the house was of the man and his wife. So after leaving the N7 at Piketberg and on arriving in Saldanha, they stopped at the police station to ask directions to 2106 Park Avenue. The man just walked out of the inspector's office and did not expect the grandparents standing in the charge office. They were equally surprised to see their son-in-law in the police station. He maintained his composure, as was his nature and offered a plausible explanation before they followed him home.

That evening was a normal family night, like any other. The warm Southern African air, off the Atlantic coast, made the evening tender with relaxing aromas of summer. Everyone seemed happy. The toddler played on the lawn in front of grandma; the baby sleeping contently, whilst the adults enjoyed a barbeque. They played cards till late that evening, talking about the week past, the new job, the new town, and their future. Life was promising, it seemed.

No mention was made about the legal expert's presence in town, the unexpected encounter at the police station, or the meaning of it all, until the man and his wife retired for the night.

Settling in bed, she shared with him that the legal expert came to the house earlier that day. She told him that there was some allegations being made and confirmed that they threatened with charges. The man told his wife that he could explain and that he would speak to her later, but not whilst the in-laws were in the house. The following day, the man, his kids, and the grandparents went for a drive.

At about 3:00 that afternoon, the man called his brother in East London. He wanted to talk about something, but was very ambiguous about what truly troubled him. He sounded unhappy, but was unclear as to what had concerned him. He was not his normal friendly and cheerful self. During their brief discussion, the man was inconspicuous about his agenda. His brother just woke up from a Saturday afternoon nap and was not in a talkative mood. He kept the conversation short, was even dismissive, as the man had a new job, in a new town, with new prospects. He had a lovely wife, two beautiful kids, why not leave the past in the past and focus on all the opportunities of the future. Life promised so many great things ahead for the man and his young family. His glumness was out of character. Annoyingly!

The conversation was brief, regrettably so, who knows how different things could have been if another choice was made. After all, the man's brother always said 'life is about choices' – how regrettable this one was.

At sunset, the family enjoyed another spectacular summers evening whilst playing canasta. Still no explanation was offered.

On Sunday morning, the grandparents left for Cape Town, to visit their other daughter. They were barely away, when the man announced that they should also go. It was as if he wanted to ensure that there was enough activity that he need not address the challenges that were threatening his family. His wife agreed, and they drove to her sister. She again told him that they needed to talk. She offered her support. She confirmed that she wanted to help, but needed to know what was going on. He agreed, but asked that they let it be for now, that they could talk about it on Monday. He promised they would talk about it on Monday.

At about 8:00 that evening, they said their good-byes and drove home to Saldanha. There was a lot of fog in the air; it was difficult to see the road. The kids were sleeping in the back of the car; the radio playing softly as they drove. Neither husband nor wife spoke much. Both were trying to see the road ahead of them. Their minds were racing through a variety of fearful thoughts. Both contemplated the threat to their family. The one desperately trying to make sense of all the information that so brutally arrived at her front door, the other, frantically trying to work out a plan to protect those he love most.

As they put the kids to bed, the man and his wife settled in bed. She asked him again, when they were going to talk. He said that he was tired. He confirmed again that they would speak on Monday, after he returned from work. He promised, reaffirming his earlier commitment. When she settled behind him, she held him tightly, lovingly, with tears running down her cheeks.

It was all too nebulous for her to take in, it made her sick with worry. Eventually they both fell asleep.

They met in dreamland. Flowers blooming everywhere, the aromas of nature, a splendid escape from reality. He was wearing a colourful bow tie and both wore matching waistcoats. They were happy, without a worry in the world. He took her in his arms, looked her in the eyes and said, "I truly love you with all my heart. You are the best thing that ever happened to me, such a great mother to the boys, don't ever forget that I'll love you forever." She looked at him, smiled spontaneously, as was her nature, and said tenderly, "I know." They could not be happier.

At 6 in the morning, he woke up. He felt better, the plan clearly shaped in his head. He got up, made some coffee, and prepared something for breakfast. It was the toddler's first day at playschool. He woke the little boy at 7:00 AM. His wife dressed their eldest son. The baby chased butterflies in dreamland.

When the time came for the plan to start, he kissed his wife, reminded her to draw the maximum allotted cash amount from the ATM she could. He told her twice, "Don't forget to draw cash, do it first thing this morning."

He kissed his wife and said, "I'll see you later… I love you."

"I love you," she replied. Her heart pounding with both love and worry for her husband.

Father and son drove off. It was a lovely warm Monday morning on the west coast of South Africa.

At the playschool, he took his little boy out of the car, took him by the hand, and led him into the school. He greeted the teacher, friendly, courteous, and caring, as was his nature. He told his little boy to enjoy himself.

"I love you, my boy," he said, "see you later."

"Bye, Daad," the little boy replied.

Before lunchtime, the man's wife made some sandwiches, expecting him to come home, as was his custom. Eventually, she called his office to inquire where he was. The receptionist guessed that he might have been out of town.

The boy was to be collected at 3 in the afternoon, and as she did not hear anything from her husband, she took the baby and walked the 5km (3mi) to the playschool. It was a very hot afternoon. The Cape southwester was cynically quiet. She stopped at the police station, en route to the playschool, and expressed her concerns for her husband. The constable made a note and took her and the baby to the playschool. They collected the little boy and the constable returned the mother with her boys to their home. Still no sign of her husband. She called his office again. This time they confirmed that he had not been in the office the entire day. She panicked; the police began a search.

Her mind raced through the events of the weekend, all the ambiguity: the vagueness, which caused such concern. The legal expert who came to visit her, the allegations, the chequebook that was found in his trousers, it all started making sense, to some extent. Her entire body was shaking with fear. She called her father-in-law in Pretoria and then her sister in Cape Town.

The latter offered to come through, the former desperately worried, but unable to do anything some 1400km (875mi) away.

At 7:30 in the evening on Monday, the police confirmed that they found the man, slumped against a sand dune. The official police report read as follows:

"According to the wife of the man, he took the boy to the crèche at 08h00 on 10 February 1997 and did not return home. She became concerned; as he was depressed over the weekend, after it became apparent that something had happened at his previous employer, who was looking to question him about a number of accusations. She reported her concerns at the police station at 13h05 and a note was made in the incident register. At 19h17 residence of the nearby village of Jacobs Bay reported a man on the sand dunes, who appeared to be dead. The body of the man was found at 19h25. Near his body was minora shaving blades, his glasses, watch, cigarettes, a lighter, a bundle of keys. His left wrist was cut open. His wife, parents and family were notified of his death."

In a suburb in East London, the phone rang at 7:45 PM. The man's brother answered the phone only to hear the distraught voice of his father. In a controlled, but distressed tone, the retired officer confirmed that they had found the man's body. He confirmed that his son was dead. He told his youngest, "Your brother is gone."

Unbeknown to his wife, our parents, and my family, this weekend would become a paradox. On the one hand, it was the beginning of the end on many levels, on the other, an ultimate sacrifice of love.

Chapter 19
Regulating the Gaming Industry

Between 1994 and 1996, Christiaan was assigned to the South African Police's VIP Protection Unit.

Previously, he worked as part of the Police's Special Protection Unit between 1986 and 1990, providing protective support to both Presidents PW Botha and FW De Klerk respectively.

However, during this time Chris was assigned to the then-Premier, Dr Popo Molefe. During this time Chris and his colleagues provided protective services to a variety of VIP's from the new South African government. This enabled him to ask President Nelson Mandela in 1998 to sign a copy of his book *A Long Walk to Freedom* for me. The President kindly agreed and on 18 January 1998, South Africa's first democratically-elected President wrote in front of one of his books "To Hein Scheffer, Best Wishes, NR Mandela", a very prized possession on my bookshelf.

Of interest would be a deduction that whilst my father incarcerated Nelson Mandela on Robin Island, my brother, as part of the VIP Protection Unit, was willing and able to take a bullet for the same man.

* * *

Prior to the 1994 elections, gambling was illegal in South Africa, and viewed by many a Church father as sinful, irrespective of the fact that a lot of prominent church members enjoyed crossing the borders to the homelands to try their luck. Casinos, at that time, were restricted to the former Homelands in the Republics of Bophuthatswana, Transkei, Ciskei, and Venda. All the casinos in these areas were owned by Sun International (South Africa) or SISA, which consisted of the world famous Sun City, Thlabani Sun, Morula Sun, Carousel, Mmabatho Sun, Molopo Sun, Thaba'Nchu Sun, Naledi Sun, Amatola Sun, Mdantsane Sun, Mpekweni Sun, Fish River Sun, the Wild Coast Sun, and Venda Sun.

In addition to holding these casino licenses, SISA also held the gaming rights at its properties situated in Windhoek, Namibia, being the Kalahari Sands, the Gaborone Sun in Gaborone, together with licenses in Selebe Pikwe and Francistown in Botswana The Royal Swazi Sun, and Hlanganu Sun situated in Swaziland, with the Maseru Sun and Lesotho Sun based in the mountain kingdom of Lesotho.

Thus, SISA held a total of 25 casino licenses within the Southern African Development Community.

Following the 1994 elections, the gaming industry in South Africa became regulated and provincial gaming boards were established for all nine provinces. This opened the prospects of new casinos being developed throughout South Africa, and as a result, SISA had to reduce some of its casino licenses before 10 May 1999. This sparked speculations that our regional offices in Bisho were to close, that the casino license at the Fish River Sun could possibly be transferred to Port Elizabeth, were SISA wished to tender for a new large casino, and that we would either move to Port Elizabeth, or to other units within SISA.

As a direct result hereof, a group of management within SISA, under the leadership of the then-Divisional General Manager of InterSun, Garth Collins, began discussions with SISA's Managing Director, Peter Bacon, about the possibility of a management buyout (MBO) of various of SISA's old casinos. The group of casinos that were ultimately agreed upon for acquisition by the new company (NewCo) were the then-Amatola Sun, Mmabatho Sun, Molopo Sun, incorporating the management function of the Mmabatho Convention Centre, Taung Sun, and Venda Sun.

A number of casinos were inevitably doomed for closure, as new casino licenses were issued, because each province was only granted a specific amount of licenses and because of the restrictions on ownership. Thus, the smaller casinos in the countryside, like Thlabane Sun and most of those in the old homelands, were to make way for larger casinos in the cities, with the exception of Sun City, The Carousel, The Wild Coast Sun, and Morula Sun. Sun City, as a matter of fact, is the only hotel resort in South Africa that can boast its own South African Post Office stamp. This destination casino resort is, thus, a remarkable emblem of the previous, the current, and the future of the gaming industry in South Africa. A monument to the genius, vision and passion of its creator, and the father of the gaming industry in South Africa, Mr Sol Kerzner. A man who started with only one hotel and became recognised as an international visionary for both the gaming and hospitality industries.

NewCo executives consisted of Garth Collins; Jeremy Franklin; John Barret, the then-Gaming Manager of InterSun; and Brett Nicholls, and the then-Divisional Human Resources Manager for InterSun. A Black empowerment component to this MBO was provided by Thebe Investments with their representative as Thabo Mokoena.

I assisted the MBO management with their road-shows in the Ciskei/Eastern Cape, as Amatola Sun was one of the casino resorts for which I was responsible at the time. We knew then that the Regional Office for the Eastern Cape was to close down and it was likely that all regional managers were to be re-deployed within the larger SISA. It was envisaged that I would move to Port Elizabeth with our Regional General Manager, Graham Vass, where it was predicted that SISA would open the Boardwalk Casino in time to come.

Eventually, Garth withdrew from the MBO and as a result of his withdrawal, so did Brett. This left Jeremy, John and Thabo, with Jeremy assuming the leadership role to drive the MBO, supported by John and Thabo. Having successfully negotiated an agreement for the sale of these casino operations from SISA, the transaction still required the approval of the various provincial gaming boards and it was to take almost a year before achieving the approval for the transfer of the minimum number of licenses which then made the sale agreement unconditional.

During this transition period, Brett asked me if I would be interested to relocate to Johannesburg and to be seconded to NewCo to assist the company with the set-up of its human resources function. SISA was very accommodating with the MBO process, as it was in their interest to ensure that their licenses were reduced, while job security for the staff at the affected casinos enjoyed high priority.

An interview was arranged for me to meet with Jeremy. We met at the InterSun offices in Sandton, and although Jeremy was a gentle and soft-spoken man, I was very nervous. He asked a number of questions about my career and my experience in human resources, which I answered sufficiently but knew I could have done better. I felt as if I did not make an exceptional impression on him that day. When I walked out of the room, it felt as if I did alright. Fortunately, Jeremy was happy with the answers provided and my secondment to NewCo was supported by both Graham and Brett.

In February 1998, Renate and I relocated to Gauteng. We found ourselves a comfortable house to rent in Rooihuiskraal, a suburb outside Pretoria, from where I drove to Sandton every day to establish NewCo's human resources function. Renate, who was still working for the same catering company she did before, also got a transfer and assumed her new position with BMW in Midrand.

That entire year, I conducted interviews, prepared contracts of employment, drafted personnel policies, and designed and implemented restructuring interventions within and for the NewCo units. I represented the units at wage negotiations, and handled all personnel administration. Although still part of SISA, we were distinctly separate as we awaited approval from the respective gaming boards that SISA may transfer its licenses to NewCo. This approval was granted in respect of Mmabatho Sun, Molopo Sun, and Taung Sun, all within the North West Province, which paved the way for NewCo to become a separate company, and the conditions precedent to the sale agreement were met. The only outstanding approvals were that for the Amatola Sun in the Eastern Cape and the Venda Sun in the far north in the Limpopo Province. With these events, NewCo vacated the SISA offices and established its own head office in Bryanston and effectively began operating as an independent new company.

In addition to dealing with the day-to-day human resources issues related to the NewCo units, the bidding processes started for companies interested to tender for the new larger casino licenses. A variety of licenses were available within the respective provinces in South Africa. I became involved with the writing of the tender documentation from a human resources perspective for these bids. NewCo wanted to expand its footprint and submitted new bids for Pinnacle Point outside Mosselbay in the Western Cape, for the Midmar Casino at Midmar Dam in KwaZulu-Natal, for Umfolozi Casino in Richards Bay/Empangeni in KwaZulu Natal, Sondolani Casino in East London in the Eastern Cape, and the Komani Casino in Queenstown, also in the Eastern Cape. An application was also submitted to transfer its existing Taung casino license to a more suitable location, being the Rio Casino in Klerksdorp, in the North West Province.

Taking into account that a number of new casino groups emerged during this time, Jeremy's NewCo was the only group that was successful to achieve preferred finalist status in all five its new bid applications. Regrettably, due to circumstances arising at that time, leading to a lack of shareholders' funds to pursue these license opportunities and settlement deals with opposition groups, NewCo eventually was only awarded casino licenses for its casino in Empangeni, KwaZulu-Natal, and for the Rio Casino in the North West Province.

During this time, Ian Mossop, the former Slots Manager at Thlabane Sun, joined NewCo and became the fourth director and shareholder within NewCo. I explored with Jeremy the possibility that I could join NewCo on a permanent basis, but it then became clear that Thebe Investments, the Black economic empowerment partner of NewCo, was keen that NewCo should appoint a Black human resources executive. This became quite a trend in South Africa at the time, i.e. that human resources posts became affirmative actions' posts, reserved for previously disadvantage individuals, albeit at a premium.

Eventually, the time came at the end of 1998 that I had to make a decision. By this time, SISA was about to begin with the Boardwalk Casino Project in Port Elizabeth, and I was given the choice to return to this project as my secondment was about to come to an end, and it seemed unlikely that I would be offered the human resources executive position within NewCo, due to the fact that I was White. However, I enjoyed my independence that I had during that year, while Renate was not keen on returning to the Eastern Cape. This was a particularly difficult decision for me, as I loved the Eastern Cape, taking into account that my family went to East London for many vacations during my childhood and I attended the last two years of my schooling there. However, Renate and I decided not to return to the Eastern Cape.

I enquired with Rob Rimmer, the human resources executive of SISA, if there were other suitable positions within the group for which I could be considered, but it became apparent that the only possibility for me within the group at that point in time, was at the Boardwalk Casino in Port Elizabeth.

As I always had an entrepreneurial spirit, Renate and I started debating the possibility that I should start my own human resources consulting firm. A daunting thought at first, as it brought great responsibility and more often than not does not create the freedom one would expect. As very few entrepreneurs truly work for themselves, you always work for a client, and although I understand the client is king, I don't believe the client is always right. However, most clients believe they are. Thus, working independently is not always as romantic as what people want to make it out to be. While the freedom and financial rewards are generally better, it has its disadvantages.

Renate and I debated late into the evenings about what I could do and how I could generate sufficient income to start my business, and more importantly, to sustain the two of us effectively. I knew that I had a sound knowledge of the South African labour legislation, and viewed myself as a dedicated and competent human resources generalist. I could be a recruiting agent, or write and conduct training programs. While I always maintained sound relationships with my current and former employers, I believed that from these relationships, I could develop sufficient support to establish a client base to at least sustain the creation of a new business, to build on into the future. However, the challenge remained, in my mind at least, that I needed an anchor client. So I decided to approach Jeremy again.

While I understood the reasons for NewCo to want a Black human resources executive, I also knew that Black executives at the time were ridiculously expensive, as one had to pay a premium to get a suitable and quality executive. I lobbied with John, Ian, and some of the other senior management within NewCo, in terms of their views in this regard. Everyone confirmed that an expensive human resources executive for NewCo was not a luxury that the new company could afford at that point in time. They further indicated that none of them would be against the idea of me assuming an interim human resources role, be it on a consulting basis, for a limited duration of time. So I made an appointment with Jeremy in the first week of October and asked him if he would consider outsourcing the human resources function to me for a period of one year. My motivation was simply that this would give NewCo some space to find its feet before incurring the cost of an expensive Black human resources executive, while it will give me the opportunity to establish my own business. Jeremy seemed intrigued, as it was not the culture within SISA to outsource any part of the human resources function to a third party. Jeremy was reluctant, but he did not say no. So I left the idea with him and his colleagues and continued with my business as normal.

In the interim, I again asked for an appointment with Rob Rimmer to solicit his support, but he directed me to Garth Collins, our Divisional General Manager. I made an appointment to speak to Garth and was granted a meeting within the following week. I knew that it would be difficult to convince my employer to support my redundancy, especially if he had a position for me. However, government published its White paper on employment equity, and in terms of this proposed legislation the same preferential employment that the National Party government legislated for 'Whites only' years earlier, was about to be passed for 'Blacks only'. It seemed that Apartheid, in the business world, at first, was about to change colour.

The majority of companies at the time felt that the human resources function was a 'soft function', so if any quotas, in terms of Black management, were to be introduced, it seemed that the human resources function would be the place where companies would try and make up their representation, which left the future for any White human resources practitioner, especially a White male, rather dim. This was precisely what NewCo and ultimately SISA and most of corporate South Africa at the time considered doing. I made a plea to Garth to support my application for voluntary redundancy, which would enable me to get some funds, and would pave the way for me to establish my own business. My meeting with Garth lasted about forty-five minutes, and to my surprise, he was very supportive and understanding. Garth, being a former human resources practitioner in his earlier career himself, seemed to understand that sometimes one needed to go outside the norms of what you studied and try other avenues. He did, with great success. He also seemed surprised at the risk that I was willing to take to start my own business. As a senior executive in a large corporate company, he understood how difficult it was to do business on your own; however, he believed that I would be successful and if I had the guts to do this, provided that I could get Jeremy's buy-in, he was willing to support me.

That evening, I was very excited and nervous. Renate and I conducted our own audit to determine what we needed to survive. What offer could we give Jeremy that would be attractive to him as a new company, without cutting our throat? My severance package was sufficient to sustain Renate and me for about four months, which is not a very long period of time. Before I accepted voluntary redundancy, I knew I needed to get Jeremy's support and sign an agreement, if possible.

Eventually on Friday, 30 October 1998, I managed to get an appointment with Jeremy. Suffering with bad case of the flu, I hardly had a voice. But I knew that meeting had to take place. During the meeting, I told Jeremy that I wanted to establish a human resources consulting firm, but would like to have NewCo as my anchor client. I told him that I needed a one year contract as I believed that if I could not make it on my own in one year, I should seek a corporate position and leave the running of a private business for those who knew better. I told him that this would provide a cost-effective solution for NewCo's need to have continuity in terms of human resources services, but would not cost the company what a full-time Black human resources executive would have cost. I explained that this in essence would buy time for us both. NewCo could find its feet in terms of establishing itself, while it would give me time to establish myself as an independent human resources consultant. Jeremy, however, had concerns about the fact that I wanted to base my office in Pretoria, as he felt that I would not give sufficient support to him and that I would be too far from their offices in Bryanston. However, at the end of our meeting, we agreed that that would be the way forward. He again indicated that he would not have the time to reduce our discussion to writing and would not be able to sign an agreement with me; however, I told him that I accepted his word and on a hand-shake between a former employer and his employee, we became client and consultant.

After our meeting, I again met with Garth who agreed to see me the same day and I told him of my meeting with Jeremy and what we agreed. Garth and I agreed that I would apply for voluntary redundancy; we finalised the terms of my departure from SISA and agreed that my last day with my original employer of choice would be 31 December 1998.

The following two months were spent to set up my business. Harry van Heerden, my friend from East London, assisted me with the establishment of a business trust, which saw the creation of 'Hein Scheffer & Associates'. Eventually, Jeremy and I signed a one year service level agreement, whereby I was to render twenty hours of consulting services to NewCo and its units, with the clear understanding that I would strive to expand my business and to grow my client base.

NewCo eventually became Tusk Resorts, the only privately owned casino group in South Africa at that time.

My parents on their wedding day on 7 February 1953, flr, my mum's parents, Suzi, Johan van der Vyver, my parents, with my dad's parents, Chris and Baby Scheffer

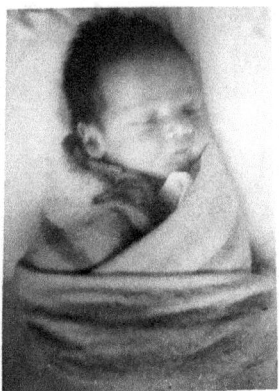

Me, six days after my birth, 1965

Christiaan holding me, with Suzanne and Johan on my Christening in Ventersdorp.

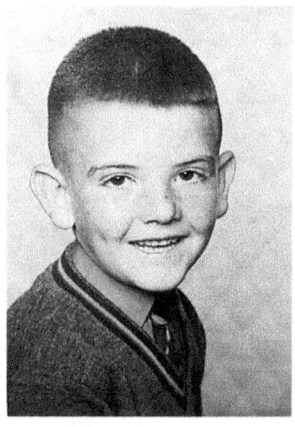

My first day of school in Kroonstad, 1972.

My parents on the R47, at the junction to Schefferspos, where my fathers' ancestral farm was.

My matric dance, with Marietta Benadie and her boyfriend, Ponti and Valerie, Harry and Heather, me and my date, on 14 October 1983

My fathers' BMW after the accident on 6 June 1984.

My parents when my dad become Chairman of the National Prison Release Board, 1984

Hennie and I in Europe: (fltr) me with my pen-friend Petra Brenner, Hennie Crowther, Claudia Brenner, with their parents, Herr u Frau Brenner, June 1985.

(Fltr) Our last vacation as students after we completed three years of studies (fltr) Willie Stolz; Halina Selwyn-Cross; Hennie Crowther; Andre de Wit; Linda Smuts; Heather McLean; Anthony Schaaf; Letitia Stols; and I, December 1986. Anina Bormann took the photo.

Working at the State Theater's Buffet de'l Opera Restaurant with Ferdi Heyns, Cynthia, me and Dawie Vermeulen, at the Jacaranda Ball, 1987.

Andre Waters and Piet Myburgh on the farm in Elliot, before I commenced with my national service, December 1987.

At my passing out parade in the Navy, with my parents, March 1988.

Graduation for my National Diploma in Personnel Management, in May 1988.

My father and his boys all in uniform. Johan in his army uniform, Christiaan when he was in the Police's Special Protection Unit, Johan in his Infantry – and me in my Navy uniform with my father in his uniform from the Prison Services.

Graduation of my Bachelors Degree in Human Resources with my parents, 1999

My father's sixtieth birthday on 28 July 1988, (fltr) me, with Christiaan, my mum, Rina, my father, Johan, Suzanne and Robert.

During our last days in the Navy in Durban in November 1989 (fltr) Mark Neethling, Eric Cleminston, Adrian Fourie, Cuan Sawyer, me and Garry.

The wedding photo of Willie and Barbara Roets, that hang in their bedroom in their home in Pretoria in February 1992.

My wedding day with Renate, (fltr) Ursula, Suzanne, my parents, Renate's parents, Mariska; at the front, Dietloff, René, Renate, me and Johan.

Renate and my wedding on 14 December 1996.

Jacobsbaai, the place where Johan died on 10 February 1997.

Alison Boshoff-Rademann with Stefan and Carla in Lytham St Annes.

My mum's seventieth birthday on 16 September 1999, with their children and grand-children.

Jeremy and Laura Franklin, when he was CEO at Tusk Resorts 2004, and my anchor client for what became Extra Expertise since 1999.

The senior management team at Celsius Hospitality Services, (fltr) Liahn Nortje, Mtheza Buya me and Renate, Michelle van Zyl, James Dyer, Anthony Hambleton-Jones with Hennie Carstens, 2007.

Tessa and Wolfgang at our home at Woodhill in Pretoria in 2007.

A fundraising effort, with the 2001 SA Big-Brother winner Ferdinand Rabie, sponsored by Celsius to raise funds for a sick boy, at the annual Cape Argus Cycle Tour, 2008.

Our three cats that came with to the UK, Gucci; with Gigi and Nuschka, 2009

Graduation day for my Masters Degree at the University of Central Lancashire in 2010.

Carla with her husband Michael and their dog Alfie in Lytham St Annes, in 2010.

My dad and his wife Madeleine during their visited to Lytham St Annes in 2010.

The HRBP's form Blackpool Teaching Hospitals, (fltr) me, with Joyce Cotton, Rachel Norris, Alison Smith, Eleanor Palmer, and Mark Green.

All our colleagues and friends at Blackpool Teaching Hospitals saying good bye and wishing us well before our departure to Plymouth, May 2012.

My dad and I on the boat, during our Mediterranean cruise, October 2012.

The wonderful Willie Roets (Bill), on the African Butler, in November 2011 shortly before he died of Lymphoma.

During a visit to South Africa, with Suzanne and my dad.

Graham and Megan Vass visiting during 2013 after my treatment.

Nick and Sue Grimshaw visiting us in Plymouth in 2013.

Renate and Cuan Sawyer outside the station in Venice, during our Opera vacation to Verona.

Renate and I visiting Johan Malan with his wife Bonnie and their daughter Melisa in the Cape.

Signing the book of condolences at the Union Buildings, following the death of Nelson Mandela in December 2013

Kevin Baber, me and Darren Mugleston in Cape Town, as *'three blokes and their bikes'* to partake in the Cape Argus Cycle Tour, March 2014.

Me, Kevin and a number of cyclists on the Cremyll Ferry, after cycling in Cornwall.

My father between his brothers Fanie on the left and Hercules on the right, with their sisters Ursula and Marie.

Receiving my LLB (Hons) in 2015.

Renate and I with my dad in Bad Saulgau, Germany July 2015, with Manuel Friedman, his baby boy and his mum Andrea.

Christiaan and my dad during one of our visits to South Africa.

Renate and I receiving British Citizenship on 23 October 2015 in Plymouth

Ponti making a speech on my 50th birthday, with Stefan and his mum in the background.

I received a surprise birthday cake, draped in both the South African and British flags.

Gerhard Sauer, me, Gerry, Renate and Frida, on the first night in our own house in Aylesbury, March 2016.

Chapter 20
Extra Expertise

On Monday, 4 January 1999, Helga, my mother-in-law, and I started with very humble beginnings. My only client was Jeremy Franklin's Tusk Resorts. Leon and Martie Nel, the management couple at the Venda Sun, sent us a large fruit basket with a bottle of champagne to celebrate the first day of Hein Scheffer and Associates (HS&A). We did very little business that first day, but I viewed the events of 4 January 1999 as the proverbial first day of the rest of my life, a new beginning. We were excited, optimistic, and were looking forward to the challenges ahead. I knew that this consulting initiative would work.

As everyone was talking about outsourcing, downsizing, or rightsizing with all companies trying to align themselves correctly for the future, I decided to embark on a process of co-sourcing, establishing mutually beneficial 'partnerships' with my new clients.

Tusk Resorts retained their HR staff in-house, but co-outsourced the executive lead role to me. So although I had no real staff, I provided support, guidance, and direction to the HR managers and staff based at the various hotels managed by Tusk Resorts. These initially were Tusk Mmabath; the Mmabatho Convention Centre; Tusk Molopo; Tusk Taung; Tusk Venda and Tusk Resorts Head Office. With my office in Pretoria, I attended the senior management meeting every Monday morning, and on my way to Bryanston, near Johannesburg, I called all the hotels to get an update to ensure that I could brief Jeremy on any HR-related matter that may come up.

I had great ambitions, and envisaged the growth of HS&A to become a Comprehensive Human Resources Services Company (CHS). With this in mind, I created all the legal vehicles to support this with a string of shelve companies ready to come alive as the business grew. I recruited Katrin Kruger, a junior human resources consultant to join us, then Hannelie van der Merwe. Soon after, Jeanette Botha joined us to help with the payroll administration and the girlfriend of a cousin of Renate, Leslie Botha, joined us as my secretary.

I decided to do recruitment work for clients, based on my own recruitment experience from Nestlé, I thought this would help me improve my turnover. I initially thought that Katrin could assist me with the recruitment work, but at that time, my old school friend Harry van Heerden contacted me and asked if I could help him find a human resources manager for their business in East

London. Katrin had all the qualifications, and was keen to go to the coast, so I promptly placed my own consultant, before she had any placement, with a client.

I also called hotels in and around Pretoria, and secured a HR co-sourcing agreement with the Manhattan Hotel where I placed Hannelie van der Merwe as personnel officer to be based on-site with the hotel, but working for HS&A doing recruitment to support the income. The business grew steadily. Three months on my own, I had both the Tusk Resorts and Manhattan Hotel contracts and also started doing pay-roll services.

During the first eighteen months of being on my own, and in an attempt to expand my revenue streams, I became a part-time Commissioner at the Gauteng Commission for Conciliation, Mediation and Arbitration (CCMA) in July. I also accepted an offer from Sonia Swannepoel, who was my first-year personnel management lecturer, as a part-time lecturer at the Pretoria Technikon. I taught first and second year students Personnel Management, Training Management and Management Principles in Practice.

Renate and I gave up our house in Rooihuiskraal and rented a beautiful house with a wild garden in the eastern suburb of Pretoria called Garsfontein.

* * *

One evening, after staying in Zimba Street just over eight months, toward the end of September, Renate and I retired to our bedroom. Eventually she fell asleep while I was reading a labour court judgment, which was relevant to the events of the time. At about 10:30 PM, I heard shouting in the street outside our house. I quietly got out of bed and went to the front door. I saw our neighbours across the road from us all standing outside their garage door, an elderly lady kneeling on the ground, and a young girl screaming hysterically. Without realising what happened, I walked closer, only to discover that two thugs had attacked them.

Later I learned that the muggers waited in their garden and as the family returned from a restaurant nearby, the two robbers jumped out on both sides of their vehicle. They grabbed the young girl and held a gun to her head. The other one shouted at the driver to get out of his car. My neighbours' mother instinctively tried to protect her granddaughter, but her reward was the back of a gun in her face. She collapsed on the ground next to the car. As if this entire trauma was not enough, the girl's grandmother became hysterical and made the entire situation incredibly volatile. Our neighbour had the good sense not to try and be brave and he allowed them to take the car, so that he could attend to his family. As the Golf spun away, my neighbour screamed in frustration and this was when I came out the front door.

I ran across the road and asked if I could help. My neighbour wanted to chase the robbers, who took his car with a lot of personal and private belongings in it. I offered to take his mother, wife and daughter to the hospital. South Africa's ambulance system is not as efficient as that of the UK, unless you have private insurance, and even then it could take a long time before they arrive.

I went back into our house and briefly told Renate, who was woken up by the commotion, what happened. I told her that I was taking the neighbours to the local private hospital. I bundled the severely traumatised people into my car. My neighbour and his son remained at the house, waiting for the police, and still visibly agitated. I gave him my cell phone number and told him to call if he needed any information, while I undertook to look after his family at the hospital.

At about 3:00 the next morning, everyone was stitched up, the adrenaline was lowered, and we returned home. The family next door were very grateful for the support that we offered, but Renate and I were very shocked about what just happened. While crime generally escalated since 1994, it has never come so close to our door.

That night, Renate and I agreed not to buy the house we stayed in; we decided that it was time to move into a security estate. The next weekend, we bought a stand at a new development about two kilometres from where we stayed, being Woodhill Country Club and Golf Estate. Over the next couple of months, we designed a house, with the help of a cousin of mine, while another cousin of mine built our house.

On 16th September 1999, we celebrated my mum's 70th birthday at the Farm Inn, just outside Pretoria. The day was made special with family and friends, and mum's only brother paying a beautiful tribute to his eldest sister. He described my mum as 'dedicated, hardworking, joyful and supportive; an inspiration to him, their siblings, and everyone who knew my mum.'

The millennium turned and none of the conspiracy theories of planes falling out of the air at midnight came true. However, just to be safe, on 31st December 1999, Renate, my parents and I had a lovely summer's barbeque in our lush garden in Zimba street, reflecting on the past year and celebrating the birth of 2000.

After nearly a year of designing, building, supervising and furnishing, we moved into Woodhill on 1st November 2000. We loved our new home, our dogs and cats enjoyed their garden and we anticipated that we would stay in this lovely house until the day we die.

* * *

I enjoyed my time with the CCMA and my role as lecturer. However, not long after these developments, Dr Brian van Zyl, the legal advisor of Sun International, convinced me to operate under his brand name, that being Van Zyl, Rudd and Associates. As the VZR: Pretoria office, we embarked on a drive to expand the concept of co-sourcing and attempted to take over the risk and management of human resources for various client companies. Although my business was doing well, Brian had a vast network of clients, which I thought would be advantageous in the longer term.

In August 2000, Renate resigned from her position as her own entrepreneurial spirit needed satisfying and she wanted to establish her own German coffee shop. I secured offices for my business in the same complex on the first floor, which resulted in me being spoiled regularly with breakfast sandwiches, the latest cheesecake experiment or a cold beer. My clients enjoyed coming to my office during this time, as they knew Renate would always have something good to eat for my client meetings. Eventually, Renate and I had difficulty going anywhere as she was always working, and with me travelling extensively during the week, we saw very little of each other. Renate decided to sell the coffee shop at the end of January 2002.

By now, my turnover was a good ZAR 1mil per annum with a variety of small clients using our services for payroll, training, human resources co-sourcing, and recruitment. In June 2002, Brian facilitated the sale of my business to Extra Expertise, a wholly owned subsidiary of Quest Personnel, part of the Adcorp Group of Companies. I sought some advice from Harry van Heerden to make sure that I get the right value for my business, whilst securing a Director's appointment with Extra Expertise. Although I had no shares in Extra Expertise, I was appointed Operations Director, as a lot of the clients to whom I provided human resources advice and services, relied on me, as consulting in its nature is very relationship-driven. My entire team transferred over to Extra Expertise, and we had great scope for expansion.

Under the guidance of the then-Managing Director, Peter Czakan, who I knew from my days in Sun International, where he was our Group Industrial Relations Manager, we grew the business effectively throughout South Africa. Our Head Office was based in Bryanston, with other offices in Kempton Park, Pretoria, Cape Town, Sun City, Zimbali, Empangeni, Venda, Mmabatho, and Taung. We continued to provide co-souring services of the human resources function to Tusk Resorts. I convinced Jeremy to transfer all his HR staff to Extra Expertise, as part of the co-sourcing model. We eventually provided the full spectrum of HR services, including payroll support to Tusk Resorts head office, its hotels, casinos, and the Mmabatho Convention Centre. We retained the contract with the Manhattan Hotel in Pretoria, and secured new clients like Lufthansa Gebäude Management, the Perishable Products Export Control Board, and Fruit and Veg City, while providing flexible staffing solutions to Sun City and a variety of other hospitality clients. I wrote various Employment Equity and Diversity Management training programmes and presented these to Quest and a variety of other ad-hock clients.

Andre Waters joined us at Extra Expertise in April 2002, and Gerhard Harmse, who worked with me at Medi-Clinic and succeeded me at Blue Ribbon Bakeries, joined the Extra Expertise in July that year.

* * *

On 7 February 2003, my parents celebrated their 50th wedding anniversary. We hosted an elaborate lunch for them at Woodhill Country Club where the now famous Nicholis Louw and his singing partner Johann performed as Cantero. Nicholis sang 'Maggie' especially for my mum, with Johann singing 'Amazing Grace' for my father. Suzanne's daughters were quite taken by Nicholas and Johann.

My mum, though, was rather bemused that day, as she had difficulty understanding what was happening. She smiled politely to the family and friends but had little insight in the true meaning of the events surrounding her own 50th wedding anniversary. Since Johan's death, my mum never really recovered from the tragic loss of her son. She deteriorated over a number of years and eventually was diagnosed with Alzheimer's disease. My father patiently attended to my mum's every need.

* * *

In September 2003, Adcorp commenced with a restructuring and decided to disinvest in the human resources consulting business and to focus on their core business, which was flexible staffing. Through a series of meetings, it was agreed that I would acquire Extra Expertise. Harry van Heerden was again my financial backer and one of his colleagues, Wayne Kluckouw, acquired a shareholding in the business.

On 21 November 2003, I assumed full control of Extra Expertise; a year later, Andre also acquired equity within the business. We were set as independent human resources consultants with a team of seventeen consultants and had offices in Gauteng, Cape Town, Limpopo, KwaZulu-Natal, and the North West Province.

In March 2004, Success Magazine ran an editorial about Extra Expertise under the heading *'Passion for People – The Birth of a Consultancy'*. The opening paragraph of their interview read as follows:

"From a position as regional HR manager for Sun International, Hein Scheffer established his own HR consulting firm in 1999. 'With the regularisation of the gaming industry, Sun International had to relinquish casino licences, which it sold to a management and empowerment consortium, resulting in the establishment of Tusk Resorts'. It was as a result of this bold initiative that I started my own consulting business as HR consultant to Tusk Resorts...."[54]

During the interview, I explained that since 1999, revenues grew exponentially, as my approach to client service was based on passion and integrity, to ensure that we make a measurable contribution to the success

---

[54] Success Magazine, March/April 2004

of our clients' business, our proactive services were compliant with respective labour legislation, and were legally defendable. It was our job to ensure our clients were kept safe, out of the CCMA and when we did go to the CCMA, that we were able to defend our actions with minimal risk to our clients.

It was only a short two years after the formation of HS&A that the business was sold to Extra Expertise. With Adcorp's 2003 restructuring, I acquired Extra Expertise out of Adcorp and established it as an independent HR and employment-law consulting firm.

On reflection, and this is no different to any other successful consulting firm, I aimed to ensure that we employed the best HR consultants, to enable them to be the best they could be, and ensure that the working environment stimulates them to bring forward the best of their own abilities. Steven Jobs articulated this principle beautifully when he said,

"It doesn't make sense to hire smart people and then tell them what to do; we hire smart people so that they can tell us what to do."[55]

We followed HR's best practice principles and constantly evaluated and re-evaluated our performance in relation to our client's needs, expectations, and experiences.

In a competitive market, a large number of consulting firms sold the same products and services; the distinct difference in terms of a competitive advantage becomes the people who make up the company. We tried to make a difference in establishing partnership agreements with our clients, co-sourcing, rather than outsourcing. The rationale for this was simple. It soon became apparent when I still had HS&A that outsourcing had a short lifespan. The agreement is signed, the relationship strong, and after twelve months, both parties start trying to squeeze as much out of the other as is possible, resulting in a deterioration of relationships and a messy end of the contractual relationship. Co-sourcing, on the other hand, is based on a collective understanding of the partnership that adds value to the business of both the consultant and its client. This required that we often went the extra mile, as the relationship was king, although the client may not always be right; advice, intervention, and innovation must be based on legal compliance, keeping the client safe, finding solutions.

This model worked well for us, as our clients engaged our services to enable them to focus on their core business, while we focused on ours. Co-sourcing established a strategic partnership between the human resources firm and the client.

In the case of outsourcing, companies often outsourced their human resources function because it was ineffective and they weren't able to measure the contribution made by the HR department. The service provider often assumed responsibility for effective HR management, becoming the service

---

[55] Steve Jobs, Former CEO of Apple

provider as the underwriter of all risk and responsibilities in terms of the outsourced solution. This, is not sustainable long-term.

Co-sourcing involved substituting our clients' entire human resources function, or partners' thereof, from the board to administrative level. Our clients did not just outsource their HR function, but formed a joint responsibility with Extra Expertise for their HR function. We got into the business of our clients, understanding the vision, their mission, and their strategic objectives. We aligned our HR strategy with that of our respective clients', respectively.

The Human Resources Business Partners (HRBP's) employed by Extra Expertise, focused on the full spectrum of HR co-sourcing solutions. HR issues such as skills development, employment equity, and wage negotiations, were tackled on a functional basis.

We listened to our clients. We ensured that we understood their needs and were flexible enough to ensure that one solution did not fit all. We did not believe in a quick fix, but rather in a long-term relationship. Our relationship with Tusk Resorts was testimony hereto. Considering that Jeremy originally only agreed to establish a one year relationship with HS&A, Extra Expertise kept the Tusk Resorts contract for eight years, until Tusk Resorts was sold to Peermont.

Whilst Human Resources in South Africa at the time was not as developed as what it is in the United Kingdom today, the provision of an effective human resources function was crucial for me to ensure we made a difference for our clients. During my interview with Success Magazine, I made a distinction between the various ways of tackling HR.

"...tackling HR include the personnel, remunerative, and strategic approaches. The personnel approach involves employing a person merely to fill a gap. This kind of company might tick over, but will never grow and expand. The remunerative approach is when companies employ people, pay them well, even incentivise them, but do not work towards developing the individual to his or her full potential. The strategic approach involves adopting a holistic view of HR. Successful companies which truly understand the importance of HR, employ the right people for the right jobs, remunerate them competitively, and incentivise them for achieving defined goals. Most importantly, it includes developing people to their full potential. It makes people happy in their jobs, and people want to be employed by those companies."

The reality is that we spent two-thirds of our day with work or work-related matters. To make a significant difference to the success of any company, it is crucial that our clients' human capital is valued. People who are focused, passionate, and enthusiastic create a positive energy with other people. To build a constructive and productive atmosphere in the workplace, people need to be happy where they are, and focused on making a positive contribution.

At the time of Extra Expertise, I truly believed that South Africa had a great future. It had a uniquely diverse society, a country with opportunity. We employed 22 consulting and back-office staff, with offices in Gauteng, the Western Cape, Kwa-Zulu Natal, Limpopo and North West Provinces.

I enjoyed my time as human resources consultant and believe that I built sound relationships with my clients who appreciated the commitment and service we delivered. As employment law has always been a personal interest of mine, I developed into a competent para-legal with a good understanding of labour legislation in general. I turned legislation like Employment Equity, which in essence discriminated against White males, for good reasons initially, to my advantage and wrote training programmes, which I used in generating income.

At that time, I never thought that in time to come I would replicate the Extra Expertise model some ten years later, abroad.

However, the travelling between the various units and our head office required of me to be out of town often, and occasionally, Renate and I had to make special arrangements to go away for weekends or traveling overseas to her father in Germany which became the only quality times that we spent together. Renate and I often debated if we could not do something else, something together, which would enable us to spend more time together, and eventually the answer came.

Chapter 21
Celsius Hospitality Services

On 10th July 2004, the General Manager of Tusk Resorts' Mmabatho Hotel and Casino Resort, Leon Nel and his wife Martie, joined Renate and I for dinner at our house. Willie, my old friend from the State Theatre, returned to Pretoria from a second visit to Turkey where he worked on the renovation of a hotel. We agreed that Willie would cook for the Nels and set the scene for a future tender to hopefully win the catering contract at the hotel.

Dinner was exquisite and Leon was especially impressed with Willie, his experiences in Turkey and was keen to get Willie to visit Tusk Mmabatho to take a look at the hotel in Mafikeng.

During the course of the evening, Renate and I jokingly suggested that we might want to tender for the upcoming catering contract at Tusk Mmabatho Casino Resort. Leon was intrigued with our line of thinking and encouraged us to do so.

* * *

In the middle of 2004, Renate and I went to Germany to visit her father, brother, and other members of her family, before we travelled to the UK to visit our friend Ponti and our god-children.

During our stay in Germany on 28th July, we were enjoying a boat cruise on the River Rhine. I phoned my dad to wish him a happy birthday. He was hosting a lunch in Pretoria for the family and some of their friends at Restaurant Salzburg. Although he was appreciative of our call, I could hear things were not well. My dad did not say much, but it sounded as if my mum took a turn for the worse. On our return, we discovered that my mum's health deteriorated tremendously and that my father did not have the expertise of how to deal with someone suffering with advanced Alzheimer's. My mum was not doing well, my dad was not doing well and something needed to be done. After consulting with both Christiaan and Suzanne, Renate and I agreed with my dad that my mum should be admitted to a facility that could look after her. This was particularly difficult for me, as I always said that I would not want my parents to be cared for by others. However, neither my dad nor we had the ability to provide my mum with the care she needed. We visited a number of homes in the following week, but could not find any that we felt were suitable.

My dad then discovered that there was a facility belonging to the Freemasons in Pretoria close to his house, so we had a look. My mum still had the odd clear moment and after we left the matron's office at Masonic Haven, she whispered to me and said, "I would rather die before I come to a place like this." This broke my heart, as we knew that my mum needed special attention. There were days and weeks that she would not have the faintest idea who my dad or any of her children or grandchildren were. Since Johan's death, my mother deteriorated gradually over the subsequent years and eventually, on 12th August 2004, she was admitted to Masonic Haven. My father visited her twice a day and a process started where we saw a dynamic and strong individual deteriorating every time we saw her. I can only describe it as a feeling of saying goodbye to a loved one that does not die. Every time we visited, she looked worse, but she was a strong woman even in this condition. Like her father, she had no intention to give life up easily.

* * *

In the meantime, Renate and I worked on preparing for the tender process with Tusk Resorts.

My business partners were supportive of the idea, with the understanding that if successful, Renate was to be appointed within the new division as Food Services Manager. This brought the reality that both Renate and I physically had to move to Mafikeng in the North West Province. We approached Jeremy and his board, and shared how we intended to turn the casino's then-failing food and beverage department into a sustainable, good quality product and service. Jeremy found it amusing that we were prepared to give up our luxurious home in one of South Africa's best Golf Estates to move to a place like Mafikeng.

I continued to provide the HR services to Tusk Resorts, and at this point, I had the contract for five years. I promised that if we were successful in the establishment of Extra Expertise Food Services, the new food services division, we would apply the same co-sourcing principles that we have delivered in Extra Expertise. Tusk Resorts remained our largest client in Extra Expertise; I would continue to manage both businesses and assured Jeremy that the HR service would not be neglected.

After considering their options, Jeremy and his board approved our proposal, which saw the birth of 'Extra Expertise Food Services', a wholly owned subsidiary of Extra Expertise.

Renate and I found tenants for our house, a high-ranking official associated with the Japanese Embassy situated in Pretoria. They rented our home – fully furnished – for the next two-and-a-half years. Renate moved to Mafikeng on 13 October 2004, and I followed on the 31st of October. We moved into a comparatively small three-bedroom flat in the staff village adjacent to the casino and took over the food and beverage function effectively from 1 November 2004.

Tusk Mmabatho, or the Mmabatho Sun, as it used to be known, was the first casino resort that Sol Kerzner built some thirty years ago. This was where the Sun King started his empire, and this was where we started our new venture.

We took over a much neglected service, financially challenged, with dubious hygiene standards and low staff morale. Considering that I have worked with the staff since 1989, when I led the HR service for NewCo before Tusk Resorts was formed – I assisted with the outsourcing of the food and beverage function to service providers like MacRib, Hole in the Cloud, and eventually to Extra Expertise Food Services – the staff morale was understandably challenged.

We provided the full spectrum of food and beverage services, including the management of the Palm Terrace Restaurant and Lounge, the pool bar, the Casino bar, Tuskers Family Diner and the Action Bar. We hosted weddings, conferences, training sessions and golf day events. The nearby Leopard Park Golf Club always used the Casino as key sponsor and service provider for their golf events. We provided the food and beverage service to this event on an annual basis for the duration of our contract at the Casino.

In the beginning of our contract, I was introduced to Anne Loots, a very competent and dynamic personal assistant. Anne was neatly dressed for our first meeting, and although we could not afford a big salary, she was keen for a new challenge and we struck a chord. Anne bought into our dream, our vision and our business. This was the beginning of a spectacular working relationship. The three of us – Renate, Anne and I – created the building blocks for a successful business.

On 14 December 2004, on our wedding anniversary, Bischi, our beautiful cat, was taken from us. He was a lovely boy with a special reconciliatory personality. We never found out what happened to him. One day he was there, and the next he was gone. We were heartbroken.

During December, we hosted a number of weddings; the first of which was held in the Leopard Room. On 18 December, while setting up for a wedding, we discovered four new-born kittens that were born that morning. The mother, a wild cat outside the hotel, deserted them, and Renate and I became surrogate parents of the Leopard Room Four. During this time, Renate would open the service at 5am and I would close at whatever time the functions were concluded, generally around 2am.

My mother-in-law, Helga, joined us in Mmabatho, as we needed someone to help with our finances. She also let her house out in Pretoria, and moved to Mmabtho with us. On the 24th of December, Renate, Willie and a friend of ours, Crystel, enjoyed Christmas dinner at my mother-in-law's house before we all reported for duty on Christmas Day to manage breakfast, lunch and dinner service on what is generally considered the busiest day of the year.

During Christmas lunch, a German friend of ours from Pretoria visited the hotel and showed us a photo of a young girl, who was only six years old. She was a resident in an orphanage in Pretoria and we were asked if we would consider adopting her.

It is worth mentioning that social services in South Africa are not as well-funded and developed as in the UK, nor do they have the robust adoption processes, as might be common practice in the UK. However, as we longed for children for many years, this was an option that we were keen to explore.

* * *

On the 26th of December 2004, miles away, the Indian Ocean cracked open, resulting in the 2004 Tsunami that killed nearly 225000 people.[56] Casualties were reported in Indonesia, Sri-Lanka, the Maldives and Thailand where the largest loss of life occurred. A week later, the real horror of the Tsunami was more evident, and I can recall standing on the casino floor on 31st December just before midnight, ready to serve champagne to the casino patrons, contemplating if I should call for a moment of silence in considering the victims of the Tsunami. However, the patrons were gambling, joyfully celebrating the birth of 2005, blissfully ignorant of the pain and suffering of so many families on the far side of the world.

* * *

On 31 December, the hotel was fully occupied and in full swing with the December festivities. I went home for the afternoon to freshen up for the evening shift. It was about 40 degrees Celsius, the height of the South-African summer. As I walked out of the service area of the hotel, past the tip, I heard the desperate pleads of little kittens, I thought I was going mad, as the four cats at home kept us busy with two hourly feedings throughout the night. But it was not my imagination. As I looked inside the bin, I discovered another five kittens that some of our Tswana kitchen staff threw in the dustbin. They were close to death, desperately dehydrated and burning in the scorching heat. I took the five kittens and ran home. On arriving there, Renate and her mum helped me cool the overheated kittens down with lukewarm water. So our family grew with the arrival of the Dustbin Five. Unfortunately, we could not save all of them, but managed to pull four through.

Willie, who was now employed by the hotel, was very critical of us, in a supportive way, as he thought that Renate has taken on too much – running the food and beverage service, raising eight little kittens who were all dependent on two hourly feeds, cleaning and nurturing. However, we managed; we loved it and over the two years at Mafikeng, we raised twenty

[56] https://www.britannica.com/place/Thailand [accessed 28/11/2016]

orphaned kittens by hand and found homes for all of them, except one. Gigi, one of the Leopard room five, managed to creep into our hearts and joined Wolfgang, Tessa, Molly, Renate and me.

During this time, we slowly won the trust and respect of the staff and patrons alike. We physically worked with the staff in the kitchen, around the pool and on the restaurant floor. We gave salary increments to all the staff just after taking over the service, which was the first increase given to the food and beverage staff in five years. We marketed the restaurant and conference facilities aggressively through the media, and successfully turned the food and beverage function around.

* * *

Our first Easter in 2005 was marked with a very successful series of functions, including a lavish Middle-Eastern evening hosted outside in a boma, with both Indian food and traditional South-African barbeques. On all accounts, everything was going great, and we made our mark as a hard-working, dedicated management couple. However, that evening, one of our staff members, who was responsible for moving tables and chairs between the boma (an enclosure used for outdoor entertainment) and the hotel, used one of our utility vehicles to take staff home to the neighbouring township. The youngsters took some beers from the store and two guys and two girls squeezed into the front cabin of the utility vehicle (a 'bakkie' in Afrikaans). Whether they consumed alcohol before they left was not clear, but driving home well after midnight and being under the influence, they hit a horse that instantly killed the two girls, and seriously injured the boys.

At this time, I was in Pretoria. Following a number of visits to the orphanage that came knocking on Christmas day, we agreed to take the young girl, whom I'll call Annabel, to Mafikeng for a visit over the Easter Holiday.

Renate phoned me on Saturday morning and told me what had happened the night before. She told me that she needed to go the state morgue to confirm the identity of the girls, who both worked for us as waitresses in the restaurant. She was very distraught. I was concerned for my wife, worried about our staff, and nervous, as I was driving with a young, vulnerable six-year-old little girl back to Mafikeng, not quite sure what to talk about.

This was a very traumatic weekend for us as four of our staff's lives were snuffed out so senselessly. The girls were killed well before their time, whilst both the boys suffered life-changing injuries.

Annabel's visit was equally challenging. Social services did not prepare us at all for what to expect. Annabel only wanted to spend time with Renate and did not want to be with me. Renate was working from early morning, which caused challenges, as Annabel did not want me to help her get dressed, resulting in Renate needing to come home to tend to her needs.

We later learned that her mother would not authorise an adoption, and the legal system failed such young and vulnerable children dismally in South Africa. This experience scarred both Annabel and us immensely. In time to come, we learned that Annabel was placed with many a potential adoptive family, but always without success.

* * *

In July 2005, Renate and I, together with my father, decided to embark on a tour of Germany, Austria and the United Kingdom. We knew that my mother was well looked after at Masonic Haven and my dad last visited Europe during a student tour in 1964. We had a wonderful trip; visited Renate's father and brother in Frankfurt, travelled to the Black Forest, then to Bad Saulgau in the south of Germany, on to Austria and ended our tour in the United Kingdom.

While in the UK, we stayed with Ponti in St Annes-on-the-Sea, and as it was close to my dad's birthday, Ponti and I arranged for a surprise party for my father at the Admirals Pub in Lytham St Annes. Suzanne flew out from Dubai, where she was working at the time to surprise my father, and surprised he was. Ponti's parents were visiting at the time, while Carla, her boyfriend, Michael, and Stefan with some of their friends made the birthday celebrations very special. On returning home, we told my dad that if he was healthy and strong when he turned eighty, which was in five years' time, we would take him back to Germany, as he truly enjoyed the country, its people and most importantly, its beer.

* * *

I remained responsible for the overall management and functioning of Extra Expertise, while Andre took over the day-to-day running of the consulting business. This necessitated a bi-weekly commute to Johannesburg, which eventually went against all Renate and I wanted to achieve originally.

Eventually, Andre and I agreed that we would split the two businesses. He took over the full functioning and shareholding of Extra Expertise, while Renate and I took over the full functioning and shareholding of Extra Expertise Food Services. This became effective in September 2005 when I relinquished all responsibility within Extra Expertise, which saw the birth of Celsius Hospitality Services (Pty.) Ltd. The latter was registered as the new name of our company with the registrar of companies on 26 September 2005.

Jeremy Franklin, the then-CEO of Tusk Resorts, described Celsius as 'a hospitality management company, driven by high standards, focusing on the needs of its patrons and clients, and managed by its owners with passion and commitment.'

During our time at the casino, we marketed the restaurant and conference facilities aggressively through the media, and successfully turned the food and beverage function around. We, in conjunction with Leon Nel and his team, hosted artists at the Casino Resort, like Nicholis Louw, Mathys Roets, The Soweto String Quartet, Nia Nel, Juanita du Plessis and the comedian Barry Hilton. All of these events were spectacularly successful.

During one of my trips to Gauteng, I visited Renate's old chef from Mercedes Benz, Shaun Cambell, who was now running a local restaurant in Pretoria. Here, I met a two-man band called the Silver Creek Mountain Band. Rod, the leader of the band, was an eccentric, talented and gentle soul. With a long grey beard and bare feet, Rod played the cello and his partner, Jean-Pierre, played the guitar. I was so impressed with their music, which is old country style, that I told Leon about them and eventually, they were contracted to play at Tusk Mmabatho the last weekend of every month.

Towards the end of our first year in Mmabatho, it became apparent that Tusk Mmabatho no longer wanted to manage the Mmabatho Convention Centre (MCC), which belonged to the North West Provisional Government.

Without really knowing what the true impact of that first supper with Leon and Martie Nel entailed, Renate and I enjoyed 'going back to the floor'. We physically worked in the restaurants, the bars, the banqueting functions and kitchens. Renate appointed Lazarus Thebe as our executive chef and this gentle soul became the heart of our food standards within the company at that time, and the group in years to come. I took responsibility for the human resources, payroll, financial and administration functions, supported by Helga, who worked as financial controller. I physically worked at functions, hosting events and building relationships with clients of our client. Renate took charge of the kitchens with the help of Lazarus, and jointly, they ensured that our food standards remained of a high calibre.

Renate also attended to our menu design and did the day-end cash-up, stock takes food and beverage control and purchases. Willie, whose contract with Tusk came to an end when we started, joined us and supported Renate with day-ends, training and admin.

In October, we went to Mauritius for my 40th birthday. We celebrated the end of an era, with Extra Expertise behind us, and planned with renewed enthusiasm what we envisaged for Celsius Hospitality Service and our future.

Although there were many challenges at this first contract, this formed the basis for us to grow our business. We also understood that we would not be able to grow the business effectively, in terms of government contracts, if we did not have sufficient 'Black Economic Empowerment'. Again, with the help of Harry, who introduced us to Mtheza Lancelot Buya, we sold an appropriate portion of shareholding to Mtheza as business partner.

With our shareholding attended to, meeting the South African government's requirement for 'Black Economic Empowerment' (BEE), we tendered for the management contract of the 5000-capacity convention centre in Mafikeng. We secured a ten-year contract, with the option to renew this for a further ten years. I think it is safe to say that everyone in Tusk Resorts thought we were crazy to take on such a large unit, which was a notorious loss maker. However, we had different plans.

In February 2006, Anne and I moved my office to the MCC, whilst Renate remained based at Tusk Mmabatho. We brought my cousin, James Dyer, who now worked as an acclaimed sales representative with a large catering distribution company, into the business. James helped with the management of the food and beverage function while I prepared to take over the general management role of the Convention Centre.

I developed a zero-based budget for the MCC, planning the turn-around of this challenging monster of a business. We took into account some of the bookings that were taken over and planned an aggressive marketing campaign. Winning hearts and minds of our staff, whilst building relationships with local government and patrons stood us in good stead.

This was a very exciting time, as it was the first time that Renate and I worked together in the same company, seeing each other every day. While many people would say that they would never be able to work with their spouse, this worked really well for us both. Although there were many challenges at this first contract, this formed the basis for us to grow our business.

* * *

On Monday, 3rd December 2006, I visited my mum at Masonic Haven. Andre, who was with me at the time, waited in the car. I walked down the familiar corridors, as I have done so many times before. That day, the staff made my mum sit in a chair next to her bed. She was wearing a blue dress and a blue jersey. Blue was her favourite colour. I kissed my mum on her head and kneeled next to her. She showed no reaction to my presence. My mum was hardly a shadow of the strong, friendly and supportive friend and mother I knew. Seeing her like this broke my heart every time I visited. I whispered in her ear and said to her that it would not be long; that I did not think her suffering would continue much longer. Unbeknownst to me, that was the last day I saw my mum alive. Andre and I flew to Cape Town the following Thursday, 6 December. At 7:00 the next morning, Masonic Haven called to say that we should come to the home as my mum's breathing was deteriorating. I called my dad and told him to go. Less than fifteen minutes later, I phoned my dad again to tell him that my mum had died. The woman, who in my mind and heart will forever remain an extraordinary and amazing human being, was at peace at last.

Anne's efficiency always struck me as remarkable, especially under stressful situations. She re-booked my flights and that same afternoon, I was back in Pretoria and on 10 December 2006 we attended my mum's funeral.

On Thursday, 14 December 2006, only seven days after my mum's death, Renate and I hosted a couple of friends, including my father and mother-in-law in celebrating our tenth wedding anniversary. It was a bittersweet celebration; whilst we mourned the loss of my mum, we celebrated our tenth wedding anniversary. Earlier that day, under the watchful eye of our trusted old friend, Willie, Renate and I renewed our vows in a private ceremony and again proclaimed our love for each other.

* * *

In April 2007, we moved back to Pretoria, where we established a head office for Celsius and moved back into our home at Woodhill. We appointed a general manager to manage the Convention Centre and developed a full set of promotional material to help promote Celsius as a real hospitality contender.

Our promotional material confirmed that Celsius provide management solutions in terms of hotel management contracts, banqueting, convention management and catering services. During 2007, we also signed a lease agreement for a new 20-bedroom hotel and branded it our first 'Red Chilli Inn'. As this was situated in Swartruggens and while the local community and churches did not support us, taking into account that Swartruggens is an immensely conservative town, the significance of 'location, location, location' was proven to be extremely important.

The fact that we were now established in Gauteng, be it with only a head office and three units, paved the way for us to tender for the management contract of the Drostdy Hotel. This monumental hotel, situated in the historic town of Graaff-Reinet, where my great-great-grandfather was born on 7 April 1816, is situated in the Karoo in the Eastern Cape. We purchased the business rights and assets from the previous management company and entered into a long-term lease agreement with the landlord being Historical Homes of South Africa.

Our promotional material confirmed that The Drostdy Hotel in Graaff-Reinet, originally a courthouse and slave quarters, was built in 1804. It went through many structural changes during its lifetime and was restored in 1977 to its original, pristine elegance when it was converted into a modern hotel. Set in the heart of the Karoo, the Drostdy Hotel should be every traveller's stopover en-route to Cape Town.

In August 2007, I saw an invitation for tenders issued by Namibia's electricity supplier for the management of their Convention Centre situated in Windhoek, Namibia. We prepared our tender documentation. Renate and I, accompanied by Helga and our bank manager, went to Namibia and presented our proposal to NamPower's representative. A couple of weeks later, they indicated that they wished to visit our contract in Mafikeng and at the end of October, a delegations from Namibia flew to Mafikeng to do a site inspection of the Convention Centre. We answered their questions and a couple of weeks later, we were notified that our tender was accepted. We concluded the final agreement in January 2008. James was transferred to Namibia where he took responsibility for the management of the NamPower Convention Centre. This new development saw the establishment of Celsius Namibia, a wholly owned subsidiary of Celsius in South Africa.

* * *

On 16 December 2007, Renate's father passed away in Germany, which brought an end to the life of an extraordinary and well-travelled gentleman. A man whom I admired and whose company I really enjoyed. Although he was difficult in the last couple of years, he remained the reason that I have a loving, friendly, funny and positive wife today. I sometimes wonder if this staunch German, by the name of Thorwalt Wilhelm Breuer, truly understood how the actions of his youth enhanced the life of an ordinary South African. He remains a person that I often think of with a smile of endearment.

* * *

Later in December, Renate and I travelled to Stellenbosch for two weeks' vacation. Sadly, on 1 January 2008, Wolfgang, my trusted dog, companion and friend, died unexpectedly, and before his time.

* * *

During 2007, it became apparent that Tusk Resorts was sold to Peermont, the only fully black-owned casino group in South Africa at that time. Jeremy retired and with the exception of Thabo, all the members of his original board went their own way. Thus, the relationship between Jeremy and I did not only last for one year, as I proposed in 1998, but Tusk Resorts continued to co-source its human resources function to my former consulting firm until 2008, well after I left. Jeremy and I changed from client and consultant to just good friends with mutual respect.

It was well-known at the time that Peermont did not subscribe to the co-sourcing of its food and beverage departments, which resulted in Celsius giving Tusk Mmabatho notice to cancel the agreement, effective 15 January 2008.

* * *

In March, my father consulted with all his children and although we expected something was brewing, he asked our permission to marry again. Everyone gave the nod and on 27 April 2008, shortly before my father turned 80, he married Madeleine Ruth Venter, a sweet, strong and dynamic 75-year-old lady.

In May, Renate and I visited my old friend, Dietloff, who was now living in Perth, Australia. We discovered that Dietloff had met the love of his life. While Dietloff marvelled over his newfound love, Renate and I marvelled over the beauty of Australia. A country where people live in absolute harmony, at least from our perspective, everyone abiding by the laws of the land. A land where people adhere to simple traffic rules. Most impressive was the cleanliness of the cities and country alike. Everything worked. Everything was on time. People took pride in what they did. We started looking at our own country – the crime, corruption, disregard for rules and regulations, and the state of our public service. We started to wonder.

Since Renate and I moved back to Pretoria, we worked diligently trying to find new contracts, building our brand, protecting our corporate image and complying with good corporate governance. Since the beginning of that year, we expanded our head office structures, we appointed Liahn Nortje, our Group Financial Manager, and later Hennie Carstens as Group Operations Manager. Renate relinquished some of her responsibilities to Lazarus in Mmabatho, who was moved from Tusk Mmabatho to be based at the Mmabatho Convention Centre. He was eventually appointed Group Hygiene and Training Manager, with the responsibility of transferring skills and establishing a training facility for young and upcoming Chefs. We appointed Nettie Erasmus our Payroll Manager and Marilyn Bredenhan as Marketing Coordinator.

On 28 July 2008, my dad celebrated his 80th birthday. By then, we secured the management contract of Woodhill Country Club, where we lived and hosted his birthday party at the Country Club. As Renate and I promised him five years ago, we departed on 29 July on our trip to Europe, accompanied by my father and his new wife, on a two-week vacation to Switzerland, Austria and Germany.

On returning from overseas, my parents moved into their new home, while Renate and I seriously contemplated our future.

During 2008, a number of our immediate family, friends and associates were attacked and became victims of the mindless and ongoing violence in South Africa. As a result of this, we decided that we do have some choices. With Celsius well established as a strong business, with a good management team, Renate and I were ready to start a new adventure. We decided to explore the possibility of expanding into international markets. We visited Australia in May that year, considered the United Kingdom and researched possibilities in New Zealand. We wanted to find a country where there was respect for the rule of law, where people's rights and dignity, irrespective of race, colour or creed, were protected.

In December 2008, Gucci, an orphaned kitten from Bronkhorstspruit, arrived at our home. I was not impressed, but Tessa really took to him.

Shortly after Gucci's arrival, Dietloff and his fiancée came to South Africa. That was the first time that we met Carla – the future Mrs Giliomee. On 27 December 2008, Dietloff and Carla exchanged their vows in an intimate and beautiful ceremony, which Renate and I arranged at a small boutique hotel. Dietloff, still the artistic and very talented writer, was so taken by his bride that he recited a personal poem that he dedicated to her as part of his speech during this special and private event in their lives.

During their short visit, we debated at great length how they found life in Australia, and reflected on our own impressions of Australia. Dietloff told us about his friends in New Zealand, his brother in Canada, while Renate and I told them about our experiences in Germany and reflected on our many visits to Ponti in the United Kingdom. We realised that residents of these countries had a few things in common. They all lived in countries that were safe, where people are law abiding and whose systems worked better than South Africa at the time. Their democracies worked, their political systems were well managed and their politicians held to account.

After exploring our options, and with the agreement of our partners in True Group, we decided to hand over the reins of Celsius to a Managing Director and prepared to move to a new country.

With the untimely death of Wolfgang, our Labrador, we could not take Tessa, our German Sheppard on her own, as she was blind. So we prepared for a new life in the United Kingdom. We sold everything we owed and with our three cats, Nushka, Gigi and Gucci, a bit of cash and a couple of boxes, we moved to the United Kingdom, via Dubai. As we frequently visited Ponti and the kids in St Annes-on-the-Sea over the preceding years, it was natural that we would move to Lancashire, where my old friend and our god-children lived.

Chapter 22
Let's Emigrate

During January 2009, we thought it would take some time to get our UK Visa. However, the period February to May 2009 became very rushed. We did not think that our Tier 1 Visa for the UK would be approved so quickly. Our three-year term for our first visa to the UK started on 8 February 2009. We had to pack our earthly belongings, sell our furniture and our house, sort out what to do with our animals and move to a country where we only knew five people.

Unbeknownst to us, moving to England would be returning to the country where most of my ancestral DNA comes from. Although history taught me that my ancestors came from the Netherlands and Germany, we were in for a few surprises.

I had a great fondness for the English language, irrespective of the fact that I only learned to speak it late in my adolescence. We always thought that in South Africa, if you could speak English perfectly, then that is surely a sign of intelligence. In fact, throughout my schooling years, English-speaking South Africans often looked down on Afrikaners who spoke English poorly. We were considered a bit of a plank.

We prepared to move to the UK, the country that influenced most of the western world in terms of its legal system, democracy, colonialism, home rule and ultimate independence. The proverbial cradle of history was also the country that changed the destiny of our own country, South Africa.

However, moving to a country we hardly knew, and leaving the country we grew up in, was very daunting. Whilst it was our choice to move to the UK, leaving our parents – Renate's mum, 70; my father's wife, 75; and my dad, 80 – was very difficult, not to mention my siblings, our respective families and friends.

When we decided to emigrate, we agreed with our family that if ever there was an opportunity for us to do an overseas adventure, this was it. I was 43 and Renate was 38 years old at the time.

Although the worldwide economic crises and recession was still gaining momentum, it seems that the UK still held a large number of HR positions available. We thought securing alternative employment could not be that difficult.

The month before our departure, we sold our cars, home and most of our

197

furniture. This was the beginning of a very painful process of saying goodbye. Paving the way for us to relocate with our cats, a few paintings, some personal and sentimental items and a few pounds sterling to make a new start. The exchange rate at that time was ZAR18 to £1.

* * *

I travelled to the UK on the 5th April 2009 for four weeks to see if I could register with recruitment agents and hopefully secure employment before we officially moved. That Sunday morning, Renate and I went to church, but I could see that it was going to be a difficult day. After church, we had lunch with our family, with all my uncles and aunts, and some friends of Renate and I. This was just too much for Renate. Her emotions got the better of her. The anticipated move was now real, a couple of weeks away and this was the first time in our marriage that we would be apart for such a long period of time. I arrived in the UK on Monday 6th April 2009 – similar to Jan van Riebeeck who arrived in Cape Town on Saturday, 6th April 1652, when the Cape of Good Hope was born. My next couple of weeks were spent registering with recruitment agents and attending interviews. I was pleased to be able to celebrate Carla's birthday with her, Michael, Ponti and Stefan on the 8th of April. However, I returned to South Africa rather disappointed that I did not secure a job but remained hopeful and in time for South Africa's national election on 22nd April 2009.

* * *

The last weekend before our final departure was the weekend of 23rd May 2009; everything was just about packed, sold and cleaned. Before we left, we checked the house one more time. Renate and I loved our home on the popular Woodhill Golf Estate in the east of Pretoria. We built this house from scratch, designing its every corner, developing its garden with the help of Josiah, our trusted gardener. As the house was cleared and cleaned, by our long-term cleaning lady Maria, we took one more sentimental walk through the house; from the bathroom adjacent to the main bedroom, with its bushman painted tiles and patio looking out on the lush garden on the one side to the green bathroom on the other side of the house. This bathroom contained the antique cast-iron bath that Andre and I fetched from 'Moreson' in the old Western Transvaal. We fetched this old bath from the farm my father grew up on, and was the bath he and his nine siblings used to bathe in as children. We had it restored before it was installed in our house. I walked through the bedrooms that were intended for our children who never came and before we left our lovely home, we buried the remaining ashes of our pets. We hold such fond memories of our time on Woodhill with all of them. We buried the ashes of Molly, who died of old age about two years before. Wolfgang, my beautiful Labrador who died pre-maturely on 1st January 2008 and Tessa, our Alsatian who was euthanised at 3:30 on Monday, 18th May 2009. We buried their ashes in the far eastern corner of the garden. I reasoned that it was unlikely for any future owner to build, plant or excavate immediately against the security wall behind the lapa.

During this last weekend in South Africa, we stayed with my dad and his wife. We did a few last-minute chores, saying good-bye to family and friends and prepared ourselves for our departure on Monday evening, 25th May 2009.

* * *

We decided not to fly directly to Manchester, but to fly via Dubai, where we visited Jacques and Shar Reijkmans and their lovely children in an attempt to alleviate the trauma of leaving our birthplace for the unknown.

* * *

We booked a taxi to collect us from my father's home, as we did not want to have a big farewell at the airport. At 12:30, we had lunch with our parents at Cappuccinos Restaurant at Woodlands. It was a light-hearted lunch but with a definite sense of anticipation. We made small talk and tried to be as upbeat as possible. After lunch, Renate and I, with our respective parents, went to my father's house; I dropped Renate at home and left to visit my mum's grave.

I bought some flowers and placed them on her grave. I sat for a while recalling the lively spirit and infectious laugh I knew my mum had. She was such a remarkable woman; so passionate about her family, dedicated to her husband, living for her children and loved her grandchildren. She did such detailed family research all her life. She was so sadly missed. I said my goodbye and went home.

Our parents drank coffee, whilst Renate and I made final preparations to leave Africa for Europe.

It was not long before the driver arrived. The final farewells commenced. I truly love my dad and leaving him behind in Africa whilst Renate and I embarked on this new adventure was very daunting. We loaded the car, Renate and I said our good-byes to Ma Madeleine, my father's wife, whilst I started saying good-bye to Ma Helga, my mother-in-law, and then to my dad. I had intended to tell my father I love him, I respect him, that I admire him deeply and that I would miss him terribly. However, I could not say any of this. I wanted to tell him that I prayed to God to keep him safe. Sadly, I could not form the words, as I knew my emotions would not hold. We hugged and said goodbye. A lot of what we both wanted to say needed not be said, as we both knew. I knew my dad loved me, we both would miss each other, and we both knew that this was the best thing for Renate and I to do.

Our parents stood outside the house; as the car pulled away, we waved and started our journey to OR Tambo Airport in Johannesburg, to Europe via Dubai and to a new life. Both Renate and I were busy with our own thoughts. She closed her eyes and I looked far over the Highveld cornfields. What would the future hold? Who knew?

* * *

We drove with the R21 past Olifantfontein. I briefly reflected on the turnoff to Bapsfontein, the old road we took so many times when we visited my mum's dad, my grandfather, the giant that was Johan van der Vyver. But before I could get too engulfed into an emotional trip down memory lane, we passed the buildings and turnoff at Pomona, heading towards the airport.

Arriving at the airport, we offloaded the car, the adrenaline kicked in. The luggage came out and we made our way to the check-in desk, through customs and down the long corridor to where the Emirates plane to Dubai was ready and waiting.

* * *

As we sat in the lounge, Renate listened to music on her iPod, whilst I watched Sky News reflecting on the underground nuclear device that North Korea detonated on Monday, 25th May 2009. The leaders of the world were one in condemning North Korea for this test. As I listened to the various speakers, I wondered what the future holds for us. Are we leaving South Africa, situated at the southernmost tip of Africa, where we have been relatively safe from international conflict, be it that we had enough of our own. I reflected that if ever international conflict was to happen, then the likelihood that this would start in the northern hemisphere is probable. President Obama added his voice to the condemnation in that *"North Korea's actions endanger people of North East Asia. They are in blatant violation of international law and their action contradicted their own prior commitments. Now, the United Nations and International Community must take action in response."*[57]

I listened to the news with a sense of unease. I looked at Renate and saw her engulfed in her music, tapping away to the rhythm of Amanda Strydom, Mattheys Roets and the Silver Creek Mountain Band; unaware of the tensions brewing in North East Asia, unaware of the unease with which world leaders were condemning North Korea. The one after the other.

The General Secretary of the United Nations Ban Ki-Moon urged for restraint and the UN Security Council unanimously condemned the nuclear tests.

* * *

---

[57] Sky News, 25/05/2009

When Renate and I decided to move to the UK, we made the entire process a matter of faith. We asked for God's guidance, assistance and help to open the door. If He supported our move to the UK, we believed; with that, our Visa was granted in less than ten days from submission to issuing. Thus, as we wanted to make a success of this adventure, in partnership with God, we knew that ultimately He is in control of the world and the universe; with that knowledge, the future, be it in Africa, Europe or wherever we ultimately ended up in the world, was in His hands.

* * *

The air-hostess called on the passengers of EK17 from Johannesburg to Dubai to commence boarding. I indicated to Renate that we had to go and get our passports and tickets ready for departure.

We arrived at 5am in the UAE. It was 30 degrees Celsius with very high humidity. After successfully making our way through customs, collecting our luggage and finding our host and friend Jacques Rijkmans, we drove through the city to their villa. On arriving at the villa, we were greeted by Shar, Jacques' wife, their three children, Mikayla, Bianca and Buddy, not to forget Bella, their housekeeper and au pair to the kids.

We haven't seen the kids since they visited Renate and I in Mafikeng during 2005. It soon became apparent that the credit crunch also hit this playground of the rich and famous as the shopping mecca of the world. A large variety of building projects was placed on hold. Thousands of ex-patriots working in Dubai returned to their respective countries. Even the cars on the highways were notably less since our last visit to Dubai, which was in 2003.

Shar predicted that after the upcoming school holidays, less people would return to Dubai, as work had become increasingly scarce.

After resting on our first day in Dubai and coming to terms with the fact that our immigration to the UK was now officially underway. Renate and I started to relax a bit. We knew there was nothing we could do. Our cats were safe in England and the quarantine agency confirmed that all three travelled well and arrived safely in Manchester.

That evening, Bella, a beautifully talented Indian girl, prepared a variety of authentic Indian curries. She made a fish curry, egg curry, bean curry and mutton curry. It was a taste sensation that we would remember for the rest of our lives.

Day two in Dubai, the temperature increased to a shocking 42 degrees. Renate and I spent the day in a shopping mall and had an afternoon nap. When I woke, I realised Renate was up and heard her talking to a man somewhere in the Rijkmans villa. I freshened up and found her talking to well-built Australian-Brit on leave from Afghanistan; a former military instructor with a sense of adventure and a philosophy of *carpe diem*. There was an especially strong bond between the soldier and Buddy, the youngest and only son of our hosts. Although the soldier was single and without children, he had a natural ability to talk, play and interact with Buddy, a third-grader with tons of energy. I watched them talk and play. I again wondered what type of father I would have been. Taking into account that after 13 years of marriage, Renate and I remained childless. I often looked at children, missing that experience.

The morning of the third and last day, we said our goodbyes to Jacques, Buddy and the girls. Shar took Renate and me to one of her jewellery friends at the Souk, where I bought Renate a custom-made puzzle ring, before Shar treated us to coffee and pastries at the 'One and Only Royal Palace Hotel'. She dropped us at the airport and the final leg of the beginning of our new life officially commenced.

We made our way through customs, checked in and wandered through the various shops, stores and brand names in that magnificent international airport.

* * *

The flight to Manchester felt shorter than from Johannesburg to Dubai; the food was definitely better on this leg as our initial experience between Johannesburg and Dubai was not great.

We arrived at Manchester on time. The sun was shining and we were delighted that the weather was so welcoming, albeit much colder than what we experienced in Dubai. This was great weather in terms of UK standards.

Ponti, my old friend from school, waited at the airport. At 6"7', Ponti towered head and shoulders above the rest of the crowed. This gentle giant was a welcoming face to see, as we would not have embarked on our UK experience was it not for him, who with his two children, our god-children, moved to the UK some eight years earlier, when he married Alison Boshoff.

Although Renate and I visited the UK regularly to see Ponti and the kids, we never considered living in the UK. The weather was predominantly the reason for Renate, whilst I was raised with a strong anti-British sentiment, as the British interned my one grandfather during the Anglo-Boer war, whilst the other's home and fields were destroyed.

* * *

According to my dad, Lord Kitchener of Khartoum burned my great grandfather's house and ruined his farm near Schefferspos as part of Kitchener's scourged earth policy, when he effectively destroyed the Afrikaner of the ZAR (Zuid-Afrikaanse Republiek), starving them into submission to British rule. Kitchener was always a name that provoked negative emotions and anti-British sentiments in my family. So living in the UK for me was never an option.

* * *

However, on Friday, 29th May 2009, Renate and I were in the UK, ready to make this unlikely destination our new home. Our Tier 1 (skilled migrant) visa allowed us to relocate to Britain, to seek employment and/or to start our own business. With the experience Renate and I gained during our 13 years of marriage at that time, we felt comfortable that our respective corporate experiences, our experience in running our businesses and our faith in God, all stood us in good stead to make a success of this new adventure. It mattered not what had happened in history, wherever we landed, we would be successful in whatever we attempted.

We arrived in Her Majesty's Great Brittan and the scene was set to commence with a brand new chapter. Within a safe, progressive and first-world country where the rule of law was adhered to, politicians were held to account and peace and harmony prevailed.

* * *

Ponti rented an apartment in Castlegate in Blackpool. Carla, his daughter, and her fiancé Michael were living in Lytham St Annes, whilst Stefan, his son, was enjoying a gap year before commencing with his studies in Psychology at Manchester University, set to start in September 2009. It was agreed that we would stay with Ponti first, when after we would move to Carla and Michael's home in Lytham until mid June, when our fully furnished flat at College Court, in St Annes-on-the-Sea was available. Michael and Carla were booked to go to Majorca to Michael's boat for a week and we agreed to look after their dog, Alfie, while they were gone.

Our first weekend in England was a bit like being on holiday. Stefan kindly gave us his room on the top floor of the house. Ponti cooked up a storm; we enjoyed some red-wine and just talk like in the old days. Renate and Stefan were reminiscing about some of our previous visits, when they talked and laughed about the neighbours in Castlegate, with people hanging out of windows and doing a variety of strange and entertaining things. Michael and Carla also made a turn later to greet us and gave us a card, in true English tradition, to welcome us to our new country. There was a sense of adventure, anticipation and excitement in the air, be it in very crisp, cold and wet air. The following day, Stefan took Renate and I to the quarantine station where our cats were held and we were very pleased that Nushka, Gigi and the youngest, Gucci, were all doing very well.

* * *

In June 2009, we moved into a fully furnished two-bedroom flat that we rented from Michael. It was situated on Kings Road, St Annes-on-the-Sea. Here, we registered with our first GP practice, opened a bank account and bought our first little car. We applied for UK conversions of our South African driving license and learned very quickly that everything is done online in the UK. Considering that we were not used to Wi-Fi in our homes in South Africa, or that everything was done online, was quite an adjustment. When we planned our move to the UK, we thought that I'll be able to secure a suitable position in the hotel industry. However, after arriving in St Annes-on-the-Sea, and visiting Blackpool a few times, I thought not. I redirected my attention to my original vocation and thought that I'll be able to secure a suitable HR position within the initial 90 days. It soon became apparent that I needed to be accredited with the UK's Chartered Institute for Personnel Development (CIPD), as all public and most private sector companies had an 'essential requirement' for HR practitioners to be CIPD qualified. We were shocked how expensive everything was in the UK, considering our base money was South African Rand (ZAR).

Chapter 23
Blackpool and UK Employment Realities

The cats flew over a week before we arrived. They were accommodated, during their six months period of quarantine in a four by six meter unit. After the initial three weeks, Renate and I rented a fully furnished, two bedroom flat in St. Anne's.

I enrolled with various recruitment websites and sent my CV to about twenty advertised positions a week. However, I received one regret letter after another. Initially this did not worry us, as we planned and budgeted for up to three months to secure suitable employment.

After two months in the UK, we bought a little car, a small Renault Modus. Every time I attended a job interview, Renate travelled with me so we visited Leeds, Manchester, Sheffield, London, Stoke-on-Trent, and incorporated a few day-trips to Lancaster, Kirby Lonsdale and Windermere in the Lake District. We discovered that the UK is a truly beautiful country, steeped in many years of unchallenged history. As I realised that I would not be employed without CIPD accreditation, I turned all my focus on the CIPD Professional Assessment of Competency (PAC) requirements.

We lived on a very limited budget. Allowing ourselves a treat once a week of one beer for me, and a pastry that we bought from Marks & Spencer's on a Sunday, which we shared. Our groceries were bought from Lidl, Iceland, and at times, from ASDA. We cut our consumption of meat and replaced this with salads, chicken, and fish. Although we were on a very stringent diet in those early days, we ate well. We lost a lot of weight, but we ate well.

During the next six months, Renate and I went to London a few times as I had to attend a number of interviews. During these trips, we always extended our time with two or three days, staying with Katrin Kruger, my very first employee from HS&A and an old friend from South Africa. Katrin lived in a small apartment in Tulse Hill in the South of London. From here we travelled by train, exploring the beauty of the most expensive city in the world. We were in London on 25 June 2009, when Michael Jackson died. We visited the Borough Market, went to Notting Hill, and visited the Portobello Market. We saw musicals in the west-end such as *Oliver* with Rowan Atkinson, *Chicago* with Jerry Springer, and *Priscilla Queen of the Dessert* with Jason Donovan. We did the Jack the Ripper walk, visited the British Museum, and the National Art Gallery. We toured the dungeons of the London Bridge – the latter is not to be recommended, everything else was fantastic.

CIPD status has various levels, being a graduate member, a chartered member and a fellow. During June to July, I completed my compilation of a Portfolio of Evidence. Once the PAC was completed, I had to attend a four-hour personal interview when a Senior HR Director interviewed me and scrutinised the evidence presented to ensure that I could meet all the requirements of the CIPD satisfactorily. After successfully passing this phase, I was awarded Graduate Membership of the CIPD and had to conduct a research report, consisting of up to 15,000 words. This had to be done in a real company.

Renate held the fort at home for us and kept me focused on looking for work, keeping me positive and ensuring that we embraced the new cuisine the UK had to offer. Restaurant dining was something left in South Africa, whilst Renate and I experimented with new UK dishes. Don't be fooled, there are some excellent foods in the UK, and with a little effort, a true gastronomical feast could be created. We enjoyed the Scottish Salmon, various types of potatoes, cheeses, fish and chips (without mushy peas), complimented by the large variety of beers and wines from all over the world. Renate also applied for positions but was met with the same treatment. Irrespective of how optimistic we were, eventually it did affect our belief in our own abilities.

* * *

By June 2009, Renate and I took a long walk on the beachfront on the South Promenade in Lytham St Anne's. We walked from our apartment in Kings Road, toward the beach, turned left at the Grand Hotel on the South Promenade, and just walked. We did not talk for a long period of time. If truth be told, I wanted Renate to say we should go back to South Africa. Perhaps, I thought, I could ask Harry for a job in Celsius Hospitals Services. Our money was nearly finished and finding a job seemed like the most difficult thing in the world. Things were about to become desperate.

Across the road from the Grand Hotel was a beautiful park with a man-made lake. There were ducks and swans. Children and grandparents would come to the lake to feed the ducks, whilst holidaymakers were relaxing on benches in the park. Renate and I sat on one of these benches. Eventually, I asked, "What are we going to do?" Renate responded, "What do you want to do?" I did not know, and it was this lack of ideas that made me think of something that Ponti's son Stefan said, *"you should phone the hospital and ask them for a job"*. So, after a long period of silence, just staring at the ducks and the children in the park, I said to Renate, "Let's go home." Initially, she thought that I meant we should return to South Africa, and whilst she was not adverse to the idea at the time, she did not respond to my comment. After I got up, we walked back to our flat in silence. However, I had no intention to throw in the towel. Not yet!

* * *

Reading through some of the newsletters I wrote home at the time, none of this last paragraph was shared with the family back home; all I wrote then was, "But as always, we persevered and worked hard to keep each other motivated."

* * *

As I had to do my management report within a company I did as Stefan suggested, I called the office of the Human Resources Director (Mr Nick Grimshaw) at the Blackpool Fylde and Wyre Hospitals NHS Foundation Trust. A large, local National Health Services Hospital with 4500 staff. Initially, his PA did not want me to meet with him; however, I employed my South African resilience and eventually managed to get her to speak to Nick, who asked his then-Acting Deputy Director, Emma Dawkins, to give me a call. I met with Emma a week later. I explained what I did in South Africa, that we immigrated and that I needed to do my CIPD report in a real company.

I offered to do any project of their choosing, free of charge, provided that I could write a report and submit this to the CIPD after completion.

I offered to work for free, as I saw this as a way in to the organisation and an opportunity to build some relationships. The title of my project was to investigate the Hospital's project management approach to HR. I spent the next ten weeks interviewing people, holding focus groups, and collecting information. I wrote the report, and submitted this to the CIPD.

On 11 September 2009, as I was finished with my project at the hospital, Nick wrote an email asking *"do you want to earn some pounds matey?"* As our stress levels continued to go up and both our bank balance and weight came down, I accepted. Renate and I were very grateful that we could get some funds. So on 18 September 2009, I began with gainful employment in the NHS. Our primary aim was to get UK experience and get some public sector exposure, which I hoped would help me to secure a better-paid permanent position in either the private or public sector, in time to come.

* * *

Within two weeks after I submitted my management report, my mentor confirmed that I passed my CIPD PAC accreditation successfully and was given the opportunity to upgrade my membership to that of a Fellow of the CIPD. This was awarded to me on 23 December 2009.

In October, the hospital indicated that they could offer me a further three-month contract to help out within the Facilities Division, with a specific remit to conduct some organisational change interventions until 31 December.

On 1 November 2009, Renate and I moved into a three-bedroom house situated at 16 Tewkesbury Road in Lytham in preparation for our earthly belongings from South Africa to arrive in the UK. We also needed to move into our own house as Nuschka, Gigi, and Gucci, our three South African cats, were due to come home on 25 November after six months in quarantine.

I started to apply for positions within the NHS as I thought my experience in Blackpool would help me to secure an interim or permanent position within the NHS. The NHS is the largest employer in Europe and the fifth largest employer in the world[58]. It should provide us with a secure and rewarding future.

During the first week of December, I applied for a Divisional HR Manager's position at the NHS Trust in Stoke-on-Trent in Staffordshire. Stoke-on-Trent is where Robbie Williams comes from, and is situated between Blackpool and Birmingham toward the South. I was delighted that they invited me to an interview. Renate and I drove down and the interview went very well. Renate's questioning and testing of my knowledge of UK employment law paid off. I was concerned, however, about the fact that I was a South African competing with four UK HR Managers with more NHS experience. We drove back to Lytham and that evening at 7:30, they called and offered me the job; we were ecstatic. On returning to work on Tuesday, I told Nick and the rest of the HR team of my experience and everyone was very happy for me. At about 11:00 AM on Tuesday, Nick confirmed that the Stoke-on-Trent hospital wrote to him and asked for a personal reference on me.

Later that afternoon, he indicated that he wanted to talk to me. During our meeting, Nick told me that neither he nor the wider HR team wanted me to go to Stoke-on-Trent. Nick offered me the position of Divisional HR Manager for Corporate Services. In this position I would be required to provide HR support to about 900 staff, including the CEO's office, and a variety of other corporate service departments. The salary placed us well within the requirements for our visa renewal, which was a requirement of the UK Border Agency (UKBA). We decided to accept Nick's offer and decline the position in the South. We decided to stay in Lytham, for now.

On Wednesday, 16 December, it started to snow in London, and the snow reached us shortly after. It is said that that year's snow was the most that fell in Lancashire in the past twenty years. It took me three hours one day to drive to work, a trip that normally only takes 20 minutes. We enjoyed a white Christmas, attended the Christmas service on the morning of the 25th, and had lunch with Ponti and our UK family in the afternoon. The cats were allowed out of the house on the 26th. With the cats home, gainfully employed, we were increasingly happy and grateful that we made the right choice in moving to the UK. We were more confident that we would make a success of our new lives in the UK.

---

[58] The Telegraph, 20/03/2012

In our annual letter to family and friends, I concluded by writing, 'Thank you to all our family and friends who supported us over the past couple of months with texts, emails, and Facebook messages.' These came from Australia, Austria, Canada, Dubai, Germany, Namibia, New Zealand, Russia, the Ukraine, and of course, everyone back home in South Africa.

Chapter 24
A Year of Adventures and Trepidations

At the beginning of 2010, Renate started working at Henry's Bar & Grill, an up-market restaurant in Lytham where she worked as duty manager. It could not be described as a new adventure as we have managed our own restaurants before and worked shifts around the clock seven days a week in Mafikeng; however, it was something to keep her busy and paid the monthly rent.

February brought an unexpected surprise, in that the Leeds Teaching Hospital in York wrote to me and confirmed that I was shortlisted for a post as Human Resources Business Partner at the hospital. This was a post that Nick Grimshaw suggested I should apply for in November 2009, prior to my interview at Stoke-on-Trent, and prior to him offering me the post as Divisional HR Manager Corporate Services. Nick heard about this vacancy during one of his networking meetings and put in a good word for me with Jackey Green, the then Director HR & OD at Leeds Teaching Hospital. As neither Nick nor I heard anything since his initial introduction, we assumed that this post was withdrawn or internally filled. I was in two minds if I should attend the interview, as I did not want to offend Nick in going for another interview, just after he appointed me. However, we discussed what to do and we both agreed that I should go for the interview, as Nick recommended me and the fact that I attend an interview did not mean I would automatically be successful in securing the post.

I drove to York and as parking in England is always a problem, I arrived slightly late, just in time to hear the last part of Jacky's welcome address to the candidates. I sat in the back of the room with about twenty people and thought that the competition was really going to be tough. It soon became apparent that the interview would be in the form of an assessment centre, with seven other candidates, facilitated by a host of HR & OD professionals. All of the candidates were younger than me and had more NHS experience than me. I was doomed. The assessment centre was interesting with my first interview a discussion of my past experience. We spoke about my time in Extra Expertise and Celsius and had a comfortable debate. The candidates were constantly rotated between rooms and I was moved to my second activity, a role play where a secretary was underperforming but externalised her inabilities and frustration with her line manager. She claimed that she was treated unfairly and started sobbing inconsolably. I listened attentively, while four assessors watched my every move. I allowed the secretary to shed her tears and spoke in a supportive but clear tone, explaining what line of action I recommend us to follow and reached agreement on a joint-solution for her and her line manager moving forward. My confidence improved and I was moved to the next activity where I was questioned on the latest developments in UK and EU employment law. I stumbled a bit on the EU part but worked my way through the latest developments of UK law. This improved my confidence further, until the first group activity, when we had to do a sales pitch on visions and values to a panel of assessors. It was an uncomfortable session as we made an uncomfortable team of candidates. The afternoon sessions increased the tension when the entire group was taken to a large room and we were instructed to build an oil drill with Legos in a restricted area. This was a group activity and I somehow became in charge of costing up our building materials. Taking into account that at times I have difficulty adding two and two together, this seemed like a disaster in the making. I felt incredibly self-conscious. I could not calculate the costs involved, overspent our budget dismally, and our every move was watched by a group of facilitators who just sat against the walls, pen in hand, recording our every move, and in my case my every mistake. The oilrig never delivered a barrel of oil and in the last seconds of the activity, collapsed on the floor. I wished I could vanish in the unseen sea on which our make-believe oilrig now was laying in pieces. Although I laughed with the other delegates, internally I was increasingly angry that we failed this task, and specifically that I allowed myself to be placed in such a position. Following this fiasco, we then were required to do wage negotiations with a time limit and a requirement to reach consensus how best to divide the available money between a number of salary bands, and unless 100% consensus was reached, no one would get an increment. During this session, the debates became more intense, and following my poor performance in the rig building, I was not going to allow no increments, so with a calculator in hand, we negotiated. Consensus was reached between the team members, just before the last second vanished, which led us into the last two sessions being numerical and comprehension tests. At 4:00 PM, everyone said their goodbyes. After we were advised that they would call the final three back within one week, I drove back to Lytham. I was glad that I attended the interview, reflecting on the activities during the assessment centre, and content that I did my best, albeit being unsuccessful for the post.

A week later, I received a letter confirming that I was called back for a second interview, and made the journey back to Leeds, this time by train. As I had to attend the second interview at the Trust Headquarters, and I was unsure where this was in Leeds, I went through early, irrespective of the fact that my interview was only at 3:00 PM. I arrived at 11:30 AM and saw one of the candidates leaving and another going in. By the time the fourth candidate left, I figured out that they called everyone back; my interview was last. As I waited to go in, the interviews varied from thirty minutes to an hour. When I eventually got my turn, the interview lasted just over fifteen minutes, followed by Jacky telling me all about Leeds Teaching Hospitals for about another ten minutes. I left the interview room with very mixed feelings. On the one hand, the interview felt as if I answered the questions well, but the timeline just felt too short. As I left Leeds station, I made peace with the fact that I had a job in Blackpool and wrote this off as part of a bigger experience. Renate picked me up at Preston station, and we drove home while I told her of all the activities and events of the day. Later that evening, Jacky called and offered me the job. I was ecstatic.

Renate and I debated late into the night what to do; should we accept this post in Leeds, which would mean that we had to relocate, or do we stay in Lytham and give myself more time to find my feet in the NHS at Blackpool Victoria Hospital. Renate was very supportive, as always, and indicated that she will go wherever I decide. She told me ample times how proud she was of me. We both praised God for what He has done in our lives and went to bed. Following my discussion with Jacky, I indicated that I would speak to Nick the following day, and undertook to phone her at midday with my response. The next morning, I kept a low profile, and when Nick came in, I asked to see him. I told him what happened. He was already aware of the fact that I was successful as Jacky called him the night before to secure a verbal reference on me. Nick was very supportive and did not want to influence me, but allowed me to make up my own mind. He confirmed that he could not offer me anything else, and ultimately this decision was one that only Renate and I could take. Nick, however, did confirm that he would be very happy if I stay but would equally understand should I decide to accept Jacky's offer. Needless to say, I was not very productive that morning. At 11:50 AM, I called Renate, and we had one more discussion on the way forward and at 12 noon, I called Jacky to confirm that I was very grateful for her offer but that we decided to stay in Blackpool for the time being. She was very understanding and even offered to be my mentor to help me develop my career in the NHS, if I so desire.

* * *

In March, Renate and I returned to South Africa for a well-deserved holiday, as I wanted to partake in my eighth Cape Argus Cycle Tour. As we still had our interests in Celsius, we were also made aware of a number of challenges which we wanted to address whilst in Pretoria. We arrived back in South Africa on the 5th of March and spent a wonderful day with family and friends at my father's bowling club on Sunday, 7 March, nearly a year after we first said goodbye to family and friends at the same club, when I left for England on the 5th of April 2009.

On Monday, 8 March, I went to Celsius' new head office in the True Group buildings in Pretoria, and what was intended to be the beginning of discussions to sell our interests to our East London based partners, turned out in a nightmare unimaginable. We discovered that the management team was in disarray, that VAT payments were not made, that staff were paid late, and that the bank returned a large number of unpaid cheques during the months prior to our return. This was devastating news, as we always proud ourselves of running a clean ship, supporting our staff, paying our customers, and staying on the right side of the taxman. Debtors were not collected and creditors not paid. The financial ratios were terrible. The business was in serious difficulty.

At a first glance, the business seemed ruined, our staff abused, and Renate and my good name in tatters. Our dream of building a good business that we may sell in time to come seemed to be dead.

We were initially overwhelmed but had 450 staff that looked up to us for a solution. As in the past, Renate and I consulted and took decisive action. I summoned the then-Managing Director of Celsius, and after a brief discussion on the state of the business, we parted company. The next two days, Renate and I took charge of our business and I tried to get to the bottom of what was going on. I agreed with our partners in East London to put an interim manager in place to see the operations through the current difficult times. By Tuesday night, I spoke to the bank to do further damage control and to our landlords who had not been paid on time. We worked hard to restore the original good relationship we once had. True Group, our partners from East London, were on hand and helped putting back the pieces. The legal team was at work and by Thursday afternoon, Renate and I were able to go to Lanceria airport to fly to Cape Town, only to discover that our flight was in fact on Wednesday afternoon. At first we thought we will not go, but then realised that our accommodation in Cape Town was already paid and unless we got out of Pretoria, we would in all likelihood not relax at all. We had to buy new tickets, but eventually we were off to Cape Town.

Arriving in Cape Town, we checked into our rented apartment, bought some food, and retired for the night. It was difficult to sleep as our minds were constantly drifting back to Pretoria, our business, our staff, the disappointing events of that week, and the absolute financial disaster that still waited to be resolved. The next morning, we collected Andre and Lynda from their hotel and went to register for the race. As was the custom, we had health checks in terms of cholesterol, sugar levels, and blood pressure. The nurse took my blood pressure and immediately asked me if I felt all right. I said, "Yes, a bit stressed but otherwise okay." She called a doctor and took my blood pressure again. Renate and I started worrying, the doctor told us that my blood pressure was way too high he described it as stage 3 hypertension. The doctor told me that they could not allow me to race and I should go and see a general practitioner as soon as possible. Needless to say, this did not help my already fragile state of mind. After registration, Renate, Lynda, Andre, and I went to meet friends for lunch at an Italian restaurant in the Cape Quarter. It was nice to see everyone again but both Renate and I were pre-occupied with our challenges back in Pretoria and my ridiculously high blood pressure. Neither of us slept much that night and as I woke up the next morning, everything unravelled. For the first time in my life, I could not see the wood from the trees. I had no idea what to do; I was devastated over the absolute chaos in Celsius and that our staff suffered so much since our departure for England. We always proud ourselves in running a 'family business', where the needs of our staff at times enjoyed higher priority than common business principles. But we received the rewards through loyalty from all our staff. We valued the people that worked for us, and they valued and trusted us. To see and hear the state of our business after one year away was devastating. The financial challenges seemed irresolvable and the money that we hoped to get for our shares in the business now had to be used to save the ship from sinking. Everything was just gone in a flash. For the first time in my life, I lost faith in myself, my judgment of character, and my ability to think straight. My world came tumbling down. As Renate woke up, I collapsed in a heap of despair. My poor wife has never seen me in such a state, inconsolable and distraught.

After Renate managed to calm me, we decided to phone Heinrich Weidmann, our former Pastor from Pretoria, who was now residing in Cape Town. We called and confirmed if they were home. I loaded my bike and we drove to the German Stadt Mission at the foot of Lions Head. On arriving there, Heinrich immediately noted that something was wrong and invited us into his house. He gave us coffee and while Renate and his wife spoke, he called me to his study, where he asked me what was going on. Again, I broke down and found it very difficult to explain what had happened with our business. Heinrich allowed me to talk and when I finished, he told me about a friend of his who cycled with him. The man was a Zimbabwean farmer who was the owner of one of the largest tobacco and dairy farms in Zimbabwe. However, following Robert Mugabe's attacks on White farmers, he was driven off his farm, which was in his family for more than 150 years. They fled with only the clothes on their bodies. Heinrich suggested that we should meet his friend, as he felt that he would be able to help me understand what I need to do. Renate, Heinrich, and I drove toward Clifton and met with Heinrich's friend, who told us about their ordeal, and how they arrived in Cape Town with nothing and started afresh. He told us about how he valued his wife and the time they have together, and how they take every bit from life they could. "Money", he said, "is not everything." At the end of the discussion, I suggested that Renate and I should return to Pretoria to attend to the challenges we have there, as we had to resolve the Celsius crises before we could return to England, and our departure date home was set for 19 March.

We left Cape Town the following day and our good friend Willie Roets picked us up from the airport and took us to the African Butler outside Pretoria. We spent a day on the farm relaxing next to the swimming pool, working out in my head what to do. By the end of that day, I had a plan. That evening, back at my parent's home, Renate and I had one of our famous bed parliaments, where we discuss the challenges of Celsius as in the past, but with a clear resolution. We agreed that we would call Harry and our East London partners to do a deal, to buy our interest for a nominal amount but to save the business from going under, resulting in massive job losses. The next morning, the proposal was tabled and a deal agreed. Again, my old friend Harry saved the day. In years to come, they made good money out of Celsius, and whilst some may think we sold our share for too little, I have peace in my mind that we got what we asked for.

On 19 March, I boarded the plane 'home', and it was the first time that I truly considered England as 'home'. I just wanted to get back to our house, the cats, and back to work. This had been the worst holiday ever. Renate stayed another week to spend some time with her mum and friends. I was relieved to be back at work and focus all my attentions on what needed to be done during the day, and at night, I spent my time with our cats. A week later, Renate joined me in England, and by that time, she was also glad to be coming 'home'.

* * *

The following week, our stresses were reduced with Renate being offered a post in Communications at the Blackpool Victoria Hospital. The post was a part-time role, but the salary was better, the hours much better, and like the old days, Renate and I worked together, for the same employer, in the same building, and even on the same floor. The future looked a great deal better.

By the end of March, the former Deputy Director of HR at the hospital was appointed and accepted the post of Director HR & OD at another hospital, and Nick invited expressions of interests to act up as Assistant Director of HR. Emma Dawkins, who at the time was the Acting Deputy Director of HR, indicated that she would be interested in the interim role as Acting Assistant Director of OD. None of the HRBP's in the team wanted to put their name in the hat, so I put my name forward for the role as Acting Assistant Director of HR. Who would have thought, on 12 April 2010, I got it!

This appointment meant that Renate and I met all our requirements for the renewal of our Tier 1 visa in February 2012, provided that we remained employed. We were now both suitably employed which alleviated a huge amount of stress. The gamble we took with the posts from both Stoke-on-Trent and Leeds, respectively, seems to have paid off. Renate and I decided to reward ourselves and booked a holiday for October for my birthday to the Kuredu Island in the Maldives.

The next two months, Renate and I dedicated all our time and effort to our new roles. Trying to learn and understand as much about the NHS as we possibly could, building relationships, and trying to forget the experiences of South Africa in March. When asked about our time in Pretoria and Cape Town, we gave positive and polite answers but refrained from going into detail. All I confirmed was that Celsius was about to be sold and that we hoped to sign the final papers around September, nothing more.

In July, Renate and I went for a week city break to Vienna, Austria. We stayed in the 'Hotel Mozart', a hotel incidentally owed by a Namibian family. We travelled on the city trams, walked, cycled on the banks for the Danu River and took a leisurely boat cruise around the city. We visited the Castles of the Habsburg Family and visited the catacombs underneath a church in the city centre. Here we viewed coffins of the dead members of the monarchy in Austria that dates as far back as the late 1400. This is the same place where Keizer Franz Josef and Keizerin Elizabeth (Sissi) were buried. We also visited the Royal Palace, Schonbrunn or 'Beautiful Fountain' residents of the Habsburg family in Vienna, where Franz Josef and Sissi lived. We walked the corridors where Marie Antoinette, the youngest sister of Franz Josef, grew up before she was married off to Louis XVII, the Dauphin of France in 1770.

The history so reach and tangible it is difficult to describe. We visited the wine lands on the outer skirts of the city and spent a day at a swimming pool retreat on top of the mountains just outside the city. We walked in forests, and got lost. We played our own 'Sound of Music' and visited Mozart's' home. We attended Mozart's Requiem performed at St. Charles' Church.

Renate and I went for coffee at the famous Sacher Hotel behind the Vienna Opera House. We visited the Vienna Opera House, and I even walked on the great stage. I wondered what my mum would have said if she saw this beautiful place of opera. I asked Renate to take me back to the Vienna Opera House for my 50th birthday. *It should be a memorable and special birthday!* The gardens in Vienna were beautiful, the people in Vienna were beautiful, and the food, wine and delicatessens in Vienna were beautiful. Life in Vienna was beautiful. A city where Renate and I would return to any day. By far, our favourite city in Europe.

On returning to Manchester, we had to fly from Vienna via Munich, and missed our connecting flight due to thunderstorms over Germany. We were given accommodation and restaurant vouchers for dinner and met Graeme Maylor, a very pleasant lad from Liverpool, who was also stranded by the same flight. We went for dinner in the Munich Airport which looked like a massive shopping centre rather than an airport. We eventually ended up in our hotel and at 6:00 the next morning, we were up and en route to Manchester, back to reality.

On Monday, 26 July, my parents arrived to visit us in Lytham and on Wednesday, 28 July, we celebrated my Dad's 82nd birthday. Friday afternoon after work, I drove to Manchester Airport and collected Manual Friedman, a German friend of ours from Bad Saulgau. My parents did not know that Manu was coming and were very pleasantly surprised. That weekend, we drove to the Lake District and enjoyed lunch at Windermere and a boat-cruise on this beautiful and picturesque lake. At the end of the weekend, we drove to

Manchester Airport to drop off Manual, and on Monday, it was back to work for me and Renate. The next week, my parents took the train to Peterborough to visit family of ours, PG and Bessie de Jager. The following weekend, we took the train to Edinburgh to the 60th Annual Edinburgh Military Taptoo. That Saturday, before the evening show, we saw 1000 pipers walking the Royal Mile playing bagpipes. At nightfall, we attended the world famous and historic military Taptoo. It was absolutely fantastic, with magnificent music, artistic displays, and fireworks. I was really proud to be able to share that evening specifically with my dad.

Sunday, we headed back home and Monday were back to work. We were worried that my parents would be stranded in our house when we were at work, but they took the bus and travelled to Preston, Poulton-le-Fylde, and even came to visit us at the Blackpool Victoria Hospital for lunch. After three weeks of visiting, they went back to South Africa. It was wonderful to have them with us and a trip I hope they would make in time to come again.

Taking into account that it is very difficult for South Africans to get a Schengen Visa to gain access to Europe, as the United Kingdom is not a signatory to the Schengen Treaty and does not have open borders like the rest of the European Union countries, when we planned our trip to Austria, we had to travel to London and applied for a multi-entry visa. Although we requested a six months' visa, we were delighted that we were granted a three month, multi-entry visa. So we had to make full use of our visa, and as the end of August had a traditional public holiday weekend, we decided to visit old friends from South Africa who now stayed in Frankfurt a Main.

During August, we contacted Liahn and Bennie and invited them to join Renate and me for a weekend to Salzburg. We intended to visit the Strobel Family, whom we had been visiting since 1999 whenever we were in Austria. So on Thursday, 26 August, we flew to Frankfurt and stayed the night at Liahn and Bennie's flat. Early on Friday morning, we all got on the train and spent the entire day traveling to Salzburg. We enjoyed catching up drinking, German coffee, and later in the afternoon, sipping Austrian wine whilst enjoying the beautiful countryside en route to Salzburg. We arrived in Salzburg in late afternoon where we rented a car and drove to the Bodensee to the house of Fanni Strobel. It was so good to see Fanni, her daughter Renate and son Peter. Renate and I last visited the Strobel Family in 2007 when Fanni's husband, Peter, was still alive, and my father joined us following his marriage to his wife, at the tender age of 80, when they joined us on a tour to Germany and Austria.

That weekend, the four of us, Renate, Bennie, Liahn and I, spent the days driving through the beautiful mountains visiting Lake Wolfgang. Friday evening, we spent at Fanni's house, enjoying a true German dinner and beer, followed by homemade nut and plum schnapps. Saturday morning both Liahn and Bennie were a bit fragile, and took some time to recover, but by the afternoon, we visited St. Gilgen, the town in the mountains, where Mozart's mother was born. On our way home, we went shopping for our evening dinner of cold meats, breads, champagne, and schnapps. The Saturday evening, Austria had their folk-music festival on television and a lifelong impression was made on us when the second runner up performed their '*Was macht das Edelweiss in meine zuppe trin...*'[59]. We held our own music festival and whilst the two Renate's with Bennie and Liahn provided hours of entertainment, Fanni and I played judges over the talent competition. Sunday we had to say our good buys and start the train trip back to Frankfurt, where we stayed with Bennie and Liahn before flying back to Manchester. A wonderfully memorable weekend.

* * *

Towards the end of September, as was agreed in March, I had to return to South Africa to finalise the sale of our interest in Celsius and formally hand over the management of the business to True Group. Again, I stayed with my parents, and the week in Pretoria was much more relaxed than what our visit was in March. I chaired my last financial and operational review with all the unit General Managers and Operational Managers in attendance. True Group had their representative in attendance and I had the opportunity to do a hand-over of management and staff. At that point, the only remaining issue that needed conclusion was a court case that was pending to take place during 2011, which I agreed to attend in support of Celsius' claim against a rouge client. Again I was grateful when I could return home to Renate and the cats.

* * *

Mid-October, the winter was clearly on its way, and as the winter came, so did our long awaited holiday to the Maldives. This was a dream come true for Renate and me, as we always wanted to visit the Maldives, and that moment was upon us. We flew from Manchester to Malé from where we took a seaplane to Kuredu Island. The brochure described Kuredu Island Resort as:

"One of the larger resorts in the Lhaniyani Atoll, and area famous for its abundant fish life. Situated 80 miles north of the International Airport and 35 minutes by seaplane, Kuredu Island is protected by one of the best house reefs in the country and has more than 3 km of white beaches and lagoons. With a glorious setting and a range of facilities, there is something for everyone. With a golf course, dive centre, water sports and beach activities, Kuredu Island Resort is an ideal choice for those seeking the joys of the sea in an informal and relaxed atmosphere..."

---

[59] Volxrock – *https://www.youtube.com/watch?v=IjqPDioHfwQ* [accessed 9/12/16]

This was a wonderful week, in fact, just too short. We spent our evenings listening to island music, dancing on a sand dance floor and practicing our best island rhythms. The days were spent in the sun, with too much food for one person to consume, and the best margaritas I tasted in a long time. We booked ourselves into the island spa and enjoyed the most wonderful treatments imaginable. The water was crystal clear, with spectacular snorkelling. The vistas in and around the island were breathtaking. At sunset one of the days, Renate turned me into a brochure model and made me swim up and down the length of a swimming pool, until she had the perfect photo. There was not a worry in the world that touched us. We celebrated my birthday with a dinner on the beach, sipping South African Chardonnay as the moon came up over the sea, enjoying wonderful seafood in a light but pleasant island breeze.

We met lovely people on the island. A honeymoon couple from Cape Town and two very nice couples from the UK. I enjoyed reading James A Michener's *The Source* and spent quality time with my lovely wife and best friend. We walked on the miles and miles of beaches, enjoying the company of a baby sand shark and young stingrays playing in the shallow waters.

During this holiday, as with so many of our choices we have made, Renate and I agreed that when we returned home, I was going to enrol to study my LLB, something I always wanted to do but never managed to do, and now the time had come.

As the seaplane lift off from the water runway in front of the island and Kuredu Island Resort became smaller and smaller below us, Renate quietly shed a tear for leaving this beautiful sun drenched island resort with its spectacularly friendly people. Returning home, I looked like a Mars Bar; I don't think I have ever been so brown than after our holiday to the Maldives.

* * *

On returning in early November, winter was clearly in full swing, and the annual Celebrations Ball of the Trust was taking place on the 4th of November in the Blackpool Tower Ball Room, the same place where the 2009 Royal Variety Show took place. Renate was wearing a beautiful brown dress and I was in my tux. We looked healthy, relaxed, and not a worry in the world.

I received my study material for my first seven modules for my first year of LLB; it looked interesting yet a daunting task. I decided not to say anything about my academic aspirations, as I first wanted to see if I could master this Achilles hill.

* * *

Unlike the year before, when the snow started on the 16th of December across the North West of England, this year it started falling at the end of November. I had to travel to Leeds for a coaching session with Jakey Green at Leeds University Hospital. I never made it to her office as the entire city of Leeds was snowed in. No taxi, bus, or any other form of transport could move in the city. It was so cold that after arriving at Leeds station, I struggled to get to a Marks & Spencer's to buy my first English ('Andy Cap') hat. After I bought my hat, I made my way back to the station only to have to wait for about an hour as the train-driver, who had to take the train back to Preston, could not get to the station as he was snowed out. Eventually, I spent my day on the train writing a short story, titled, 'A Letter to my Daughter'. (See Chapter 26).

* * *

Two weeks later when South Africa celebrated the 'Day of the Covenant' on the 16 December, the snow covered the earth in Lytham with a beautiful white blanket. Christmas was upon us and the time for us to go to visit our parents and friends in South Africa had come. However, the snow started to cause havoc with airlines and Heathrow was the first airport to close. Flights were delayed with more and more people stranded at airport buildings. At one point, around 19 December, there were over one million people stranded inside Heathrow airport. Eventually, the day before our flight had to depart from Manchester, we were told that the flight had been cancelled due to bad weather. This was devastating, as with all the drama we had earlier in the year in Pretoria, we wanted to spend Christmas with our parents and planned to spend the 24th with Renate's mum, enjoying a traditional German Christmas, and the 25th with my parents and siblings. This soon became only a dream. As the airline cancelled our flight, they refunded us in full. Trying to get new flights that didn't go through Heathrow, as our closest airport was Manchester, and was not closed on account of the weather, was a difficult task. Eventually, we managed to get tickets with Swiss Air but the departure date eventually was Christmas Eve.

It soon became clear that whilst we considered 2010 to be a year filled with both adventures and trepidations, not in our wildest dreams did we anticipate that we would spent Christmas Eve in airports and planes. However, while saying that, the food on Swiss Air was wonderful, the service was wonderful, and the fact that we made it to South Africa, albeit only arriving at lunchtime on 25 December, was wonderful.

We were grateful that we were able to spend the time with family and friends, and especially the fact that we could go back to Cape Town for a week, with our old friend Willie, to face my demons of March. We stayed in the same apartment, and I reflected on all the emotions of the past year. We visited Heinrich and friends from the Stadtmission in Cape Town. Considering the ups and downs of all that 2010 brought, we made peace with the fact that there was more to life than money. Don't get me wrong, it would have been nice if we made millions from Celsius, but we didn't; she served us well, we travelled the world, and created employment opportunities for more than 450 people. We had peace that Celsius, now in the True Group camp, was in good hands. Renate and I were in a better place than where we have been before, and 2011 promised to bring new adventures, new challenges, and a brighter future.

As we spent Christmas day with my family in glorious 30 degrees Celsius under the African sun, we thanked God for all the blessings that He brought over our lives during that year and prayed that 2011 would bring new blessings, adventures, and good health.

Chapter 25
International Politics, Ill Health and the English Riviera

The beginning of 2011 started with good news when we received my results of the first year of my LLB and was advised that I passed 2010 with a distinction. The first in my academic career!

This year truly was a year to remember. Reflecting on the past twelve months, it is amazing what happened both in Renate and my lives, but also in the world generally. It all started on the 14th of January, when the 'Arab awakening' inspired the people of Tunisia to oust their President following weeks of unrest. This was quickly followed by unrests in both Libya and Egypt, as the people of these countries increasingly got fed-up with their oppressive governments. I must confess, this sparked a bit of hope in my heart for places like Zimbabwe.

In February, I started with European Law and was assigned to a tutorial group in Liverpool. Renate travelled a few times to Liverpool with me, and whilst I was in the tutorial, she explored the shops of the city. Our tutor was Paul Flodman, an ex-policeman and expert on European Law – an interesting man, but more about him later.

Renate continued to enjoy her role in Communications at the hospital; however, massive restructurings were required due to the recession and the financial challenges of the country. In March, we embarked on an ambitious restructuring intervention at the hospital with just over 640 posts identified to be made redundant within the next financial year.

These restructurings also created opportunities, and it emerged that Renate's role could become permanent while my role was also under review.

At the beginning of April, we received a call from a friend of Renate in Pretoria. She informed us that Ma Helga, Renate's mum, was very ill with pneumonia and was in ICU. We were obviously concerned but were reassured that our friend would keep us posted on her progress. I tried to contact Ma Helga's Doctor to find out what was going on, but the receptionist refused to provide us with any information in fear of breach of patient confidentiality. Eventually after two failed attempts to speak to her in person, I wrote to her instead. On Tuesday, 12 April 2011, we received an email from Ma Helga's doctor confirming that they have conducted preliminary tests, and in addition to being a diabetic she also suffered with a variety of serious complications including possibly cancer. Needless to say, this came as a massive shock, as it was only a week ago that Renate spoke to her mum who said that she was fine, a bit of bronchitis, but fine nevertheless. The big challenge for us, however, was that the doctor also asked us to come to South Africa, as she proposed that they had to operate, but indicated that Ma Helga's prognosis was very poor, due to all the complicating factors.

This caused massive stress for both Renate and me, as we could not afford to be away from work at that point in time, taking into account all the changes that were busy unfolding at the Trust. However, both our respective line managers agreed that we could go to South Africa, and we found tickets on Swiss Air to travel. We landed in Johannesburg late on Friday afternoon, 15 April, and went straight to the hospital. Ma Helga looked surprise, and whilst she was irritated that her friend and the doctor told us what was going on, she was pleased that we came. Ma Helga had lost a lot of weight and looked very frail. Renate and I were really shocked. That weekend, we spent all of our time with her and after Ma Helga indicated that we should speak to the doctor to hear first-hand what needed to be done, Renate confirmed an appointment for us the following Monday.

During the weekend, we went to Ma Helga's home to check on the cats and her dog who were looked after by a family friend. Irrespective of what the doctor was to tell us on Monday, it became quickly clear that Ma Helga was no longer capable to look after her house. We realised that the time had come that she would require specialist care. However, we did not approach this subject, as we knew how sensitive this would be. We spent the balance of the weekend at the hospital and tried to be as positive and supportive as possible, while allowing Ma Helga to instruct us on what she wanted us to do.

After the visit to the doctor on Monday, 18 April, she confirmed that Renate's mum had an obstruction, which she suspected to be cancerous. The only way to determine the true state of her health was to operate. However, taking her frail condition into account, they were concerned that her lungs would not be able to cope with the anaesthetic. The fact that she was diabetic also did not help. To add to these complications, they discovered an aneurism on her aorta. The options for us to consider were that if they do nothing, Renate's mum would die, potentially a long and painful death; if they operated, she could die on the table but had a chance to survive. The doctor confirmed that subject to what my mother-in-law decided, she would require post-op care and could not live on her own. Renate and I went back to the hospital and shared these facts with her mum to get an idea of what she wanted to do. Ma Helga said that if her time had come, then so be it, and indicated that the operation should go ahead. In the meantime, Renate and I started to look for space in old age homes and visited a number of facilities but were unsuccessful in finding a place, with some places having waiting lists of over ten years! Care homes in South Africa is a great scarcity and if found, very expensive.

We debated what best to do after the operation and it was agreed that we should look for a place of care where her mum could recover. Renate's Aunt found a room for her in a retirement home, and we put that forward as an option. However, we braced ourselves as we touched on the subject of the house and the animals. To our surprise, Renate's mum agreed to go to Ermelo and indicated that we should try and find a home for the animals, and if all else fails, should put the cats down. She advised Renate where her Will was and agreed to sign a power of attorney in favour of her daughter, should anything happen. With regard to the house and its contents, she instructed us to clear the house, except for a short list of items that she wanted to take with her to Ermelo.

The following Monday afternoon at 4:00, I started working on clearing and sorting the house in Capital Park. Later that evening, Renate joined me, and we worked until nearly 10:00 at night when we drove back to the East of Pretoria to my parents. Tuesday we spent the morning at the hospital and were just in time to speak to Renate's mum before they gave her pre-op medication. It did not take long before she was out. We stayed with her and walked with her to the Theatre. While waiting for her to go in, the Specialist came to talk to us and indicated that if he feels that her blood pressure was taking too much strain, with the constant threat of the aneurism, they could abort the operation before its completion.

Renate and I waited. Later my sister Suzanne came to the hospital and kindly waited with us. The first two hours were the worst. We knew if they have not aborted the operation by then, then there was hope. After three and a half hours, they pushed my mother-in-law out of theatre and declared the operation a success. She was breathing on her own and while in immense pain, she was all right. The doctor predicted that Ma Helga would go to ICU after the operation, but she was transferred to the High Care Unit and responded to us. Both Renate and I were relieved. We returned to the house and spent the next three days working at the house from early morning until late at night.

It is truly the most difficult thing to clear someone else's house, something I do not wish on anyone. I called Nick Grimshaw, our Director of HR at the hospital, to ask if I could stay an additional week to help Renate, but he was not keen for me to be away from work for such a long period of time, so I had to get back to England by the next Friday. We had three days to sort out the house. To add insult to injury, it was Easter, and South Africa, like most of the Christian world, comes to a standstill during this time. We had to pay a premium for cleaners, painters, and furniture removers. I called on a number of our friends in Pretoria who kindly agreed to come and help us to clear the garage, and the balance of the stuff in the house. By sunset on Thursday afternoon, the house was just about empty, nearly ready to be cleaned, re-painted, and placed on the market.

That night, a friend of ours called to say that she knew of a two-bedroom home in Amandasig Retirement Village in Pretoria and if we wanted it, we could have it immediately. We arranged to go and view the place at 10:00 that night and took it. We felt it would be easier for Ma Helga to recover in Pretoria. It was closer to her friends, my parents, and when we came to visit, we would not have to drive out to Ermelo to see her. My father's wife, was managing a frail-care home at the time and kindly agreed that Ma Helga could come to her for a couple of weeks. I had to return to South Africa in any event in a couple of weeks' time to testify in a court case for Celsius.

That Friday night, I said my goodbyes to Ma Helga, Renate, and my parents and flew back to England. Leaving Renate to oversee her mum's transfer from hospital to the care-home, from where I would collect her in four weeks' time to re-settle her in Amandasig. I was exhausted but relieved. I again realised what wonderful friends we have in South Africa. They sacrificed key parts of their long-weekend to help Renate and me sort out the house and everything associated with it. Although the support from family and friends during this time was absolutely wonderful. Renate stayed for another week, overseeing the cleaning of the carpets in the house, the re-painting inside, and preparing the house at Amandasig to ensure that everything was ready for her mum's arrival in May.

* * *

The long talk about Royal Wedding eventually took place on 29 April, which seemed to give the world a reprieve of all its madness. For a brief moment, everyone focused on the fairytale love story of Prince William and Kate Middleton. However, this was followed by an announcement by President Obama on 2 May when he confirmed that Osama Bin Laden was shot dead by US operational forces, while hiding out in a compound in Abbottabad, Pakistan.

* * *

Back at the Blackpool Victoria Hospital, I attended an interview on 5 May for the post of Deputy Director of Human Resources at the hospital and was told that evening that I was successful. Renate returned on 9 May, and we had to refocus our attention to the events at work but were relieved to know that her mum was discharged from the hospital and recovering at the care home. According to my dad, she was doing exceptionally well.

* * *

In addition to the proposed restructurings we were working on at the hospital, an additional proposal was being worked on to incorporate two community health care service providers, which would effectively increase the head-count of our hospital with an additional 1600 people to a total of 5000 people. With government's intention to run the NHS more like a business, rather than a public sector service provider, it was important for us to be successful in this bid and all plans were that we would take over the two community Trust's by 1 October 2010.

* * *

I returned to South Africa on 20 May in preparation for the Celsius court case. My first stop in Pretoria, however, was at the care home, where Ma Helga was recovering. I was very impressed with her recovery, although still very thin and frail, she was clearly much stronger and better than what she was when I saw her a couple of weeks earlier. I took her to Amandasig and quickly realised that she was much better than what we thought. She quickly regained her feistiness, so I knew she would be all right. We arranged with Willie's sister to come and live with her to help for a four-week period. As the court case was not concluded, but postponed, I returned to England.

On returning to England, I brought Renate's aunt, Karin, with me to stay with us for the next six months. Karin has learning difficulties. It was absolutely fantastic to have her with us, as she only saw the beauty in life, loved unconditionally, laughed uncontrollably, never regretted anything, she made us smile, and taught us to be thankful for all the gifts and graces we have been granted. She heralded in the beginning of a wonderful six months of our lives.

Renate attended her interview for a permanent post on 1 June and was confirmed as the new Volunteers Coordinator and Community Engagement Officer of the Trust. In this role, she was responsible for the day to day management of 350 volunteers working at the hospital. We were both very pleased, and taking into account that our UK Visa applications were due for renewal in February 2012, it could not have come at a better time. This placed us in a good position in meeting the balance of the UKBA requirements to ensure a successful extension of our visas in the UK.

On 13 July, Renate, Karin and I attended my Graduation Ceremony where I received my master's degree from the University of Central Lancashire. As I sat in the auditorium waiting for the proceedings to commence, I could not help in feeling so incredibly grateful that I had the opportunity to study and complete my master's. The dissertation, dedicated to my father, considered the impact of a matrix approach to project management in delivering change within an NHS organization, something I could not have done without Renate's support. That day, while enjoying every moment of the event, I thought of my mum, and thought that if she were there, she would have been proud.

The following week, Renate, Karin, and I left on vacation to what we were told is the English Riviera. We travelled south to see Graham and Megan Vass at Cheltenham and explored the villages of the Cotswolds. From there, we visited Bath and did an open-top-bus tour of this beautiful city. Eventually, we arrived in Torque, in the "English Riviera". We spent a couple of days exploring the town and surrounding villages. After three days, we made our way toward London, via the historic Stonehenge. It was absolutely spectacular to see and experience these ancient stones, and as Graham so correctly predicted, at the end of our tour of Stonehenge, we would still not know where the stones came from, who brought them, how they were transported and planted, nor what their purpose was. What we did know was that they were a historic marvel and a visit that all three of us would remember for life. From Stonehenge, we set off to Seven Oaks, south of London. On arriving there, we took a brief detour to Tonbridge, the twin town of Heusenstamm, Renate's late father's hometown in Germany. We stayed in Seven Oaks for three days and took the train into London every day. We spent half a day in the South African Consul to apply for new South African passports, as our passports were nearly full. We visited Buckingham Palace, Westminster Abbey, Big Ben, saw the Houses of Parliament, and Clarence House. The latter is where HRH Prince Charles and Camilla, the Duchess of Cornwall, stay when they are in London. We took an open-top bus tour and saw Kensington Palace and its gardens, the former home of Diana, Princes of Wales, and discovered a huge variety of places we never would have seen were we on foot. The last evening in London, Karin was so exhausted that she fell asleep on the train back to Seven Oaks. After our time in London, we started the long trek back to the North West, but drove via Oxford where we spent the mid-morning walking through this beautiful University Town. The closest comparison to a South Africa university city would be Stellenbosch or Potchefstroom in mid-summer, definitely a town Renate and I agreed to visit in time to come.

The trip to the south opened our eyes to the beauty of this Island nation and we agreed that if it was our destiny to stay in the United Kingdom, then we would endeavour to find a suitable position in Devon, like Plymouth, in time to come. That part of the world reminded of the rolling hills of Kwa-Zulu Natal, absolutely beautiful.

* * *

Since February that year, I suffered from a blocked submandibular gland, which, due to a 5mm stone inside it was decided that the gland needed to be removed surgically. This was done on 20 September, and after three days in the hospital, I recovered at home. Karin was a caring nurse ensuring that I have sufficient coffee and tea to enjoy. I used some of my time at home to study in preparation for my European Law exams that were set for 13 October. I recovered fully and returned to work a bit earlier than what the doctor wished.

I wrote my exam and as my father said, "I did my part; I just hope the lecturer would do his." Paul Flodman, our tutor, was such a remarkable lecturer, he made European Law interesting and alive, and I managed to start the exams with a year mark of over 70%. I was optimistic.

* * *

On 25 October, I submitted a 4000-word short story, titled *'A Letter to my Daughter'*, to the Brit Writers Awards (see Chapter 26).

November was upon us, and on 4 November, Renate and I attended the Trust annual celebration ball, which again proved to be a huge success. The next day, however, Renate, Karin, and I departed for South Africa. Sadly, Karin's time had come to an end, and the six months that she was with us were over. Both Renate and I, and indeed our cats, would miss Karin very much as she became such an important part of our lives, a breath of fresh air in our home.

Our first week in South Africa was spent with my parents and Renate's mum, respectively. We had a spectacular lunch with my fathers' brothers and his sister, the latter being a very glamorous 89-year-old. I had the opportunity to talk to my uncles about the politics and history of South Africa. We enjoyed a very insightful debate about the politics of the day, Alan Elsdon's book *'The Tall Assassin' (Die Lang Generaal)* and a book that I bought titled *'I Write What I Like'* by Steve Biko. Imagine the debate. Reflecting on the lunch and discussions with my dad and uncles, I can only say it was a memorable lunch with the elders of my family. The second week of our vacation, Renate and I spent a week on the *African Butler*, with Willie, a privately owned and managed game farm, and just enjoyed the beauty of Africa. Although we managed to see a few of our friends in South Africa, time was just too short, and before we knew it, we were heading back to the cold and dark winter awaiting us in England for Christmas.

* * *

At the beginning of December, we received the terrible news that Paul Flodman, my European Law tutor, died suddenly of a heart attack.

On 5 December, Renate and I attended our first Royal Variety Show in Manchester, which was performed in the company of HRH Princess Ann, the Princess Royal, in celebration of our 15th wedding anniversary. The following week, I received the good news that I passed my European Law exam, and whilst I did not get a distinction, I was still happy with the results.

As Christmas drew closer, we anticipated the beginning of yet another snow-covered UK, as it was predicted that this winter would be worse than the previous two.

On Christmas Eve, Renate and I hosted a dinner at our house with friends staying in Lytham but who originated from Cape Town, and following the church service on the 25th, we enjoyed a spectacular Christmas dinner at Ponti's house with Carla, Stefan, Renita and partners in attendance. We ate, sang *'Dreaming of a White Christmas'*, and enjoyed the most memorable Christmas in England thus far.

As 2011 drew to a close and we reflected on the previous twelve months, we thought that, generally, 2011 had been a good and blessed year for us, albeit not a good year for the world economy, politics, or world peace. However, our parents were well, healthy and happy. Father Christmas brought an invitation for Ma Helga to come and visit us and I sincerely hoped she would accept this invite during the summer of 2012.

Chapter 26
A Letter to My Daughter

On a train in York, while being delayed by snow and waiting for an absent train driver, I reflected on that day your mother and I decided it was time to start a family. We were married for just over a year, living in a renovated railway house in East London, in the Eastern Cape, South Africa.

I was 31 years old and mum five years younger. The timing was perfect, we both had excellent jobs at the time, we were well-settled in our roles as husband and wife, and we had a lovely two bedroom house, situated on a large piece of land. The house was positioned in the front of the yard with a big garden to the back. We had two dogs, a Labrador called Wolfgang and an Alsatian puppy called Tessa; and three cats Molly, Nuschka, and Bishop (or Bischi). Bischi was a young kitten and destined to become your cat in time to come. Our home was ready, our yard had plenty of space, and our pets were set to welcome you into our home.

It was a summer's day in 1987, mum and I had a barbeque in the garden, and Wolfgang was slightly irritated with Tessa as he viewed her to be a busy and annoying puppy. Nuschka visited the old lady next door more than what she stayed with us and Molly did not like the fact that there was another dog in the house. When the dog activities became too much for her, she sought sanctuary in one of the large trees in front of the house. Bischi was always at home, a young inquisitive kitten, a beautiful cat. Mum and I watched the sun set while the dogs played in the garden. Bischi was sleeping on Mum's lap, purring happily. Suddenly, mum said, "I think we should start a family." I was ecstatic. I really wanted to have children, be a good father, to provide our children with a happy home and opportunities that will enable them to achieve their wildest dreams. I always dreamed to have four children, hopefully I thought, before my thirtieth birthday; however, this was not meant to be. Hearing mum's suggestion was fantastic. It did not matter that I was over thirty already; we were both young enough and the time could not have been better. The thought of you coming into our lives were electrifying.

That evening, after mum's great announcement, I thought of writing you a letter, a welcome note to our lives if you will, a letter of introduction to our family. I was so proud, just thinking of becoming your dad was a spectacular thought. I wanted to give you a glimpse into my thoughts and emotions prior to your birth. What I thought, what I imagined for you. That evening, while mum was asleep, I looked at her, listed to her voice, slowly breathing as she wondered in the garden of her dreams. While she was picking flowers in her dreams, I composed a letter for you in my head. I thought how you might look and try to visualise your beautiful face, even before you were born. Mum is beautiful, you know, and I am not bad looking either. So it was not difficult to imagine that you will be a beautiful girl, exquisite, elegant and graceful, like your mother. I imagined that you'd have her build, her features and sense of humour. I also imagined that you would have my sense of adventure, both your grandmother's talent for music and the arts, the one granddad's ability to keep family together, and the other's ability to laugh. In fact, all four of your grandparents loved to laugh. An excellent characteristic, in time to come you will learn that laughter is good for the soul. Secretly, I imagined that you will have my hair and knew that you would thank me for this in time to come.

Molly came into our room and saw Nuschka and Bischi sleeping on the end of the bed. She jumped up and nestled herself in mum's arm. The dogs were also sleeping quietly somewhere in the house. Everything was quiet and peaceful.

My thoughts got distracted and I wondered how you would react toward all the animals in the house. As both your parents were animal lovers, I knew you would have a natural instinct toward animals. I considered how Wolfgang would be your playmate; Tessa would grow up to be your protector. Molly, I regret to admit, would initially tolerate you with some level of irritation, but in years to come would accept and love you as an important member of our family. As you grow up, Nuschka would come and sleep with you rather than with us, and Bischi would be your cat. These thoughts pleased me and I was content that our family was ready to fall into place.

I briefly reflected why I thought that you would be a girl as the eldest, as both my brothers had boys. Only my sister had daughters, and I made a calculation that rationalised this for me in a perfect mathematical manner, at least in my own mind it did. There was a difference of six days difference in birth between me and my eldest brother. He was born on 19 October and I on 25 October, and then six days' difference between my sister and my brother just older than me. She was born on 15 June and he was born on 21 June, be it that there were ten years between the eldest and the youngest, and five years between my sister and brother (the middle two). So I calculated that as the oldest and youngest were six days apart and the middle two were six days apart, it would follow that if the eldest first child was a boy, the second sibling, my sister's first born was a girl, and as my other brother's first born was a boy, it is natural that as I was the youngest, and based on the above calculation, my firstborn was definitely going to be a girl. There you have it, that's how I did it. I drifted off with a smile on my face, as I realised how silly this rationale must sound. It did not matter as both mum and I, and I hoped the pets, as well, were happy that you were on your way.

An old friend of mine, who claimed to have been knowledgeable of Buddhism, told us that prior to the birth of a child, the spirit of that child came to visit its future parents, to see if they are indeed the correct parents for him or her. My last thoughts that night were wondering if you have been to visit us, to see your future home and room, your parents and pets, and wondered if you approved. "Of course, you did," I said, as I helped mum lifting her basket of flowers that by now was full to capacity.

Over the next couple of weeks, I often reflected on the letter I wrote to you in my head, altering it, adding new thoughts, and deleting the bits I knew made no sense. I had to get it right. I could not put to paper, write to you your very first letter, if the content was not 100% correct. I wanted it to be a masterpiece. Something you would read in years to come, perhaps read to your children, and with a smile on your face proclaim to their eager minds that "Granddad wrote me this letter long before I was born, to welcome me into their home and to help me understand how special I am in their lives," perhaps adding, "This inspired me to write your letter to the two of you, and I hope one day when you have children of your own, that you would do the same for your children." You see, it was so important for me that your letter was perfect, as I hoped to create a legacy, a family tradition, if you will, that I could not afford to mess up. It had to be right. So I continued to amend, improve, and update the letter that was lying on the study table in my head.

Six months went by, and month after month I waited for the news that you gave your nod of approval, that you came to look at our home, your room, at us your parents and our pets, and that you approved by giving notice of your intention to arrive in nine months' time. However, our eagerness to welcome you in our home was not yet to be satisfied.

With the turn of the millennium, we stayed in another city in a different province or county, in a bigger house with four bedrooms, within a lush garden in the front of the house and a beautiful swimming pool toward the back. There was plenty of space for you to play, to learn how to swim, to paint in the garden, and to play your piano. Everything was ready for you.

One Sunday evening, I was reading a paper from work; mum was sleeping when I heard a commotion in the street. I went outside, only to discover that our neighbours across the road had been hi-jacked. Their little girl, who was nine at the time, was held at gunpoint while the thugs assaulted her grandmother and then stole their car. As our neighbours were in shock, I offered to take the woman and little girl to the hospital, while the man waited for the police. Mum was very shocked that something so terrible could happen at our front door.

Those were difficult years in South Africa, and in time to come, it would become worse, with an increase in criminal activity and a general disregard for human life. The next weekend, mum and I drove around the new Golf Estate Developments near us and bought a piece of land. Mum designed a beautiful home for us, a beautiful three-bedroom home, situated in a lush garden with a big water fountain. I planted a stunning rose garden and we built a refreshing swimming pool. There was lots of space for

Wolfgang, Tessa and the cats. Mum designed an entire section of the house for you. I thought I'd use it as a study until you came. Once you arrived and grew big enough to have your own room, you would move to the other side of the house. I knew young ladies needed their own space. So we made sure that you would have plenty thereof.

While the house was being built, we stayed with mum's mother. That was the year mum turned thirty and I reached the big thirty-five. We were young enough and had sufficient time, but thought that we would seek some medical help to see if we could entice you to join our happy home. We had to pay a lot of money to have a private in-vitro fertility (IVF) procedure performed. I haven't told you yet but mum is petrified of needles. I hope you don't inherit that from your mother. She truly could faint at the sight of a needle. Don't laugh; it is terrible if someone is so afraid of needles. Anyway, IVF required of mum to have injections every day, for a long period of time. But we were both keen to have you, so the sacrifice was done gladly. One day, following one of the procedures, the doctors showed me some of the embryos that were fertilised, but that were not as good as what you were, and those were not implanted. However, I was amazed to see how the embryos were all at different stages of development. The sells divided 4, 8, 16, 32, 64…it eventually looked like a strawberry. After the procedures, I treated mum like a goddess; she was not allowed to do anything as we wanted to make sure that you, or the embryo representing you at the time, could settle and grow successfully. We had to wait two weeks for the news. The doctors indicated that they would confirm your 'notice of arrival' i.e. that mum was pregnant with you, by phone. When they did not call on the designated time, we called the surgery. The doctors confirmed our worst fear. The IVF did not work. Mum was not pregnant, and you remained a treasure in my heart.

Four years later, I became anxious that time was fast beginning to run out, as my fortieth birthday was uncomfortably close. I did not want to be an old man by the time I could walk you done the isle. As I pondered my age, I imagined you on your wedding day, your lovely long, thick hair beautifully done, your fine-looking dress, you looking radiant, ready to give your hart to the other special man in your life.

Eventually, mum and I wondered if you are to come to us in a different form. Traditionally, families have their own children, but after trying for our own child for so many years, with all the highs and lows that go with it, the rollercoaster had taken its toll. In desperation, we started considering alternatives, and a practical alternative was to explore if we could adopt. We talked with a friend who fostered children from challenged families, and was eventually introduced to an adoption agency. We registered and underwent a number of probing interviews. You would appreciate that when people adopt a baby, the authorities must make sure that the prospective adoptive parents are suitable guardians of a baby who is dependent on the state to act in its best interest. We were deemed very suitable parents, but the challenge was much more complex. As White parents, we wished to adopt a White baby, but living in South Africa at the time, this was not easily achieved. However, we wanted you to join our family and were prepared to be creative in stretching our own parameters. Once we reached agreement that we would be prepared to look at a Black, Asian, or mixed-race child, we faced the challenge of telling our conservative White South African parents. Let me just say the grandparents did not approve. Mum and I were devastated and decided to just allow Mother Nature to take her course.

Just as we decided to stop looking for you, a friend of ours came to visit for Christmas lunch and brought a photo of a six-year-old White girl who was residing in an orphanage and who our friend thought would be a perfect match for both you and us. While looking at your photo, mum and I wondered if this was the way in which you intend to present yourself. A meeting was arranged and we came to visit you. The house had a lot of children, too many children for the house. This served as affirmation of so many sad stories that made its way into the heart of modern day family life. You were shy, but inquisitive, petite, with small features. Your hair was thick, and you sported a gentle smile. We arrange for you to visit us a few days, as the housemother seemed very keen that this worked for you and for us. Mum and I were excited and thought that a 'fast forward' girl was a good solution, considering that we were not as young as when we were at the time we first decided to start a family. Having our little girl at the age of six turned back the clock for us. It settled the books a bit, balancing the age difference there, otherwise, would have been between parent and child. We hoped with enthusiasm that this would set the scene for you to have loving parents and for mum and me to have our dream daughter. Your visits from the start could only be described as difficult. In discussions with the housemother and the social worker, respectively, it became apparent that in your short life, your biological parents treated you with little respect, if any. We learned that your father abused you at so many levels. We discovered that you were neglected, assaulted, and suffered cigarette burns, to mention a few of the horrors that you had to endure in the first few years of your life. This resulted in you developing a deep-rooted distrust in men, generally, and that you could not believe that there are men who are trustworthy, who could give you safety, unconditional love, care, and a happy future. I was sickened to hear that your father allowed your brother to molest you, not to mention the pain you suffered at your father's hands when he burned your little arms. This scarred you physically, but more importantly, the emotional damage this caused was more than what any of the adults around you could understand. A few months later, we arranged for you to come and visit us for a school holiday. We were stunned that the home packed all of your clothes and indicated that after the school holiday, we could enrol you in a local school near us. This, they explained, was due to the fact that your biological mother had not made contact with you for nearly five years, and if that was maintained, the law could allow an adoption without your biological mothers' approval. During your stay with us, I so longed to care for you, to talk with you, to be a father to you. But for reasons I do fully understand, you did not feel safe in the company of a man. You only wanted mum all the time. Only mum could comb your hair, could talk with you, feed you, or walk with you. My dear child, I so regret everything that had happened to you in your short life. By the end of your holiday with us, your biological mother made contact with the home, and as she was within the five-year time frame, it soon became apparent that your adoption would remain a dream, for at least another five years for both you and any prospective adoptive parents. This experience scared both you and us. You, for yet another family you nearly had was lost, as we learned in your short life you had been assigned to a large number of potential families, but with your biological mother refusing to allow a legal adoption, this remained complicated. Us, because for a brief moment had a glimpse of what it would be to have a little girl in our home, and then you were gone.

That December, Bischi disappeared, and our beautiful youngest cat, that was intended to be your cat, vanished from our lives, just like you did, and was no longer part of our family. Mum and I were heartbroken. It was a sad, lonely, and terrible Christmas for mum and I. We remained in contact with you and the home, and I remained hopeful that things would change, that it would work out for the better, for both you and us.

During the next three years, the adoption agency with which we initially registered, sent our application documentation back with a cover note confirming that the waiting list for White babies was longer than three years, and as the list was static for a number of years, they could not add us. They suggested we approach them again in three or four years' time, if indeed we were still interested in adopting a White baby. However, it also came with a note that the agency could not indicate if, in four years' time, the situation would have changed for the better.

During this time, we still had not been graced by your presence, Molly became older and had difficulty eating, Nuschka was also not young anymore, Wolfgang became more and more fearful of loud noises like lightning and thunderstorms, and Tessa became partly blind due to a unique illness often befalling Alsatian breeds. Although our time was generally dedicated to work to keep ourselves busy, the dream to have you became fading with mum dedicating a lot of her time caring for orphan kittens. She raised more than twenty little ones by hand. We found homes for all of them, but one kitten joined our family, with the glamorous name of 'Giggi'. I remained confident though that one day you would come. I knew that we had to remain positive and that there was still hope. I knew we would meet soon.

In the year that mum and I celebrated our tenth wedding anniversary, my mother died. I was especially sad to have lost my mum, as she was a very special lady, and more so, that I really wanted her to meet you and for you to have met her. Later in that same year, Molly, mum's beloved cat, died, and the first day of the next year, my dear Wolfgang died unexpectedly.

Another two years later, mum and I decided that to truly give you the best opportunities, we would probably need to consider moving to another country. We visited Perth, Australia, and when it became clear that we wouldn't be able to move there, we considered Christchurch in New Zealand. We nearly bought a lovely home there but when that fell through, we considered moving to the United Kingdom. Our first application for a visa went missing in the post so that was another year gone. Eventually, in February 2009, we received confirmation that we could move to Britain.

Mum and I became very busy planning our move to the UK. Tessa was very dependent on Wolfgang for guidance, as she was now totally blind, and with Wolfgang gone, we were very worried how she would cope with such a big move. Nuschka and Giggi settled well and became very good friends. We knew they would be fine. A new kitten joined our home, and mum gave him the impressive name of Gucci. During this time, all our attention was focused on our move to the UK. We decided to take the pets with but realised that they would have to go into quarantine for six months. It soon became apparent that Tessa would not be able to join us. We thought it would be cruel to put her through six months of quarantine when she would be in a kennel for such a long period of time all by herself. It was also difficult to give our beloved dog to someone else, due to her unique and special needs. The day we said goodbye to Tessa was particularly sad as both your dogs, which were intended as playmates and protector, were gone.

I often think of both of them, and how they would have reacted when they met you. Wolfgang would have allowed you to pull his ears as you played with him, while Tessa had a gentle air about her; she was such a marvellous nanny to Gucci when he was a very small kitten. I know you would have loved both Wolfie and Tessie very much.

The day we left the country of our birth, we said all our good-buys to family and friends and had sent the cats off to quarantine in the UK for six months. We followed a week after them and arrived at the beginning of spring in England. We had a lot to deal with in our new country, finding new jobs, visiting the cats most weekends, and trying to understand the very strange dialects people spoke in Lancashire. We found the people to be very friendly and the safety in the country refreshing. Everything worked, the trains were on time, the police protective and helpful, and cities much safer than what we were used to. I must confess, though, that those first couple of months were very difficult, and visiting the cats was great as they were happy to see us. Molly, Wolfgang and Tessa often came to visit mum and me in our dreams.

By 2010, both mum and I found good jobs. The cats came home, with Nuschka now 'the old one', Giggi and Gucci fully grown and entertaining each other to our great delight.

At the beginning of winter that year, I had to attend a meeting in Leeds, and the first snow caused havoc in the North and Eastern parts of the country. Trains were delayed and entire cities were frozen to a grinding halt. While I was caught between train delays due to the snow and humbled by both the absolute beauty and brutal force of Mother Nature, I decided to write to you.

'Why?' You may ask, after all these years? After all the mental debates, the dreams, the hopes, why now do I eventually write my long awaited letter to you?

Well, my beautiful little girl, I can tell you why I have spent most of this terribly cold and icy day, reflecting on our relationship over the past thirteen years, and finally penned this letter to you. Firstly, mum and I decided to again explore the possibility of doing three cycles of IVF in an attempt to entice you to join our home. Prior to this decision, we did explore a variety of alternative options like UK adoption and surrogacy. However, adoption in the UK reminded us too much of the pain we experienced with the little girl we had with us for a short while in South Africa, and surrogacy was just too expensive, while the risks generally remained very high. Earlier today, before leaving for Leeds, I received an e-mail from the fertility clinic confirming that because mum and I are now 40 and 45 years old, respectively, we had a very poor chance for success, while the risk to mum's life would be significantly higher due to her age. Lastly, we have used all our savings to emigrate to the UK; mum and I only have twenty years left to build up a new pension for our old age. This prompted me to make the calculation, that if you were to be born during the next year, I would be 67 years old by the time you celebrate your 21st birthday.

So my dearest child, I guess that on this cold, icy, and sad day, I am writing to you to say how much I wanted you in our lives. How difficult it is for me to understand why you were so elusive over the past thirteen years. I am writing to you to reflect on our journey to date.

I could make a last plea, in promising you that we will be good for you. We would love you; give you all you want within our means; we would teach you about all the places we have visited before your arrival, to encourage you to be adventurous, courageous, and willing to learn about various diverse places, peoples, countries, cultures, and languages. But you have heard all of this before; you have seen the tears in my eyes and know about the heaviness of my heart. You have listened to my prayers and pleas in the dark of night. You have witnessed the questions and frustrations and have been party to all of the initiatives mum and I have tried to have you as part of lives. As mum and I love each other very much, are happily married, and content with our lives, I know we would have made a great family. Why you never came, I may never know. Thus, as I cannot force you to come, and time is no longer on our side, not to mention that finances are also not readily available, I suppose my child, I am grieved in writing to you to say goodbye.

Your loving father, Always.

Chapter 27
Good News, Bad News

At around Christmas of 2011, I received an advertisement in my inbox for a post of Director of Human Resources & Organisational Development at Plymouth Hospitals NHS Trust, in Devon.

We agreed that I should apply, and after being shortlisted, I attended the interview on 20 January. I was the second of three candidates. After my presentation, I was bombarded with a variety of industry-related, employment law and human resources strategy questions. However, at the end of the interview, I thought things could have gone either way, as there were some questions that I thought I could have answered better. On completing the interview, Helen O'Shea, the then-Interim Chief Executive, indicated that she would give me a call later. Five hours after I left Plymouth returning home, I arrived back in Preston. Renate collected me from the railway station. At 7:00 PM, the phone rang; it was Helen O'Shea. She started in the traditional NHS manner of thanking me for my application, and giving me some positive feedback, but then indicated that some of the panel members thought that I needed more development. I turned my thumb down to indicate to Renate that I was unsuccessful, while listening to Helen's feedback. At the end of the conversation, she indicated that whilst she thought that I did very well and understood that I needed some development, she would be happy to offer me the post and to support me with those development areas. I thanked her for her support, and only once I terminated the conversation did I indicate to Renate that I was offered the job. We were both ecstatic.

* * *

Our excitement was dampened a week later when I received a note from Gillian Wood, a very dear friend of ours, who worked with me at Nestle South Africa. She confirmed that her husband died unexpectedly in Perth, Australia. We were speechless. Needless to say, I did not share my good news with her at that time, as she had enough to deal with.

* * *

On 18 February 2012, Renate and I wrote our International English Language Tests (IELTS) exams to see if we may qualify for an Australian work visa. As part of the verbal testing, we needed to talk about an older inspirational person; I choose my dad, and Renate talked about our mutual friend Willie Roets. This prompted us to try and phone Willie, as we knew that he fell ill with what he described as flu on the 26 December 2011. We had not spoken to him in recent weeks and were not successful in reaching him. The next morning, 19 February, I called Willie again and was delighted when he answered the call. Imagine our disbelief when we heard our friend's tired voice on the other side of the line, telling us that he had cancer. We were shocked and desperately tried to get friends of ours in Pretoria to see Willie so that we could get a better understanding of what was going on. The feedback was not positive, and on 26 February, it was confirmed that Willie was diagnosed with lymphoma. He was transferred to the Steve Biko (or Pretoria Academic) Hospital. He had lost about 15kg (or 2.36 stone). The prognosis was not looking good.

On Saturday, 24 March Renate and I loaded a photo album on Facebook titled "*Memories with Willie Roets*", and on Sunday morning, 25 March 2012, Willie's brother sent us a message to confirm that that morning, Willie had passed away. We were devastated. I still can't believe that it all happened so quickly and that we were not able to see him to say goodbye.

In the meantime, I started with my induction for my new post in Plymouth, and as I had to give three months' notice, it was agreed that I would take up my new post on 1 June. I attended one week in February, one in March, and one in April getting to know some of the key people at Plymouth Hospitals NHS Trust. Willie's funeral was on 29 March and I had to be in Plymouth for induction. Whilst traveling down to Plymouth the day before, I contemplated the events of the funeral and regretted that Renate and I could not be in Pretoria. I had five hours on the train to reflect on our friendship, our lives together, and how Willie touched both Renate and my lives. I made some rough notes of what I thought would happen that day of his funeral, from what I knew of the man, his family, and friends. As the clocks turned back the last weekend of March, and spring had sprung, the seeds were sown for another short story yet to be finalised.

The first week of April brought yet another shock to our family, when Renate's uncle died unexpectedly in Ermelo. Uncle Dieter was such a talented artist and painted the most remarkable landscapes of Southern Africa. We hoped that this was the turning point and that we would be spared any additional bad news for the remainder of the year.

At the end of April, Renate finished off at the Hospital and started planning the great preparation for our move to Devon, which was set for the

end of May. On the 2nd of May, Andre came to visit from South Africa and he and I were set to attend the final two legs of the 2012 Sevens Rugby World Series. I had some leave planned for May, so when Andre arrived, Renate and I took him for traditional fish and chips with mushy peas at our local pub,

'The Villa', an old manor house just outside Wray Green. On the 4th of May,

Andre and I drove via Thornton and Kirkby Lonsdale to Windermere in the Lake District. The following day, we took the road less travelled, and rather than taking the M6 motorway north to Scotland, we took the very scenic A591 from Windermere to Keswick. The road seemed to climb indefinitely up through mountains; we stopped at Ullswater Lake in the distance while the stonehedges on the various farms formed an interesting pattern on the mountainous landscape. Eventually we followed the A66 past the Bassenthwaite Lake to Cockermouth before we turned right on the A595 to Carlisle in search of Hadrian's Wall, which we never found. At Carlisle, we re-joined the M6 and travelled north to Glasgow. En-route was the largest number of wind-turbines I had ever seen.

On arriving in Glasgow, we checked into our hotel, a Premier Inn, on the outskirts of the city, and visited a local pub where, by luck, they launched the Caledonia Best, 'Scotland's Perfectly Balanced Beer', a new and very tasty Scottish Beer. The next day was Andre's birthday and day one of the sevens rugby. At the end of day one of what was continuous rugby, we took the bus into the city centre and were pleasantly surprised in the beautiful architecture of Glasgow. We met a South African Scotsman, called Andrew McKenzie, who took us to a pub called the Blackfriars. We celebrated Andre's birthday drinking beer, and listening to Stretch Dawrson and the Mending Hearts, a contemporary Scottish jazz & blues band. The next morning, we felt worse for wear, and decided the best way to face the day, was to start with a hearty Scottish Breakfast. Andre had the real thing with haggis, black pudding, bacon, eggs, and beans. I managed to have some haggis, but could not stomach the black pudding. At the end of the second day of rugby, I succeeded in getting a rugby ball signed by the South African Sevens' team for the son of a friend of ours in South Africa who was rugby mad. I was pleased with the weekend and the result.

The following day, Andre and I drove to Edinburgh, where Renate joined us after taking the morning train from Preston. We gave Andre a whistleblow tour of Edinburg, the Cathedrals, the Royal mile, and the Edinburgh Castle. At lunchtime, the three of us drove back to Lytham.

Back in Lytham St. Anne's, Andre made us our first Potjie in England, a traditional South African dish that is cooked in a cast-iron pot over an open fire. Two days later, Andre and I took the train to the capital and spent two days walking the streets of London. We met Garth, a cousin of his that we last saw when I lived in Bethal, in Mpumalanga in the old Eastern Transvaal, some eighteen years ago. The likeness of Andre's cousin to his father was so striking, that when Garth walked into the pub, we simultaneously recognised him as cousin Garth. Kathrin Kruger joined us later that afternoon and the four of us went for dinner. The next day we headed out to Twickenham, where the final leg of the sevens rugby played out.

Andre departed for South Africa on 16 May, and our final days in Lancashire were upon us. My staff hosted a South African dinner for me to say good-bye, and it was a truly remarkable evening.

On Monday, the 28 May, Pickford's collected our furniture and boxes. After Pickford's departed, Renate and I cleaned the house and slept on the floor in the lounge for our last night, as we did the first night, some three years ago. Early on the morning of 29 May, we loaded the two cats (Gigi and Guci) in the Land Rover, and Stefan (our godson) and a friend of his took Renate's car to Devon and the Southwest.

Stefan stayed with us for a week to help us unpack. On 1 June, I started at the hospital as Director of Human Resources and Organisational Development. The Trust had some 6000 employees, and as everyone was very pleased that I joined, I could only imagine that there would be a lot for me to do. I was not wrong. The first weekend in our new home, Renate, Stefan, and I worked diligently to get the house sorted.

Two weeks later, on 15 June, Renate's mum, Ma Helga, arrived to visit us for three months. During the next two months, while I was at work, Renate spent some quality time with her mum, showing her the beautiful hills of Cornwall and villages in Devon. They started doing crafts together, and in the evening, while I was working on my final assignments for my law studies, Renate and her mum did beading.

On 1 August, the hospital's new Chief Executive, Ann James, started, as Helen O'Shea took up a post in Jersey. She was a very warm and engaging individual who I was confident would be good for the hospital, someone with whom I would be able to work well together.

At the end of August, Renate and I had planned a holiday to Verona, Italy, which was pre-planned long before we knew that we would move to Plymouth. On 20 August, Renate and I left for our first visit to Verona, Italy, to attend the 99th Annual Opera Festival. My old friend from the Navy, Cuan Sawyer, agreed a year earlier that if we go, he would join us. We arrived at the 'Residence Adige', our self-catering apartment in Verona. Cuan was waiting for Renate and me. It was good to see my old friend again.

* * *

Verona is a beautiful historic city. We visited the 'Basilica di San Zeno', took the most beautiful night photos of the bridge leading to the Verona Castle, shopped at the 'Torre dei Lamberti', an 84m high tower that dates back to 1172, and Renate cooled her feet in the large fountain on the old square. As we had some time before the Opera festival began, we took a train to Venice to explore this spectacular city. This small city in northern Italy, was situated on 118 small islands, separated by canals and linked with bridges. We were in awe. Back on the train, after an insightful but hot day, Renate and I agreed that once we have our UK Passports, we would come back to this beautiful city.[60]

---

[60] https://www.italyguides.it/en/veneto/verona [accessed 9/12/2016]

Arriving back in Verona, we decided that we'd go directly to the 'Piazza Bra' for dinner, outside the Verona Amphitheatre. We enjoyed Italian Pizza, beer, and really good grappa. We left the Piazza by taxi at about 2:00 AM, Cuan placing all his shopping and backpack in the boot of the taxi. As the taxi pulled out form the hotel grounds, Cuan realised that all his bags, his passport, the gifts for his girlfriend and family, were all still in the back of the taxi. We desperately tried to phone the cab company. The hotel owners were very supportive and helpful. At 4:00 AM, we realised that it was unlikely that they were going to get back to us. We retired for the night. The next day everyone was a bit subdued.

That evening, we went out for dinner and Grappa. Cuan and I decided that if we haven't heard by the end of the next day, we will travel to Milan to seek assistance from the South African Consulate. On Thursday morning, I called the Consulate in Milan, and we agreed to get tickets for the 6:30 AM train to Milan on 24 August. That morning, we woke up at 4:30 AM. We were downstairs before 6:00 AM to get our taxi to the railway station. As we came into the lobby, the hotel owners and some of the staff were all talking excitedly. They just received a phone call to confirm that Cuan's goods were all found in the boot of the taxi. As the tickets to Milan were bought and paid for, we decided to go anyway. What was intended as an emergency trip, became an unplanned outing.

Arriving in Milan, the railway station was very impressive with shopping malls, coffee shops and patisserie's everywhere. We had some coffee and tackled the big city, took the underground to the Milan Cathedral, walked the streets of Milan, Cuan did more shopping and the three of us had lunch at a street side café. Milan was not that impressive as a city. The little bit we saw was impressive, but not a city that would lure us back for a second visit. Later in the afternoon, we made our way back to the station and took the train back to Verona. Unwittingly, we visited all the main capitals in northern Italy, when we only planned an Opera Festival in Verona.

The Opera weekend arrived, and we attended Bizet's *Carmen*, Puccini's *Tosca*, and Verdi's *Aida*. The first two nights were beautifully warm, clear skies and a full moon lying low over the amphitheatre. The music was soothing and the ambiance mesmerising.

While listening to the three operas, I could not but think of my mum who loved opera, and our friend Willie, whom I met at the State Theatre when we both sang for the PACT Ad-hoc Opera Choir. Our long awaited first holiday to Italy was at its end, as the following morning, Renate and I had to make our way back to the airport to fly back to England, while Cuan had his flight that evening, back to Johannesburg.

* * *

It was amazing how quickly Ma Helga's three months went by. Not long after our return from Italy, Renate and her mum drove to London, to spend one last day trip in the city before she returned to South Africa on 15 September. I submitted my final assignment on Criminal Law and had to start preparing for the exams, while my parents' trip to Europe, another holiday we planned a year ago, was also imminent.

Monday morning, 24 September, we checked in for our flight and went to the departure hall. After fifteen minutes of waiting, my dad and Ma Madeleine appeared. We were delighted to see them.

We departed for Barcelona where we spent the first night in a beautiful self-catering apartment. The next day, we took a taxi to the harbour and boarded the Costa Magica. We spent a day at Mallorca. From Mallorca we stopped at beautiful Valletta, the capital city of Malta; we sailed towards Italy and stopped at the cities of Sicily and Naples. We marvelled at Mount Etna and at Naples; Renate and I did a quick walk through one of the old castles, bought chilies from a local merchant, and tasted a rum baba, a small yeast cake saturated with rum filled with whipped cream. We continued our journey to Savona, from where we did a day trip, by coach, to the beautiful principality of Monaco. It was raining, so my parents decided to shop while Renate and I took on the elements in search for the 'Cathédrale Notre-Dame-Immaculée' where Princess Grace and Prince Rainer are buried. Monaco was beautiful, with spectacular botanically gardens; we saw the starting point of the Monaco Grand Prix, the hairpin bend, and the famous Monte Carlo Casino.

On the ship, we were treated to two Captain's Dinners, one of the evenings we dressed up in black tie and evening dress. Renate and Ma Madeleine looked beautiful whilst father and son were equally dashing. The final leg back to Barcelona was before us and we still had three days to explore in that beautiful city.

We visited the world heritage site that is the spectacular 'Sagrada Familia', and enjoyed an open bus tour viewing the impressive architecture. We walked down the pedestrian 'Ramblas' and had lunch and cheap sparkling wine at the great market in Barcelona. Our last evening was topped with seafood ' Paella' near the harbour, Sangria, and later in the evening, on our way home, some Gelato.

We returned to London on Friday, 5 October, but took my parents for an open-bus tour to see the city.

During the week in Plymouth, I returned to work whilst Renate brought my parents to make a quick turn at my work where they met Anne and some of my colleagues. On Monday 15 October, as I set off to write my final law exams, Renate and my parents took the National Express to London to enable them to fly back to South Africa.

On 29 October, I received an email form the Brit Writers' Awards, confirming that my short story 'A Letter to My Daughter' was a finalist in the short story category, and the final award ceremony was set to take place in the Thistle Hotel in London on 1 December. I was delighted as I never thought it would make it to the short-list.

November was a hectic month at work and it felt as if the pace of the year just continued to increase. The highlight of the month was our attendance of the 100th annual Royal Variety Performance at the Royal Albert Hall in London, and that in the company of HRH's Queen Elizabeth II and Prince Phillip. Renate and I were so taken by the evening that afterwards we walked the streets of London for a while, before we took a black cab back to our hotel in Hyde Park.

The month went by in a flash and it was not long before we had to return to London for our evening at the Brit Writers' Awards, which was equally impressive.

On 14 December, Renate and I celebrated our 16th wedding anniversary and spent the evening at Borringdon Hall, a spectacular old Manor House less than ten minutes' drive from our house. We discovered this by accident, and learned that it was recorded in William the Conqueror's 'Doomsday Book' of 1086. This book recorded all land, its owners, holding, and livestock in England at the time. We had a spectacular dinner in the Gallery Restaurant, and over breakfast, the restaurant manager told us about the ghosts of the House. I thought we would go back to this beautiful, historical and allegedly haunted gem, in time to come. Perhaps we'll meet the ghosts of years past.

On 17 December, I received my results for my law studies and to my utter surprise, I was informed that I successfully completed my studies and after three years, was now the proud holder of a Diploma in English Law. Renate and I spent Christmas Eve quietly at home, attended the Christmas Day service at the Hospital's Chapel, and enjoyed a bit of quiet time at home. I finalised my second short story *'A Friendship Treasured'* just after Christmas (see Chapter 28).

Talking of years past, and whilst there were a number of events that called for our reflection, remembrance, and even despair, 2012 will also be remembered for the amazing year that it was. We were truly blessed with all the good things that happened during the year. We thanked God for the grace that He had bestowed on us. We prayed that 2013 would be an exciting year, a year that will see us well-settled in our new surroundings, and like any new year, unarguably, will bring new opportunities and adventure for us all.

Chapter 28
A Friendship Treasured

Spring came early that year and promised England a sunny, warm summer, if there is such a thing. It was the beginning of a new season. Birds were chirping happily in the early morning. The sky appeared bluer and brighter, whilst the air had a fresh crispness about it. A sea of daffodils and a few colourful tulips announced brightly that spring has sprung.

Travelling south on a train to Devon, the vistas of the English countryside were afresh with life. Like the spring announced its presence in youthful colour and splendour, so will seasons mature in summer, age in autumn, and die in winter. This is how it will be with us all.

As I observed the beauty of spring in all its joyous splendour, I reflected on a good life of a remarkable man, an inspirational human being, a 'master' in his own right, who, I hoped, would be with us for many years to come. However, this was not to be, and that reality required my presence, albeit in spirit, in a church in Pretoria, South Africa.

While my train pulled out of Birmingham New Street Station, picking up speed toward Worcestershire, Gloucestershire, the beautiful green hills of Somerset and ultimately Devon, I retreated to that space in my head, where everything is quiet and peaceful.

Settling down, I imagined the front entrance of the large, conservative Dutch Reformed Church, situated in one of the affluent suburbs of Pretoria. I visualised the lush green gardens, before I entered through the large wooden archway.

The organist played Pachelbel's Canon in D. The smell of wood, furniture oil, and years of religious tradition was nearly tangible in the air. I made my way through the pews and looked at the sea of family and friends who filled the church. There were faces of people I saw as recently as November last year, and then I recognised others I last saw more than twenty-five years ago. There was a wide spectrum of mourners from close family and friends to farmhands, domestic workers, nursing staff, and carers.

For a widower, with no children, there were a lot of people coming to say their good-byes. It was clear that this man touched the lives of many people. I greeted some of the familiar faces I recognised from the past, enquired quietly how they were and nodded my head in confirmation that I was fine while making my way to my seat.

It was 11 AM when I sat down on the hard, upright wooden bench, in the sixth row from the front. In front of me, there was an open space of pews that were reserved for close family.

Looking at the funeral leaflet, it pained me to see the photo of my dear friend, a photo I took of him when we visited in November, and today, less than four months later, we were here to say goodbye.

* * *

My thoughts were interrupted when the Reverend willed the congregation to stand as the coffin was brought into the church. I watched the procession and reflected on the twenty-eight years that I had the privilege of knowing Bill.

As the organist played Bach's *Adagio* from *Toccata*, my mind wandered off again, thinking of the time that Bill and I worked at the Pretoria State Theatre and reflecting on the operas we sang in. There were Giordano's *Andrea Chenier*; three operas by Puccini, *Madam Butterfly, Tosca,* and *Turandot*; Verdi's *Rigoletto*; and Wagner's *Tristan und Isolde*. We were in the same voice group, bass baritone, and were always placed together, the slender, tall, experienced man next to the not so tall, younger, inexperienced lad.

* * *

The Reverend started the service by asking the congregation to sing *How Great Thou Art*. I pondered the meaning of the words and thought of Bill's life, his sense of humour, artistic flair and love for fusion cooking. Just as a smile crept to the side of my mouth, the Reverend asked the congregation to be seated and began the service with a reading from 1 Corinthians 13.

"If I speak in the tongues of men and of angels, but have not love, I am only a resounding gong or a clanging cymbal...."

Bill's family made a collage of photos in celebration of his life that played in a loop on a big screen in front of the Church. Seeing these pictures of his life, adventures and travels, prompted many memories, and made me think of the lives of both Bill and his wife Barbara.

She was an American citizen, whom he met when they were students in Alaska, working as missionaries. They made the perfect couple.

Thinking of Barbara, I remembered the Easter weekend many years ago. They wanted to go away for on a short holiday, and asked me to housesit to feed their dog Ludwig. I reflected on the car accident that killed Barbara and injured Bill so badly that he was hospitalised for more than three months. I thought about the bond that developed between Ludwig, Barbara's dachshund, and me; the subsequent time that I looked after Bill and cared for him after he returned home. It created such a special bond.

From the time I met Bill, he had shown the ability to rise above any difficult circumstance and always considered others first. He never disclosed any of his personal pain or hardship to anyone around him. He was always positive and openly thanked God for the grace and blessings he received in his life. At the end of the reading, the congregation was asked to rise again to sing *Dear Lord and Father of Mankind*. I stood up, but did not sing as I was deep in thought.

* * *

Eventually, Bill returned to work and a couple of years later, accepted early retirement. He decided to go to Turkey where he was invited to help a friend to renovate and redecorate a country hotel on the outskirts of Istanbul. He immersed himself into this project. Sadly, he also allowed his 'friends' to convince him to spend just about his entire pension as a 'loan' on their hotel refurbishment. This saw Bill returning to South Africa with no savings and in a situation that as a pensioner, he had to find work again. Amazingly, while we were angry because of the manner in which he was being used, he just said "it's fine, it's only money" and "the Lord is good to me, I know He will provide". This made me even angrier as I am a pragmatist. Although a Christian, I do believe and trust in the grace of God but also believe that God helps those who want to be helped. So, I reprimanded Bill as I thought his actions were careless. I told him that he should not have spent his life savings on strangers. He should not expect God to be providing when he was wasting what he should look after. Unbeknown to me, while I was worried about Bill's money, he was more worried about the well-being of others.

The service continued and I tried to focus on the sermon and listened to the Reverend's words about living a caring life for others, despite his own needs, a life that was 'Christ-like', and that is how I know Bill lived, always showering others with love and considering their needs above his. The Reverend spoke about the meaning of love not being self-seeking, not easily angered, and not keeping record of any wrongs; I reflected on my own life as my wife and I had used the same section of scripture at our wedding.

At the end of the service, the congregation was informed that family and friends would present a musical programme, which seemed perfectly apt, as he came from a wonderfully musical family. The congregation was asked to rise to sing *Amazing Grace*, to allow for some time to enable Bill's family to prepare. It consisted of some vocals, solo instrumental interludes, and finished with a duet of *He Touched Me,* a recording of Bill and one of his sisters. All of this was very special, as Bill was truly loved by all.

* * *

As time moved on, I had established a successful consulting firm. Bill was working as a recruitment consultant in Kiev in the Ukraine. His contract came to an end, so he returned to South Africa just in time for my wife's birthday. I wanted to surprise her, and he agreed to cook a special dinner for us. We converted our lounge into a formal 'restaurant' with a candle-lit table for two. Bill did an elaborate three-course menu. He did not speak to us during the dinner, other than a few Russian words, like "*Da*", "*Horosho*", "*Pozhalusta*", "*Ya Ne Znayou*", and a number of other Russian gems that we never understood. After dinner, Bill joined us with a glass of wine, which sparked a debate that led us to agreeing that I would try and help him to get work with a client of mine who owned a hotel in Mafikeng.

We created a plan of action and the following week, the General Manager of the hotel was invited to our home for dinner. This time, both Bill and my wife were in the kitchen, cooking up a storm. The evening was a great success and Bill cooked himself into a job, while inspiring my wife and me to tender for the overall catering contract at the same hotel.

The next couple of months were hectic. Bill moved to the historic town of Mafikeng in August, and after we were awarded the catering contract, we finalised the creation of our catering company and followed in November. Once everything was in place, Bill transferred over from my client to our books and remained our employee. He was responsible for the front of house, customer relations, and ensuring that all functions were running smoothly.

We shared excellent times in Mafikeng. Bill and my wife alternated in doing 5 AM cash-ups. He reprimanded her, in a caring way, as in between our work pressures, and over a two-year period, she raised 20 stray kittens. Bill, always concerned for others, was worried that my wife had taken on too much. This, however, did not prevent him from adopting a kitten of his own, and one day, dressed in his Russian snow hat, appeared at our front door to book his kitten into 'Molly's Crèche' to play with the other kittens. The next day he produced a letter of complaint in that Molly, our eldest cat, and 'crèche principal', was too strict in handling the little ones.

We also had a cook that was supposed to prepare *Coq au Vin*, but decided to grill the chicken and drank the wine instead. When I proposed action against the cook, Bill intervened on his behalf. The staff loved him, as he continued to lend them money and played taxi to staff, late at night at the end of their shifts.

* * *

Eventually, my wife and I immigrated to England and while we spoke regularly, it was very difficult being so far from the ones dearest to us. Fortunately, we were able to go back to South Africa on a fairly regular basis.

* * *

As the service was drawing to a close, the Reverend indicated that there were a few people who would do obituaries in memory of Bill. While the day had been emotionally draining, as the pinnacle of the preceding eight weeks, my anxiety and stress levels increased throughout. I tried to listen attentively as people spoke about their times and experiences with Bill. How he was described as a 'pillar' for his family and I reflected on my own experiences as recent as the last two years.

Two years before Bill's death, my wife and I visited South Africa for two weeks and the three of us w e n t t o Cape Town to herald in the New Year. We enjoyed many wonderful dinners in Cape Town. Bill and my wife continued their fusion cooking, and we enjoyed the rich and versatile wines of the Western Cape. The sunsets over Clifton beach were beautiful, while we had fish and wine for lunch in Simonstown and sunset cocktails at the old Club Med. We visited an array of wine farms, attended the site where my late brother died many years ago in Jacob's Bay, and enjoyed crayfish in Paternoster on the Cape west-coast. Eventually, before we returned to Pretoria, we had dinner with Bill's nephew in Blouberg Strand, with beautiful vistas of Table Mountain. We ended that year with champagne, as the old year made way for a new one. Bill, my wife, and I agreed to do something similar every year.

The following year November, we returned for our annual holiday. Bill collected us on 6 November from the airport; it was his birthday. We had lunch with my mother-in-law at the Ocean Basket (a seafood restaurant) with wine, chilies, and garlic. At first, we went to stay with my parents for a few days, and then went to Bill. We stayed at the 'African Butler' for a week of safaris, sunshine, peace, and quiet, the African way. We talked about Steve Biko, politics, the challenges of the land, crime, the economy, and we philosophised about humanity. We entertained mutual friends and prepared various menus so when our guests arrived Bill would shout, "Menu number five – let's get this show on the road." Later in the evening, when the guests left, Bill would promptly sing, "I'm a little noddy boy I always nod my head..." and the three of us would clean the kitchen before we retired for the night. It was such a special time with such a special human being.

* * *

As people talked about how inspirational Bill was, and how they would miss him, I reflected on how big our shock was in early February, when we spoke to him to hear a tired voice saying "I have cancer". We were speechless. We knew he was not well since Christmas, but we originally thought he had bronchitis, that developed into pneumonia. Two weeks later, we managed to speak to him again and it was clear that he was critically ill, yet, he proclaimed that he was fine, "God is so good to me," he said. "I am truly blessed to have you as my children, I love you both."

Bill was diagnosed with lymphoma, and although it is considered a very aggressive cancer, if treated aggressively, its impact could be delayed. However, the South African National Health System is appallingly inept and

Bill had no medical insurance. I frantically wrote to everyone in South Africa who we thought may be able to help. I wrote to local radio stations, private healthcare service providers, family, and friends.

* * *

As the first two obituaries were concluded, it was my turn to do the third and final one. I clutched my piece of paper and nervously moved to the front of the church. I looked at Bill's brother, sisters, and other members of his family. I looked at my friend's coffin briefly, and referred to the paper before me. I read anxiously.

"What does one say about a wonderful human being like Billy?

I got to know him as a humanitarian, who found jobs for the jobless, arranged accommodation for the homeless, gave some of the little money he had to the needy and has always been a positive and inspirational person to many, many people. The amount of messages that came from the Ukraine, Russia, the USA, Australia, Europe and from all over South Africa is testimony to this.

When my wife and I got married, he adopted her as his daughter, and instantly changed roles from my friend, to my 'father-in-law'. The best 'father-in-law' any son could ask for. We enjoyed his comfort foods like his home made Spaghetti Bolognaise and a variety of dishes inspired by his style of fusion cooking.

It was Bill who inspired us to start our business, after he came back from a stint in Kiev; and then he came to work with us in Mafikeng. We had so many fun times together. It was also in Mafikeng that Bill met the owners of the African Butler, a place that was very close to his heart.

My wife and I often stayed with Bill. We loved his musical talents, as he played his piano, or sang impromptu. Together, we listened to classical music, drank red wine and talked at length about religion, creation, and politics.

Bill loved to travel, he enjoyed doing things differently and irrespective of having difficult times, he never complained. When-ever I asked him how he was, he always replied, 'the Lord is very good to me, I have lots to be thankful for'.

When my wife and I celebrated our tenth wedding anniversary in 2006, he took us to the hills 'on the farm', as he liked to refer to the African Butler, and at sunset he guided us to renew our vows. Bill personified love. I often referred to him as a modern day 'master'. He had the perfect balance between being silly, full of fun, with a sense of peace and serenity. T r u l y inspirational.

We spoke to Bill briefly before his death, when he told us that he had cancer. Even then he said that he was happy and content, grateful and thankful.

I have known Bill for 28 years and have known him as an optimistic, sometimes stubborn, but always very kind man.

Today should be a day we celebrate his life. We are grateful for that and will cherish his guidance and teachings; his mannerisms, quirks and sayings; and the remarkable impact he had on all of us.

Let me end in saying: We will miss you my friend. Thank you for making our lives richer."

* * *

As I made my way back to my seat, I looked out of the window, and noticed the absolute clear blue skies. I had a quick glimpse of a dove on the branch of a tree, seemingly looking just at me. I smiled and resumed my seat. The Reverend called on the congregation to stand for one last time, to sing *Nearer My God to Thee.*

* * *

As the imaginary pallbearers carried Bill's coffin out of the Church as my train pulled out of Totness, in Devon. I slowly left the room in my head. Returning to reality, I realised that Plymouth, my final destination was the next stop. As the mourners in the church in Pretoria, made their way out of the imagined building, I held court with Bill in the spirit.

The beautiful green hills of Devon and the crystal blue skies of that spring day in England seemed the perfect way to say my own goodbye to a dear friend, be it from afar.

Chapter 29
The Illumination of 2013

At the end of 2012, we expressed the hope that 2013 would be a year that will see us well-settled in our new surroundings. As with any New Year, we expected a lot. However, we never anticipated the curveball that 2013 would bring. Like any new year, we hoped that this year would bring new opportunities and adventure for us all. The year did not disappoint; we did settle well in Plymouth and considered buying our own home. My job was going well, irrespective of the ongoing financial challenges that we faced as a hospital and generally within the wider NHS.

We followed the news about the ongoing civil war in Syria, Oscar Pistorius, the resignation of Pope Benedict, and the death of former President Nelson Mandela. Renate was delighted to be appointed on a flexible basis to work at the hospital. Health-wise, the year was definitely an illumination, whilst Renate's mum came to visit for six months. We took trips to Landsend, Penadlake, and Looe in Cornwall. There were a few trips to London, a summer vacation to Scotland, and we returned to Lytham St. Anne's to see dear friends and to say good-bye to another. The year 2013 ended with a warm African summer; we celebrated Christmas with family and friends, whilst the world said goodbye to Nelson Mandela.

* * *

Whilst we were basking in the aftermath of 2012, we started the first of January with the sad news that Herman Hanke, a friend of Renate's mum died in a plane crash outside Phalaborwa on New Year's Day. What made this even worse was that Herman retired on the 31 December 2012.

During January, the world watched in horror as the Civil War in Syria entered its third year. It seemed the Assad regime of President Bashar al-Assad, who has ruled Syria as President since 2000, had become untouchable to the world. Following the Arab Spring of 2011 and the on-going war on terror, the western world appeared to have lost its appetite for war. That was until Assad reportedly used chemical weapons on his own people, resulting in thousands of refugees leaving the country. This prompted American President Barak Obama to draw his proverbial red line, threatening Assad with military retribution unless he turned-over all chemical weapons to UN weapon inspectors. This was done, but Assad remained in power. Syria remained at war, and by the winter of 2013, millions of Syrians had been displaced from their homeland. The UN projected that an estimated 11 million refugees had left the country, without an end in sight. The world would see many years of war to follow, resulting in a further estimated 13.5 million Syrians in need of humanitarian aid, without any inclination of when normality would return to that ancient land.[61]

* * *

By the end of January, Renate and I went to see our first 3D Movie, being the *Life of Pi*, and what an epic experience that was. I read this fantasy adventure novel by Yann Martel during our 2005 holiday to Mauritius and always wondered whether they would make a movie. We were not disappointed, definitely a must see. During the second week, I published my second short story, titled *"A Friendship Treasured"*, and started working on a third one.

Meanwhile, following what was a routine health check back in 2010, resulted in four sets of blood tests and two rounds of prostate biopsies by December 2012. Ultimately a third biopsy was required, but this time it was done under general anaesthetic. This was deemed necessary following a steady increase in my PSA or prostate-specific antigen levels that increased steadily and were all higher than what is generally considered normal levels. PSA levels should be between 0–2.5. By November 2010, it was 164% higher than the maximum normal ratio; May 2012, 256% higher; Sep 2012, 288% and Dec 2012, 344%. The UK's National Cancer Institute described the PSA test as a "test that measures the blood level of PSA, a protein that is produced by the prostate gland. The higher a man's PSA level the more likely it is that he has prostate cancer. However, there are additional reasons for having an elevated PSA level, and some men who have prostate cancer do not have elevated PSA levels"[62]. We learned that it's likely that most men will die with prostate cancer, but not of it.

On Tuesday, 29 January, I went to theatre, and on Friday, 1 February, I was diagnosed with prostate cancer.

Both Renate and I were shocked. At 47, this was far too young for me to have such problems. We called a friend of ours in South Africa who had the same problem a couple of years ago and following surgery was cleared with a very active and normal life. He patiently and supportively explained to me that there were options, and that I needn't make a decision in haste. Prostate cancer is traditionally one of the slowest growing cancers there is. I was advised to do my research, not to be intimidated by the doctors, family or friends, and to make sure that I make the right decision for me. He also suggested that I should 'interrogate' the doctors, which traditionally as a

---

[61] *http://syrianrefugees.eu* [reviewed 22/12/16]
[62] http://www.cancer.gov/cancertopics/factsheet/detection/PSA [reviewed 22/12/16]

South African patient, we are not good in doing. He advised that I ask the doctor about his success and failure rates, to inquire about different treatment regimens and techniques, and to read arguments for and against treatment, irrespective of what the doctor recommends. Too often we just go with what the doctor said. I started to do research and talking to a number of specialists at Plymouth Hospitals Trust, where I worked. A large number of websites confirmed three options for Renate and me to consider.

Option 1 was to do nothing: This option, also referred to as 'watchful waiting', is where the PSA levels are monitored over a period of time, normally at three to six monthly intervals, to see if the PSA levels changed. This is a good option initially, especially in the early stages of an elevated PSA test, as a number of factors could contribute to an artificial elevation. These could include inflammation that would normally settle resulting in the PSA level dropping to within normal levels. It is said that a 'normal' PSA level for men under the age of 50 is a PSA level of below 2.5.[63] Considering the steady increase over the preceding twenty-five months, this sounded like an option that we could not follow.

Option 2 was to go for the many variations of radiation treatments such as Intensity Modulation Radiation Therapy (IMRT), Proton Beam, and Brachytherapy. According to a radiology information website, "Intensity-modulated radiation therapy (IMRT) is an advanced mode of high-precision radiotherapy that uses computer-controlled linear accelerators to deliver precise radiation doses to a malignant tumour or specific areas within the tumour"[64]. IMRT is a more scientific approach to terminating or delaying the development of cancer cells. However, it could have long-term side effects such as damaging the intervening and surrounding tissue when radiating the prostate area. In later years, it could also manifest in colon and rectal problems, infertility, secondary cancers, or even new cancers.

Another technique, according to the Birmingham Prostate Clinic's website, is Brachytherapy treatment, which "involves the use of radioactive seeds to deliver radiotherapy directly into the cancerous prostate gland"[65]. Whilst this is not a suitable treatment for aggressive tumours, it allows the patient to get back to a normal life very quickly. The treatment involves the insertion of a radioactive cell near or in the cancerous area. It then releases its content slowly and hopefully kills the cancerous cells. There is, however, no way to know whether the cancer is contained within the prostate or whether it spread to secondary areas. Brachytherapy does not remove the cancerous cells from the body, and one of the downsides of this treatment, according to Dr Richard Whittington, Associate Professor of Radiation Oncology at the University of Pennsylvania, School of Medicine, is that "there are few surgeons who will do a prostatectomy after radiation therapy.

[63] http://www.nlm.nih.gov/medlineplus/ency/article/003346.htm [accessed 22/12/2016]
[64] www.radiologyinfo.org/en/info.cfm?pg=imrt [accessed 22/12/2016]
[65] www.birminghamprostateclinic.co.uk/treatments/brachytherapy.php [accessed 22/12/2016]

The reason for this is fibrosis or scarring, caused by the treatment that would make surgery more difficult to do after radiation"[66].

Option 3 was surgery to remove the prostate, which is generally done through two approaches. This is either done through abdominal or by way of perineal surgery. The first has three options. The first is keyhole surgery, the latest technological advances being the DaVinci Robot, or the second more traditional option, by way of open abdominal surgery. The perineal and third approach requires more technical skills but has additional advantages in that there is less blood loss, whilst its outcomes in terms of incontinence and impotence are much better. According to the Department of Urology at Tulane University, there also appeared to be less chances for long-term bowel problems.[67]

After careful debate with Mr Paul McInerney, the Urologist Specialist with specialist interest in Prostate and Renal cancers at Plymouth Hospitals NHS Trust, who specialised in the perianal approach, we decided that that was the best way forward. As we planned to go to South Africa in March, Mr McInerney suggested that we should try and speak to Dr Lance Coetzee, an Urologist Specialist at the Pretoria Urology Hospital whom he trained with in America. He rated Dr Coetzee among some of the best in his field. We agreed that we would finally decide on the way forward following our return from South Africa. Renate made an appointment for me with Dr Coetzee.

Initially we told no one, other than our friend in Johannesburg who recovered from prostate cancer, as Renate and I thought we needed to reflect on this matter first, consider the options for ourselves, and then intended to tell our parents, family, and friends when we visited South Africa in March.

On 7 February, I had a discussion with Ann James, our Chief Executive. It was initially awkward to discuss this rather personal matter with Ann, as generally South African men do not talk about these things, but I felt liberated after my discussion with her. She was understanding, supportive, and reassured me that she and the Executive team at the hospital will support me in whatever I decided to do. I continued to do my work and found the busy daily schedule a welcome distraction.

* * *

By the next week, South African sport and indeed the world sporting fraternity, was shocked with the news that Oscar Pistorius killed his girlfriend, Reeva Steenkamp, at his luxury home in Silverlakes on Wednesday, 14 February. This became a particularly sombre day, as the feast of Saint Valentine is intended to celebrate love. This is also the same date that we buried my brother Johan in 1997.

---

[66] www.oncolink.org/experts/article1.cfm?c=90&id=2599 [accessed 22/12/2016]
[67] www.jurology.com/article/S0022-5347(05)65988-5/abstract [accessed 22/12/2016]

Renate and I were, like most of the world, captivated by the press releases, police statements, and journalists, their comments and speculations. The next couple of days, the UK media had a daily update on the Pistorius/Steenkamp saga. Alex Crawford, the Sky News reporter in Africa, who previously reported on the Arab Spring and ultimate death of Gaddafi in October 2011, gave regular updates outside the Brooklyn Police Station. Eventually, she moved to outside and inside the court, where Pistorius's bail application was heard. Of interest was that the response from people in support of Oscar was widely across the racial boundaries, and irrespective of one's individual view on this matter, Oscar Pistorius was viewed by many as a national treasure. Most people just did not want to believe that that fatal day could be anything but a terrible accident. We followed the bail application hearing day by day, and sighed a collective sigh of relief when he was granted bail on the 22nd of February. This was in light of the mess the South African police had made with the investigation process. The truth of that terrible day was still to be uncovered, with the court case being scheduled for March 2014. This promised to be a second OJ Simpson court-case, with Britain and most of the western world captivated.

* * *

On Saturday, 2 March, Renate and I were ready to go to South Africa for a short holiday to seek out some well-needed sunlight, and to visit our family and friends. Everything was ready, our luggage packed, our train tickets booked to Heathrow all in preparation for our flights to Johannesburg later that evening. I drove to one of the recycling stations to throw away the last of our rubbish, while Renate took the cats to the cattery. After I cleared my car of all the garden rubbish, I went for a quick hair-cut, knowing that when I got home, Renate and I had about an hour before we would take a taxi to the rail-way station and for our holiday to start. However, after I had my haircut and paid, I noticed that there was a piece of paper lying on the floor, and why I do not know, but I bent awkwardly sideways to pick this up, and collapsed on the floor. I had this intense, sharp pain in my lower back that prevented me from moving. I could not get up from the floor, the pain was so intense. One of the ladies at the hairdresser helped me up and eventually walked me to my car. It felt like it took forever, as I could not walk properly and looked like a very old man, with a serious case of scoliosis. I managed to drive home, and on arriving back at the house, I noted that Renate was still not back from the cattery. However, I realised that our holiday was not going to happen, at least not on that day. Whilst waiting for Renate, I called Stefan Bruijn, a South African Emergency Medicine specialist who worked at the hospital, to inquire what I could do. He suggested some anti-inflammatories, which I took, but also suggested that if it was not getting better, I should go to the emergency department for a check-up. When Renate arrived, we contacted British Airways to see how to place our tickets 'on-hold' and phone the train-line to cancel our train tickets. We thought that if we delay our trip with a couple of days, we might be able to go by the 6th, so we re-booked everything for Wednesday, the 6th of March.

I also tried to phone Ann James, as I wanted to clear with her that I could come back a couple of days later than originally planned; however, I did not manage to get hold of her. By 2:00 that afternoon, as our train departed for Heathrow, Renate and I checked into the hospital's emergency department. Initially, the doctor on duty suggested that it would be good if I could sit, to go to South Africa, as the warm weather would do me well, so I took the medicine they gave me, went home, and hoped that I would be more mobile. By Wednesday, I still could not walk and I now had additional pain with pins-and-needles down my right leg. Again, we postponed our flight, this time to December, and went back to the emergency department. They gave me morphine, and referred me for a computed tomography (CT) Scan. This revealed that there was no major problem, other than a herniated disc between the L4 and L5 discs in my lower back. I was given more tablets, and referred to physio. The next couple of days I walked with crutches, as I needed to remain mobile, attended a couple of sessions with the physiotherapy department, and also attended four sessions of hydrotherapy. By 13 March, I was nearly fully mobile again, although my back was still very stiff.

Ann sent a message that I could convert my two weeks annual leave to sick leave, but as I felt much better by Monday the 13th, I agreed to take one week of sick leave and the second week remained on annual leave. Renate and I spent the next couple of days at home, exploring Plymouth, and investigating the possibility of buying our own home. I felt terrible that Renate could not see her mum and that we could not go back to South Africa. I felt guilty that we had to wait until December to see our family and friends. Most of all, I felt dreadful for all the trouble my dad went through to arrange a lunch for us with family and friends that was supposed to have taken place on Sunday, 3 March, and which he had to cancel at very short notice. So let me formally apologise to those of you who agreed to join us for lunch on that day, and then had the plans cancelled.

The following week, I went back to work, and Renate returned to her routine at home. During our time, Renate and I debated at great length what line of treatment I should follow. We initially agreed that Mr McInerney was to perform a perineal radical prostatectomy. Although the initial date was proposed to be the 10 April, I had some unfinished work that needed to be done at the hospital. In agreement with Mr Paul McInerney, we postponed my surgery to Thursday, 18 April. Renate and I met with Paul before the operation and he explained all the pros and cons to us and answered all our questions. I started working with Martin Bambir, my very competent and trusted deputy, to develop a plan for continuity, to ensure that our human resources and organizational development (HR and OD) agenda continued successfully in my absence. It was envisaged that I would be away from work for at-least six weeks following the operation.

On Friday, 29 March, Renate and I drove the four-hour trip to London to pick up her mum. Ma Helga offered to come and visit us for six months, to support us both during my recovery. Her flight arrived at 6:00 AM on Saturday the 30th, and after we collected her, we drove straight back to Plymouth.

* * *

The next couple of days went by very quickly, with performance review meetings, engagement workshops, and a Board meeting on 12 April. It offered effective distractions and kept my mind constructively busy. I had little time to contemplate the pending operation and what may follow after that. However, after sunsets in the evenings and after Renate went to bed, I often spent time reading about the consequences of treatment, and no treatment, and the required after care that would follow. This often overwhelmed me and the anxiety started to increase. Renate was very good, though, because in her positive and optimistic manner, she could pick up when I was down, and constantly gave positive reassurance that this is the right thing for us both.

* * *

On 17 April, I went to work as normal until about 2:00 PM. After completing my handover with Martin, I was admitted and prepped during the night for the operation the following morning. I was in theatre at 9:00 AM on 18 April and woke up after the operation without the anticipated pain that I thought I would have. The next day after the operation, Ann and other colleagues from the hospital came to visit and I felt surprisingly well. Renate came to see me every day and spent most of the day with me in the hospital. Her mum held the fort with the cats at home. I was sent home on Saturday, 20 April, and on Monday morning had my first home visit from the community nurse.

* * *

As a South African immigrant, this was my first experience of community nurses. Their function is to make sure that whilst recovering at home, that I was all right, a truly remarkable system of quality care. The balance of that week I tried to get used to living with a catheter and to regain my strengths.

* * *

The first week following the operation was uneventful, with the wound healing. Friday night, March 26, was a difficult night. I could not sleep and became increasingly uncomfortable. I noted that my urine drainages were substantially less than before. Saturday morning, I got up feeling really unwell, and it felt as if I needed to go to the toilet, yet there was nothing coming out. I got out of bed, hoping that gravity will give a hand, and it did. The urine started flowing, past my catheter. I was able to hold it back, and then noted that the bag sock the community nurse provided caused a constriction. When I corrected this, 500ml of urine drained into the bag instantly. The rest of Saturday went by uneventful. I felt all right and spent most of the day writing and watching TV. At about 5 in the evening, I wanted to watch a game of South African rugby, but started feeling a bit uncomfortable sitting, so I lay down on the couch.

This was where things started to go wrong. The wound felt very sensitive, painful, and hard. I developed a cold fever and just could not get warm. My entire body was cold and by 6:00 PM, I got into bed, Renate covering me with three blankets. This was very out of character, as I traditionally am always warm. I had a headache that just did not want to subside. Renate took my temperature but it was only slightly elevated at 37.8. We called the community nurse and they came out a couple of minutes later. By then my fever was 38.4. They had a look at the catheter and discovered that it was turned causing another restriction.

At this time, although my face was red, my body felt cold. The community nurse had a look at the wound and the entire wound was inflamed. Renate said that she could not see any stitches due to the swelling. The community nurse described the wound to be "very unhappy, but not really angry"; it felt darn furious to me. Devon Docs, an out-of-hours GP service, prescribed a seven-day antibiotic; however, again, I had great difficulty to sleep during the night. The fever and headache remained persistent. At about 3:00 on Sunday morning, the fever settled, but the headache remained. Renate gave me something to eat at about 8:00 AM, I drank all my tablets. The wound however, remained bitterly sensitive.

I went for a shower at about 11h00 and whilst I was in the shower, Renate noted stuff running down my legs. Initially she thought that I was having diarrhoea. However, on closer inspection, it became clear that this was blood clots, and other nasties, coming out of the wound. A huge amount of 'stuff' came out. The shower floor was covered in it. Whilst this was taking place, the community nurse called to follow-up on her previous visit. Both Renate and I were relieved that she called at that specific point in time. Renate asked her to come and have a look. We cleaned up, got me into bed, and when the nurse came, both Renate and the nurse felt the wound looked much better. Although the left-hand-side (opposite to where the original drain was inserted) still felt hard, swollen and red, but according to Renate, not as bad as the night before. My fewer remained at a constant 37.8 but without any headache.

I spent most of Sunday in bed, and at about 5:00 PM, I checked the wound, and it oozed quite a lot again. The side of the drainage pipe was not swollen anymore and felt soft, although there was still watery-blood oozing. The opposite side still felt hard and red. I spent a bit of time sitting on the side of the bath, to see if anything will drain, and again a lot of thick black blood clots drained out.

On Monday morning, my fever and headaches were back, and when Renate inspected the wound, it was clear that it was now bitterly angry. My wound was septic. We agreed to contact the community nurse again. She had one look at the wound and called our GP. He was at our house within about 30 minutes, and after he inspected the wound, confirmed that he wanted me back in the hospital. He suggested that they either had to drain the wound, or administer a stronger, focused, intervenes anti-biotic. As the wound was so inflamed, I now could not sit at all. An ambulance form the South West Ambulance Services collected me from home and took me back to the hospital. The doctor on duty had a look at the wound, cleaned it, and first placed me on a strong dose of antibiotics, followed by liquids for the night. By the next morning, the wound looked much better; most of the inflammation was cleared, with only a bit of infection around some of the stitches. The medical personnel cleaned the wound, gave me more antibiotics, and by lunchtime, I was discharged.

* * *

In the meantime back in Blackpool, my former boss, Nick Grimshaw resigned from his post as Director of HR&OD, and during the past five months, my former team and some of the Executive colleagues campaigned very diligently that I should come back to Blackpool as Director of HR&OD. Initially I said no, and reminded both them and myself that I have often said that once you left a place of work, you should not return, as it is never the same. However, they remained persistent and when I came out of the hospital, I received a beautiful card from all our former colleagues on the top floor at Trust Headquarters. Everyone wished me well and reminded both Renate and me how much we were missed. I thought this was very touching until later in the week, when a massive bunch of flowers were delivered, with a card, with the message:

"*Hope you are recovering well and enjoying being pampered, from all your friends at Blackpool,*" followed by a post script that read, "*Please come back, we need you!*"

I was so touched. This was followed by a couple of telephone calls from other colleagues at Blackpool who all asked that I should consider coming back to Blackpool.

Eventually, Renate and I debated what to do, and ultimately, I called my dad for some advice. Whilst both Renate and I were very happy in Plymouth, we were disillusioned about the distance of Plymouth from everywhere else.

Lancashire is six hours away whilst London a good three or four hours. However, after careful consideration, we decided that this was not the time for a major change in our lives.

On Saturday, 1st of June, Renate and I drove to Penadlake, just across the border into Cornwall, to the home of Gordon and Beth Roberts, a remarkable couple we met in the Emergency Department in March when I injured my back. Beth suffered of Parkinson's disease, but invited us to join them on the 1st of June, for their annual Chestnut Appeal and Cure Parkinson's Trust fundraising event. The Chestnut Appeal is a charity at the hospital, raising funds to support men with prostate cancer. Gordon and Beth, who also lived in Botswana many years ago, now lived on a beautiful countryside estate, next to the most remarkable lakes and woodlands. We had a lovely day and visited them again later in the year, developing a strong friendship between us.

During the week before I returned to work, Ponti and Ian came to visit from St. Anne's-on-the-Sea and we took a few day trips into Cornwall, visiting the famous Port Isaac, where the popular Doc Martin television serious is filmed; we visited Padstow, Penzance, and Landsend, the most southern point of England.

Monday, 10th of June, was my first day back at work. I agreed to a 'phased-return', just to see how things are going. However, within the next two or three days, I was back in full swing, working my normal hours. It was good to be back at work, to be with my colleagues, and feeling that the nightmare of the past was behind me.

This optimism was short-lived, as I developed some complications. Fortunately, I had a follow-up meeting with Paul McInerney on Wednesday, 12 June, to discuss the histology report following my operation. During this consultation, my challenges became secondary, as there was more bad news to follow. It was confirmed that they discovered a small percentage of 'tertiary grade 5 patterns', at the top of the prostate near the bladder neck. Cancer cells are graded from 1-5. One being very slow growing cells, and unlikely to spread or cause serious harm. Grade 5 cells are the most aggressive, likely to grow fast and spread invasively to other organs. Ultimately, all of this meant that most of the cancer cells found in the biopsy look likely to grow at a moderately quick rate, whilst some cancer cells were likely to grow faster. The tumour was classified as T3a, meaning that the tumour extended beyond the prostate capsule.

A follow up PSA test was taken, and, traditionally, following a radical prostatectomy, the PSA should drop to 0.1, mine was 1.4. As indicated before, this could have been a false elevation, due to the long time that I had a catheter in, so it was decide to review that again in July. I had a follow-up appointment on the 2nd of July when my PSA was 2.1; Paul suggested that I consider radiotherapy. However, as the most common side effects, according to MacMillan cancer support information, is tiredness, effects on the skin, urinary, bowel, and sexual problems, this was not something I wanted to rush into. We agreed with Paul that we would do one more PSA at the end of August and that I will see him again first week of September.

* * *

The weekend of 14 July was Renate's birthday, and we decided to go to London with her mum, to visit some friends. We took a first-class train trip to London and on arriving at our hotel, ensured that my mother-in-law was comfortable in her room, before Renate and I took the tube into central London. On Thursday evening, we had a dinner appointment with Jeremy and Laura Franklin, friends of ours from South Africa, who were about to return home after a trip to Scotland and a short stay in the capital. We met at Henry's Café Bar in Covent Garden and had a wonderful evening with two special friends. The following day, we made the same journey into London, however, this time via Liverpool station to meet with our solicitors Breytenbachs, South African migration specialists in the UK. We gathered information about the possibility to apply for Renate's mum to come and stay with us in the UK, once we have secured permanent residence. However, Breytenbach's confirmed that, whilst possible, this type of application was very expensive, with high risks as the rules for parental visas had become very strict. We debated the detail of our meeting over brunch at the Lord Aberconway, a beautiful old pub in Bishop's gate. Later that day, we took a slow walk through London's streets, and by mid-afternoon made our way toward the South of London, where we visited Katrin Kruger. We were treated to a lovely dinner, good Argentinean red wine, and lovely German schnapps. On Saturday the 13th, the three of us took a short train trip to Westfield Mall, where we joined up with Graham and Megan Vass at Bill's Restaurant. Renate, her mom, and I, spent lunch and a good part of the afternoon with Graham and Megan reflecting on our respective adventures and developed life-long memories. After my mother-in-law retired for the evening, Renate and I went for a walk. We took a long stroll through a suburban woodland and, eventually, wandered the streets of Hanger Lane, a west London suburb. Before we retired for the night, we met some German tourists and an American in one of the local pubs. The next day, Sunday the 14th, we took the train back to Plymouth and just enjoyed the beautiful scenery on the three-hour train trip from London. We reflected on the remoteness of Plymouth and debated the possibility of securing a post in the NHS closer to London in time to come.

On returning home, it was as if we were away for a week. It felt as if we had not had a bit of trouble in the world. However, returning to Plymouth also meant that we were returning to reality and the challenges that faced us pertaining to my health.

* * *

On 25 July, I flew to South Africa to surprise my dad in celebrating his 85th birthday. I went for just over a week. Andre collected me at the airport and arranged to have lunch with my dad on Friday the 26th. On arriving at the restaurant, Andre went inside and chatted with my dad. I waited a few minutes to allow them time to settle, and went inside. My dad sat with his back facing the door, so I managed to walk until I was behind him before I could hold his shoulder and said hello. He was pleasantly surprised and it was absolutely amazing to be with him. My siblings and I, with my dad's remaining brothers and sisters with their significant others, celebrated a very special birthday on Sunday, 28 July. I stayed with them for a week. Andre and I visited his family and also celebrated the 80th birthday of an Aunt of mine in Witbank before I returned to Renate and her mum on the 5th of August.

When I returned to work, we learned, with shock, that Alison Boshoff, a dear friend of ours in St. Anne's-on-the-Sea, was diagnosed with cancer. This was not good news and made me reflect on my own situation with renewed focus. We told Alison that we would see her soon when we made our way north to Blackpool, en route to Sterling in Scotland. We planned to visit Scotland during the week following the August bank holiday weekend. With all the challenges at work, time flew, and before we knew it, it was the end of August. I had my third PSA test done on Friday, 23 August, and the next morning, Renate and I drove north. Although we invited Renate's mum to join us, she was not keen, and suggested that she would look after the cats. On Saturday evening, we arrived in Blackpool, where we first stopped at Alison's house to see how she was doing. She remained positive and looked surprisingly well. We promised to come and spend a bit of time with her on our return from Scotland and left to see Dean and Jayne Quinn.

Dean, Renate and I used to work together at Blackpool Teaching Hospitals, and on Sunday morning, the four of us travelled north, past Glasgow to Stirling, just south of the Scottish highlands. We stayed at the Double Tree, by Hilton Hotel, Dunblayne Hydro. A beautiful old hotel situated on the hills of Dunblayne, the hometown of the 2013 Wimbledon Champion, Andrew Murray. We visited Stirling Castle the Monday morning, a remarkable part of Scottish/British history, dating back to 1107, home of Alexander I, James VI of Scotland, who became James I of England and Ireland in 1603, which saw the union of England, Scotland and Ireland. The Castle's bloody history is synonyms with Scotland's greats, like William Wallace and Mary Queen of Scots. In the great hall, we were told how to make haggis which consists of finely chopped sheep's lung, heart, kidney, liver, and mixed with oatmeal, onions and spices, wrapped in a sheep's stomach, and slowly cooked for about three hours.

The Castle had an impressive distant view of the William Wallace monument, built some 140 years ago. The monument celebrates the man and story of Sir William Wallace, defined as patriot, martyr, and Guardian of Scotland. We were fortunate enough to see a live play on the life and history of William Wallace and the battle for the Stirling Bridge. We followed the William Wallace story, visited the Hall of Heroes, and climbed the very narrow staircase of 246 steps to the top, where we marvelled at the brilliant Scottish vistas before making the steep climb down.

On our way home, Jayne started feeling unwell, and by the time we got back to the hotel, she was clearly not herself. We agreed to stay in and agreed to meet later that evening in the pub. However, Renate, Dean and I had dinner on our own, as Jayne was still not feeling well. The next day, we decided to have a quiet day in. We enjoyed the beautiful lounge of the hotel and marvelled at the panorama from the hotel. We read our respective books until about 2:00 PM, when we enjoyed high tea. Jayne and Dean retired to their room, and Renate and I went to sit on the porch in front of the hotel, enjoying the summer sun. The weather was spectacular that week in Scotland. At about 3:00 PM, I called my GP's surgery to get my blood results and was told that they could not give it to me as the doctor needed to speak to me. This did not bode well and the next half hour became rather tense. Eventfully, my GP called back and confirmed that my PSA was 3, which was terrible news indeed. It was consistently rising, and fast. I started realising that radiotherapy was on the cards. Renate and I discussed the pros and cons of the treatment, but concluded that if that is the only option left, then that is what we needed to do.

Returning to work the first week of September, I made an appointment to see Paul and he referred me to Dr Francis Daniels, Consultant Clinical Oncologists at Plymouth Hospitals. Francis met with both Renate and I and again explained the pros and cons of radiotherapy and agreed that before we start, we will do another PSA to give us the assurance that we are doing the right thing. This was done two weeks later, when the PSA was again higher at 4.2, 4200% higher than what it should be after my operation.

* * *

In the meantime, I was sent for a bone scan and a revised CT scan, just to ensure that the cancer did not spread to my bones or other organs. Both these tests were clean. Radiotherapy was all that remained, and 32 sessions over six weeks, every day, Monday to Friday, was planned between 7 October and 19 November. MacMillan Cancer support described radiotherapy as a method to treat cancer by using high-energy rays to destroy the cancer cells, while doing as little harm as possible to healthy cells. In men, pelvic radiotherapy can be used to treat cancer of the prostate gland, bladder, rectum or anus.[68]

Although I could have stayed at home during the six weeks treatment, I elected to continue work and coped very well, with the exception of two days when I was just too tired. Fortunately, Ann was very supportive and

---

[68]http://www.macmillan.org.uk/Cancerinformation/Cancertreatment/Treatmenttypes/Radiotherapy

intervened by sending me home to go and rest. Thinking back at my treatment and sitting in Oncology day after day made me realise that there were many patients suffering with cancer that were worse off than me. I remained, grateful that I was able to maintain a positive approach to life, for at least most of the time.

On 1 November, Carla and Michael, our goddaughter and her husband, came to visit to help raise funds at a charity dinner for the Chestnut appeal.

* * *

After I concluded my treatment, there were only a couple of weeks left for me to do a handover to Martin, before Renate and my long awaited holiday to South Africa and Namibia was due to start on 7 December. I desperately needed some respite after my treatment, and we decided that we would spend our time in southern Africa to relax, recover, and to enjoy the company of family and friends.

However, just before we left, I walked past a couple outside the Hospital's car park speaking in Afrikaans and struggling to figure out how to pay for parking. "Now that is a language that I don't often hear in this part of the world" was my introduction to Gideon and Bualah Maas, an academic couple formerly from Stellenbosch University, who recently moved from Coventry to take up posts at Plymouth University. We arranged for them to visit before we left for South Africa, and had a cup of coffee, talking about our respective experiences of immigration and other challenges that we shared. This accidental meeting in a hospital car park was the start of what promised to be a long and mutually enjoyable friendship.

* * *

Just before we left on vacation, President Jacob Zuma announced on 5 December that "…our beloved Nelson Mandela, the founding President of our democratic nation had departed". Although most people knew that Nelson Mandela was critically ill and anticipated his imminent death, the world was shocked. British commentators were perplexed and amused with the singing and dancing in the streets in Houghton outside Madiba's house, as this appeared out of place following the death of an international icon.

* * *

Renate and I drove the three and a half hours to London to start our leave on the evening of 7 December and although Heathrow had some technical issues, we departed on time. Arriving on the 8th, we went to my parents' home to freshen up, before Renate and I left to collect her mum and to go to Andre's farm in Cullinan where we were joined by the family of Willie for the burial of his ashes in the rocky ridges of KwaMahlanga. We spent the next couple of days with my parents, visiting friends nearby and just enjoying the fresh warm African air. We visited the Union Buildings and signed the book of remembrance for Nelson Mandela. On the 12th, we departed by plane to Windhoek, where we stayed at the Kalahari Sands hotel and had dinner with old friends form the hospitality industry. The next day we took a leisurely drive to Swakopmunt to visit my cousin and her family for a couple of days. They treated us with typical Namibian hospitality. We drove in the dry riverbed of the Swakop River, celebrated our seventeenth wedding anniversary with a drink at sunset at the Tugboat Restaurant, and enjoyed the impressive family dynamics of the van Rensburg family.

On the 15th, when the rest of the world said goodbye to Nelson Mandela at his funeral in Qunu, Renate and I drove to Gobabis to spend another few days with Renate's family on 'Stoetzer', a beautify and large game farm between Omitara and Gobabis. We listened to the speeches of the various dignitaries at the Mandela funeral, but were most impressed by the American President Barack Obama's speech. He paid tribute to Nelson Mandela the man, reprimanded the leaders in attendance that claimed solidarity with Madiba's struggle and reminded the world that Nelson Mandela knew he was not a saint. Whilst his entire speech was spectacular, I particularly hoped that people like Robert Mugabe, Jacob Zuma, and the wider ANC listed to his words when he said "There are too many leaders who claim solidarity with Madiba's struggle for freedom, but do not tolerate dissent form their own people. And there are too many of us who stand on the sidelines, comfortable in complacency or cynicism when our voices must be heard". For all the critics of Nelson Mandela who like to remind the world that he was no saint, President Obama confirmed that "…Madiba himself strongly resisted such a lifeless portrait. Instead, he insisted on sharing with us his doubts and fears, his miscalculations along with the victories. 'I'm not a saint' he said, 'unless you think of a saint as a sinner who keeps on trying'"[69].

* * *

The couple of days at Stoetzer were fantastic. No Television, radio, or internet. Just the beauty of Namibia, the sounds of Mother Nature, healthy food, good company, and lots of rest. It was perfect. In fact, it is safe to say that both Renate and I fell in love with Namibia, and consider it a country that we would love to see much more.

On returning to Pretoria, we attended a college reunion with some of Renate's Technikon friends, spent a couple of days at the Hartebeespoort dam with Renate's aunt, and took long walks at sun set in the afternoons. On the 24th, we went to Renate's mum for Christmas Eve before the three of us went to my dad's house on the 25th to spend Christmas with him, his brothers, children,

---

[69] http://edition.cnn.com/2013/12/10/politics/mandela-obama-remarks/

and grandchildren. It was a spectacular day and Ma Madeleine pulled out all the stops.

Our time in Southern Africa was very special. We had a very relaxing time. We enjoyed seeing everyone we did and were ready to return to the United Kingdom, to go home, after a very special and memorable vacation. My only regret is that we were not able to see my brother during our time in South Africa.

On returning to the UK, Renate and I were relieved to sleep in our own bed again. We spent the last couple of days of the old year with friends in and around Plymouth and reflected on the past year. The support we have had from family and friends, from South Africa, Australia, Dubai, Germany, and England, was absolutely spectacular. We cannot thank enough those who called, emailed, prayed and supported us that year. Their kind words of support, or just inquiring how we were doing, or that they were thinking of us, were what gave Renate and me the strength to get through the challenges of 2013.

Chapter 30
The Wars of 1914 and 2014

The New Year started with optimism, renewed energy, and a belief that this will be a good year all round. Our visit to South Africa and Namibia last December revitalised us, and we thought we were ready to face the adventures and challenges the new year promised to offer.

On 13 January, Renate started working on a flexible basis through NHSP (a flexible staffing agency for the national health services) providing administrative support to a number of wards, at the hospital. She loved it, and the people she worked with quickly realised that she was a great asset to their teams.

The weekend of 16 January, Renate and I went to Reading in Berkshire, west of London. We visited the Jamie Oliver restaurant, looked at the Thames River breaching it banks as it flowed through the city. We enjoyed a spectacular dinner at the China Garden Restaurant, where a Chinese lady taught us how to eat with chopsticks, and visited the South African shop in Reading, enjoying the best biltong we have had outside South Africa.

The following week, I had to attend a medical follow-up, to determine whether I won the battle against cancer. A week before my appointment, I had new blood tests done, and the ideal target was a PSA reading of 0. My blood tests confirmed a reading of 0.39; I was given the all clear, with a follow-up test planned for 28 July. I gave thanks in the hospital Chapel with sometime of reflection. Although both Renate and I were very relieved and grateful, 2014 had some unexpected consequences for us.

February saw the beginning of the new academic year, and following the stressful events of the year before, I originally thought I'll stop my studies, being content with the fact that I received a Diploma in English Law. However, after receiving my clear bill of health, I decided that I started out to complete an LLB and decided to enrol again to complete my law degree. The subjects for this year were Contract Law and the Tort of Negligence, which consisted of a number of law tutorials in Exeter, an old Roman city near Plymouth.

The end of the month, Renate and I drove to Blackpool to join Nick Grimshaw, his wife Susan and their friends in the celebration of his 50th birthday. Nick, my former boss at Blackpool Teaching Hospitals became a very good friend to Renate and I. We stayed with Ponti in St. Anne's, and as always, it was great to see him and the family.

I enjoyed studying again and found the module on contract law very interesting. We had a great tutor; Vince Johns who reminded me of Paul Flottman, our late European Law tutor. They both brought their respective subjects alive, with stories, examples and illustrations. I always enjoyed contract law, but Vince made it especially interesting. I submitted my first assignment in March and passed with good grades, something I repeated six times during the year, as the various assignments on both contract law and the tort of negligence fell due.

During March, my very first employer from Medi-Clinic came to visit. Johan Malan came on a healthcare visit to England and was the then-Regional Human Resources Manager at Medi-Clinic in 1992, who employed me as Personnel Officer for Sandton Medi-Clinic. I was particularly pleased to welcome Johan to the South West of England. I always tried to maintain good relationships with my past employers. I was particularly pleased that our friendship of more than twenty-two years placed me in a position to show Johan the impact of the Human Resources function in the National Health Services. He wanted to understand what we did from a shared services point of view, how we promote employee engagement, reduced sickness absence, did workforce planning, (or not, as the case may be), and the challenges that we faced within this complex, but nationally treasured institution of health. I took Johan and his colleague to a number of NHS Hospitals across the South West, and it would be fair to say that he was suitably impressed with the quality and scale of the NHS in the United Kingdom. Medi-Clinic sent another delegation later in the year to have a look at our shared-services and other back-office support structures.

* * *

With April upon us, Renate and I were preparing for our 'Life in the UK Test'. This is a requirement by the United Kingdom Border Agency (UKBA) for all people who apply for indefinite leave to remain. The test is generally done after completing five years of residency in the United Kingdom.[70] A book titled *Life in the United Kingdom*, "an overview of Britain's history, values, laws and constitution". This acts as a guide for new residents. The purpose of this book and test is to give an overview of the history of the United Kingdom, since the 3rd and 4th centuries AD. It considers the departure of the Romans in 410 AD, the invasion of the Vikings in 789 AD, the arrival of William the conqueror in 1066, right up to the Second South African (Boer) War (1899–1902) and modern day life in the United Kingdom.[71] It is a historic journey which describes the people that shaped this country, defined its values and principles, and considers the traditions and cultures across the United Kingdom. It also provides valuable insight into its legal and constitutional

---

[70] https://www.gov.uk/life-in-the-uk-test
[71] Life in the United Kingdom: A Guide for New Residents, 3rd Edition

system, the history and role of the monarchy, and the implications of the devolution of authority to countries like Scotland, Northern Ireland, and the principality of Wales. This is a good way to equip immigrants for their life in the UK, to integrate us, and to ensure we understand and conform to the British values. The latter being defined as:

- democracy
- the rule of law,
- individual liberty,
- tolerance of those with different faiths and beliefs, and
- participation in community life.[72]

Something that was striking of this journey for me was that the British people always protect their history. Irrespective of whether the events were good, bad, or indifferent, you can trace back British history to before the Roman occupation of 43 AD. As one government takes over from another, the ruling government does not destroy the legacy, statues, street names, or town names left by the former. In fact, they protect the past, as history is both a celebration of admirable achievements, and a reminder of atrocities that should never be repeated, but should also never be forgotten.

This, sadly, is not the case in South Africa. When the ANC came into power, millions of rands were spent to change street names, to remove all the apartheid statutes, everything that was vaguely representing of South Africa's White past, even before the establishment of Apartheid had to go. This is being called 'decolonisation'[73].

* * *

Midway through our studies, Renate was appointed substantively as Project Assistant in the Oncology team, funded by MacMillan[74], a cancer charity based at our hospital. We were both delighted, and Renate would spend the rest of the year working with a team of dedicated people, supporting people with and who survived cancer.

In April, Renate and I drove to Cardiff, to do our 'Life in the UK' test, only to be turned away as we used our work-permit to register and only had our passport with us for identification. As ridiculous as this sounds, bureaucracy is well and alive, even in first world countries. We drove back, re-registered, paid another £75 per person, and eventually took our test on Friday, 11 April. We spent the weekend and visited the Cardiff Castle, Mermaid Quay, and wandered the streets of this beautiful city and capital of Wales.

---

[72] https://lifeintheuktests.co.uk/study-materials/chapter-1/

[73] Sam C. Noluthungu, South Africa in Africa : A study of ideology and foreign policy, p102

[74] http://www.macmillan.org.uk

On 15 April I travelled to Amersham in Buckinghamshire for a meeting and stayed in the Kings Arms. A beautiful Tudor exterior hotel where a scene from Four Weddings and a Funeral was filmed.[75]

The good news that we passed our 'Life in the UK Test' was dampened with the news that the Trusts' financial position had deteriorated, with a £20m deficit and an increase in public demand. A sense of tension was emerging in the hospital, as everyone was aware that services needed to be delivered, that funds were limited, and that the expectations of the public were ever increasing.

A year after my operation, I was physically recovering well. However, the psychological impact of being diagnosed with and treated for cancer, with the associated after-effects, caused a number of internal wars and was taking its toll. I remained tired, felt stressed most of the time, with ever increasing levels of anxiety. This, I was told, was normal and will decrease in time to come. However, the only thing that decreased was my own levels of self-worth. I had a constant fear that the cancer will come back, and that ultimately, I was no longer the man I used to be.

* * *

Kevin Baber, a colleague of mine from the hospital at the time, and I became good friends. He has a special disposition in that he often say what he thinks, without thinking what he said, much like Hugh Laurie's television character Dr Gregory House, MD from the drama "House". But like his film equivalent, Kevin has a good heart. He is a keen cyclist, and as I brought my bike back from South Africa in 2013, he insisted we should go for a ride.

We started off cycling around Mount Edgcombe in Cornwall, which delighted Kevin as I fell off my bike. However, we went up to the All Saints church at Millbrook, before we made our way back down the home straight to the Creyml Ferry. We boarded the ferry only after we had a beer at the Edgcombe Arms. This paved the way for many a cycle ride with Kevin, a friend of his Darren Muggleson, Phil Hughes, our medical director, and other colleagues and friends of Kevin or Darren. All the rides were named, and traditionally related to something that happened on the ride. During 2014, we did 707 km (439mi) before the end of December.

An evening ride with Kevin	19 km
Sore Ass	66 km
Long hill evening ride	34 km
Not that bad evening ride	26 km
A very slow Sunday afternoon	28 km
31 day ride	20 km

---

[75] *http://www.movie-locations.com/movies/f/4wandf.html#.WG-zx7GcZ-U* [accessed 06/01/2017]

The Baber revenge	30 km
The Boer, the Scot and two Englishmen	32 km
A crashing finish	32km
Reservoir Dogs	30 km
Schwalbe is the best	47 km
A quick one up St Anthony's	20 km
Boys in the suburbs	23 km
A sunset with sheep	27 km
A good Sunday afternoon	47 km
Wet feet, slippery chains and grumpy	26 km
Lots of hills and slippery slopes	69 km
How very slow was Baber today	48 km
South Africans are useful	28 km
Darren came off again, Phil and the Lodger got lost, and Baber… is just Baber	30km
Slow and icy, with great new gears	25 km

Kevin encouraged me to go out regularly, although I did not go as much as I could have.

Some of the rides took us past St. Anthony's, up Crafthole, via the Military Road on the Rame Peninsula, to Siblyback Lake Reservoir, Prince Town, Ivybrindge, and Yealmpton. My oncologist did say that cycling was good, whilst Kevin and Darren were adamant to take me through my paces. All of this set the scene for us taking part in the Cape Town Cycle Tour[76], which is the world's largest timed race with 37000 participants cycling the 109km around the Cape Peninsula. March 2015, three blokes and their bikes would take on the Cape Town cycle tour, albeit the Cape southwestern, and devastating wildfires had different plans with us (see Chapter 30).

* * *

Although not much happened in Renate and my life other than what was already stated, this year saw its share of news-worthy events. There was the on-going war in Syria, the flooded Somerset levels, the Sochi winter Olympics, the Oscar Pistorius murder trial, elections in Afghanistan, the European Union, Egypt, India, South Africa, and the independence vote for

Scotland. There was the 100th anniversary of the First World War and the disappearance of Malaysian MH370 with its 239 passengers and crew. Russia annexed Crimea, and on 17 July, another Malaysian Airline (HM17) crashed, with Russian separatists being blamed, causing the death of

---

[76] http://www.capetowncycletour.com

another 298 civilians. The latter resulted in the breakup of the G8 nations and threats of another cold war.

*　*　*

I can only describe Monday, 4 August 2014 as a remarkable day of remembrance. Most of Europe commemorated the 100th anniversary of the beginning of the First World War. I never knew the reason the war started. I was surprised to learn via a BBC documentary, that it was on 28 June 1914, when Gavrilo Princip, a Bosnian Serb, assassinated the Archduke Franz Ferdinand of Austria. He was the heir apparent to the Austro-Hungarian throne. This act of murder, aimed to destroy the Austria-Hungary relationship with the then South-Slavic provinces, an event that would cost the world more than 17,000,000 lives.[77]

Through numerous documentary and radio programs on the BBC, and 'live twitter feeds' of the events of that dreadful day, it became apparent that the rising German Empire, Austria-Hungary, and Italy had an alliance, known as the 'Central Powers', whilst the then-Imperial Powers, France, Russia, and Great Britain, had an alliance known as the 'Triple Entente'. So when Austria-Hungary declared war on Serbia, Russia, who had a history of clashing with them over the Balkan States, backed its ally. Germany, who had an ever-increasing navy and was gaining confidence through its industrial strength, backed its ally Austria-Hungary. Initially, the three cousins, King George V of Britain and Tsar Nicholas II of Russia, worked frantically through diplomatic means to prevent conflict with Kaiser Wilhelm II, but without success. The first declaration of war was on 28 July 1914, one month after the assassination of Archduke Franz Ferdinand, when Austria-Hungary, backed by Germany, declared war on Serbia. Four days later, on 1 August 1914, Germany declared war on Russia, and two days after that, on 3 August 1914, with France. On Tuesday, 4 August 1914, Germany marched on France, taking the shortest route, through Belgium and Luxembourg.

The British Government, we were told, issued an ultimatum to Germany to withdraw from Belgium by midnight on 4 August 1914. It was 11:00 PM in Britain.

A hundred years later, we spent the final hour, between 10:00 and 11:00 PM, in reflection. At 10:00 PM, Renate and I switched off our lights in Plymouth, and so did the rest of Britain. In Blackpool, the lights on the Blackpool Tower were switched off; in London, Tower Bridge, and the lights at the House of Parliament fell dark. I lit a single candle, as we also remembered. It was an interesting reflection, as we watched the various memorial services across the UK and Belgium; I could not but wonder how that last sixty minutes before the declaration of war felt for the people of Britain, 100 years ago.

---

[77] http://www.bbc.co.uk/news/magazine-25776836

As the cities across the UK became dark, we remembered those who sacrificed their lives in the battles of the First World War.

The Royal Family was out in full force, remembering. Queen Elizabeth II attended a memorial service at Crathie Kirk in Aberdeenshire, in Scotland. Prince Charles, also in Scotland, was at Glasgow Cathedral with a number of Commonwealth dignitaries. Prince William and Catherine, the Duke and Duchess of Cambridge, and Prince Harry attended the commemorations at St. Symphorien Military Cemetery in Mons, Belgium. The latter was a spectacular evening of remembrance. There were readings of letters from soldiers, both British and German, and reflections on what it meant to them. The London Symphony Orchestra and the Berliner Philharmoniker played Butterworth's rhapsody *'On a Shropshire Lad'*. Butterworth himself died in the battle of the Som. There was also music from Bach and Brahms. But what was most striking of this evening was the brilliant participation of both British and German artists, dignitaries and attendees. Both sides remembered all the fallen in respectful reverence.

Camilla, the Duchess of Cornwall, attended a candle light service at Westminster Abbey. The Very Rev Dr John Hall, Dean of Westminster, led the service from the Abbey. As the service progressed, candles were extinguished systematically. Until only the candle next to the grave of the Unknown Soldier was flickering. It was a very poignant evening of reflection, of remembrance, but also of remorse. Remembrance, as we should never forget those who sacrificed their lives for our freedom, for our safety, for our liberty; remorse, for the cruelty of man, that humanity has the capacity to cause such devastation on each other, such loss of life, such destruction.

I reflected on South Africa's own wars, and wondered why it was that man is so blood thirsty. Also, why does the people in Southern Africa destroy its history so persistently. It just seems as if we never learn, considering the atrocities of 2014, in Syria, Russia, Nigeria, Kenya, Somalia, Israel, Gaza, and Iraq; our ability to be at war is never ending.

British and Commonwealth soldiers who sacrificed their lives in the war were all remembered. The Tower of London looked as if its moat was covered in blood, where 888,246 red ceramic poppies were planted in their memory. At 11:00 PM, at the grave of the Unknown Soldier, the Duchess of Cornwall extinguished the last candle, which marked the darkness of the moment when Britain declared war on Germany.

As the hour drew to a close, and the moment of Britain's entry into the war, a hundred years ago, drew nearer, a reading was done from Churchill's historic recollection titled 'The World Crises'. Winston Churchill was the First Lord of the Admiralty at the time, and he recalled the atmosphere of that fateful night. It was 11:00 PM and 12:00 AM by German time when the ultimatum expired. Churchill wrote:

"The windows of the Admiralty was thrown wide open, in the warm night air. Along the mile, in the direction of the Palace, the sound of an immense

concourse, singing 'God Save the King', floated in; and on this deep wave,
their broke the chimes of Big Bed; and as the first stroke of the hour boomed
out, a rustle of movement swept across the room. The war telegraph, which
meant 'commence hostility against Germany', was flashed to the ships and
the establishments under the white ensign all over the world. [Churchill said],
"I walked across the horse guards' parade, to the cabinet room; reported
to the Prime Minister, and the Minister were assembled there, that the deed
was done.'[78]

Looking at the documentaries of commemoration at the time, we were
again filled with awe as to how the British nation protect their history,
remember the fallen, on both sides of the war, and the impressive display of
respect for all of those who have been affected by the war. We were again
reassured that we made the right choice in coming to the United Kingdom.

* * *

During August, we had a number of our friends from Blackpool and
Fleetwood in Lancashire coming to visit. We showed off our beautiful county,
with visits to the Barbican, the Hoe, and Cornwall. It is becoming increasingly
evident how fortunate we were to be able to live in the beautiful South West
of England in that time. Its beauty, diversity, and good weather all
contributing factors to our happiness in Plymouth.

With the last visitors saying their goodbyes, I had to turn my attention to
my exams in September, and after a surprisingly good academic year, I
started preparing for my exam, which took place on 18 September. The
thought of writing a three-hour paper on Contract Law and the Tort of
Negligence was very daunting, but I was relieved to get three of the areas
that I hoped for, and prayed that I did enough on the fourth area. As my dad
always said, "I did my bit; it is now up to the examiner to play his part." I
was truly relieved when this exam was done. Renate met me in town and we
had a relaxing lunch with some much needed white wine to celebrate the end
of the academic year. I knew this would be short-lived, as my final stretch to
the end of my degree was due to start on 4 October.

* * *

Renate and I attended the St Ives music festival in Cornwall from 25–28
September, and enjoyed the music by the famous Fishermen's Friends
from Port Isaac's; we met a brilliant and talented blues guitarist, Sarah
Gillespie, and attended a performance by the South (formerly the Beautiful

---

[78] The World Crisis 1911–1918, by Winston Churchill

South). This fisherman's town on the far south-western coast of Cornwall truly touched both Renate and me.

* * *

On 4 October, 2014, the final leg of my studies began with the last modules in Land Law, Trusts and Equity. This time I had to go Taunton for the bi-monthly tutorials.

The week of 14 October, we were supposed to join Ponti, Stefan, and Carla with their partners for a week in Turkey to celebrate his 50th birthday. However, things did not work out that way, and he decided not to go. Renate and I stayed at home and focused on work.

The hospital pressures mounted with financial challenges, non- delivery of consultant job plans, and a general rising sense of tension in the hospital.

At this time, Gerhard and Frida Harmse, my former colleague, employee, and friend, and his wife decided to immigrate to the UK. Frida held a Belgian passport, and we offered for them to come and stay with us for a couple of weeks to see how things are. Frida had to return to South Africa, but Gerry stayed behind to complete his CIPD conversion, similar to what I had to do in Blackpool. After he completed his academic side, I offered for him to complete his report at the hospital and took him with us on our weekly cycle outing. Kevin quickly nicknamed Gerry 'the lodger', who proved his worth very quickly with cycling, as he can change a flat tire in the dark, next to a busy road, in five minutes flat. Kevin was duly impressed and saw some worth in the South African.

Eventually, that December, Gerry successfully completed his CIPD qualification and returned to South Africa for Christmas before he returned to stay with family near Manchester. Renate and I went to Manchester for Christmas, where we stayed with our godson Stefan and his partner, before we all went to Ponti for Christmas day. As always, Christmas is a time of reflection. This one was no different. This year, we reflected on the wars of both the past and our current time, whilst I battled a number of internal wars. We had a great time with Ponti, as always, but driving back to Plymouth gave some headroom to make a number of personal choices for 2015. The year of my 50th birthday, was the year that I was going to take charge of my life again. I had to help a couple of people check out of my head.

Chapter 31
Three Blokes and Their Bikes

On 12 January 2015, I asked for a meeting with Ann James, the Chief Executive of the hospital. During that meeting, I thanked her for her support during the previous two years. She had been remarkably understanding from the time I was diagnosed with cancer, through my various tests, the operation, and the subsequent radiation therapy.

I told Ann that during the last December, I thought a lot about the previous two years. As a natural reflector, I indicated that 2014 had been a particularly challenging year for me. This was not as much due to the work that needed to be done, but rather more on a personal level. The consequences of my illness, its treatments and lasting effects had a massive psychological impact on me. Ann was very understanding, and as we spoke about the challenges of the hospital, she pointed out that I should not take the challenges of the NHS personally. She suggested that I have to face my own demons, deal with the wars within and should not have sleepless nights about things over which I have very little or no control.

To say that Ann was surprised by my announcement that it was time for me to move on from Plymouth, is an understatement; however, she was very supportive. On reflection, this is also not something that I would ever do again. Transparency has its place, but sometimes it is better to keep one's thoughts to oneself. However, at that time, expressing my intent to seek an alternative appointment provided me with much needed relief, as suddenly, I started to feel more relaxed.

Ann's advice and our discussion reminded me of Stephen Covey's in *7 Habits of Highly Effective People*.[79] Covey's seven habits that he offered were:

1. Be proactive
2. Begin with the end in mind
3. Put first things first
4. Think win-win
5. Seek first to understand, then to be understood
6. Synergise
7. Sharpen the saw

---

[79] 7 Habits of Highly Effective People, pg.53

Covey's first habit had some striking importance in my life at that point, as it offered the following advice:

"Your life doesn't just 'happen'. Whether you know it or not, it is carefully designed by you. The choices, after all, are yours. You choose happiness. You choose sadness. You choose decisiveness. You choose ambivalence. You choose success. You choose failure. You choose courage. You choose fear. Just remember that every moment, every situation, provides a new choice. And in doing so, it gives you a perfect opportunity to do things differently to produce more positive results."[80]

Good advice, I know, and an approach with which I agreed. However, it felt incomprehensible that the anxiety, the insomnia, the inability to focus, is 'carefully designed by' me. Deciding to leave Plymouth was the first step in choosing to take charge of my own life again.

As I was about to go to South Africa with Kevin and Darren to partake in the Cape Town Cycle race, Ann and I agreed to regroup on my return and to see how things were going.

* * *

Renate and I travelled to South Africa nine days before Kevin and Darren, to spend some time with our parents in Pretoria, see a few friends, and relax for five days at the Magalies Park Golf Club with Renate's mum. I recovered from sunburn obtained at Andre's lodge, after spending only one hour in the sun, without sun-block. What could a 35-degree African sun do to a former resident of Pretoria in any event? I looked like a Cape Lobster!

* * *

On 28th of February, we left for Cape Town in anticipation of the arrival of Darren and Kevin (Mr B), and spent the day with friends in Blaauwbergstrand before their arrival. I received a frantic text message from Kevin instructing me to "get beer and wine; apparently, it's a third world country that doesn't sell alcohol on Sunday..." Although alcohol is sold on Sundays in South Africa, a developing country, I may add, I procured some wine and beer as instructed, before sunset.

DAY 1 (Sunday)
After Renate and I checked into the Big Bay Beach Club, we off-loaded my bike and our luggage and went shopping for some basic groceries. I went to the airport to see Emirates flight EK0770 from Dubai touch down thirty minutes earlier than anticipated, at 4:00 PM on Sunday, 1st of March.

---

[80] https://www.stephencovey.com/7habits/7habits-habit1.php

The Cape was hot with a light southeastern blowing. Water bottle in hand, I saw Darren first, and then Kevin hobbling behind him. His ankles were swollen with his toes looking like little piglets. I was surprised to see how light they both travelled, only to realise that their bikes were still in Dubai. After getting them into the car to go back to the Beach Club, Kevin placed his feet on the dash to get the piglets under control and get his swollen ankles back to normal. Truly a sight it was. On our way back to the house, Kevin wanted to buy some bread, bacon and eggs, and insisted that I stop at Woolworths (South Africa's version of Waitrose).

That evening, after freshening up with some cold Windhoek Draft Beer, we had dinner with Darren's parents-in-law, Craig and Pat, and their friends Eric and Geraldine from Padstow, Cornwall. Two lovely couples who made all of us feel very welcome. We ate South African beef fillet, and drank Pinotage from Zonnebloem and Beyerskloof Wine Estates respectively.

Back home, Kevin opened some Chenin Blank from Leopards Leap, Neil Ellis, and Boschendal. We stargazed and tried to pinpoint the Southern Cross, Orion's belt, and some formation Kevin created. We were not sure whether this was wine induced hallucinations, dehydration or just general exhaustion. With all Mr B's comments, the time in Cape Town promised to be a very entertaining one. Dr House was in the house. Retiring for the night, we all slept like logs, or at least most of us did.

DAY 2 (Monday)

Darren and I were up first, meeting in the kitchen for tea and coffee, respectively. We were all bemused to hear that, in the middle of the night, Kevin was looking for the toilet, only to wander into Darren's room. The latter, rather confused, or perhaps disturbed, about why this larger than life figure was standing at the end of his bed. Eventually, Kevin found his way to the correct door, and the rest of the night was peaceful.

After all four of us were up, Kevin proceeded to make some breakfast, consisting of boerewors that he baked in a frying pan in the oven, and some eggs on buns. Renate did some washing for us, after which the three blokes went to the local bike shop. We bought some new kit, and I made arrangements for my bike to be re-assembled, the latter at a cost of R150.00 (£8.50). On returning home, we stopped at the local Pick n Pay (like Morrison's) to get some additional groceries. Although there is nothing wrong with my driving skills, Kevin became increasingly anxious when I forgot to put the brake on, and as we disembarked, the car started rolling backwards. Kevin criticised my driving skills, defining it as 'chaotic'. I can confirm that no harm was done to any animals or humans.

We had to wait for the other two blokes' bikes to arrive on the 11:00 AM flight from Dubai. As it was not clear when these would be delivered to our house, there was not much we could do on the second day, other than wait. We went for a walk on the beach. The miles of white beaches on

Blaauwbergstrand, stretching in front of us, the ice cold Atlantic Ocean looking more inviting than the reality of its temperature. The vistas of Cape Town, at the foot of Table Mountain directly in front of us, were breath-taking. Robben Island was only three miles away from us. Situated west from the coast at Blaauwberg, we could see the Minto Hill lighthouse, the village where my parents and I stayed, when my father worked on the island, and the ferry that commutes between the Victoria and Alfred (V&A) waterfront and the island harbour on regular intervals. We ended up at 'Eden on the Bay', a shopping complex with coffee houses, restaurants, and surf shops. We drank coffee and ate South African flapjacks (a small pancake), with fruit and yogurt, before we walked back to the Beach Club. We continued waiting for the bikes. Kevin fell asleep on the couch, as we waited, and waited some more...

The heat mounted, and initially it looked like the island disappeared below a cloud of heat. However, later when Craig came to visit, he told us that the 'clouds' we saw were not 'meteorological clouds', but smoke. We later learned that most of the southern peninsula was ablaze with wildfires. Key areas like Constantia, Fishoek, Ou-Kaapseweg, and Chapman's Peak, covering both the original and alternative routes of the Cape Town Cycle route, were under threat. The fire brigades across the Cape Metropole were working diligently to bring the fires under control. However, the heat and strong southwesterly wind did not help. We all received emails confirming that the race organisers are consulting with all relevant stakeholders and confirmed that a press conference will be held on Wednesday at 4:00 PM to confirm the way forward.

At 4:00 on Monday afternoon, both Darren's and Kevin's bikes were delivered. Darren took me to the bike shop to collect my re-assembled bike. On cycling back to the Beach Club, my Orbea felt like a brand new cycling machine. Kevin and Darren sorted their bikes, while Renate and I prepared dinner.

Renate made a spectacular Mediterranean salad, prepared some gem squash (a local small pumpkin), beetroot salad and garlic bread. I prepared some mielie-pap (maze), tomato and onion relish, boerewors, cheese-grillers, T-bones and beefsteak. Considering both Kevin and Darren's comments after dinner, it must have been a success, which obviously was accompanied by some Chenin Blanc from Neethlingshof, Neil Ellis, and Leopards Leap. Darren and I enjoyed some Windhoek Lager with Renate having some JC le Roux bubbly. All in all, everything was ready for our first ride on Tuesday.

DAY 3 (Tuesday)

I woke up at 6:30 AM and started to convert some of the previous night's pap into porridge for breakfast. Kevin and Darren rose; we all got dressed in our 'three blokes on their bikes' gear, just to make sure that everything fits, and took a leisurely ride out on the Cape West Coast. We took the R27 north and stopped at the Farmstall restaurant for some coffee and muffins, the latter being served with cheese and jam. We had two blueberry muffins and a date and nut muffin. Kevin commented later to Renate saying "you [South Africans] are a strange lot, serving cheese with sweet muffins...!"

We cycled toward Melkbostrand, a beautiful coastal village with large holiday and residential homes, good quality seafood restaurants adjacent to a spectacularly large white beach, the lilac blue waters looking as inviting as the Caribbean. This was a cool relief as the temperatures quickly rose to 43 degrees Celsius, the sea breeze providing a welcome relief to the stifling hot atmosphere. We returned on the coastal road and completed the first 29km, testing our bikes, stretching our legs, with Kevin and Darren trying to bond with some of the locals. The press reported that the temperature of the day was the highest the Cape had seen in 100 years!

After we freshened up, uploaded Strava (the GPS App we use to monitor our rides) with the aptly named rides of '*Bike Testing & Leg Stretching at 43 Degrees Celsius*', Darren titled his ride '*43 Degrees in Melkbos*' and Kevin '*Thumbs up to the caddy boys!*'. We picked up Renate and drove north, direction Stellenbosch. After going past Simonsig wine estate with its large wine bottle outside, we arrived at Fairview Wine Estate. We listened to the local 'Smile 90.4 FM', a predominantly music show, playing 'hits of the eighties, nineties and now'. We sent them a shout-out but were not sure if they ever played it as we had arrived at Fairview. Here the heat was still standing at 42 degrees as there was no wind. Getting out of the air-conditioned car felt like going through a time warp from Plymouth to Dubai in a second.

On arriving at the estate, we took photos of the goats and their tower. Kevin was concerned that it was not safe for them to walk up and down the tower, and suggested a hand railing should be installed to comply with required health and safety regulations. We tasted some wine, and cheese, and more wine. The emphasis for me was on tasting – rather than drinking, as I was the designated driver. There were some Goats du Roam cycling shirts for sale and both Kevin and Darren tried to get their sizes, but these were not available. Disappointed that they could not get their desired merchandise, we settled on the veranda outside the restaurant for some lunch, and of course, some more wine. Renate enjoyed a selection of Fairview Cheeses, Kevin and I had a steak salad and Darren treated himself to a Springbok salad. Kevin made an observation that my demeanour had changed since back in South Africa, not something that I noted. He suggested that I was more aggressive, 'more South African', than what I was in England.

After Fairview, the heat was still surprisingly high. We started driving back. Driving long distances would become a key element of this cycling trip, as everything is 30-60 minutes far. We stopped at Simonsig Wine Estate and first took a photo outside the entrance in front of a massive bottle of wine. Kevin dubbed this 'three blokes, a large bottle of wine, after a bottle, before another bottle...' We obliged and tasted some more wine, watched a bit of cricket, and enjoyed the air-conditioned facilities.

Driving home, it did not take long before Kevin demonstrated his 'Chenin Blank Shuffle', which was within ten minutes back in the car; he made himself comfortable and fell asleep. He awoke to his name being mentioned on a shout-out on Smile 90.4fm. On returning home, we all felt that the lunch was sufficient to sustain us through the night, however Kevin needed some chicken. So, we got some peri-peri chicken on our way to the Beach Club and stopped at Craig and Pat's for sundowners. Craig told us how the people from antiquity navigated in the old days, using the stars, and explained the various types of light-houses the weathermen used as points of reference when forecasting the weather. He used the Minto Hill lighthouse on Robben Island as an example.

Getting home, we placed some washing into the washing machine. Renate retired for the night, and I prepared the chicken. Although neither Darren nor I were particularly hungry, the chicken tasted good, Kevin finished half of it, calming his craving for chicken.

DAY 4 (Wednesday)

I rose to make some porridge for breakfast before we did our second ride on the Cape West Coast. We took the same route north, but in reverse, explored Melkbostrand a bit, and rode direction Veldrift, before we turned due south to return to Blaauwberg. We stopped for coffee at the Farmstall, this time without the muffins.

As we were invited to lunch with Johan Malan, Group Operational Human Resources Manager for Medi-Clinic, on Wednesday, Kevin suggested that we plan our day a bit, as we could not arrive at Johan's place 'three sheets to the wind'. I have never heard this saying before, but was intrigued. Before we left, I wanted to make sure I understood the saying and suggested that I should remember this, 'three sails to the wind', causing both Kevin and Darren to hackle me, as I got the saying wrong.

We cycled back to the Beach Club, freshened up, and uploaded the ride on Strava titled 'A pleasant ride–like three sails in the wind', Darren titled his 'Reliability ride' and Kevin got frustrated with the time robots (traffic lights) took to change in South Africa, so he called his 'Robot invasion...'

We took a drive out to Cape Town city centre to visit the V&A Waterfront, where we showed Kevin some of the high quality specialty stores at this big iconic development, with its large number of restaurants, pubs and branded store outlets. We enjoyed a light lunch, as we had dinner with the Malans that evening, before we drove back to the Beach Club to relax a bit before we needed to drive out to Durbanville.

Late afternoon we took the N7 and N1 north direction Stellenbosch and Durbanville. It was confirmed over the news that the Cycle Tour had been amended, and Darren quickly checked his emails, only to find the following announcement in his inbox:

It's been an extremely worrying and tense week for Cape Town. For the last four days, our beautiful Southern Peninsula that the iconic Cape Town Cycle Tour traditionally passes through, has been on fire. It's been devastating....

...For the Cycle Tour to be able to safely cater for the 35000 anticipated participants, we need to start placing infrastructure on the ground by tomorrow morning. For this to happen, a decision on the route needs to be made today. The decision we have made is unanimous and has not been taken lightly. It has involved extensive discussion and collaboration by all stakeholders...

...Having carefully assessed all available information, it has become clear that the safety of cyclists cannot be guaranteed on Chapman's Peak and this rules out using this famous landmark for the 2015 event...

We understand that many visitors have travelled from far afield to participate in this iconic international bucket list cycling event. We are also keenly aware of the need to reduce the impact the event will have on traffic and other emergency services that are desperately needed elsewhere in the South Peninsula.

With this in mind, we have taken a bold decision and will be staging a vastly shortened version of our beloved Cape Town Cycle Tour in solidarity and support for those affected by the tragic fires burning on the mountains around Cape Town.

The route will be a 47km circular route from its normal start at the Civic Centre to the end of the M3 and back the same way to a slightly altered finish in Green Point. The unfortunate set of circumstances we face this week is unprecedented in 38 years of the Cape Town Cycle Tour....

We were all very disappointed as we turned off toward Durbanville and arriving at the Malan residence. We tried to see if the evening news had any more details, but there was nothing other than the absolute devastation the fire caused to people's houses, their cars, and their lives. As we tried to make peace with the fact that we will not be doing the 109Km traditional route, we settled and enjoyed traditional South African hospitality, with a braai (barbeque) at the house of Johan and Bonny Malan, with their daughter Melissa. Just before dinner, as is custom in most Christian Afrikaner homes in South Africa, Johan said grace before we ate. As per the local custom, everyone held hands, and as this was not something Darren expected; taking Kevin's hand, he said, "This is all a bit bufty." No one heard, other than Kevin. Grace was said and we were treated to some South African boerewors, chicken skewers and salads, topped off with Milktart and cream for dessert. As I have been the designated driver for most of our outings, Darren offered to drive us home. On our way, Kevin told us about Darren's comical comment. All in all, a very successful day, other than the news of the shortened route of the Cape Town Cycle Tour.

283

DAY 5 (Thursday)

Waking on Thursday, everyone was still a bit disappointed about the dramatically shortened route that was planned for the 2015 Cape Town Cycle Tour, titled the 'Solidarity Ride'. This shortened route was to ensure safety comes first. The 'Cape Town Cycle Tour 2015 – Solidarity Ride' was in support of the firefighters who risked their lives getting the fire under control and for the people whose lives were devastated by the raging fires.

We were disappointed by comments from some donors on the just-give page who inquired whether they could get their money back, as we were not cycling the full 109km. Whilst it was clear that some were made in jest, others appeared to be serious. However, considering the funds raised went to the Chestnut Appeal, prostate cancer awareness and the race was dedicated to the firefighters who placed their lives at risk, our critics should have doubled their contributions.

We did not cycle on Thursday, as we wanted to register early and took in some of the scenery in and around Cape Town. Arriving in the city, we registered, got our timing-chips sorted, and had to wait for new cycle numbers, as they misplaced ours. That eventually sorted, we walked through the large exhibition of cycling merchandise. Kevin was getting hungry, so the exhibition was cut short, and on our way out, both Kevin and Darren were lured into an Oakley shop. Kevin bought a new frame 'Racing Jacket' for his special prescription lenses, and convinced Darren to buy a pair of 'Radar Lock's', as well. I abstained from the shopping frenzy.

We did not drive directly toward Camps Bay, but took a slight detour via Constantia toward Hout Bay. Around the back of Table Mountain. I wanted to show them a part of the alternative route that we would cycle on Sunday. I hoped we could see some of the fire damage that was reported on the radio around Contantia, whilst the beauty of that part of Cape Town is normally truly breathtakingly. We drove past both Groot and Klein Constantia, through Hout Bay, over Suikerbossie, passed Llundudno and the Twelve Apostles, before we arrived in Camps Bay and Clifton Beach. The scenery did not disappoint, as serene as I remembered the beautiful Cape of Good Hope to be.

In trying to find a restaurant on the sea front, Kevin considered the first three sub-standard. Eventually, thanks to some help from trip-adviser, he selected a restaurant for us called the Cod-Father. We enjoyed delicious Kingklip, Langoustines, and King Prawns, with some excellent Saxonburg Chenin Blanc. After lunch, we wandered to the sea front, got some ice-cream and enjoyed the beautiful vistas across Clifton Beach. Darren made himself comfortable on the lawn above the beach for some vitamin D loading, while Kevin and I heckled a local street artist to reduce the price of some paintings. I managed to reduce the price from R300 to R180; however, Kevin offered R200, and the deal was done. Not sure who was happier, Kevin or the artist, as the artist reminded Kevin, "Today is your lucky day."

We drove back direction Cape Town, but stopped at the old La Med Sports Bar, which is situated at the Glen Country Club in Clifton. The Sports Bar is under new management, with some extensive investments, called the Bungalow Restaurant and Lounge, Clifton, situated adjacent to Camps Bay. This sports bar-cum-restaurant-cum-lounge-area is situated high on the sea, with a spectacular view of the Atlantic Ocean in front of it. Camps Bay is situated toward its left, with the Twelve Apostles (mountain range) holding stately watch over the various holidaymakers and local residents. On the deck adjacent to the restaurant were large comfortable couches, where we spent most of the afternoon, enjoying the view, the fresh sea breeze, some cocktails and wine. On our way out, we took panoramic photos of Camps Bay and the Twelve Apostils, whilst Renate took a photo of the 'three blokes'. Everyone was of one mind that that place was fantastic and we should spend more time there.

Getting back home, everyone was still in high spirits, reflecting on the day's events, the exhibition, Kevin and Darren's expensive sunglasses, in comparison to my high quality Lidl sunglasses, our excellent meal at the Cod Father, and the afternoon at the Bungalow. We prepared some cheese and wine for dinner before everyone got to bed.

DAY 6 (Friday)

As the race was dramatically shortened, we agreed that we need to ensure we keep our miles up and decided to go for a few more rides before we go back home. On Friday, we again took the R27 north and rode up the west coast of South Africa, direction Duynefontein and Velddrift. Before getting to the Melkbos turnoff, I needed a loo, as I often do, and had to make an emergency stop next to the R27 at a large tree. You can't argue with Mother Nature. The highway police coincidently stopped across the road at the same time, which caused Kevin to have visions of me being arrested. Our brief interruption was uneventful, the police continued on their journey and we continued ours to Melkbos. We stopped at the Dam Huis for coffee. Kevin and Darren had some scones, with cheese and jam, while I had coffee and rusks.

After cycling back to the house to change, we upload our rides on Strava. Kevin was creative with the naming of his ride, being 'Flack Jacket meets racing jacket meets £4.99 from Lidl...', Darren calling his, 'Duynefontein and back leg stretch', and mine just simply 'Melkbos Morning Ride'.

After collecting Renate, we drove to Franschoek to collect a ring Darren bought for his wife Jo. We spent a bit of time walking through some of the shops in this beautiful and historic town; while Darren obtained the ring, Renate and I bought some exquisite chocolates, talked to local shopkeepers, and Kevin bought himself a leather bracelet.

We drove to La Motte wine estate, where Johan Malan suggested we should stop for lunch. La Motte is part of the Rupert Family Estates and produces high quality wines. A very impressive wine estate; however, on arriving, it soon became apparent that we would not be able to get a place in the sun and drove direction Cape Town. We stopped at Antonij Rupert Wine Estate for lunch. As the temperatures started to drop, we decided to sit outside. We enjoyed a rather disappointing lunch at 35 degrees Celsius in the Olive Grove. Whilst the food was not much to write home about, the wine was good – or as Kevin would put it, "okay." Kevin ordered his first ever £2.50 wine, a Chenin Blanc Protea, which tasted very good. However, he soon ordered a more appropriately priced wine, which was equally palatable. We spoke about the beautiful ring Darren bought Jo, and how he would transport this back home. We debated my parent's imminent arrival in Cape Town, to meet Darren and Kevin, and to have a last meal with us on Monday before we returned to the UK. Mr B's wit, sharp as ever, provided some excellent comic relief.

Friday evening, Kevin and Darren cooked Jamie Oliver's' famous Fish Pie for us. Darren took charge of the kitchen as Executive Chef with Kevin as his Sous Chef. Craig and Pat came over to join us, with Craig spending most of the evening telling us stories about his days as *the weatherman* at the BBC. It's a pity that all his experiences, originally in the merchant navy and later as *the weatherman* for the BBC, were not penned down. Craig has had such an extraordinary and colourful career, with detailed knowledge of the stars, navigation and the weather, crowned by an exceptional ability to tell a story. Truly a remarkable and entraining human being. Dinner consisted of crisps and dips as a starter, lovely creamy baked fish-pie served with Koo bake beans, and creamed sweet corn, finished off with traditional Malva pudding. It was a very enjoyable evening, the food was great, wine was good, and the company excellent.

DAY 7 (Saturday)

On Saturday morning, we decided to rack-up more miles. We decided to take one more leg stretcher before the real race. We followed our now traditional route on the R27 up north, I had to navigate some quick manoeuvres to avoid being mowed down by a local taxi driver, but the rest of the ride was uneventful, albeit at pace.

Arriving at Melkbosstrand, we stopped at the Dam Huis for coffee. Kevin complaining about the slow service, whilst Darren pointed out that according to the history page on its menu, the sight allegedly used to be a Fish Shed in 1806 and played a big part in the Battle of Blaauwbergstrand.

British soldiers attacked the then-Dutch colony, as they feared that the French were planning to use the Cape Colony to block British ships going to India and the Far East. The battle lasted for ten days, when the then-Lt Gen Sir David Baird accepted the surrender from the Dutch Lt General Jan Willem Janssens. This saw the occupation of the former Dutch Cape Colony, by Britain, until 13 August 1814, when it became a permanent British Colony. This was maintained until 31 May 1910 when the Cape Colony with the other three Southern African British Colonies, Natal, Transvaal (the former *Zuid-Afrikaansche Republiek*), and the Orange River Colony (the former *Republiek van den Oranje-Vrijstaat*), were incorporated into the Union of South Africa. The Union of South Africa, a dominion of the British Empire, became the Republic of South Africa on 31 May 1910 and became an independent country from Britain on 31 May 1961.[81]

After our coffee arrived and we ate some Melktert, we headed home to upload our rides on Strava. I named my ride *'The last Melkbos ride, dodging taxis waiting for coffee and melktert'*; Kevin, clearly still not impressed with the service and Darren and my choice of early morning substance, titled his *'When did milk tart became a blokes breakfast'*; with Darren a more practical *'Pre Argus Leg Loosener'*.

Renate and I went to Stellenbosch to visit her cousin. We stopped en route for a Wimpy brunch, which was utterly disappointing, before going to Delheim Wine Estate, where we tasted a few wines and purchased some Delheim Chenin Blanc and Cabernet Sauvignon Special Reserve as our celebratory wines for Sunday afternoon. Later we spent time with Renate's cousin, whom we hadn't seen in eight years, before we drove back to Blaauwberg to join Kevin and Darren.

They spent lunch at Eden on the Bay, having a few beers either side of a brisk walk along the beach, and had a short visit to Pick n Pay for Jelly babies and sports drinks.

On Saturday evening, Craig booked us a table at Col' Cocchio Restaurant for some carbo-loading. Daren and I stayed clear of the wine and had a Peronni each, while Kevin had some wine with Craig and Pat. Renate had a very healthy salad and appeletizer. I felt nervous, even for the shortened route, as whilst I had done seven Cape Town cycle tours before, I aborted three attempts between my seventh and the 2015 race. I had to start and complete this race, even if it was just to break the fear this race provoked in me.

Arriving home, we did the final checks with our gear. Our duties were for me to make some mielie-pap for breakfast and sort out the coffees and tea for the morning. As Craig brought his car over the night before to enable us to load the bikes, Darren was in charge of loading the bikes and Kevin sorted the water bottles.

We agreed that as there was a strong southwesterly wind forecasted for Sunday, we would cycle home to Blaauwberg after the race, as we should have the wind behind us, and the route is fairly flat. That would aid us in getting more miles in than what we would have done if the full cycle tour was taking place, hopefully silencing any possible critics.

---

[81] http://www.southafrica.net/za/en/articles/entry/article-southafrica.net-the-battle-of-blaauwberg

DAY 8 (Sunday)

The long awaited day arrived. Sunday, 8 March 2015, the alarm clocks went off at 4:45 AM. Darren tackled the bikes and loaded them on the car. Kevin measured some energy drinks for our water bottles, and I started the porridge. Setting the gas stove too hot, I promptly burned the mielie-pap but was able to salvage it. We had our coffee and tea and got our 'Three Blokes on their Bikes' kit on.

After breakfast, there was a clear sense of anticipation in the air. It was still dark outside; the wind was blowing intensely and the Atlantic Ocean adding to the chill morning air. We were all busy checking and double-checking whether we had everything we needed.

Our ID cards to gain access into the race were all ready. Trying to hydrate, we started to drink our energy drinks. We had enough energy gels, wine gums, and food bars to keep us alive for two races. At 6:00 AM, we were ready, loaded, and geared to go.

Craig drove the three of us into Cape Town, via the Duncan Docks, and off-loaded us at the Mercedes-Benz motor dealer in town. It soon became evident that the wind was much stronger than what we anticipated. We made our way through Cape Town's city centre, following other cyclists to the start line. The city echoed with loud music that was being piped form the start line. Every five minutes we heard the gun announcing another group of cyclists who started their race. There were thousands and thousands of cyclists in Cape Town. According to the press, some 33,000 cyclists were taking part.

We made our way to the toilets before our group, 5C, started. Our new cycling gear was proving to be more challenging that what we anticipated; however, we soon got the hang of it. I asked another cyclist to take some photos of the three of us, and it became evident that the nerves started to kick in, probably a combination of the horrifying known and the fear of the unknown. As I have done the Argus seven times previously, I have never done the circular route, whilst the entire Cape Town cycle experience was a new one for both Darren and Kevin.

While waiting, we watched on the big screen how the men's elite group came into the finish line, with a time of 1 hour, 1 minute. The winner of the 2015 was a South African called Nolan Hoffman. Five minutes before we had to depart, Mr B decided he needed to go to the toilets, again. Considering how he pesters me for always looking for a bathroom, Darren and I took great joy at giving him a hard time. He arrived one minute before we had to go.

Although the unprecedented shortened route was the first in its 38-year history, we made peace with the fact that we were part of making history in this spectacular event. The organisers asked cyclists to wear red, or something red, in participating in the 'Show You Care Solidarity Ride', in support of all the people who worked for and volunteered in the battle against the fires that battered the Cape's Southern Peninsula. Fortunately, The Three Blokes and their Bikes, kit was suitably red.

At 8:14 AM, the gun went off, the crowd shouted "Woopa!", and the Three Blokes on the Bikes started the 2015 Cape Town Cycle Tour, named the 'Solidarity Ride'. We started to make our way out of the city centre. It started initially very slow, in Hertzog Boulevard, underneath the Nico Malan Theatre complex and Civic Centre, out on the Nelson Mandela Boulevard and the N2 in the direction of Muizenberg. It did not take long for Darren to shoot off. Kevin and I remained together and cycled at a steady pace. We went past Hospital Bend, then the Rhodes Memorial, past Bishops Court and Constantia, before we prepared to go over Edinburgh Drive, the Newlands Forest, and the ladies mile in the direction of Tokai to the end of the M3 and the old Blue route.

The road was lined with people, cheering, clapping, music playing, and generally having a great time. The atmosphere, the entire race was energising. The wind calmed a bit as we went through Bishops Court, but we could feel the wind on the Tokai flat that took us to the end of the M3 and the ultimate turnaround point. It was interesting to see how slow we moved toward the turnaround point, with the wind against us, in comparison to the people who had turned around and were returning to the city centre, on the other side of the motorway, with the wind in full force behind them.

As we approached the turn-around point, I thought I saw Darren on the opposite side heading back to Constantia, moving very fast. However, it could have been any of the thousands of other riders. It took Kevin and me just over an hour to complete the first half of the 47km and to reach the turnaround point at the junction between Tokai and Ou-KaapseWeg. It was a great relief to turn with the wind behind us. We were accelerating back up the M3 direction, the city centre. The painful hills coming out to Tokai became exhilarating down hills heading back to Cape Town. Darren reached an average speed of 26.78km (16.73mph), with a top speed of 39.8km; (24.87mph) Kevin did an average of 22.42km (14mph); and I achieved 21.82km (13.64mph), with a top speed of 36.5km and 39.6km, respectively.

On our way back, I went past Lynda, an old friend of mine, en route, who started doing the Cape Town Cycle tour (then called the Cape Argus) with me in 2000 for the first time and who continued to do it year after year since. Although she is a stronger rider than me, we always struggled on the hills. However, this year, I managed to be stronger and faster up-hill than ever before. I just had time to shout a "hello Smutsy" followed by a "send my regards to the kids" before I was off again. That alone was invigorating for me.

Making our way back into the city centre, Darren finished first with a time of 01h45:18, followed by Kevin at 02h05:47, while I completed the race in 02h09:16.

As I drove into Cape Town and toward the finish line, this Solidarity Ride also became my own thanks-giving ride. I felt humbled and thankful that we have managed to raise more than £2000 for the Chestnut Appeal. I was appreciative that we finished the race without incident or injury, despite the strong winds and the large number of cyclists on the road. Lastly, I remained deeply grateful that I regained my full health and recovered fully from prostate cancer.

We met on the lawn of the McDonald's outside Cape Town stadium developed for the 2010 football world cup in Greenpoint. We congratulated each other on a good race, uploaded our times and stats on Strava, and had some refreshments.

It was not long after that when we started our way back to Blaauwberg Stran, some 20km outside the city centre. We cycled past Duncan Docs, took a short detour on the N1, before we took the R27 back to the Beach Club. Mr B got his wires slightly crossed and nearly took the N1 north to Johannesburg; however, we managed to wave him down, and once he joined Darren and me, we cycled northwest to Blaauwberg.

Just after arriving back in Blaauwberg, and about 3km from home, Kevin took a wrong turn, going onto the pavement, where he went over a bad piece of paving which punctured his front wheel. It took a few minutes before Darren and I noticed that he was way behind us, and then seeing him walking. We waited for Kevin before we agreed to make our way to the News-Café in Blaauwberg for beer, food, and an assessment of the situation. He should have said he needed a beer; he did not need to wreck his front wheel for a beer.

Darren called Craig and asked if he could collect Kevin. While we waited, we had some toasted sandwiches and beer, just to celebrate the successful completion of our day. After Craig arrived, we settled our bill, Kevin loaded his bike, while Darren and I cycled home.

After we inspected Kevin's bike and the possible damage to his front wheel, Kevin and Darren went to Craig's for a few celebratory drinks and to watch some football, while I went for a shower and an afternoon nap.

We had dinner at the Ocean Basket in Blaauwberg. The fish, with signatory sauce tartar, garlic, and chilies, was a perfect ending to a great day. Craig and Pat joined us, and as always, we enjoyed their company before retiring for the night.

DAY 9 (Monday)
Kevin and Darren rose early to do a last ride before we return to England. They fixed Kevin's tire and agreed to cycle past the local cycle shop, just to check that Kevin's wheel was not permanently damaged. As we had lunch booked with my parents, I agreed to do some writing to ensure our cycle tour is preserved for perpetuity.

By the time they returned, we learned that Kevin had another puncture; they uploaded their last ride on Strava, appropriately titled '*Tyre off three times, two tube changes, a coffee but, no cake!*' Darren titled his ride '*Melkbos reliability ride?*' After everyone freshened up, we made our way to Cape Town to meet with my parents.

My dad, Chris (or the Great Lion as I like to refer to him) (aged 86), and his wife Madeleine (aged 81), flew down from Johannesburg to see us for one more lunch and to meet our English friends. I made a reservation at the Glen Country Club, with the Bungalow Restaurant and Lounge, in Camps bay. We drove into Cape Town, where Darren, Kevin and Renate dropped me at the hotel where my parents stayed, while they drove on to the restaurant. I picked up my parents, traveling with them, I directed my father toward the restaurant in Camps Bay. We had a splendid afternoon. The weather was great, with no wind, excellent food, and Great Contantia wines. My dad told Darren and Kevin about Robben Island, about the origins of the Bisley (a shooting competition with English origins from Surrey), and the rifle he and my grandfather hid before and retrieved after the Second World War, in the old Western Transvaal's district of Ventersdorp, (in the now North West Province), on the family farm. My father had some great fish and chips, while Ma Madeleine enjoyed a spectacular seafood platter for one. Renate had a salad, and I enjoyed a fillet on a creamy Dijon mustard sauce, Kevin had some prawns and beefsteak, and Darren enjoyed Cape sushi and steak.

After lunch, Renate and I walked with my parents to say goodbye, and as always, it was very difficult to say goodbye to my dad and Ma Madeleine. He is such a remarkable man, who had such an inspirational influence in my life, living so far from him makes moments together so much more special. On saying our goodbyes, my parents were very complimentary of our English friends. I think it gave my father some peace of mind to know that we have settled well, in our new country, with good jobs, and supported by good friends.

After my parents returned to their hotel, Kevin, Darren, Renate and I spent the remainder of the afternoon at the lounge area of the restaurant, enjoying the beautiful vistas of the Atlantic Ocean, at the foot of the twelve apostles in beautiful Camps Bay.

Darren drove us home. We had a very relaxing afternoon back at the Beach Club. We packed our bikes ready for the long flight back, and on Monday evening, Craig and Pat came to visit for old time's sake. We enjoyed some of the last red wine we had in the house and talked about sports, the race, next year's cycle tour, and politics.

DAY 10 (Tuesday)
On Tuesday morning, we rose slowly, finalised our packing, cleaned the house, and went to Craig to print our boarding passes. As our flight was only at 6:10 in the evening, we arranged for a late check-out. Kevin and Darren went for a last visit to the Eden on the Bay restaurant complex, while Renate and I stayed at home, having a bit of a nap before the very long flight back to the UK. At 2:30 in the afternoon, we left the Beach Club. Bikes and some luggage were loaded in the rented car with me and Kevin, with Renate and Darren traveling with Craig to the airport. After we returned the rented car, checked-in our luggage, and made our way to the waiting area for boarding,

291

I had a last Windhoek Lager, Kevin and Darren a couple of glasses Chenin Blanc, while Renate got the latest Gucci perfume. As we flew home, via Dubai, we all reflected on the past trip to Cape Town. So long in the planning, so quickly gone, but memories created for life. A great experience, I hope we will go back for the full 109Km Cape Town Cycle Tour on Sunday, 6 March 2015.

* * *

Arriving back in the UK, I returned to work to prepare for the Care Quality Commission (CQC) inspection in April. During the weeks preceding the CQC inspection, there was a feeling of togetherness in the hospital, a great sense of camaraderie. Management and staff worked diligently in preparing for the planned quality inspection.

Staff survey results over the past three years confirmed that employee engagement and communication between staff and senior management steadily increased. The Plymouth Way, a defined cultural methodology as 'the way we do things around here' was well embedded and Ann James' open door approach for everyone had gone far in creating an open and supportive culture.

* * *

I mentioned earlier that I had been suffering some internal challenges during the end of 2014 and the beginning of 2015, but on reflection, these were the culmination of the psychological impact of everything that happened in 2013. After my operation, I wanted to get back to work as quickly as possible, and returned within six weeks after my surgery. I met and worked with my colleagues, some of whom were my physicians as a patient, attended board meetings as Director of HR, and listened to cancer statistics being reported on a monthly basis.

I endured one particular board meeting when the hospital debated whether it should invest in a Di-Vinci Robot, which would ultimately be used for *inter alia*, prostate cancer patients. It was suggested that a Di-Vinci prostatectomy would allow surgeons to operate with enhance vision, precision and control, with minimal side effects to the patient. During this specific board meeting, the presenting clinician went into great detail in describing the benefits of the Di-Vinci Robot, and explained in graphic detail (I say graphic, as it was very intense on a personal level) as to the consequences of the illness, the side effects and impact on men living with prostate cancer. Whilst I was in attendance, it felt as if he was just talking about me, and everyone was listing. Clearly he was not, and was probably not even aware of my own circumstances at the time, but the impact of 2013, only manifested towards the end of 2014 and the beginning of 2015.

Previously I mentioned that Ann had been incredibly supportive during this time. After the board meeting, she noted that the presentation struck a chord with me, and inquired quietly if I was OK. I was very cautious not to be perceived as weak, so obviously I said I was fine, but in hindsight, was deeply affected.

On reflection, when I was diagnosed with cancer, I should have taken time out, I should have sought help, and I should have spoken to professionals who would have reassured me that what I was feeling was normal. I was not unique and ultimately, it was likely that for me everything would be OK. However, my Afrikaner male pride prohibited and inhibited me.

Although I was back at work six weeks after my surgery, a couple of months later I again embarked on a further seven weeks of very intense radiotherapy without taking any time off. The consequences of living with and beyond cancer directly contributed to an over sensitive, emotional and at times paranoid state of mind. Yet, Ann James, my colleagues and friends in the hospital were spectacular in supporting me, although I may not have perceived it as such at the time.

* * *

Everyone at the hospital was nervous about the CQC inspection, ultimately, the hospital did well, and although there were areas that required improvement, I was particularly pleased with the fact that the Trust was rated as 'outstanding' for caring and 'good' for culture and leadership. An extract of the CQC report read:

"...We found that the current leadership team has promoted a positive open culture, which aspires to put patients first, despite the significant financial pressures in Devon. It is a credit to all the staff that we found caring to be outstanding overall..."[82]

The CQC result was a testimony to Ann's leadership and the culture that she had established at the Trust.

* * *

I thought that after the cycling trip to South Africa my resilience would have been re-established and I would be able to determine what it was that I wanted to do. Staying or leaving. Considering the challenges I faced internally about the impact of my treatment, its consequences and what the hospital started to mean to me, as a former patient, it soon became clear that I would need to find an alternative place of employment. My resilience declined, my anxiety increasing and I was suffering increased insomnia.

---

[82] http://www.cqc.org.uk/content/cqc-rates-plymouth-hospitals-nhs-trust-outstanding-caring-overall-trust-requires

I referred earlier to having people staying rent free in my head. This I can only define as when you think more about other people than what they think about you in terms of what you have done, said, or not done. This resulted in me having difficulty to eat, sleep, and concentrate. Everything that happened around me started to make me concerned that I was not performing at my peak, that I was not as good as what I could be. I started worrying about everything. I worried about other people's workload and their responsibility, their view of my performance, and everything became an issue for me. Eventually my friend Kevin convinced me to seek help and suggested I do a self-referral for cognitive behavioural therapy (CBT). CBT is described as talking therapy that helps people manage the way they think or behave.[83]

However my internal challenge continued, and whilst the CBT helped greatly, the hospital, its environment and what it represented for me, from a patient's perspective, remained a challenge. The fact that I had to write my final two papers for my LLB on 8 June did not help.

At the same time, an opportunity arose within a number of Clinical Commissioning Groups (CCGs) in the home counties near London. I read all the documentation about the post and realised that the shared service was very similar to what I did in Extra Expertise. I submitted my application via an agent the week before my exams, and was delighted when I was shortlisted. Renate and I were also keen to relocate closer to London, near international airports, that would enable us to visit our parents in South Africa. We wanted to buy a house in the not so distant future, but one that was more centrally located.

Shortly before my final exam, and in discussion with Ann, it was agreed that I could take some study leave to prepare for my exam.

I did a short hand-over to Martin, and withdrew to our house, where I focused on my studies and tried to forget about the challenges the hospital represented in my life.

* * *

During this time, Gideon and Beulah, our friends from Plymouth University, announced that they were returning to Coventry.

* * *

On Monday, 8 June, I wrote my final paper for my LLB, and although it was a challenging paper, I thought I did all right. Following my exam, I returned to work.

On Sunday, 15 June, I took the train from Plymouth to London to attend the interview, scheduled the following day. Whilst en-route, I bought a Sunday Telegraph and noted a small article about Nelson Mandela. The

---

[83] http://www.nhs.uk/Conditions/Cognitive-behavioural-therapy/Pages/Introduction.aspx

reading of this prompted me to write a reflective narrative about this remarkable statesman. (See Chapter 32)

The interview on Monday, with the CCGs went very well. I competed with three other candidates, and was pleased when Nicola Bell, the then Accountable Officer at Herts Valleys CCG, contacted me at 4:00 that afternoon to offer me the post for Director of Workforce at the CCGs in West Hertfordshire, Bedfordshire and Luton.

I called Ann to advise her of my appointment, and tendered my resignation with the Trust on 22 June 2015. We debated when I could be released from the Trust, and eventually it was agreed that I could start on 1 September.

Considering that my dad indicated that he wanted us to join him for a holiday in Switzerland, Germany and Austria, Renate and I had leave booked for July, everything turned out fine. I finalised the various projects I was working on at the hospital, prepared a hand-over report to Ann, Martin and the future Director of People and looked forward to seeing my dad in Zurich.

* * *

The long awaited holiday with my dad was upon us, and on Thursday, 9 July, Renate and I waited to board the Brittany Ferry leaving Plymouth Harbour. Just before we boarded, Luke Homan, a friend of mine who studied law with me, sent me a text to confirm that our results were out. I quickly checked my OU account, and was delighted to learn that I passed my LLB (Hons). I was overwhelmed with joy.

Kevin sent us a photo confirming that he watched the ferry leaving from his apartment at the Royal William Yard, whilst we enjoyed, with renewed reason to celebrate, our first ferry trip following our immigration. Renate had the best beef bourguignon on board she had ever had. I had roasted lamb with delicious French red wine.

After crossing the English Channel overnight, we arrived on the 10th in Roscoff in France, from where we drove to Renate's godparents in Blumberg in the Black Forest.

My dad arrived the following day in Zurich where we picked him up on the 11th. We stayed in Blumberg a couple of nights to enable my father to recover from the flight. He was nearly 85 years old at the time. His wife did not join us, as she had a knee replacement earlier in the year and was concerned that the travel and walking may be too exhausting. In Blumberg, we visited a schnapps distiller and had traditional food at the Scheffellinde Restaurant in Achdorf. We enjoyed a special train trip on the Sauschwaenzle Bahn, through the Black Forest countryside. This caused Renate great joy and lots of laughter. She could truly laugh like her late father and like my late mother. When they start, they just can't stop. Truly special to witness.

On the 13th, we drove to Austria to visit Fani Stroble at Krispl on the Mondsee, just outside Salzburg. We visited the Mondsee and enjoyed the great Austrian lakes and vistas. We celebrated Renate's birthday at the Mondsee Restaurant, and visited Bad Ischl, a spa town situated in the southern part of Upper Austria, near the Traun River in the centre of the Salzkammergut region. On the 16th, we left for Bad Feilnback, in Bavaria. Here, we stopped to see the sister of a school friend of Renate, before we arrived in Essenbach, to visit a college friend of Renate whom we've not seen for a long time. The following day, we travelled by train into Munich, the capital of Bavaria, where we visited the world famous Hofbrauhaus Munich. My dad surprised us with lunch to celebrate the successful conclusion of my law degree. It was a very special day.

On 18 July, we arrived in Baden-Württemberg, where we stayed at a beautiful hotel in Bondorf and Hohenfels.

We came full circle with my dad, who visited most of these places five years earlier with us when he and Ma Madeleine got married. We celebrated his 80th birthday at Andrea Friedmann's Stern Restaurant in Bad Saulgau in 2010, and returned, albeit a week too early, to celebrate his 85th birthday with the Friedmanns.

Renate's brother Rene and his partner Whipke joined us with Andrea and Manual Friedmann in Bad Saulgau, where we attended the Baechlefest.

By 21 July, we were back in Blumberg and spent another couple of days with Adi and Hannah, Renate's godparents, visiting Ehrenkirchen in Freiburg, before my dad returned home to South Africa from Zurich. As always, it was so difficult to say good-bye to my dad. He is such a remarkable man, such a force in Renate and my lives.

The following day, Renate and I drove back to Roscoff to catch our Ferry back to Plymouth, and on 27 July, I returned to work.

* * *

Kevin organised a couple of farewell events for us during August; friends of ours form Blackpool came for a weekend visit, and we hosted a number of farewell dinners at our home. I spent a couple of weeks in Hemel Hempstead during August as part of my orientation for my new role and rented a cottage, whilst Renate continued with her work in Plymouth. I started my new role on 1 September, commuting the 242mi (389km) every weekend between Hemel Hempstead and Plymouth.

Eventually, in October, we rented a house in Aylesbury, and during the weekend of 23 October, we returned to Plymouth to finalise our move from Devon to Buckinghamshire. However, we first stopped at the Plymouth Register Office. Here we swore allegiance to Her Majesty Queen Elizabeth II, listened with gratitude to the playing of God Save the Queen, and received a coin each to commemorate the granting of our British citizenship.

That evening, we had dinner with friends of ours in Plymouth at the Rod & Line pub in Saltash. Saturday night, we gathered our closest friends with Ponti and our godchildren, including Renate's godparents form Germany, when on 24 October, we started to celebrate my 50th birthday at Jolly Jacks Restaurant. The evening was a great success, with a spectacular surprise birthday cake containing both the national flags of the United Kingdom and South Africa.

On Wednesday, 28 October, we packed our house, stayed for one last night on the Hoe before we collected the cats and drove northeast toward London. To a new county, a new role, and a new future.

Chapter 32
A Reflective Narrative in Memory of Nelson Mandela

On a train between Plymouth and London's Paddington station, I read a copy of the Sunday Telegraph of 15 June 2015. A small reflective article titled *'From the Archives'* grabbed my attention.

Arthur House, the paper's correspondent, wrote about the events some fifty years ago, when the 1964 journalist, Douglas Brown, reported on the life sentence that Nelson Mandela started on Robben Island. As I came from South Africa, lived on Robben Island, albeit for a short period of time, but visited this world heritage site many times in my life, it captured my interest.

House commented how Brown reported on Mandela's speech *"spoken with dignity and without bitterness, he spoke for free rights of man"*. The 1964 journalist was quoted to have said, *"Nelson Mandela will become the most effective martyr in the history of Africanism"*. House added, *"... that Mandela was guilty as charged was not in doubt. He had 'willingly confessed that he was party to a conspiracy to destroy the South African state by force.'"* But the real issue was, *"outside the competence of a South African judge to decide"*; namely, whether *"a people deprived of any peaceful means of asserting their rights are justified in resorting to violence"*.

This short article made me muse about the years gone by, on Mandela, his life and legacy, but also on my own life, growing up in White dominant South Africa, as a White Afrikaans-speaking South African.

My wife and I lived and worked in Plymouth, Devon, England, and planned a holiday to Southern Africa in December 2013, to visit our parents for Christmas. When we made our reservations some months earlier, we were unaware that we would arrive in Johannesburg two days after the passing of the iconic, first democratically elected President Nelson Rolihlahla Mandela.

Like the rest of the world, South Africa was shocked about the passing of the great Madiba. Nelson Mandela was often referred to as 'Madiba' in South Africa, which refers to his Xhosa clan name, a reference of respect or a sign of endearment. The name 'Madiba' became widely used internationally following his death. Everyone knew that it was imminent; he was 95, frail, and struggled with his health. Yet, his passing left a massive gap, both locally and internationally.

On 10 December, whilst South Africa's political and social good and great attended a memorial service in Johannesburg, my wife and I drove to the Union Buildings in Pretoria to sign the book of remembrance. This magnificent seat of government, designed by Sir Herbert Baker and completed in 1913, to celebrate the Union of South Africa when the country was still under British control, kept spectacular watch over the city. The sky was dark grey with thick clouds, yet the temperature was pleasantly warm. There was an ominous atmosphere in Pretoria. A light rain fell softly, nearly respectfully, over the Jacaranda city, named so for its beautiful Jacaranda trees which line the streets and covers the city in a lilac blanket of blooms every year during October. It was as if everyone paused reflectively, remembering, but also contemplating, 'what will happen next'?

As my mum died seven years earlier and was buried on the 10th of December, this day was a particularly poignant day for me on a personal level. My simple entry into the book of remembrance read: *"You were an inspiration for all of humanity. You were the hope of a free South Africa. Thank you Madiba."* We took a photo in memory of that historic day. We looked at the huge number of flowers that were covering the base of the First World War Memorial in front of the Union Buildings, and thought the inscription on the base of the monument was equally applicable to Mandela as it read *"Their ideal is our legacy, their sacrifice our inspiration"*. We absorbed the beauty of our former hometown and reflected in silent contemplation on its people, challenges, and on our own roots.

Our time in South Africa was truly insightful, as the South African people, both Black and White, talked persistently about Madiba. They talked in the banks, in the streets and in restaurants, about Mandela the boxer, the human rights fighter, the lawyer, and the family man. They talked about Mandela the leader, the prisoner, the strategist, and the president.

People discussed how he was imprisoned for 18 of his 27-year sentence on Robben Island. They reflected on the small cell he came home to, after a day's hard labour in the island quarry, the floor he had to sleep on, the bucket he had to use for a toilet, and how he was deprived of contact with his loved ones. Yet this prison island was also the place that converted a man of violence – although he died, never renouncing the use of violence – into a man who used insight, intellect, compassion, and stately disobedience to convince the government of the day to transform South Africa from a historical dictatorship into a multi-cultural democracy.

Describing Apartheid South Africa as a dictatorship may cause offense to some, specifically the Afrikaners of the 1940s to the 1990s who wanted to protect themselves, preserve their own, and ensure a stable future for their kind. The reality of that time is undeniable, that during this time, unless you supported the Nationalist Party, belonged to the correct Afrikaans church, and towed the party line, you were quickly branded as a communist, the anti-Christ, or an enemy of the state.

The novel by Alan D Elsdon, *The Tall Assassin*, explains the reign of terror, the paranoia of the Afrikaner government and propaganda on which we were raised. It tells a spectacular tale of the dark dealings of General 'lang' (tall) Hendrik van den Bergh, the head of the then- Bureau of State Security (BOSS), who was responsible for the ultimate arrest and incarceration of Nelson Mandela. Elsdon suggests links between BOSS and the deaths of HF Verwoerd, Nic Diedericks, Steve Biko, Anton Lubowski, and Prof Johan Heyns. He implies that there was a stately flirtation between the Nationalist Party leadership of old and the ideology of Nazism. Whilst the ideology of Apartheid, or 'separate development' as Verwoerd clarified in 1960, in theory may have been an effort of the Afrikaner to protect itself, its consequences were paradoxical.

It was this paradox that Mandela used to defeat the Afrikaner government. Whilst in prison, he made it his duty to understand his enemy. My father, who was the deputy commanding officer on Robben Island in 1966, confirmed that, when we lived on the island, Mandela treated his captures with condescending respect.

However, Nelson Mandela studied his enemy and understood their history during colonial South Africa; the constant battles between the Brits and the Dutch since 1652; the establishment of the various Boer Republics, the devastation of the two Anglo Boer Wars in 1887 and 1899, respectively; the formulation of the Union of South Africa in 1909; the ascent to power of the Nationalist Party in 1948; and the ultimate establishment of the Republic of South Africa in 1960. He studied the language, read Afrikaans poetry, and knew both the history and fears of his captors.

Mandela knew that the Afrikaner had no-where to go. Although they referred to themselves as 'Europeans', South Africa was their homeland, as much as it was the homeland of Black South Africans. The impact of the various colonial powers, the Boer's desire for freedom, self-determination and independence, set the scene for a brutal, suspicious and self-preserving nation that would sustain Apartheid for nearly fifty years.

This inherent fear of domination, Mandela knew, came particularly from the devastation caused by Lord Kitchener of Khartoum. What Kitchener did to the Boers, following the Second Anglo Boer War (1899–1902), caused the Afrikaner to draw laager, a stronghold, to protect itself at all cost.

It was also this fear of domination that Mandela addressed on 12 February 1990. In his first press conference after his release, he talked about the proposed principle of 'one man, one vote'. "We understand those feelings [of fear]," he said, and reassured the people of South Africa that, "...the ANC is concerned to address that problem and to find a solution which will suit both the blacks and the whites of this country."

When Mandela became President on 10 May 1994, he expressed hope for a united and magnificent South Africa, defined as his rainbow nation, and declared that "... out of the experience of an extraordinary human disaster that lasted too long, must be born a society of which all humanity will be proud of. Our daily deeds as ordinary South Africans must produce an actual South African reality that will reinforce humanity's belief in justice, strengthen its confidence in the nobility of the human soul and sustain all our hopes for a life for all".

Madiba was buried on Sunday, 15 December, in Xuno in the Transkei in the Eastern Cape of South Africa. One international speaker after the other paid tribute to the life of Nelson Mandela. President Barack Obama spoke of Mandela's legacy, confirming that Madiba "taught us the power of action, but he also taught us the power of ideas; the importance of reason and arguments; the need to study not only those who you agree with, but also those who you don't agree with".

Throughout our stay, I was acutely aware what people said about Mandela. They commented on his time as President and compared him to his successors. They speculated about Thabo Mbeki, who was the President passionate about an African renaissance; sadly, he was too academic for his own people, his position on HIV Aids cost him dearly. This resulted in a loss of the momentum established by Mandela. His successor, President Kgalema Motlanthe, had the statesmanship and presence to do Mandela proud, but was generally seen as an interim caretaker. His successor, the then President Jacob Zuma remained an embarrassment for the people of South Africa. He provided excellent material for stand-up comedians and was a far cry from Mandela's ideology. Under Zuma, some of the doctrines of Apartheid had been re-established under the guise of 'Black economic empowerment'. Corruption, nepotism, a disregard for the rule of law and violence are again a part of everyday life.

Today, the concerns of all the people of South Africa are as real as those referred to by Mandela at his first press conference. Whilst he tried to address those fears, the incumbent President seems to do the exact opposite.

People deliberated about Mandela's humanity, what he originally stood for, what he did, what he eventually achieved, and the legacy that he left behind.

My own view on Mandela had changed over the years. Originally I, like most White South Africans, was programmed to consider him a criminal, a terrorist, and an enemy of the state. Today, I know, in reality, all he wanted was equality, wishing to be respected as a human being, being treated in a free and fair way in the country of his birth, in South Africa. He wanted the freedom that the Afrikaner fought for all their lives, even if it meant through means of violence, as they have done. The Afrikaner was deprived of that freedom by the British, and then deprived Black South Africans of the same. Mandela wanted to see a unified South Africa, Black and White living successfully in harmony, one country for all.

I saw Madiba as the hope for a free and fair South Africa, a country where everyone, irrespective of their background, colour, or religion, would be equal and respected. I saw a man transformed; from the creator of the Church street bomb in 1981, where 17 people died with 197 people injured, including my own brother, to a global peace-maker.

Nelson Mandela became an inspirational human being, a statesman the likes of whom the world has yet to see, and an inspiration to me and many others. He was the best and most charismatic leader that South Africa has ever produced.

It is a pity that he only stood for one term of office. However, even in that, Mandela was an example to other African leaders, to try and teach them not to become power- hungry dictators, as was the case with Robert Mugabe of Zimbabwe and so many other leaders who cannot let go.

Remembering Mandela since his passing, the world seems a chaotic place. There does not seem to be leaders like him, nor people who can teach or inspire us, as he had done. President Obama, speaking at Mandela's memorial, considered Mandela's words at the 1964 Rivonia trail when he proclaimed that "I have fought against white domination and I have fought against black domination. I've cherished the ideal of a democratic and free society in which all persons live together in harmony and [with] equal opportunities. It is an ideal, which I hope to live for and to achieve. But if needs be, it is an ideal for which I am prepared to die".

Who knows how South Africa would have looked like, was Nelson Mandela President for a second term? I am confident that it would have been better than what South Africa is today. Perhaps less violent, less corrupt, perhaps more equal, free and fair, for all.

I am grateful that we had the privilege of being able to be a part of this historic point in time. We were there to say good-bye, to remember, to bear testimony, and now we can pay tribute to this remarkable man in absolute admiration. He was and remains an inspiration for all of humanity. He was the hope of a free, non-racial South Africa; let's not forget the man called Nelson Rolihlahla Mandela. (18/07/1918 – 05/12/2013).

Chapter 33
A Journey of Choice

During the past fifty years, I have stayed in 29 different cities and 41 different homes. I attended seven different schools and stayed across all of the then four provinces of South Africa, being the Cape, Orange Free State, Transvaal, Natal, and ultimately, moved across continents.

Some of these moves were compulsory, as my father was transferred between various Prison reserves. I hated this as a child, as we had to make new friends, leave old friends behind, and never really settled. This early nomadic existence directly contributed to me feeling that I don't quite fit in. It created a sense of 'otherness' or being 'outside the margins', as described by Silvia Rodgers.[84] She was the wife of Lord Rodgers of Quarry Bank, who was a founder of the Social Democratic Party, SDP, in 1981, and escaped from Poland via Berlin to the UK as a child.

This 'otherness' continued after school and college, during my national service in the Navy, and for most of my working career. However, although I might not have had much of a say in the moves I had to endure as a child or during my national service, the remaining 24 house moves across 16 cities over a span of 26 years and two continents were my choice.

Although a source of great frustration as a child, it did equip me to be less reliant on others and to be more dependent on myself. I liked the definition of my 'otherness' as articulated by Rodgers, when she wrote 'perhaps my problem is that my otherness is free-floating. It has no one root but an anchor that can be put down anywhere and as easily dislodged'.

My forbears were inherently adventures. Through the family research that my mum dedicated her entire life to, it became apparent that my forefathers left the Netherlands in 1691 and 1696, [van der Vyver and De Jager] respectively and Germany in 1762, [Meyer and Scheffer] respectively, to settle in South Africa. However, as we explored our ancestral DNA, I was very surprised to learn that although I am 87.8% European, I am 53.8% English, 29% Iberian and only 5% North West European. In addition hereto my adventurers forefathers ensured that my DNA also included 4.9% North West African, 4.6% Ashkenazi Jewish with 1% Eskimo, 0.9% Baltic and 0.8% Papuan.[85] This adventurous characteristic, the survival instinct of the

---

[84] Rodgers, S.: *Red Saint, Pink Daughter*, p. 278
[85] www.myheritage.com

Afrikaner over the years, and our own desire for a safe and functioning world saw us return to Europe and, eventually, becoming British citizens.

I have written about a large variety of people who crossed my path, people who shaped my character from the day I was born, to the day I wrote matric (A-Levels). Those who influenced my thinking when I studied and taught me my first lessons as an employee. There were individuals who shaped my value system and beliefs while I did my national service, friends I laughed and cried with. I have written about those who hurt me but also about people that I have hurt. Reflecting on the mistakes I have made in my own life, I came across a quote by Vincent Lombardi, who fittingly wrote about what we do with our lives. He said:

In spite of what many think, none of us are really born equal, and the talented have no more responsibility for their birthright than the underprivileged for theirs. The measure of each is what each does in a specific situation.

I believe that the obstacles in our lives are part of the process of building our character. I could surely blame a variety of people for making my life difficult, but I could equally thank each one of them for challenging me and, thereby, contributing to making me a more resilient human being. A stronger me.

Initially, when I started writing about this journey, I intended to write a story of an ordinary South African. A story that followed the birth and childhood of a White South African boy in mid-Apartheid, his indoctrination into the chosen religion and politics of his family, and the initial experiences of his childhood, which formed the bases of his being. I reflected on the natural and normal rivalry between siblings. My first experiences of life but also of trauma, heroes, achievements, courage, a variety of life lessons, and the choices I made.

However, as the storyline unfolded, influenced by the clarity of hindsight and a career in human resources, it became evident that this was no ordinary story. I may be an ordinary immigrant, but the sibling rivalry, the political realities, the influence of religion, and the hard lessons of life turned an ordinary life into an extraordinary journey through life. A journey of life lessons, tolerance, sympathy, achievements, reconciliation, self-assessment, self-awareness, and ultimately, a journey of hope and meaning.

Although I may not have had total control over everything that happened in my life, like most of us, I do have control over what I choose to do, as a consequence of those events. Stephen R. Covey[86], wrote in the late eighties how our lives are made up of 10% of things that happen to us, of which we have no control. But he also defined a 10/90 rule, in that 90% of life is determined by how we react thereto. He argued that we have no control over

---

[86] Stephen R. Covey, 7 Habits of Highly Effective People

10% of our life, i.e., I had no control over the fact that my sister wanted a sister and not another brother; I had no control over the fact that one summer's day, a motorbike rider drove down a specific road at breakneck speed; and I had no control over the fact that I was diagnosed with cancer.

However, according to Covey 90% of life is determined by our reactions to the things that happened in our life. We do have control over our own actions, our behaviour, and the way we respond to events in our lives. This is not always easy, and mental health issues play a contributory factor in this regard; however, our actions generally remain within our gift. Taking the examples above further, whilst my sister chose to reject me at my birth, I chose to accept and love her; whilst the court felt I could have prevented the death of the motorbike rider, whilst I disagreed, I chose to learn from this and to make me stronger; whilst cancer is a shock to anyone, I chose to keep on working, remaining positive, and working through the treatment in a systematic and constructive manner, with negative consequences I know, but that was some of the unforeseen outcomes of my choices in life.

As part of Covey's habit 1, being pro-active, he offered his view on a 'circle of concern and circle of influence'.[87]

Instead of reacting to or worrying about conditions over which (you) *have little or no control, proactive people focus their time and energy on things they can control. The problems, challenges, and opportunities we face fall into two areas – Circle of Concern and Circle of Influence.*

Proactive people focus their efforts on their Circle of Influence. They work on the things they can do something about: health, children, (and) *problems at work. Reactive people focus their efforts in the Circle of Concern – things over which they have little or no control: the national debt, terrorism, the weather. Gaining an awareness of the areas in which we expend our energies in is a giant step in becoming proactive.*

Don't get me wrong. I know that some of my decisions in life could have been better or were plain wrong. I have many regrets about how I responded to some of the challenging situations or how I behaved in these moments. However, I also know that I don't have to rationalise my wrong choices. Instead, I try to learn from them, as there is no excuse. I know that my life is determined by my behaviour and actions to the choices I make. Ultimately, my response to life's events will determine my own happiness.

I have reflected a lot during the time of penning my journey thus far. The choices I have made and the reactions I have had, and still have to make, about that 10% of life over which I have no control.

Victor E. Frankl, explained in his book *Man's Search for Meaning*, the term 'logotherapy' which comes from the Greek word 'logos' and represents 'meaning'. The methodology of logotherapy, he explained, is to take a

---

[87] Stephen R. Covey, 7 Habits of Highly Effective People, Pg 84 & 85

forward view, rather than being retrospective or even introspective.[88] It is not to consider what happened to me during the past fifty years, or even how I interpret the experience, perceptions, and my realities of those events. It is more to consider the significance of my life on this earth, today and tomorrow, to take control of the 90% that Covey spoke about. Frankl believed that if we could define the meaning of our life – and there is meaning for us all – that that will become a powerful motivating force to propel us forward, facing, embracing, and dealing with each challenge life has to offer, giving it meaning, shaping the choices we make, enhancing the journey of our lives that helped Renate and me to adapt to UK life.

This was evident on the eve of 24 October 2015, when we gathered a group of our closest friends in the UK to celebrate my fiftieth birthday. My god-children, Carla and Stefan, in true South African tradition, said the most beautiful things about me, as what any father would love to hear form their children. My dear friend Ponti paid tribute to our friendship and our collective journeys. Was it not for him moving to the UK, it would have been unlikely that our journey would have taken us here. After I thanked Renate for her love and support during our journey thus far, I reflected on the six and a half years in the UK up to that day.

We started the UK part of our journey in Lancashire; I reflected on the fact that I could not understand the dialect, and my Afrikaans accent did not help. We felt 'alien', to use Silvia Rodgers' phrase. She defined her own journey from Poland, via Berlin, to London, as a 'cultural bereavement'. One of suffering the *'loss of the familiar and ejection into the new is ... [a] culture shock'*[89].

My lack of insight into the intricacies of the English language caused for many consternations. I used the wrong words or phrases at the wrong time or out of context, causing grave offense to a group of ladies at Blackpool Teaching Hospitals, albeit unintentionally. My South-Africanisms raised many an eyebrow, from having 'telephonic discussions' to 'saddling a horse that was going nowhere very fast' (*om die verkeerde perd op te saal*).

On the journey to becoming British citizens, we have learned more about the British history and experienced its culture, traditions, and customs. One could say we got educated, integrated, and ultimately, accepted in our new country. We learned that a circle was a roundabout, a robot is a traffic light, the highway was the motorway, and pants were trousers. We swam in the Atlantic Ocean off the Cornish coast at Polzeath. We ate 'banjo butties'; fish and chips with mushy peas; baked beans on fried toast; and haggis. We tried scotch-eggs and ate Skate but could not eat black pudding. We enjoyed Kevin's fish pie; drank Indian Pale Ale, Doombar, Cornish Siders, and Chablis. I cycled in the rain, wind, and snow, and played fancy football – albeit once, for a short season, and very poorly. We gained some insight into

---

[88] Victor E Frankle, *Man's Search for Meaning*, p104
[89] Red Saint, Pink Daughter, p. 191

the UK's historic past as we learned about William the Conquer (1066–1087); William Wallace (1270–1305), and William Shakespeare (1564–1616), to mention a few. We saw documentaries and learned about the Tudors (1485–1603); the Stuarts (1603–1714); the Hanovers (1714–1901); the House of Saxe-Coburg and Gotha (1901–1917); and the Windsors (1917–). We learned so much more about British history than what our South African schoolbooks, or Afrikaner folk law ever taught us.

Renate and I created the most spectacular memories with my dad and Ma Madeleine – traveling Europe, cruising the Mediterranean, and visiting them annually back in South Africa.

My father has always been a man of strong character, a family and career man. He became an outstanding, insightful family man, a person who always tried to keep the family together, to keep peace among his children, his family, and his friends. At the time of writing this, my dad (the great Lion) was in his 89th year. Strong, wise, and humble. A man that I can only describe as one of my closest friends, greatest confidants, and the most wonderful sound board anyone could wish for. He will always be a man whom I respect deeply and admire greatly. He most definitely gave my life meaning.

My mum was the same. My love for music, the finer things in life, the beauty of laughter, the importance of family and friends, and the ability to turn the other cheek come from her. My mum and I had great times together. It was true what my sister claimed for most of her life that there was something special between my mum and me – a unique bond between mother and child. Whether I became the story my mother told me about as a young boy, I don't know, and that is no longer important. However, I do know that throughout our lives together, even at the end of hers, we had a very special bond.

All of my siblings had a notable impact on my life. Chris, during my early years, to a lesser extent, more so later in our lives. I can only describe him as a gentle giant. A big man with a very small heart, a kind man. Suzanne influenced me to a greater extent. While our early years have been troublesome, we have developed a very loving relationship. I can honestly say that I love her very much, not because she is my sister, but rather despite thereof. When the two of us are alone, we always had a special and loving relationship.

Johan was by far my closest sibling, and that was not just because we were born sixteen months apart. He had been my protector when we were small, my friend as we grew up, and was a remarkable human being. He was very considerate, looking out for his loved ones, even if it meant, and we wish it wasn't like that, an ultimate self-sacrifice.

Two hundred and one years after the birth of my first South African great grandmother on my father's side – albeit an immigrant from Indonesia, six generations removed from me – I entered my fiftieth year and my seventh as an immigrant to the United Kingdom.

During those fifty years, I had a happy and interesting, albeit at times stressful, youth. At the age of 30, I met the most remarkable and beautiful German-speaking South African girl, who cried of joy listening to Augstin Lara's 'Granada'. Throughout the next twenty years, we embarked on several adventures and moved house too many times. We started two businesses. We travelled extensively in Southern Africa, visiting the Portuguese Islands, Mauritius, and Namibia. We explored Europe, Australia, relaxed in the Maldives, and, eventually, immigrated to the United Kingdom. Throughout this journey, we made wonderful friends.

On arriving in the United Kingdom via Dubai, with only a couple of suitcases, three cats, and our paintings, we lived on a tight budget, looking for work. We lived on a tight budget looking for work. This proved to be difficult, so I started studying and became a Fellow of the Chartered Institute of Personnel Management (FCIPD), completed a Master's Degree and eventfully was awarded, a LLB (Hons).

Ultimately, desperation nearly pushed us to consider giving up and returning to South Africa. But then, I agreed to work for free, just to get a foot in the door. This paid off as we both secured good positions, and I, eventually, became a Human Resources Director in the National Health Services.

We lived in Lytham St. Anne's; worked at the Blackpool Teaching Hospitals NHS Foundation Trust in Lancashire in 2009; moved to Devon in 2012, where we worked at Plymouth Hospitals NHS Trust until 2015; and, eventually, settled in Buckinghamshire.

In 2013, I was diagnosed with, treated for, and survived cancer. I received the best treatment the NHS could offer. With the love and support of Renate, reinforced by my faith, and the help of remarkable colleagues, family and friends, I ultimately won the battle.

I embarked on cycling expeditions, which was two-fold, partly to help me regain my strength, but also so that Kevin could educate me about British history, culture, practices, and customs. A task he set to doing with passion, dedication, and his own special approach to humour. I think all of this was part of Kevin's bigger plan, perhaps unplanned, to turn a brass Afrikaans-speaking South African wannabe Brit into a proper English bloke.

By 2015, opportunity knocked, and we settled in the Aylesbury Vale District, in Buckinghamshire, a stone's through from Waddesdon Manor, the French Renaissance Châteaux of Baron Ferdinand de Rothschild, built between 1884 and 1890.

Here, we bought a house, with beautiful vistas of the countryside. I returned to my consulting roots, managing a HR and ODL Shared Service, which did the same type of work as Extra Expertise in South Africa. A completed circle. Like my ancestors immigrated to South Africa, we completed the circle, a journey of immigrants.

On reflecting on my life, the question that I often considered was not who to blame for what happened in my life, but rather what I choose to do with those experiences, those learning moments, those events.

Considering Victor Frankle's logotherapy and the futuristic view thereof, it may not always be good to reflect too much on the past. We have no control over it. It can't be changed. We should consider the events of the past, learn from it, but then move on.

The journey is not over yet.

In my life, thus far, I can honestly say that my parents, all of my siblings, family, friends, and colleagues reflected herein, all enhanced my life. Whether I did the same for them is not for me to comment on. What I do know is that this journey taught me that the way we live our lives, or conduct ourselves with others, directly impacts how we inspire or fail to inspire the people around us.

Who would have thought that in 2016, David Cameron would nearly destroy the British Union, Great Britain would vote to leave the European Union, and Donald Trump would secure the democratic nomination for the Presidential election. Moreover, that 2017 would start with Donald J. Trump becoming the 45th President of the United States of America and Britain triggering article 50 of the Lisbon Treaty, setting the scene for becoming independent from the European Union.

My father had one career his entire life; I have a wonderful life divided over a variety of interesting careers. Life, I would argue, is indeed a journey of choice.

Annexure 1
VAN DER VYVER

Here follows an overview of the family tree of Willem van der Vyver from Haarlem, Holland in the Netherlands.[90, 91][* - birth; ≈ - christened]

<u>1st Generation [1691]</u>

Willem van der Vyver was born 1691 in Haarlem, Northern Holland in the Netherlands. The town is famous for its flower-bulb-growing districts and extensive tulip fields, art museums and cobblestone streets.[92] Willem arrived in the Cape of Good Hope, South Africa in 1714 and married **Elizabeth Bastiaanse** on 31/07/1719 in Drakenstein. They had no children. Willem had a second marriage and married **Marie Viviers** on 08/09/1726. They had six children. Five sons and a daughter.

(1) Anna Maria (*30/11/1719)
(2) <u>Willem Jacobus</u> (*04/10/1727)
(3) Bartolomeus (*05/10/1732)
(4) Abraham (≈24/04/1734)
(5) Jan Abraham (≈11/09/1735)
(6) Izak (*11/08/1737).

<u>2nd Generation [1727]</u>

Willem Jacobus van der Vyver was born 04/10/1727 in Paarl and married **Johanna Dorothea Debes** on 15/02/1761 until 03/12/1769. They had five children; two sons and two daughters.

(1) Willem Jacobus (*04/04/1762)
(2) Maria Elizabeth (*24/12/1763)

---

[90] Coetzee, S, *Geslagregister van Willem van der Vyver van Haarlem, Nederland.*
[91] van der Vyver, Tom en Johannes Daniel van der Vyver, *van der Vyver Stamboom.*
[92] https://www.holland.com/global/tourism/destinations/more-destinations/haarlem.htm

(3) <u>Hendrik Cristoffel Lourens</u> (*06/04/1765)
(4) Bartholomeus Jacobus (≈12/04/1767)
(5) Anna Margaretha (*25/03/1769).

He had a second marriage to **Judith (de Wit) Sandenberg** in December 1769. They had six children; three sons and three daughters.

(1) Frederic Johannes (≈13/01/1771)
(2) Cornelia (≈04/10/1772)
(3) Christina Gezina (*14/11/1773)
(4) Izak Jacobus (*08/04/1775)
(5) Johannes Petrus (≈17/07/1777)
(6) Maria Helena (≈01/08/1779).

3rd Generation [1765]

Hendrik Christoffel Lourens van der Vyver was born on 06/04/1765 and married **Maria Elisabeth Erasmus** on 23/09/1798. They had eight children; three sons and five daughters.

(1) Margarita Susanna (*13/03/1800)
(2) Willem Bartholomeus (*09/06/1802)
(3) Johanna Christina (*04/12/1804)
(4) <u>Lourens Stefanus</u> (*03/10/1806)
(5) Maria Elizabeth (*18/11/1810)
(6) Martha Louisa (*18/11/1810)
(7) Hendrina Christina Wilhelmina (*04/03/1819)
(8) Hendrik Christoffel Lourens (*05/01/1825).

4th Generation [1806]

Lourens Stefanus van der Vyver was born on 03/10/1806 in Tulbach and married **Jacomina Jacoba Ströh** on 02/04/1832 until 04/06/1850. They had nine children; three sons and six daugthers.

(1) Hendrik Christoffel Stephanus (*12/06/1838)
(2) Dorothea Cornelia (*1840)
(3) Anna Maria (*20/05/1841)
(4) Maria Elizabeth (*20/12/1842)
(5) Jacomina Jacoba (*02/05/1844)

(6) Lourens Stefanus Hendrik (*18/07/1845)
(7) <u>Johan David</u> (*11/02/1847)
(8) Johanna Magdalena (*1850)
(9) Elsje Johanna (*04/06/1850).

Lourens Stefanus had a second marriage to **Elizabeth Rosina Green** on 20/09/1850 until 11/01/1856. They had three children; one son and two daughters.

(1) Hendrik Christoffel Jacobus (*1851)
(2) Hester Petronella (*06/02/1853)
(3) Elizabeth Rozina Anna Susanna (*28/12/1855).

Lourens Stefanus had a third marriage to **Helena Catherina Klopper** and three more children; two sons and a daughter.

(1) Willem Bartholomeus (*1857)
(2) Jacomina Hendrina (*20/02/1860)
(3) Barend Christiaan (*17/10/1864).

5th Generation [1847]

Johan David van der Vyver was born 11/02/1847 at Tweefontein in the district of Steynsburg and married **Louisa Maria Maartens**. They had five children; three sons and two daughters.

(1) Johanna Barendina (*21/07/1874)
(2) Lourens Stephanus (*25/02/1877)
(3) Matthys Daniel (*1879)
(4) <u>Johan David</u> (*09/10/1883)
(5) Jacomina Jacoba (*26/09/1886).

6th Generation [1883]

Johan David van der Vyver was born 09/10/1883 in Steynsburg and married **Hester Lesya van Zyl**, on 01/08/1904 in Venterstad. They had six children; four sons and two daughters.

(1) <u>Johan David</u> ("Ouboet") (*20/04/1905)
(2) Jacob van der Vyver (*21/10/1907)

(3) Louwrens Stephanus ("Loutjie") (*25/03/1910)
(4) Maria Magdalena Hester Johanna ("Miem") (*26/06/1925)
(5) Louisa Maria ("Wiesie") (*17/10/1928)
(6) Matthys Daniel ("Thys") (*30/04/1930).

7th Generation [1905]

Johan David van der Vyver was born on 20/04/1905 in Venterstad and married **Susanna Elizabeth De Jager** on 10/07/1929 in Pietermaritzburg. They had four children; three daughters and one son.

(1) <u>Hendrina Cecilia</u> (*16/09/1929)
(2) Hester Louisa ("Hettie") (*09/10/1930)
(3) Susanna Elizabeth ("Koer") (*09/11/1932)
(4) Johan David (*21/02/1934).

8th Generation [1929]

Hendrina Cecilia van der Vyver was born on 16/09/1929 in Pietermaritzburg and married **Christiaan Johannes Scheffer** on 14/02/1953 in Pietermaritzburg. They had four children, three sons and one daughter.

(1) Christiaan Johannes (*19/10/1957)
(2) Suzanne Elizabeth (*15/06/1959)
(3) Johan Dawid (*21/06/1964)
(4) <u>Johann Heinrich</u> (*25/10/1965).

9th Generation [1965]

Johann Heinrich Scheffer was born on 25/10/1965 in Aliwal-North and married **Adriana Maria Margareta Nolte** on 22/11/1992 in Pretoria. They divorced on 13/01/1995. They had no children. He had a second marriage with **Renate Hoffmann** on 14/12/1996 in Pretoria. They had no children.

Annexure 2
DE JAGER

Here follows an overview of the detailed family tree of **Pieter Christiaan De Jager** as researched and recorded by Cecilia Scheffer.[93]

1st Generation [1696]

Pieter Christiaan De Jager originated from Zutphen, in the Netherlands, a city in the province of Gelderland. It lies some 30km north-east of Arnhem on the Eastern bank of the river Ijssel at the point where it is joined by the Berke.[94] He arrived in the Cape, South Africa and married **Hermina Karelse** in Swellendam on 19/02/1696. They had four sons.

(1) <u>Andries</u>
(2) Carel
(3) Lourens
(4) Christiaan.

2nd Generation [1726]

Andries De Jager married **Elizabeth Potgieter** on 29/09/1726. They had four sons.

(1) Pieter (baptized ≈02/06/1731)
(2) Jan Hermanus (≈19/04/1733)
(3) Andries Christoffel (≈05/08/1736)
(4) <u>Frederik</u> (≈31/01/1740).

---

[93] Scheffer, HC, *Geslagregister van Pieter Christiaan De Jager soos nagevors deur Cecilia Scheffer*, Unpublished register and research notes on the De Jager family in South Africa.
[94] https://nl.wikipedia.org/wiki/Zutphen_(stad) [27/08/17]

3rd Generation [1768]

Frederik De Jager was baptized on 31/01/1740 and married **Maria Strydom** on 14/02/1768. They had six sons.

(1) Andries (≈09/02/1772)
(2) Johannes Petrus (≈12/02/1775)
(3) Frederik Johannes (≈21/02/1779)
(4) Johannes Petrus (≈23/12/1781)
(5) Christiaan Jacobus (≈01/10/1789)
(6) <u>Matthys Godliep</u> (≈15/04/1792).

4th Generation [1792]

Matthys Godliep De Jager was baptized on 15/04/1792 and married **Antoinette Elizabeth Weeber.** They had six sons.

(1) Frederik Johannes (born *1822)
(2) <u>Johan Hendrik Valentyn</u> (*30/06/1824)
(3) Petrus Jacobus (*1829)
(4) Matthys Michiel Andries (*1832)
(5) Hendrik Johannes (*1834)
(6) Carel Pieter (*1838).

5th Generation [1824]

Johan Hendrik Valentyn De Jager was born on 30/06/1824 and married **Maria Johanna Dorothea du Plessis**. They had six children; three sons and three daughters.

(1) Matthys Godliep (*1853)
(2) <u>Pieter Willem</u> (*12/04/1854)
(3) Antoinette Elizabeth (*06/08/1864)
(4) Maria Catharina (*18/11/1867)
(5) Catharina Johanna Dorothea (*10/09/1869)
(6) Johan Jacobus Valentyn (*12/01/1872).

Johan Hendrik Valentyn had a second marriage, to **Francina Janette de Villiers**, and had six children; all sons.

(1) Matthys Michiel Andries (*02/11/1877)
(2) Daniel de Villiers (*25/08/1880)
(3) Frederik Johannes (*30/06/1882)
(4) Hendrik Jacobus Cornelius (*13/10/1883)
(5) Willem Francois (*07/06/1888)
(6) James Alexander (21/03/1892).

6th Generation [1854]

Pieter Willem De Jager was born on 12/04/1854 and married **Johanna Hermina Pritchard de Villiers**. They had eight children; six sons and two daughters.

(1) <u>Pieter Gideon</u> (*05/04/1878)
(2) Johan Jacobus (*23/06/1880)
(3) Anna Johanna (*12/07/1882)
(4) David Hendrik (*21/09/1884)
(5) Maria Johanna (*13/03/1887)
(6) Pieter Willem (*22/06/1889)
(7) Daniel Charles (*27/04/1893)
(8) Matthys Michiel (*14/09/1895).

7th Generation [1878]

Pieter Gideon De Jager was born on 05/04/1878 and married **Hendrina Cecilia Oberholzer**. They had seven children; four sons and three daughters.

(1) Pieter Willem Gideon (*26/05/1907)
(2) Johan Albert (*22/07/1908)
(3) <u>Susanna Elizabeth</u> ("Suzie") (*18/04/1910)
(4) Cornelius Johannes (*25/04/1912)
(5) David Hendrik (*29/03/1914)
(6) Johanna Hermina Pritchard (*17/03/1917)
(7) Hendrina Cecilia (*15/07/1918).

Pieter Gideon had two more marriages. His second wife died giving birth to twins who were stil-born. His third marriage was with **Maria Susanna van Zyl ("Ouma Maraai")**, born Scheepers. They had two children; a son and a daughter.

(1) Pieter Gideon ("PG") (*15/02/1939)
(2) Maria Susanna (*31/05/1942).

8th Generation [1910]

Susanna Elizabeth De Jager was born on 18/04/1910 in Venterstad and married **Johan David van der Vyver** on 10/07/1929 in Pietermaritzburg. They had four children; three daughters and one son.

(1) Hendrina Cecilia (*16/09/1929)
(2) Hester Louisa ("Hettie") (*09/10/1930)
(3) Susanna Elizabeth ("Koer") (*09/11/1932)
(4) Johan David. (*21/02/1934).

9th Generation [1929]

Hendrina Cecilia van der Vyver was born on 16/09/1929 in Pietermaritzburg and married **Christiaan Johannes Scheffer** on 14/02/1953 in Pietermaritzburg. They had four children; three sons and one daughter.

(1) Christiaan Johannes (*19/10/1957)
(2) Suzanne Elizabeth (*15/06/1959)
(3) Johan Dawid (*21/06/1964)
(4) Johann Heinrich (*25/10/1965).

10th Generation [1965]

Johann Heinrich Scheffer was born on 25/10/1965 in Aliwal-North and married **Adriana Maria Margareta Nolte** on 22/11/1992 in Pretoria. They divorced on 13/01/1995. They had no children. He had a second marriage with **Renate Hoffmann** on 14/12/1996 in Pretoria. They had no children.

Annexure 3
MEYER

Here follows an overview of the detailed family tree of **Johann Justus Wilhelm Meyer** as researched and recorded by Cecilia Scheffer.[95]

1ˢᵗ Generation [1762]

Johann Justus Wilhelm Meyer, came from Hameln in Lower Saxony, south of Hannover in Germany. It is the capital of the district of Hameln-Pyrmont and is best known for the tale of the Pied Piper of Hameln.[96] **Johann Justus Wilhelm Meyer** arrived in South Africa in 1786 where he married **Helena Maria Kerkhoff** on 14/09/1788. They had five children; three sons and two daughters.

> (1) Johanna Maria (*09/06/1789)
> (2) Johanna Frederica (*19/07/1790)
> (3) Johan Frederick (*28/04/1792)
> (4) Justus Wilhelm (*14/06/1795)
> (5) Justus Hendrik (*30/09/1799).

2ⁿᵈ Generation [1799]

Justus Hendrik Meyer was born on 30/09/1799 in George and married **Margaretha Catherina van der Lith** on 15/10/1801 in George. They had ten children; five sons and five daughters.

> (1) Justus Wilhelm (*17/03/1821)
> (2) Elizabeth Catharina Johanna (*24/02/1823)
> (3) Andries Ludolph (*17/11/1824)
> (4) Johan Frederik (*14/01/1827)
> (5) Hendrik Oostwald Albertijn (*28/09/1828)

---

[95] Scheffer, HC, *Geslagregister van Johann Justus Wilhelm Meyer soos nagevors deur Cecilia Scheffer*, Unpublished register and research notes on the Meyer family in South Africa.
[96] https://www.roughguides.com/destinations/europe/germany/lower-saxony-and-bremen/hameln-hamelin/ [17/09/17]

(6) Helena Christina (*09/09/1830)
(7) <u>William Ferdinand</u> (*19/10/1832)
(8) Johanna Frederica (*27/07/1834)
(9) Charlotte Maria (*23/12/1836)
(10)   Margaretha Catharina (*19/09/1838).

3rd Generation [1832]

William Ferdinand Meyer was born on 19/10/1832 in George and married **Maria Orsila Magdalena Terblanche** in George. They had six children; three sons and three daughters.

(1) Stephanus Johannes
(2) William Ferdinand
(3) Maria Orsilia
(4) Susanna Francina
(5) Helena Christina (*12/03/1875)
(6) <u>Justus Hendrik</u> (*05/01/1859).

4th Generation [1859]

Justus Hendrik Meyer was born on 05/01/1859 in George and married **Maria Johanna Gouws** at Skurwedraai in the district of Kroonstad. They had eight children; six sons and two daughters.

(1) <u>Christina Johanna</u> ("Baby") (*16/06/1896)
(2) William Ferdinand ("Ferrie") (*25/04/1898)
(3) Marthinus Pieter ("Tien") (*06/06/1900)
(4) Justus Hendrik ("Jus") (*08/03/1903)
(5) Gerhardus Andries ("Gert") (*23/04/1905)
(6) Stephanus Esais ("Fanie") (*24/04/1908)
(7) Pieter Johannes ("Piet") (*22/02/1911)
(8) Maria Ursula Terblanche ("Miem") (*27/07/1914).

5th Generation [1896]

Christina Johanna Meyer was born on 16/06/1896 in Parys, in the Orange Free State, and married **Christiaan Johannes Scheffer** on 29/12/1918 in Ventersdorp. They had ten children; six sons and four daughters.

(1) Johann Heinrich ("Hein") (*01/12/1920)
(2) Maria Johanna ("Marie") (*22/05/1922)
(3) Hendrina Margaretha ("Henna") (*11/02/1925)
(4) Justus Hendrik ("Jus") (*02/07/1926)
(5) <u>Christiaan Johannes</u> ("Chris") (*28/07/1928)
(6) William Ferdinand (17/06/1930)
(7) Hercules Jacobus (*09/04/1932)
(8) Christina Johanna ("Issie") (*24/09/1934)
(9) Maria Ursula (*24/08/1936)
(10)   Stephanus Hermanus ("Fanie") (*01/06/1938).

<u>6th Generation [1928]</u>

Christiaan Johannes Scheffer was born on 28/07/1928 in Ventersdorp and married **Hendrina Cecilia van der Vyver** on 07/02/1953 in Pietermaritzburg. They had four children; three sons and a daughter.

(1) Christiaan Johannes ("Chris") (*19/10/1957)
(2) Suzanne Elizabeth (*15/06/1959)
(3) Johan Dawid (*21/06/1964)
(4) <u>Johann Heinrich</u> ("Hein") (*25/10/1965).

Cecilia died on 07/12/2006. **Christiaan Johannes** had a second marriage, with **Madeleine Ruth Venter** on 27/04/2008, Madeleine died on 07/02/2018.

<u>7th Generation [1965]</u>

Johann Heinrich Scheffer was born on 25/10/1965 in Aliwal-North and married **Adriana Maria Margareta Nolte** on 22/11/1992 in Pretoria. They divorced on 13/01/1995. They had no children. He had a second marriage, with **Renate Hoffmann** on 14/12/1996 in Pretoria. They had no children.

Annexure 4
SCHEFFER

Here follows an overview of the detailed family tree of **Christiaan Johannes Scheffer** as researched and recorded by Cecilia Scheffer[97].

Christiaan Johannes Scheffer was born in 1762 in Einbeck, Hanover, Germany. A town in the district of Northeim in southern Lower Saxony, part of the German timber-frame road, a tourist route leading from the river Elbe in the north to Lake Constance in the south.[98]

Johann Steenvat arrived in the Cape, South Africa, from Westheim, a small village in the district of Germersheim in the state of Rhineland-Palatinate in Bavaria, Germany[99], and married a girl from Dutch Batavia, modern day Indonesia, recorded as **Rachel from the Cape**. Rachel was born c. 1764. They had two children; one son and a daughter.

(1) Margaretha Elizabeth (*20/05/1787)
(2) Johannes Carolus Frederick (*1789).

1st Generation [1762]

Christiaan Johannes Scheffer was born in 1762 and married **Margaretha Elizabeth Steenvat** on 31/03/1802 in Cape Town. They had four children; one son and three daughters.

(1) Catharina Bartholomina Elizabeth (*31/08/1806)
(2) Johanna Sophia Henrietta (*04/07/1808)

---

[97] Scheffer, HC, *Geslagregister van Christiaan Johannes Scheffer soos nagevors deur Cecilia Scheffer*, Unpublished register and research notes on the Scheffer family in South Africa.
[98] http://www.germanywanderer.com/the-german-timber-frame-road/ [27/08/17]
[99] https://ipfs.io/ipfs/QmXoypizjW3WknFiJnKLwHCnL72vedxjQkDDP1mXWo6uco/wiki/Germersheim_(district).html [27/08/17]

(3) Margaretha Frederika Carolina (*17/11/1810)
(4) <u>Christiaan Johannes</u> (*07/04/1816).

2nd Generation [1816]

Christiaan Johannes Scheffer was born on 07/04/1816 in Graaff Reinet and married **Johanna Frederika Wilhelmina Schimper**. They had nine children; four sons and five daughters.

(1) Catharina Hendrina (*1843)
(2) Christian Johannes (*1844)
(3) Margaretha Elizabeth (*1846)
(4) <u>Johann Heinrich</u> (*22/05/1851)
(5) Johanna Frederika Wilhelmina (*04/03/1853)
(6) Henrieta Carolina (*31/05/1859)
(7) Carel Daniel (*08/10/1861)
(8) Johannes Carel Frederick (*1864)
(9) Martha Etricia (*07/02/1871).

3rd Generation [1851]

Johann Heinrich Scheffer was born on 22/05/1851 in Aberdeen and married **Hendrina Margaretha Visser** on 09/04/1877. They had twelve children; five sons and seven daughters.

(1) Hendrina Margaretha ("Ousus") (*09/11/1884)
(2) Catharina Hendrina ("Kitty") (*28/03/1886)
(3) Hercules Jacobus ("Ouboet") (*19/06/1887)
(4) Johann Heinrich ("Hennie") (*01/01/1889)
(5) Jacomina Margaretha ("Jakkie") (*25/10/1890)
(6) Margaretha Elizabeth ("Bettie") (*25/02/1892)
(7) Henrietta Carolina ("Jettie") (*24/06/1893)
(8) Maria Isabella ("Maraai") (*06/12/1894)
(9) <u>Christiaan Johannes</u> (*24/07/1896)
(10)   Stephanus Hermanus (*27/03/1898)
(11)   Carel Daniel (*30/11/1899)
(12)   Johanna Frederika Wilhelmina (*23/03/1903).

4th Generation [1896]

Christiaan Johannes Scheffer was born on 24/07/1896 at Kafferskraal, Ventersdorp and married **Christina Johanna Meyer** on 29/12/1918. They had ten children; six sons and four daughters.

(1) Johann Heinrich ("Hein") (*01/12/1920)
(2) Maria Johanna ("Marie") (*22/05/1922)
(3) Hendrina Margaretha ("Henna") (*11/02/1925)
(4) Justus Hendrik ("Jus") (*02/07/1926)
(5) <u>Christiaan Johannes</u> ("Chris") (*28/07/1928)
(6) William Ferdinand (17/06/1930)
(7) Hercules Jacobus (*09/04/1932)
(8) Christina Johanna ("Issie") (*24/09/1934)
(9) Maria Ursula (*24/08/1936)
(10)   Stephanus Hermanus ("Fanie") (*01/06/1938).

5th Generation [1928]

Christiaan Johannes Scheffer was born on 28/07/1928 in Ventersdorp and married **Hendrina Cecilia van der Vyfer** on 07/02/1953 in Pietermaritzburg. They had four children; three sons and a daughter.

(1) Christiaan Johannes ("Chris") (*19/10/1957)
(2) Suzanne Elizabeth (*15/06/1959)
(3) Johan Dawid (*21/06/1964)
(4) <u>Johann Heinrich</u> ("Hein") (*25/10/1965).

Cecilia died on 07/12/2006. **Christiaan Johannes** had a second marriage, with **Madeleine Ruth Venter**, on 27/04/2008. Madeleine died on 07/02/2018.

6th Generation [1965]

Johann Heinrich Scheffer was born on 25/10/1965 in Aliwal-North and married **Adriana Maria Margareta Nolte** on 22/11/1992 in Pretoria. They divorced on 13/01/1995. They had no children. He had a second marriage, with **Renate Hoffmann** on 14/12/1996 in Pretoria. They had no children.

Bibliography

Alzheimer's institute: www.alzheimers.co.za

All Scripture quotations in this publication are taken from the *HOLY BIBLE: New International Version* (NIV).

Archives of the Union of South Africa, 1946: http://www.sahistory.org.za/archive/memorandum-on-the-national-union-of-south-african-students-%28nusas%29.-part-one-nusas-the-trade-union%0A?page=1186

Bell, B. and Mitchell J., (2008). *Insight Guide South Africa*, Insight Print Services, Singapore

Botha, Retha., (1995). *A poem for Barbra*, Private Collection

Churchill. W., (2007). *The World Crisis 1911- 1918*, Penguin, London

Covery, Stephen R., (2004). *7 Habits of Highly Effective People*, Simon & Schuster UK Ltd.

Coetzee, S, *Geslagregister van Willem van der Vyver van Haarlem, Nederland*, on https://www.wikitree.com/wili/Van_der_Vyver-74

Criminal Law Amendment Act, No 08 of 1953

Deacon, H., (1996). *The Island*, A History of Robben Island 1488 – 1990, David Philip Publishers, Cape Town

Frankl, Victor E., (1992). *Man's Search for Meaning,* Beacon Press

Godley, G. A., (1920). *Report of the Inter-departmental committee on native pass laws*, Union of South Africa

Giliomee, D., (1995). *Young Days*, A Private Collection

Goleman, Daniel., (1995). *Emotional Intelligence*, HarperCollins Publishers

Hewaarachichi, T., (2013). *Apartheid in South Africa*, on Prezi,

Home Office., (2013). *Life in the United Kingdom, A Guide for new Residents,* 3rd Edition, TSO, also https://www.gov.uk/life-in-the-uk-test

Hoge, J., *Personalia of the Germans at the Cape, 1652 – 1806,* Cape Town and also Deutsche Einwanderer in der hollandischen Kapkolonie 1651-1806 – http://www.safrika.org/Personalia_de.html

Jackson, Gordon S., (2003). *Never Scratch a Tiger with a Short Stick,* NevPress

Johnston, R.P., (2013). *Burnout,* Private publication

Kruger, (1980). *Headmasters Journal,* Erasmus Highs School, April 1980

Lombardi, Vincent., (2000). *Winning is a Habit,* Quoted in The Launch Issue of '*Motivation of Champions*', Strobe Communications

Maslow, A. H., (1943). *Theory of Human Motivation,* Originally Published in *Psychological Review,* 50, 370-396

Mandela, Nelson R., (1994). *Long Walk to Freedom,* MacDonald Purnell (Pty.) Ltd.

Mandela, N.R., (1996). http://www.sahistory.org.za/letters/second-letter-nelson-mandela-hendrik-verwoerd-26-june-

Mandela, N.R., : *http://awakenthegreatnesswithin.com/50-inspirational-nelson-mandela-quotes-that-will-change-your-life/*

Michener James A., (1980). The Covenant, Martin Secker & Warburg Ltd., London

Noluthungu Sam C., (1975). *South Africa in Africa: A study of ideology and foreign policy,* Manchester City Press

Pretoria News. '*Motorcyclist Killed*', 7 June 1984

Public Safety Act, No 03 of 1953

Quotation from a private conversation

Reader's Digest (The)., (1994). *Illustrated History of South Africa – The Real Story,* Expanded Third Edition, South Africa

Rodgers, S., (1997). *Red Saint, Pink Daughter: A Communist Childhood in Berlin and London,* Carcanet, London

SABC, *News* on 10/04/1993

Scheffer, H.C., *Geslagregister van Pieter Christiaan De Jager soos nagevors deur Cecilia Scheffer*, Unpublished register and research notes on the De Jager family in South Africa.

Scheffer, H. C., *Geslagregister van Johann Justus Wilhelm Meyer soos nagevors deur Cecilia Scheffer*, Unpublished register and research notes on the Meyer family in South Africa.

Scheffer H. C., *Geslagsregister van Christiaan Johannes Scheffer*, soos nagevors deur Ceclia Scheffer, Unpublished Register and research notes on the Scheffer family of South Africa.

Scheffer, J.H., (2001). *Friends*, Private Collection

Scheffer, J.H, quoted in Success Magazine, March/April 2004

Scheffer R., The Dailey Dispatch, East London, 15 March 1982

Schoonees, M.A., *et al.*, (1972). *Verklarende Handwoordeboek van die Afrikaanse Taal* (HAT), Voortrekkerpers

Sky News, 25 May 2009

Sky News, 22 May 2013

Soanes, C. et al., (2008). *Compact Oxford English Dictionary of Current English*, Third Editions, Revised, Oxford University Press

The Telegraph, 20 March 2012

van der Vyver, J.D., http://www.law.emory.edu

van der Vyver, Tom en van der Vyver, Johannes Daniel., (2017). *van der Vyver Stamboom*. CD publication

Vermeulen, Stephanie., (1999). *EQ Emotional Intelligence for Everyone*, Zebra Press

Volxrock – https://www.youtube.com/watch?v=IjqPDioHfwQ

Wicomb, R. and van der Merwe, A., (2015). *Kleur, my leve, my lied, Randall Wicomb*, Nadeli

Welsh F., (2000). *A History of South Africa*, HarperCollins Publishers, London

Internet Searches: -

http://www.bbc.co.uk/news/magazine-25776836

http://www.biblica.com/en-us/bible/bible-faqs/how-were-the-books-of-the-bible-chosen/

http://www.biblica.com/en-us/bible/bible-faqs/how-were-the-books-of-the-bible-chosen/

www.birminghamprostateclinic.co.uk/treatments/brachytherapy.php

https://www.britannica.com/place/Thailand

http://www.cancer.gov/cancertopics/factsheet/detection/PSA.

http://www.capetowncycletour.com

http://www.centrepompidou.fr/

http://www.cqc.org.uk/content/cqc-rates-plymouth-hospitals-nhs-trust-outstanding-caring—— overall-trust-requires

http://edition.cnn.com/2013/12/10/politics/mandela-obama-remarks/

http://uk.encarta.msn.com/encyclopeida_761557321/South_Africa.html

http://famousdiamonds.ripod.com/cullinandiamds.html

http://www.germanywanderer.com/the-german-timber-frame-road/

https://www.holland.com/global/tourism/destinations/more-destinations/haarlem.htm

https://www.italyguides.it/en/veneto/verona

www.jurology.com/article/S0022-5347(05)65988-5/abstract

http://www.loeser.us/flags/south_africa.html

http://www.macmillan.org.uk

http://www.macmillan.org.uk/Cancerinformation/Cancertreatment/Treatmenttyp
es/Radiotherap

http://www.movie-locations.com/movies/f/4wandf.html#.WG-zx7GcZ-U

http://www.nhs.uk/Conditions/Cognitive-behavioural-
therapy/Pages/Introduction.aspx

http://www.nhs.uk/conditions/post-traumatic-stress-
disorder/Pages/Introduction.aspx

http://www.nlm.nih.gov/medlineplus/ency/article/003346.htm

www.oncolink.org/experts/article1.cfm?c=90&id=2599

http://www.platinum.matthey.com/about-pgm/production

www.radiologyinfo.org/en/info.cfm?pg=imrt

www.roman-empire.net/decline/constantine-index.html

https://www.roughguides.com/destinations/europe/germany/lower-saxony-and-
bremen/hameln-hamelin/

http://www.sahistory.org.za

http://www.sahistory.org.za/archive/black-uncivilised

http://www.southafrica.net/za/en/articles/entry/article-southafrica.net-the-battle-
of-blaauwberg

http://www.sahistory.org.za/dated-event/military-service-becomes-compulsory-
white-south-african-men

http://www.sahistory.org.za/article/gandhi-and-passive-resistance-campaign-
1907-1914 http://www.sahistory.org.za/topic/congress-south-african-students-
cosas

http://www.sahistory.org.za/indian-indentured-labour-natal-1860-
1911#sthash.zzl0KKmd.dpuf

http://startupquotes.startupvitamins.com/post/118845639623/it-doesnt-make-
sense-to-hire-smart-people-and

https://www.stephencovey.com/7habits/7habits-habit1.php

http://www-cs-students.stanford.edu/~cale/cs201/apartheid.hist.html

https://www.theguardian.com/news/2006/nov/02/guardianobituaries.southafrica

https://nl.wikipedia.org/wiki/Zutphen_(stad)

https://ipfs.io/ipfs/QmXoypizjW3WknFiJnKLwHCnL72vedxjQkDDP1mXWo
6uco/wiki/Germersheim_(district).html

Acknowledgements

Although all the people reflected in this book made a difference in my life, I do wish to thank a few, starting with those who helped with the editing, flow and layout of *A Journey of Choice*. A special word of thanks to Vinh Tran and the team at Austin Macauley Publishers, without whom this book would not have been possible. A special thank you to Graham Vass for the kind words he wrote as preamble to this book. Thank you for all the people who have crossed my path over the past fifty plus years. Thank you to all my family and friends, and during my career, especially thank you to Johan Malan, Terry Lavery, Graham Vass, Jeremy Franklin, Nick Grimshaw, Ann James, and Nicola Bell. Dietloff Giliomee and Retha Botha thank you for the use of your poems. Jeremy Franklin for his original review of the chapter on the gaming industry, and for his subsequent support during difficult times. For the late Willie Roets I am eternally grateful for his friendship, support and encouragement in my life. A special word of thanks to my parents Chris and Cecilia Scheffer, my siblings, Christiaan, Suzanne, and my late brother Johan. To my late mother Cecilia Scheffer, I feel honored to have been able to publish your family research, be it an overview, you have made such a huge contribution to my life, and I know that this book containing all four of our family lines, would have delighted you. Lastly, a massive thank you to my lovely wife Renate, for all your patience, support and love. Without your help, this would not have been possible, in Graham Vass's words, '*I salute you*' and love you!

Printed in the USA
CPSIA information can be obtained
at www.ICGtesting.com
CBHW072146140624
10091CB00008B/148